STATE OF THE NATION

STATE OF THE NATION

British Theatre since 1945

MICHAEL BILLINGTON

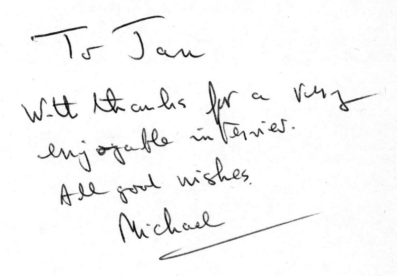

To Jan

With thanks for a very
enjoyable interview.
All good wishes.
Michael

faber and faber

First published in 2007
by Faber and Faber Limited
3 Queen Square London WC1N 3AU

Typeset by Faber and Faber Ltd
Printed in England by Mackays of Chatham, Chatham, Kent

A CIP record for this book
is available from the British Library

ISBN 978-0-571-21034-3

2 4 6 8 10 9 7 5 3 1

Contents

CONTENTS

Plate Illustrations

STATE OF THE NATION

Introduction

I have been a theatre critic for the bulk of my working life. I spent six years from 1965 to 1971 as Irving Wardle's deputy on *The Times*. Since October 1971 I have been privileged to be theatre critic of the *Guardian*. In all that time, I must have spent around eight thousand nights sitting in theatres. But a professional preoccupation with drama does not, I hope, preclude a fascination with the wider world. And this book has been driven by two strong impulses. One was a desire to explore the pattern and shape of British theatre since the end of the Second World War. The other was to try and discover the links between theatre and society. It is obvious that politics has been a recurrent theme of modern British drama. But I began with an insatiable curiosity about the extent to which theatre was influenced by the political temper of the times and about the way it may even have propelled social change. Does theatre simply reflect society? Or does it, in any way, help to create and modify it? I didn't begin with a preordained thesis: simply with a set of questions to which I hoped to find an answer.

I would describe the book as a 'personal view' because it is one man's subjective take on sixty years of British theatre. But, having said what the book is, it also may be helpful to say what it is not. It is not a comprehensive, encyclopedic history of British theatre: that would require a team of authors and a book roughly five times the current size. The book also focuses more on England than Scotland, Wales and Northern Ireland largely because that is the territory with which I am most familiar; a critic based in Edinburgh or Belfast would have an entirely different story to tell. And, although I recognise that theatre is a collaborative art, the book undeniably pays more attention to writers than to actors, directors, designers, producers or composers. In part, that is a reflection of my own bias towards text, which itself stems from an education that was geared more to an analysis of language than to an exploration of sound or image. But I also believe, in spite of a recent shift towards collectively devised art, that the dramatist is the key creative figure in theatre. To some, this may seem a provocative stance. But the interpretative arts of acting and directing depend upon the existence of an author's words. And it is predominantly, although not exclusively, through the work of dramatists that one is able to trace the fluctuations of post-war British society.

This is a book that will doubtless have something for everyone to dislike: your own favourite plays, performances or significant events will probably go unremarked. But I can only plead again that this is one man's personal vision of momentous times in theatre and society. Having said that, the book has been informed by a lifetime's discussion of theatre with friends and colleagues. It also stems from forty years as a critic. And I should like to pay tribute to the late John Lawrence who, as arts editor of *The Times*, set me off on the reviewing trail in 1965. I also owe an immense debt to three editors under whom I have worked at the *Guardian*, Alastair Hetherington, Peter Preston and Alan Rusbridger, and to a succession of arts editors at the paper who over the years have shown an astonishing mixture of faith and forbearance. At Faber and Faber itself, I was also encouraged by Peggy Paterson to write the book in the first place while Dinah Wood, as my current editor, has offered an exemplary mixture of stick and carrot and has scrutinised the text with patience, skill and critical insight. Finally, I have to pay public thanks to my wife, Jeanine, who in the years it has taken me to write the book has helped to keep body and soul together and shown a patience that would have been the envy of Chaucer's Griselda.

I

1945–50

The Age of Austerity

Where does the story of post-war British theatre really begin?

Some would claim on VE Day – 8 May 1945. That was the day when a grateful nation celebrated the defeat of Nazism and street parties erupted up and down the land; but the touching image of Noël Coward and Ivor Novello, fresh from their evening's triumphs in *Blithe Spirit* and *Perchance to Dream*, joining the euphoric crowds streaming towards Buckingham Palace reminds us that the West End's twin icons were still regally intact. Others might say that it was only much later in the decade, with the arrival of the verse dramas of Christopher Fry and T. S. Eliot, that a decisive cultural shift took place. An even more popular view, enshrined in countless academic texts, is that you have to wait until the premieres of *Waiting For Godot* in 1955 and *Look Back In Anger* in 1956 for British theatre to shake off its post-war sloth and get down to serious business; that until then, for all the heroic individualism of actors like Olivier and Gielgud, British drama was still governed by quilted escapism and bourgeois refinement.

For me, however, the story really starts on 26 July 1945. That was the date on which it was announced that Labour, with the slogan 'Let us face the future', had won 393 seats in the General Election as against 213 for the Conservatives and twelve for the Liberals, with twenty-two Independents. Churchill, the great wartime symbol, had been swept from power to be supplanted by Clement Attlee: a decent, supposedly dull Labour leader who looked like a suburban bank manager, listened eagerly to the county cricket scores and relished the novels of Agatha Christie. It says much about Attlee's modest demeanour that on the night of Labour's electoral triumph, his wife, Vi, drove him to the Palace to see the King and waited outside in the car. After a victory rally in Central Hall, Attlee went home to bed and recorded in his diary: 'It had been quite an exciting day.'

The ensuing six years of Labour government were to be momentous domestically and internationally; but argument still rages over how much was achieved. Some see the Attlee years as a lost opportunity: a time in which Britain failed to confront its diminished world status, missed the boat on Europe and left the old class system more or less intact. Others point to the creation of new structures for health, welfare, education and housing, a progressive decolonisation including the establishment of a democratic India and a transition from postwar austerity to burgeoning affluence. When a poll was taken in 2004 of 139 historians and political experts, who were asked to name the most successful prime minister of the past hundred years, Attlee came out a decisive top, defeating Winston Churchill. Even so, as John Charmley points out in *The Folio History of England*, the post-1945 period is a peculiarly difficult one to pin down:

> Images crowd around in such conflicting forms that it is tempting to ask the real post-war forties to stand up: food queues, rationing, frozen water pipes, grey bread, Evelyn Waugh excoriating the Attlee regime for its levelling ways; or a truly egalitarian era, where moral purposes counted above profit and individual advantage, and a united people strove successfully to overcome the effects of the most devastating war in history; a false dawn when time and energy were wasted on nonsense like nationalisation; or a bright new morning when the foundations of a better, more decent Britain were laid.

Everything depends on your point of view. Those touched by interwar prosperity still shudder at the recollection of post-war austerity. But, having been born in 1939 into an aspiring working-class family, I recall the years from 1945 to 1951 differently. I remember the dismal diet, the powdered eggs and milk, rationed sweets, the brutal cold in the winter of '47 with my mother literally begging for a sack of coal. But other, happier memories also come to mind: food parcels from American relatives, endless visits to the five local cinemas, cricket at Edgbaston, Dick Barton and *ITMA* on the radio, my first taste of a banana, my first circus, my first *Peter Pan* (Phyllis Calvert in Coventry), even my first Shakespeare (astonishingly, *Troilus and Cressida* at Stratford-on-Avon). For wartime children, as Susan Cooper has written, 'the world opening before us was not a pale imitation of one we had lost but a lucky dip of extraordinary things we had never seen before.'

On the national level, what also strikes me is the renewed sense of purpose in the post-war years. Britain may have been plagued by serial economic crises and an unforgiving Arctic winter, followed by serious floods, in 1947. But there was also a hunger for enjoyment and a sense of crusading idealism. Sport, for the nation at large, provided a therapeutic release after years of struggle and hardship. Crowds packed into soccer and cricket grounds and the golden summer of 1947 was dominated by the cavalier, record-breaking batting of Compton and Edrich for Middlesex: as Neville Cardus wrote, 'there was no rationing in an innings by Compton.' And, even at the height of post-war austerity, what Richard Hoggart called 'the bump of social purpose' helped to galvanise and liberate the culture at large. In 1945 the Arts Council – an extension of the wartime Council for the Encouragement of Music and the Arts – dispensed its first public funds. In 1946 the BBC's Third Programme began daily broadcasting. The same year saw the launch of Penguin Classics with E. V. Rieu's best-selling translation of the *Odyssey*. Serious weeklies were eagerly devoured: in 1949 the BBC's magazine, *The Listener*, had a circulation of 151,350. Long-lasting festivals were created in Edinburgh, Aldeburgh and Cheltenham. And, although you could say that none of these events impinged on the mass public, constant attempts were made to increase access to high culture. Billy Butlin, a cheery entrepreneur whose cut-price holiday camps dotted the British coastline, persuaded the Old Vic to do Shakespeare at Filey and the San Carlo Opera to stage *La bohème* at Skegness. Butlin may have been a publicity-seeking showman but his determination to show that holiday camps could offer more than beauty contests and talent shows was a sign of the affirmative idealism of the times.

Not everyone, of course, shared this belief that a Labour government could, or would, create a better Britain. Winston Churchill in a notorious election broadcast in 1945 had warned that any Labour government, in order to carry out its socialist programme, would have to fall back on some form of Gestapo, 'no doubt very humanely directed in the first instance'. The Tory press reacted with horror when Labour, within eighteen months of being elected, took twenty per cent of the economy into public ownership. And it should never be forgotten that the National Health Service Bill – the Attlee government's greatest legacy – was venomously opposed back in 1946 by the GPs' trade union, the British Medical Assocation: 'I have examined the

Bill,' wrote Dr Alfred Cox in the BMA's house journal, 'and it looks to me uncommonly like the first step, and a big one, towards National Socialism as practised in Germany.' Not all opposition to Labour was that hysterical; but there was a clear division in post-war Britain between those anxious to return to pre-war values and those who believed in change and progress.

As so often, the theatre offered a perfect microcosm of a conflict being enacted on the national stage; and what is astonishing is how quickly the battle-lines were drawn up. On the one hand, there were those who saw the chance to create a new kind of theatre in post-war Britain; on the other, there were those anxious for a return to the status quo. In a way the battle could be crystallised as a conflict between an institution and an individual: between the Old Vic and Hugh (Binkie) Beaumont, managing director of the dominant producing firm of the day, H. M. Tennent Ltd. Beaumont, who took over sole running of 'the firm', as it was known to initiates, was a silky Welsh authoritarian who had enlisted many of the star actors, writers and directors and who exercised huge commercial influence: on VE Day there were twelve Tennent productions running in thirty-six West End theatres. For Beaumont, in fact, the war had provided a tremendous opportunity and had allowed him to break into classical territory by presenting John Gielgud at both the Phoenix and the Haymarket in seasons embracing *Hamlet*, *A Midsummer Night's Dream*, *Love for Love* and *The Duchess of Malfi*. In the years to come Beaumont's power vastly increased, to the point where it became a national issue, through his skilful use of subsidiary, non-profit companies as a way of avoiding Entertainment Tax.

The Old Vic could not begin to match Beaumont's awesome commercial dominance. What it symbolised was a visionary idea that harked back to its eccentric founder, Lilian Baylis, and that chimed in with the new national mood: a dream of a permanent classical company with educational duties and the capacity to train the next generation of artists. After Baylis's death in 1937, Tyrone Guthrie had inherited her missionary fervour. With the onset of war and the bombing of the Old Vic's Waterloo Road base, Guthrie sent two companies out to the mining villages of South Wales and the industrial towns of the North-West. The former, headed by Sybil Thorndike and Lewis Casson, had taken *Macbeth* to the miners and been ecstatically received: indeed, in one small town in west Wales, a kindly cleric

8

announced at a lunch: 'We have to welcome Dame Sybil Thorndike, a member of the oldest profession in the world.' But Dame Sybil, then a grandmother in her fifties, embodied the Old Vic's pioneering spirit. And even when the Old Vic company returned to London in August 1944 and, unable to occupy its old home, began its now legendary seasons at the New Theatre in St Martin's Lane, it had not lost its idealistic vision. Those seasons, under the directorship of Laurence Olivier, Ralph Richardson and John Burrell, could be said to have anticipated Labour's post-war dream of building a better future.

Cynics hinted that Olivier and Richardson were a pair of carpet-baggers treating a great institution as a vehicle for their own star talents. In fact, both had been part of the pre-war Old Vic and inherited its values: Olivier had even suggested, in a speech from the Vic stage in 1937, that it should become the National Theatre. While sharing the leading roles, the two stars also surrounded themselves at the New with actors of the calibre of Sybil Thorndike, Margaret Leighton, Joyce Redman, Harcourt Williams, George Relph and Alec Guinness. Even more significantly, they broke all the West End rules by pioneering revolving repertory and cheap tickets: half the seats were sold at prices ranging from a shilling and sixpence to four shillings and sixpence, amounts that would have bought between ten and forty cigarettes.

Those lucky enough to have seen the 1944–46 seasons at the New always speak of them as one of the high-water marks of modern British theatre. They yielded performances that are part of theatrical history. Olivier's Richard III, his Hotspur and Justice Shallow in *Henry IV Parts I and II* and his performances of Oedipus Rex and Sheridan's Mr Puff on the same evening are spoken of with awe alongside Richardson's Peer Gynt, Falstaff, Uncle Vanya and Cyrano de Bergerac. The Olivier–Richardson years also influenced impressionable teenagers from Kenneth Tynan to Peter Hall. The latter, in *Making An Exhibition of Myself*, wrote of that first heady season:

> It was still wartime and there was the danger of bombs, sometimes buzz-bombs or V2s. Nobody seemed to take much notice of them. There was a determination that life must go on. London was outwardly grey and boarded-up with deserted streets and a few noisy cars; but inside the buildings there was a sense of an immense party in full swing.

But there was something more than a party going on at the New Theatre. What Olivier, Richardson and Burrell were doing was show-ing what could be achieved by a permanent company playing in reper-tory; and the long-term potential of this did not go unnoticed. Ivor Brown in the *Observer* wrote of 'presentations of the classics worthy of a National Theatre with every resource of staging and casting at its disposal'. The Old Vic was also seen as a highly exportable national asset. After VE Day, the company toured to Antwerp, Brussels, Ghent and Hamburg where the Schauspielhaus had miraculously survived wartime bombing raids. The company even gave a special matinee of Shaw's *Arms and the Man* to British troops stationed in Belsen before going on to the Comédie-Française where *Richard III* enjoyed a spec-tacular triumph. And at the close of the 1945–46 London season the company headed off to New York where they offered an ambitious rep comprising *Henry IV Parts I and II, Uncle Vanya, Oedipus Rex* and *The Critic* and where, according to Olivier in his memoirs, 'the recep-tion was as happy as a marriage-bell'.

The post-war idealism that drove the Old Vic company, however, went far beyond the work on stage. It was clear that what Olivier, Richardson and Burrell intended to create was an embryonic Nation-al Theatre. In January 1946, at the peak of their success, they recom-mended to the governors the Vic Expansion Scheme. This was an astonishingly ambitious five-year plan: one that envisaged the creation of two Old Vic companies alternating between London and the provinces, the earmarking of key repertory theatres as regional bases and the creation of a Theatre Centre to encourage training, experi-ment and the development of young audiences. In the ramshackle world of British theatre, dominated by the fitful brilliance of commer-cial adventurism, this was the equivalent of the Attlee government's plans for a cradle-to-grave welfare state. It was nothing less than a vision of the future in which the theatrical balance would shift from the individual to the ensemble, from the private entrepreneur to the state provider and from commercial short-termism to the search for tomorrow's audience.

The most radical part of the scheme was the creation of a Theatre Centre, comprising a children's theatre, a school and an experimental stage all operating under the umbrella of the Old Vic. The whole oper-ation was to be run by three remarkable men whose careers thread their way through post-war British theatre. Michel St Denis, nephew of the legendary Jacques Copeau, was an inspirational Frenchman whose Compagnie des Quinze had astonished West End audiences in the Thirties and who had founded the pioneering London Theatre Studio in Islington in 1936. George Devine, who had worked with St Denis at the Studio, was a highly regarded actor-director who radiated an air of mature wisdom, thanks partly to the pipe on which he constantly puffed. The third member of the trio was Glen Byam Shaw, who came from a distinguished artistic family and who, like Devine, had been a member of Gielgud's pre-war companies before deciding to turn to directing.

The first fruits of the Centre were visible in the winter of 1946 when Devine launched the Young Vic Company with a production of Carlo Gozzi's *The King Stag* at the Lyric Hammersmith; and, even if the Young Vic never created the repertory of children's plays it hoped for, it had great success in taking high-class productions to an expanded touring circuit. It was the prototype of those theatrical commando units, such as the RSC's Theatregoround and the National's Mobile productions, that were to spring up in the Sixties; and both its name and its principles lived on in the breeze-block building of the Young Vic, created by Frank Dunlop in The Cut in 1970. And it was no accident that Dunlop paid homage to that post-war dream. He himself was one of the distinguished alumni of the Old Vic Theatre School which Michel St Denis set up inside the bomb-damaged Waterloo Road building in the freezing January of 1947. One sad victim of its inauguration ceremony was the pioneering Labour Education Minister, Ellen Wilkinson, who once said she wanted to make Britain 'a Third Programme nation' (later to become BBC Radio 3), who contracted a severe chill from which she died ten days later. But, even if the students were sometimes frozen stiff, they were never bored rigid. At a time when drama academies were often comparable to finishing schools, the St Denis regime was based on a rigorous Stanislavskian approach and the dismantling of the students' personalities in order to acquire greater expressiveness. If descriptions of the School sometimes make it sound like the aesthetic equivalent of boot-camp, its list of graduates was phenomenal: actors such as Joan Plowright, Prunella Scales, Denis Quilley and Alan Dobie, directors of the calibre of Peter Zadek, Michael Cacoyannis, Christopher Morahan and Casper Wrede and such notable designers as Richard Negri (later principal architect of Manchester's Royal Exchange), Alan Tagg and Carl Toms.

Given the fervent idealism that surrounded both the Old Vic's New Theatre seasons and the Theatre Centre, it is legitimate to ask what went wrong. Why was the great vision never fully realised? On paper, the Old Vic looked like a model organisation. While the parent company fulfilled its national responsibility, satellite groups carried out the vital business of training, research and development. But in the end the whole scheme was scuppered by a complicated mixture of factors: the natural ambitions of the key actors, the British belief that administrators and governors are more trustworthy than mere artists and the lack of any coherent financial structure to underpin the grand plan.

Olivier and Richardson were inspirational company leaders and artists with their own personal agenda. Having worked non-stop for two years from 1944 to 1946 in a gruelling repertory for forty pounds a week, both felt the need to recharge their batteries and restore their bank balances. After the success of his wartime film of *Henry V*, Olivier went off in 1947 to direct his black-and-white *Hamlet*: Richardson stayed with the Vic playing Inspector Goole in J. B. Priestley's *An Inspector Calls* and Face in *The Alchemist* while directing Alec Guinness in *Richard II*. Without its twin stars operating in tandem, however, the Old Vic company suddenly lost much of its lustre. Reviewing Shaw's *Saint Joan*, starring Celia Johnson, in 1947, T. C. Worsley in the *New Statesman* described the production as large, broad and coarse: 'so coarse indeed, that at too many moments, instead of watching a company that pretends to the rank of a National Theatre, we might have been assisting at a pageant organised by the YWCA' – although it's only fair to point out that Worsley had a strong aesthetic and sexual allegiance to Binkie Beaumont's West End camp. But 1948 was to prove an even more decisive year for the Old Vic in that both major stars were away from home. Olivier, for ambassadorial as well as artistic reasons, led an Old Vic company on a punishing and lavishly acclaimed six-month tour of Australia and New Zealand. Richardson, trying to fit in enough film work to give himself two clear years at the Vic from 1949, went off to make *Anna Karenina*, *The Fallen Idol* and *The Heiress*. But, in the temporary absence of its twin stars, the Old Vic began to look, in Worsley's words, like 'a moderate stock company' and temporarily ran up a bank overdraft of eight thousand pounds.

Turning a blip in the Old Vic's fortunes into a major crisis, the chairman of the theatre's governors, Lord Esher, drew up a 'Private and

Confidential Memorandum on Future Administration' which proposed termination of the three directors' contracts when they expired in 1949. They would be replaced by a full-time Adminstrator and a seasonally appointed Artistic Director. Given that Olivier and Richardson had planned their working lives around a long-term commitment to the Old Vic, it was a shattering blow. What made it worse was that they both received Esher's news by formal letter while working abroad: Richardson while filming in Hollywood and Olivier while preparing to do a matinee and evening performance of *Richard III* in Sydney as well as suffering from a torn cartilage and the crack-up of his marriage to Vivien Leigh. You could accuse Olivier and Richardson of reckless naivety in being simultaneously absent from London and of leaving too much in the hands of the overworked Burrell. Even so, nothing can excuse either the brutal manner of their sacking or its disastrous short-term consequences for the British theatre. Had they been allowed to stay at the helm of the Old Vic and fulfil all their plans, a National Theatre would quickly have become a living reality.

Who was to blame for their sacking? Some pointed the finger at Tyrone Guthrie who allegedly resented the dominant presence of the two star actors and who felt rebuffed when knighthoods were conferred on Richardson and Olivier in 1947 ahead of himself. Others viewed the icily ambitious Lord Esher as the villain of the piece. Still more blamed Llewellyn Rees, the Drama Director of the Arts Council. Having officially recommended the creation of the post of Old Vic Administrator, he took on the job himself with a show of reluctance worthy of Richard III accepting the English crown.

But, behind the whole shabby manouevring, what one really sees is the triumph of English committee-itis and distrust of the working artist. The irony is that, while Olivier and Richardson were attempting to create a *de facto* National at the New Theatre, bureaucratic moves were afoot to set up a *de jure* institution. In 1945 discussions had begun under the chairmanship of Oliver Lyttelton, a blustering member of Churchill's wartime Cabinet, to unite the existing Shakespeare Memorial National Theatre Committee and the currently renascent Old Vic. In 1946 a formal agreement was reached between the two parties which Lyttelton described as 'a contract of marriage pending the consummation of a marriage'. By 1948 the austere Labour Chancellor of the Exchequer, Sir Stafford Cripps, had even provisionally committed the government to making a contribution of

up to a million pounds towards the building costs: a remarkable gesture at a time of financial restraint. But, as the great and good engaged
in their machinations and the Old Vic was brought to the edge of the
bridal bed, the actual artists who might make a National Theatre
work were marginalised: something that Ralph Richardson had
already grasped with his usual poetic prescience. Olivier in *Confes-
sions of An Actor* recalls how he and Richardson were walking back
one day from one of the endless 'let's-have-a-National-Theatre' committee meetings. As they did so, Ralph foresaw the end of their Baylis-
inspired dream. 'It won't', he said prophetically, 'be our dear, friendly,
semi-amateurish Old Vic any more, it'll be of government interest now
with some appointed intendant swell at the top. They're not going to
stand for a couple of actors bossing the place around any more. We
shall be out, old cockie.'

In fact, the National Theatre was to remain a pipe dream for a
decade or more. Otherwise, everything fell out much as Richardson
predicted. By the end of 1948 he and John Burrell had formally
departed from the Old Vic to be replaced by Llewellyn Rees as Administrator and Hugh Hunt as Artistic Director. Olivier, after his triumphant Antipodean tour which was intended to boost the image of
Britain and train a new company, returned to the New in 1949 for one
last packed-out season. He reprised his Richard III and added Sir Peter
Teazle in *The School for Scandal* and the Chorus in Anouilh's
Antigone to his astonishing post-war portrait gallery. Kicked out of
the Old Vic, he once more became an actor-manager setting up his
own independent company at the St James's Theatre. And, although
the Old Vic company reclaimed its Waterloo Road home in 1950, the
ambitious Theatre Centre fell apart under a welter of mutual recrimi-
nations. The whole saga came to a melancholy climax in May 1951
when the three directors offered their resignations, which were
promptly – even enthusiastically – accepted by Lord Esher. But it had
been clear for a long time that there was no place for this kind of
visionary project in Rees's pragmatic world. Irving Wardle, who
admirably recounts the whole story in *The Theatres of George
Devine*, quotes Rees as saying: 'I went into a class of St Denis and
these boys and girls were all being animals; it was like going into a
lunatic asylum . . . It seemed to me that they were practising a sort of
amateur psychoanalysis. I felt they were preparing the students for a
theatre that didn't exist.' There you have it in a nutshell: the bureau-

cratic mind that fails to grasp the point that only by preparing students for a Platonically ideal theatre does one ever help to bring it about.

All this haemorrhaging of talent sparked a good deal of public indignation: letters to the press, critical editorials, questions in the House. And not without reason. In the space of three years, under Lord Esher's chairmanship, the Vic had managed to get rid of Olivier, Richardson, Burrell, St Denis, Devine and Byam Shaw. Esher's ultimate justification was that he was seeking to give the organisation a stability and fiscal responsibility that would allow it to evolve into the seemingly imminent National Theatre. But, although the Queen laid one of the serial foundation stones on the South Bank in July 1951, the building itself proved to be as much of a mirage as ever. And, even though Guthrie livened things up when he succeeded Hunt as Artistic Director, all Esher did was to terminate a radical vision, treat great artists like improvident schoolboys and usher in a period of prolonged uncertainty in which the Old Vic was constantly outshone by the Shakespeare Memorial Theatre in Stratford under the inspired command of Anthony Quayle. The only consolation is that the work of the artist outlives that of the political fixer; and, while men like Esher and Rees are largely forgotten, the memory of the post-war Old Vic seasons survives. As Harcourt Williams wrote in *The Old Vic Story*: 'It was an undertaking that required great courage, foresight and patience. I sometimes think it could never have been done but for the old friendship that existed between Richardson and Olivier.' Important seeds had also been sown. The Theatre Centre's mandate of better provision for young audiences, more systematic training for actors and even a redefinition of stage space (St Denis's personal dream) was not merely vindicated but actually executed in the years ahead. A glimpse of glory had been vouchsafed; and that was to outlive the boardroom backstabbing and private politicking that accompanied the Old Vic tragedy.

If the Old Vic embodied the idealism of post-war theatre, J. B. Priestley represented that same spirit on a truculently personal level. Born a Victorian in 1894, coming of age in the Edwardian era and famously successful as a novelist and playwright in the Twenties and Thirties, Priestley had acquired a whole new reputation during the war. His Sunday-night broadcasts, delivered on BBC radio throughout the summer of 1940, had combined a pleasure in things English with a sombre confidence in final victory that led Priestley to rival Churchill in national popularity. Indeed when the BBC mysteriously dropped him, Priestley assumed it was because he had excited the wartime leader's jealousy. Whatever the truth of that, Priestley was a national treasure, humane socialist and man of the theatre; and through his plays, books, lectures and articles he became a passionate advocate of the new, post-war idealism. Indeed no playwright of the period charted so accurately the hopes and dreams, as well as the disappointments, of the socialist experiment.

An alliance between Priestley and the Old Vic seemed inevitable; and in October 1946 his play, *An Inspector Calls*, became only the second premiere ever to be given by the company. Written in the winter of 1944–45, the play was first performed in Moscow and Leningrad. But, as a prophetic appeal to the spirit of universal brotherhood, it seemed exactly the right piece to be staged in London in 1946. Like a lot of Priestley's work, it uses an Edwardian setting to convey a modern message. Admittedly there is something schematic about the way each member of the Birling family is held morally responsible by the ghostly Inspector Goole for the death of a young girl, Eva Smith. But the play differs from Priestley's pre-war moral thrillers like *Time and the Conways* and *I Have Been Here Before* in its forthright anger at England's class-ridden, commercially exploitative, sexually chauvinist society. When the young Sheila Birling expresses her horror at the sacked Eva's desolate, half-starved life, the Inspector points out that if it weren't for the numberless Evas of this world, 'the factories and warehouses wouldn't know where to look for cheap labour'. And when Sheila's fiancé defiantly claims that 'we're respectable citizens and not criminals', the Inspector sardonically replies, 'Sometimes there isn't as much difference as you think.' Which makes Priestley sound less like an Edwardian throwback than an early example of a British Brecht. But Priestley had the instincts of a social engineer as well as a demolition expert. He not only suggests there is hope in the younger generation's readiness to confront its guilt. He also gives the Inspector a rousing exit speech that eloquently encapsulates the play's philosophy:

But just remember this. One Eva Smith has gone – but there are millions and millions of Eva Smiths and John Smiths still left with us, with their lives, their hopes and fears, their suffering, and chance of happiness, all intertwined with our lives, with what we think and say and do. We don't live alone. We are members of one body. We are responsible for each other. And I will tell you the time will soon come when, if men will not learn that lesson, then they will be taught it in fire and blood and anguish. Good night.

What is fascinating is the timeless application of Inspector Goole's, and Priestley's, rhetoric. You can imagine the speech being warmly applauded in the Soviet Union in 1945. But it must also have stirred a few consciences in the London winter of 1946–47: it was both a clear warning against the danger of returning to the old stratified, pre-war ways and a plea for a new communitarian society. And the message could hardly have been more timely. While the Attlee government had launched an ambitious nationalisation programme and laid the first foundations of the Welfare State, many of Britain's traditional vested interests remained intact. As Anthony Howard points out in that vital book of essays on post-war Britain, *The Age of Austerity*: 'The public schools quietly set about building up their fee-paying waiting lists, the ancient universities made use of their wartime convalescence to develop a stronger power and prestige than ever and even the House of Lords devoted itself to peaceful recuperation.' Priestley's play was a direct assault on the entrenched forces of Forties conservatism, but it has had a long afterlife. In 1993 Stephen Daldry gave it a brilliant Expressionist production at the National Theatre in which the play suddenly seemed a topical attack on the rancorously divisive, selfishly individualistic society that was Mrs Thatcher's personal legacy. And in 2003 Priestley's play was the prototype for a lively satirical squib by Justin Butcher, *A Weapons Inspector Calls*, about the lies and evasions surrounding the Iraq war. The frightening thing about Priestley's play is its perennial relevance. It is as if the forces of reaction in Britain are always either boldly resurgent or doggedly quiescent. But the theatrical significance of *An Inspector Calls* lies elsewhere. What it reveals is that obsessive concern with using the stage to symbolise and analyse the state of the nation that was to become the animating force in British drama over the next fifty years.

Priestley's claim to be the inventor of 'state-of-the-nation' drama was enhanced by *The Linden Tree*, which opened at the Duchess Theatre in October 1947, backed by the author's own money. No play anatomises more accurately post-war Labour England; and, when it was vivaciously revived by Christopher Morahan at the Orange Tree in 2006, it seemed not just a period piece but, like *An Inspector Calls*, a vibrant play for today. Priestley's passionate, though not uncritical, defence of Labour's peaceful revolution is all the more remarkable when you consider that he wrote it during the freezing, crisis-ridden month of January 1947 when the country was enduring its worst four weeks of winter weather since 1881. Villages were cut off. Factories were closed. Fuel supplies were catastrophically low. On 6 February Emanuel Shinwell, the Minister for Fuel and Power, announced to the Commons that electricity for industry could no longer be guaranteed in various parts of the country, that current for domestic use would have to be rationed and that some power stations would have to be closed. Labour blamed the shortages on the weather and the fuel industry's former capitalist proprietors. The Tories said it was all the fault of doctrinaire socialism: as Lord Swinton wittily observed in the Lords, the crisis was due 'not to an act of God but to to the inactivity of Emanuel'.

Not, you might have thought, the most propitious time to weigh up the pros and cons of Labour's post-war revolution. But Priestley's skill lies in using a domestic crisis to examine the state of England; and, as so often, he makes a family gathering the focus. The action takes place on the sixty-fifth birthday of Professor Linden, an idealistic historian who has forsaken Oxford to teach in a dreary provincial city (christened 'Burmanley') and who is under fierce pressure from the university's Vice-Chancellor to retire. As Linden's family assembles for the birthday, they come to represent different aspects of post-war England. Linden's son, Rex, having seen his best friend killed in the war, is a jaundiced super-spiv who quotes old Chinese poems in order to justify his hedonistic individualism. Sharing Rex's bilious dislike of socialism, daughter Marion has married an aristocratic Frenchman, converted to Catholicism and lives a life of expatriate grandeur. Of the other children, Jean is a dedicated doctor who believes strongly in public-service principles while seventeen-year-old Dinah lives at home, studies the cello and is buoyed up by dreams of an exciting future. But what drives the play forward is Linden's enforced retirement. And when he decides to stay on and fight the university authorities, his wife abandons him, leaving Dinah and a sturdily reliable housekeeper to champion his cause.

The arguments against the play are obvious. The characters all embody Anglo-Saxon attitudes. The longed-for confrontation between the humanist Linden and his new-broom opponent never happens. And few women today would endorse Linden's assertion that 'a man stays where his work is and the woman stays with the man'. What makes the play so impressive, however, is Priestley's ability to do two things at once. On the one hand, he explores a recurrent human dilemma: the enforced retirement of a sixty-five-year-old still at the height of his powers. By making his hero a dedicated teacher who believes that even modestly gifted students deserve the best, Priestley also anticipates Terence Rattigan's *The Browning Version* which surfaced in the West End a year later. But Priestley uses the Linden family as a microcosm of modern England and thereby opens up a debate about post-war society. In a key moment Marion, from the comfortable vantage point of exile, attacks England's crude materialism. Professor Linden responds by invoking the miracle of the loaves and fishes and the post-war vision of social equality:

> Call us drab and dismal if you like, and tell us we don't know how to cook and wear our clothes but for Heaven's sake recognise that we're trying to do something that is as extraordinary and wonderful as it's difficult – to have a revolution for once without the Terror, without looting mobs and secret police, sudden arrests, mass suicides and executions, without setting in motion the vast pendulum of violence which can decimate three generations before it comes to a standstill. We're fighting in the last ditch of our civilisation. If we win through, everybody wins through.

That is the most vigorous defence of the Attlee government and its aims to be heard on the British stage: it also gives the lie to the myth that post-war drama, before the intervention of the Royal Court, was all French-windowed irrelevance. But Priestley's play is anything but flag-waving propaganda. While endorsing Labour values, Linden also questions the 'grey, chilly hollowness' of the trade union and Civil Service machines and the lack of gaiety and colour in contemporary life. Even at his most passionate, Priestley always supplies a grumbling appendix or a moment of mysticism; and music, as always, provides a metaphor for the spiritual values that are in danger of being lost in the drive for higher productivity and technical efficiency. In one highly charged moment, as Dinah plays the Elgar Cello Concerto offstage,

Linden reminisces about the period it evokes and the mood behind the music:

> An old man remembers his world before the war of 1914, some of it years and years before perhaps – being a boy at Worcester – or Germany in the Nineties – long days on the Malvern Hills – smiling Edwardian afternoons – Maclaren and Ranji batting at Lord's, then Richter or Nikisch at the Queen's Hall – all gone, gone, lost for ever – and so he distils his tenderness and regret, drop by drop, and seals the sweet melancholy in a Concerto for 'cello.

It's hard to believe that John Osborne didn't have that speech in mind when Jimmy Porter in *Look Back In Anger*, after a dismissive swipe at Priestley, later admits that 'the old Edwardian brigade do make their brief little world look pretty tempting'. But, far from being nostalgic, Priestley's play addresses the immediate present and looks to the future. It also, with Lewis Casson and Sybil Thorndike in the cast, caught the public mood, running for 422 performances at the Duchess. Even conservative critics saw that this was more than a play about mandatory retirement. As J. C. Trewin wrote, 'Burmanley is the country in little: Priestley symbolises our present struggle, the need to work our passage from the dark.' The state-of-the-nation play had, in fact, been decisively launched.

But Priestley was a polemicist as well as a playwright; and in 1947 he published a brilliantly pungent book, *Theatre Outlook*, which expressed his dissatisfaction with the current mismanagement of the theatrical industry and outlined his vision for the future. It was a book that applied practical socialist principles to reactionary theatrical structures; and, even if it took time for many of Priestley's ideas to come about, it offers exemplary proof of the aspirational idealism that ran through Forties England. Priestley begins by attacking those he sees as the enemies of good theatre. Amongst them are 'English politicians who, taking part in the non-stop drama of Westminster, have usually neither the time nor the inclination to do much serious playgoing'. Priestley also has a go at hidebound playgoers, especially 'the half-witted mobs in provincial cities who visit theatres only to see film stars in the flesh': a temptation even more transparent fifty years on with the transformation of the West End into Hollywood-on-Thames. And he fiercely attacks the Treasury which, via the Arts Council, disburses sixty-five thousand pounds to theatre while at the same time clawing back millions in Entertainment Tax. But Priestley's chief venom is reserved for fat-cat theatre owners in both the provinces and the West End. As Priestley points out, the property owner benefits from a hopelessly one-sided deal: the producer of a play or musical guarantees the theatre owner a weekly minimum covering all the owner's charges and expenses but, over and above that, the owner takes a substantial share of the returns. 'Clearly for the owner,' as Priestley points out, 'this is gambling without losing. If you win, he wins but if you lose, he is no longer with you.'

Having done a swashbuckling demolition job on the casino-like nature of theatrical capitalism, Priestley then sets about supplying socialist remedies. He advocates the creation of a publicly controlled Theatre Authority which would look after the bricks and mortar and prevent any one producing management, such as H. M. Tennent, enjoying a monopoly of prime West End sites. Warmly praising the work of the Old Vic triumvirate, Priestley also advocates the creation of three more national companies on the same lines financed by Entertainment Tax revenue and committed to nationwide touring. In addition, Priestley envisages a chain of Civic Theatres run by public corporations and reflecting local character and outlook: 'Thus Manchester's Civic Theatre would be determinedly, and even grimly, Mancunian.' Even smaller towns and villages are included in Priestley's plan with monthly visits from commando units sent out by the larger Civic Theatres. Priestley's sexual conservatism occasionally shines through. 'We need too,' he suggests, 'a theatre that attracts to itself plenty of virile men and deeply feminine women and is something better than an exhibition of sexual oddities and perversions. We need, in fact, more psychological maleness and femaleness and a good deal less sexiness.' This not only sounds uncomfortably like Shaw's satirical notion of the 'manly man' and the 'womanly woman' but also reflects a growing heterosexual suspicion of the power allegedly exercised by a close-knit gay mafia of producers, playwrights and directors.

Whatever Priestley's sexual hang-ups, he offers a radical vision of an ideal theatre and one imbued with his own brand of poetic feeling. At the end, in an attempt to probe the mystery of theatre, he asks whether there is a profound symbolism in the art of theatre that appeals directly to the unconscious:

Does this little dream of the playhouse somehow chime and match with the long dream of man's life? Does it hint at profound truths for which we have never been able to find the right words? Is there in all this business of setting the stage and donning wigs and costumes and raising the curtain on tragedy and comedy some queer suggestion of symbolic ritual?

Priestley's mysticism was accompanied, though, by a good deal of robust common sense. And it is striking that, at the British Theatre Conference held in February 1948 and bringing together various sections of the industry, many of his proposals were ringingly endorsed. The Chancellor, Sir Stafford Cripps, also announced to the Conference a clause in the Local Government Bill empowering local authorities to spend sixpence in the pound on civic entertainment. One has to remember, however, that any display of idealism in post-war Britain was always met with vehement opposition. The Theatre Managers Association (TMA) not only pulled out of the Conference but sent a circular to MPs raging against the new powers granted to local authorities which they feared would dent their dominance of the provincial touring circuit. They also sought to smear anyone advocating controls on theatre ownership. A review of Priestley's *Theatre Outlook* in their house journal tartly observed: 'Mr Priestley's book costs 7s. 6d. (about nine roubles)' – a propagandist tactic reminding us that post-war progress was often accompanied by 'Reds-under-the-bed' scares.

But the idea of Priestley as a covert communist is laughable. He was too much of a pugnacious individualist ever to accept a system of rigid state control. The truth is, I suspect, that Priestley was both an enlightened internationalist and a deeply English social reformer. You see both these strands in two of his post-war plays which suffered dismally brief runs. *Home is Tomorrow*, produced in 1948, is set on a fictive Caribbean island and argues that the First World owes a moral debt to the Third, that international idealism and global capitalism are natural enemies and that Washington will always do its best to undermine the work of the United Nations: ahead of its time in 1948, the play now looks horrifically topical. Equally remarkable is *Summer Day's Dream*, which expired after fifty performances at the St Martin's Theatre in 1949. Set on the Sussex Downs in 1975, the play combines Priestley's fears of nuclear catastrophe and hatred of superpower arrogance with his love of pastoral England. What is impressive is Priestley's instant alertness to the dangers of nuclear development. Britain's decision to develop its own atomic bomb had been secretly made by a Cabinet committee in January 1947. And that decision only emerged through an off-the-cuff remark by the Defence Minister in the Commons in May 1948. But Priestley had served in the First World War, lived through the Second and seen the images of Hiroshima and Nagasaki, and now viewed nuclear re-armament, of which he became a militant opponent, as a threat to our civilisation. Even more striking is Priestley's passion for what the social historian, Angus Calder, has called 'deep England': that pastoral landscape, celebrated in our literature, 'that stretched from Hardy's Wessex to Tennyson's Lincolnshire, from Kipling's Sussex to Elgar's Worcestershire'. In *Summer Day's Dream* Priestley draws heavily on that rural idyll. He not only shows the Dawlish family, survivors of an implicitly nuclear Third World War, living off the land. He also depicts an invasive American industrialist, Russian bureaucrat and Indian research chemist departing spiritually enriched by the Shakespearean and Kiplingesque magic of rural England. The play is a fantastic, and not always plausible, comedy. But, having initiated the state-of-the-nation play, Priestley shows a faith in deep England that was to be both endorsed and sceptically sabotaged by later generations of writers.

While Priestley was a pioneering writer operating within the existing framework, other artists believed that a radical vision demanded new ways of working and a fresh audience. Out of this belief emerged Theatre Workshop: a penniless collective that stomped the country in the post-war years earning itself a glittering provincial, and European, reputation in the face of Arts Council indifference. Before the war Joan Littlewood, a RADA-trained actress, and Ewan MacColl, a folk singer and socialist writer to whom she was briefly married, had worked together in Manchester-based groups called Theatre of Action and Theatre Union. What linked the groups was fierce political commitment, rejection of naturalism and fascination with the European theories of the Swiss designer, Adolphe Appia, and the Russian experimentalist, Vsevolod Meyerhold. Even though war led to an inevitable diaspora, individual members of the Manchester groups were assigned research projects. And even before VE Day a hard core – comprising Littlewood, MacColl, Gerry Raffles, Howard Goorney and Rosalie Williams – met in Manchester to talk about creating a full-time company. They eventually decided on a new name, Theatre Workshop.

They also drew up a Manifesto:

> We want a theatre with a living language, a theatre which is not afraid of the sound of its own voice and which will comment as fearlessly on Society as did Ben Jonson and Aristophanes. Theatre Workshop is an organisation of artists, technicians and actors who are experimenting in stage-craft. Its purpose is to create a flexible theatre art, as swift-moving and plastic as the cinema, by applying the recent technical advances in light and sound and introducing music and the 'dance theatre' style of production.

The heroic story of the group's battle for survival, tireless travelling and dependence on a handful of enlightened supporters has been well told by Howard Goorney in *The Theatre Workshop Story* and by Joan Littlewood in her autobiography. Characteristically, the group began its post-war life in August 1945 in Kendal thanks to the practical support of John Trevelyan, the local Director of Education and later secretary to the British Board of Film Censors. But what is striking about Theatre Workshop from the start is its attempt to achieve a double revolution: one that embraced both form and content. And you could see that in a first-year repertoire that comprised MacColl's *Johnny Noble* and *Uranium 235*, Molière's *The Flying Doctor* and Lorca's *Don Perlimpin*.

The famous Theatre Workshop style, based on a synthesis of all the arts, clearly evolved from the plays they were doing. MacColl's *Johnny Noble* was a ballad opera about the love of a young merchant seaman and his girl played against a background of Thirties unemployment, the Spanish Civil War and the Second World War. And the opening sequence of MacColl's script shows just how far Theatre Workshop had moved from the British tradition of scenic naturalism and laborious exposition:

1ST NARRATOR (*singing*): On this dead stage we'll make Society appear.

An acting area flood fades up discovering three YOUTHS *playing pitch and toss up stage centre.*

The world is here.
2ND NARRATOR (*speaking*): Our world.

Up boogie-woogie music. A WOMAN *enters, dances across stage and off. Fade out music.*

1ST NARRATOR (*singing*): A little gesture from an actor's hand creates a rolling landscape.

1ST NARRATOR (*speaking*): Or a desert.

2ND NARRATOR (*singing)*: A word from us and cities will arise. The night be broken by screaming factories.

Up burst of machinery. A red spot is faded up discovering a half-naked figure of a MAN. *He mimes raking out a furnace in time to machinery. The light and machine noise fade out together. The* MAN *goes off.*

Already the Theatre Workshop trademarks are there: the fluid mixture of speech and song, expressive use of light and sound, the suggestion of the stage as a metaphorical world. But, in a company which had its origins in pre-war agitprop, there was a political purpose behind the aesthetic grace. And this fusion of radical form and content found its fulfilment in a study of nuclear fission, *Uranium 235*, which became one of the company's greatest successes and stayed in its repertory for five years. The show was a direct response to the dropping of the atomic bomb on Hiroshima in August 1945 and sprang from an urgent need to explain to audiences the history of atomic energy. Bill Davidson, an actor who had trained as an engineer, and the company electrician, Alf Smith, who had a degree in physics, explained the fission process to MacColl and the rest of the group. Out of this came a show that made science thrillingly manifest. There was an atomic ballet in which neutrons and protons danced to create a character called Alfie Particle. Energy was depicted as a gang boss in a Hollywood film noir. Max Planck and Niels Bohr explained the quantum theory as a couple of knockabout comics with phoney German accents. Far from being patronising, the show was endorsed by nuclear scientists: one physics professor even wanted to use it as a teaching aid for students. And it proved equally popular with audiences up and down the country including happy holiday campers at the Filey Butlin's in 1946. It is also worth noting that a similar show, $E=mc2$, was produced more or less simultaneously by America's Living Newspaper, dedicated to instant documentary theatre. As Kirsten Shepherd-Barr notes in *Science On Stage*: 'It is a remarkable coincidence that demonstrates the vital role of theatre on both sides of the Atlantic in the post-war public discourse on nuclear energy. Theatre did not simply reflect but *actively helped to shape* this public discourse.'

Theatre Workshop's ability to reach a wider audience was also helped by influential friends. Tom Driberg, the left-wing Labour MP, was an early supporter and when the company made its London debut in Hanwell in 1946 he brought along a group of parliamentary colleagues including Nye Bevan, Ian Mikardo, Benn Levy and Alf Robens. Critics and audiences in West Germany, Czechoslovakia and Sweden, where the company toured in 1947–48, were wildly enthusiastic. They also grasped the key point that Theatre Workshop was achieving an aesthetic revolution. A Prague critic wrote of *Johnny Noble*: 'With extreme skill and artistry the producer was able with a few shining metal bars to produce a decor of gaol. She uses light, movement and music to perfection.' When I caught up with Joan Littlewood's work in later years, I too was constantly overwhelmed by the one thing people rarely talked about: its sheer aesthetic beauty. But what is staggering is the indifference, often bordering on rank hostility, of the Arts Council to the company's work. Here was a genuine collective offering high-quality work to new audiences throughout Britain; yet, because they were not building-based and were blatantly left-wing, they met with stonewalling, bureaucratic rejection. The Arts Council's constant suspicion of Theatre Workshop – the blackest mark on its post-war record – was to have far-reaching consequences. But the company's achievement was to prove that it is possible, in Sir Philip Sidney's phrase, 'to instruct through delight'. As Kenneth Tynan said, they wiped the puritan frown off the popular image of socialist art; and their belief in communal celebration reminds us that, even in the austerity-conscious Forties, there was a hunger for joy.

At the opposite end of the spectrum from the peripatetic Theatre Workshop stands the poetic revival that flourished in Britain in the late Forties. Theatre Workshop was a socialist, secular, provincial collective: the poetic revival was often thought to be reactionary, religious and metropolitan. And it is true that it is as hard to imagine Joan Littlewood directing *The Cocktail Party* as it is to contemplate T. S. Eliot enjoying a rough night with Theatre Workshop in Barrow-in-Furness. Yet, although they were leagues apart stylistically and the poetic dramatists were eagerly embraced by the theatrical Establishment, these two separate strands of post-war theatre had more in common than one might suppose. Both were suspicious, to varying degrees, of the prevailing naturalism. And both viewed the new post-war Britain with a mixture of hope and disappointment born out of moral idealism. It was just that Joan and her gang wanted more red-blooded socialism and the poetic dramatists more Christianity.

Before the war the poetic revival had in fact largely been identified with a Marxist analysis of society, thanks to the Thirties dramas of Auden and Isherwood. And echoes of their playfulness, if not their Marxism, lingered on in the first landmark of the post-war poetic movement: a satirical verse drama by Ronald Duncan, *This Way To The Tomb*, which opened at Ashley Dukes' Mercury Theatre in Notting Hill Gate in 1945 and proved so popular that a year later it moved to the Garrick for matinees. Rereading it now, one is struck by its mixture of Eliotesque piety and Audenesque verve. Conceived in the form of a Masque and Anti-Masque, the first half deals with the temptations of St Antony while the second half is a boisterous attack on the hucksters who exploit the saint's tomb and on Forties intellectual poseurs. 'I like my painting muddy and all my verse obscure, / My music without melody, You see I'm most mature,' cries an effete Man of Culture in lines that might have come from a Hermione Gingold revue sketch. But, even if Duncan is now largely forgotten, he himself has vital links with the very culture he affected to despise. Having struck up a friendship with Benjamin Britten, who composed the incidental music for *This Way To The Tomb*, he was invited to write the libretto for *The Rape of Lucretia*. Duncan was also a founder of the Taw and Torridge Festival in Devon which in 1955 invited Theatre Workshop to stage the British premiere of Brecht's *Mother Courage*. And it was Duncan's desire to set up a festival circuit for the production of new, non-commercial plays that led, by a roundabout route, to the creation of the English Stage Company.

In the second half of *This Way To The Tomb* the pleasure-seekers and culture-vultures, who flock to a sanctified TV studio dedicated to St Antony, are said to be 'searching for Faith and Love'. And it was the quest for those suitably capitalised qualities that animated much of Forties poetic drama: certainly that of Christopher Fry who achieved the movement's first major breakthrough. Before the war, Fry had been a schoolmaster, rep actor and lyricist for intimate revue penning songs with titles such as 'I'll Snatch The Man From The Moon' and 'You Must Be Very, Very Careful', which sounds like either a contraceptive ad or an embroidered motto by Noël Coward. After the war, Fry first attracted attention in 1946 with *A Phoenix Too Frequent*: like Duncan's play, it offered a tomb with a view in that it was based on the classic story of an Ephesian widow who, under the influence of a handsome officer, reawakens to the joy of life. The production was mainly notable for the London debut of Paul Scofield, who had already won golden opinions in Birmingham and Stratford-on-Avon. But Fry's theme, the triumph of love and life over death, clearly struck a chord in a society debilitated by war and hungry for affirmation.

Fry's belief in 'Faith and Love' also helps to explain the phenomenal success of *The Lady's Not For Burning* which opened at the Arts Theatre in 1948 and enjoyed a nine-month West End run terminated only by John Gielgud's prior commitment to Stratford-on-Avon. Fry's play had a fanciful medieval setting but its themes spoke directly to the post-war world. Its hero, Thomas Mendip, was a discharged, bitterly disillusioned soldier: a recurrent figure in post-war drama. But Fry's real theme was the Christian one of redemption through love. Out of the mutual desperation of Mendip, a soldier seeking to be hanged, and Jennet Jourdemayne, a woman desperate to avoid being burned as a witch, sprang love and acceptance of life. Salvation by love is an old theme. But, in Fry, the language of love was shot through with specifically Christian imagery. After Thomas has portrayed himself as nothing more than 'a perambulating vegetable patched with inconsequential hair', Jennet replies:

> By a quirk
> Of unastonished nature, your obscene
> Decaying figure of vegetable fun
> Can drag upon a woman's heart, as though
> Heaven were dragging up the roots of hell.
> What is to be done?

At the play's end Thomas also replies to Jennet's query as to whether she is an inconvenience to him by saying 'As inevitably as original sin', and their future union is sealed with his cry of 'And God have mercy on our souls'. This was earthly love with a Christian tag: something which in a post-war world, where fifty per cent of parents still sent their children to Sunday school, was regarded as neither exceptional nor offensive. And although Fry's play with its neo-Elizabethan linguistic exuberance is now out of fashion, its title is sufficiently part of our consciousness for Ronald Millar to have adapted it for a speech by Mrs Thatcher to the Tory Party Conference in which she ringingly cried: 'The lady's not for turning!'

If Fry's Christianity was based on compassion and tolerance, that of T. S. Eliot was more associated with guilt and atonement; which is the standard charge made against *The Cocktail Party* whenever it is revived today. Always an advocate of poetic drama, Eliot had explored its possibilities before the war in a tantalising, pre-Pinteresque fragment, *Sweeney Agonistes,* in the sonorously impressive *Murder In The Cathedral* and in the studiously Aeschylean *The Family Reunion.* But Eliot's willed determination to crack the difficult form of poetic drama only bore popular fruit with *The Cocktail Party.* And, whatever our modern reservations, it is worth recalling that, after its initial appearance at the 1949 Edinburgh Festival, it ran for 325 performances at the New Theatre and for almost a year on Broadway. It was a highbrow play with popular appeal; and despite the familiar claim that poetic drama 'remained obstinately on the margins of public taste', the combined runs of Eliot's and Fry's successes would, as Dan Rebellato pointed out in *1956 And All That,* have filled the Royal Court for decades. The success of Eliot's play was obviously boosted by the appearance of first Alec Guinness and then Rex Harrison in the leading role of Sir Henry Harcourt-Reilly, the cocktail party's mysterious Unidentified Guest; but the picture of ordinary theatregoers eagerly queueing up outside the New Theatre, reproduced in Peter Ackroyd's biography of Eliot, suggests that the play tapped some contemporary nerve. If so, what was it?

David Pryce-Jones in *The Age of Austerity* is in little doubt that *The Cocktail Party* appealed to the snobbery of those who felt disenfranchised by a Labour government. In fact, Pryce-Jones sees the play as an extension of the arguments Eliot advanced in 1948 in *Notes Towards The Definition of Culture*: that culture was the highest expression of man; that, if you accepted culture, you must also accept the things that fashioned it such as religion and wealth; that the people most fortunately placed to enjoy and improve this culture should have every opportunity to do so; and that, if you didn't believe this, you shouldn't dabble in culture. Seen from that perspective, *The Cocktail Party* becomes, for Pryce-Jones, 'a play defending a minority culture at a time when the barbarian nomads appeared to have got the upper hand, even to have elected a government of their own choice'. For Pryce-Jones it is 'a play of mood' putting the case for a beleaguered and increasingly isolated cultural elite.

That's a possible interpretation. But, if Eliot were seeking to defend the embattled citadel of a cultural minority, why would he choose the form of a Shaftesbury Avenue adultery comedy? Why also would he fill the play with social satire on the prattling small talk of wealthy partygoers? Right from the start Eliot seems to be slyly subverting the upper-class milieu he depicts. Edward Chamberlayne, hosting a cocktail party from which his wife Lavinia is conspicuously absent, is wryly ironic about a young socialite, Celia Coplestone, with whom he is involved. When a guest remarks that Celia, apart from being interested in cinema, has her poetry, Edward retorts, 'Yes, I've seen her poetry – interesting if one is interested in Celia': a remark whose world-weariness was presumably shaped by Eliot's years as Faber and Faber's poetry editor. But Eliot's love of music hall is signified by the Unidentified Guest's first exit prankishly singing 'What's the Matter with One Eyed Riley?' Eliot's comic use of repetition was also something from which Pinter, among others, was to benefit. At one point a party guest refers to 'the only man I ever met who could hear the cry of bats'. Which is chimingly followed by 'Hear the cry of bats?' – 'He could hear the cry of bats' – 'But how do you know he could hear the cry of bats?' – 'Because he said so. And I believed him.'

Behind the social satire, however, lies a play about the search for what Ronald Duncan, as explained earlier, capitalised as Faith and Love: a constant yearning in the post-war era. But what makes the play so disquieting – and off-putting to many – is Eliot's suggestion that Love may require a passionless acceptance of the status quo while Faith may demand an ecstatic atonement. Harcourt-Reilly, both earthly shrink and surrogate god, finally reunites the separate Chamberlaynes in a loveless, ironic echo of Euripides' Alcestis and Admetus. He then offers to reconcile the disturbed Celia to the human condition in a manner that he has applied to other members of the upper class suffering temporary breakdown:

> They do not repine;
> Are contented with the morning that separates
> And with the evening that brings together
> For casual talk before the fire
> Two people who know they do not understand each other,
> Breeding children whom they do not understand
> And who will never understand them.

On the one hand, Eliot poses a world of stability, decorum and passionless habit: one which many of his original audience would have easily recognised. Against that lies the harder path taken by Celia. She works out her salvation by becoming a Christian nurse and missionary in an African village where she ends up crucified 'very near an anthill'. Rationalist critics have jibbed at this ever since the play's premiere and found something disgustingly disproportionate in Celia's willed martyrdom; and it is perfectly true that the Celia of the opening scenes – a fashionable woman with an appetite for concerts and exhibitions – is transformed rather precipitately into a figure of ant-ridden angst. But the real point is that Eliot, far from offering bromides to the bourgeoisie, was both holding up a mirror to the bland routine of material comfort and arguing that faith, taken to its limits, demands extreme sacrifice. It may be true, as Ackroyd suggests, that there was something strenuously determined about Eliot's attempt to turn himself into a dramatist; but at least in *The Cocktail Party* he imbued modern drawing-room comedy with mystery and pain, moved easily from quasi-naturalistic party talk to passages of melancholy beauty and appealed to an element of spiritual rigour and self-sacrifice that was a component of Forties idealism.

The Cocktail Party was presented in the West End by a shrewd, gargantuan gourmet, Henry Sherek; *The Lady's Not For Burning* by the more quietly fastidious Binkie Beaumont under the banner of Tennent Productions Ltd. Both, in short, were commercial ventures. But I would still rank Eliot and Fry with J. B. Priestley, Joan Littlewood's Theatre Workshop, the Olivier–Richardson–Burrell Old Vic and the St Denis–Devine–Byam Shaw Theatre Centre as embodiments of post-war Idealism. As individuals and institutions they were all wildly different. In personal philosophy they ranged from Christian asceticism to revolutionary socialism and in theatrical style from broad-based classicism to European Expressionism. But what they had in common was an unbudgeable belief that the post-war world required a radical new outlook and approach to theatre.

Against the Idealists I would place the Pragmatists: those who, whether as producers, dramatists, actor-managers or critics saw theatre primarily as a customer service and who tapped into a middle-class nostalgia for pre-war values. Turn the faintly mildewed pages of a pictorial theatre magazine, *Theatre World*, and you find Eric Johns writing in the edition for August 1946 with its cover image of a camp

revue: 'Bit by bit London's pre-war glory is being restored. The foun-
tains are playing in Trafalgar Square, the statues are back on their
plinths but, most significant of all to the playgoer, John Gielgud is
back in St Martin's Lane.' You can almost hear the audible sigh of
relief. After the horrors of war, Gielgud is strutting his stuff at the New
Theatre, where he once starred as Richard of Bordeaux, Hamlet and
Romeo, God's in His Heaven and all is right with the world.

Inevitably, a key figure in the restoration of the West End's pre-war
glory was Binkie Beaumont. As the managing director of H. M. Tennent, he strove to keep a well-shod foot in both the Idealist and Pragmatist camps while ultimately embodying a conservative asesthetic
and fighting tenaciously to sustain the dominance of commercial theatre. Beaumont was responsible for many of the best West End productions of the Forties, played an astute political game and backed talent;
but, in the end, it's difficult to see that he had a genuine vision of theatre beyond simply delivering the goods. In the apt words of Irving
Wardle, 'Beaumont's West End flourished like a traditional grocery
shop selling reliable brands to regular customers.' He was, in fact, the
Fortnum and Mason of London theatre.

What is hard to understand now is the intense resentment and envy
Beaumont's business aroused in the post-war world. But that was
because of its commercial power, tentacular reach and astute manipu-
lation of the financial system, which takes some unravelling. H. M.
Tennent Ltd, of which Beaumont became managing director in 1941,
was the parent company and a large commercial producing management. But under that umbrella were three non-profit-making sub-
sidiaries: Tennent Plays Ltd (wound up in 1947), Tennent Productions
which succeeded that company and stayed in business till 1967, and
the Company of Four created at the Lyric Hammersmith in 1945 and
feeding work into the West End.

The arguments at the time arose from Beaumont's skill in outwitting
his managerial rivals and playing the system to his advantage. Entertainment Tax, a temporary levy placed on theatre tickets in 1916 to
help the war effort, had never gone away: in fact, during the Second
World War it had reached 33.3 per cent. Which meant that a third of
all box-office income went direct to the Treasury. But Beaumont
astutely spotted a loophole in the Finance Act: that a not-for-profit
company presenting 'educational' plays was exempt from the tax. So,
with encouragement from the glamour-loving Maynard Keynes who

was chairman of CEMA (the forerunner of the Arts Council), Beaumont successfully applied for exemption and set up Tennent Plays Ltd in 1942. What that meant in practice was that Beaumont had bigger budgets than his rivals to spend on actors, designers and writers. It also enabled him to bankroll Gielgud's wartime seasons at the Haymarket and Godfrey Tearle's post-war ventures at the Piccadilly as well as West End productions of Thornton Wilder's *Our Town* and *The Skin Of Our Teeth*. And, when in 1947 the Inland Revenue started to ask awkward questions, Beaumont simply wound up the company and formed Tennent Productions Ltd, to which the Arts Council lent its benevolent imprimatur. It was under that banner that work by Euripides, Shakespeare, Vanbrugh and Chekhov was presented as well as, more controversially, plays by Arthur Miller and Tennessee Williams, not to mention such blatantly commercial dramatists as Wynyard Browne and Daphne du Maurier. Meanwhile the Tennent organisation gradually acquired a controlling interest in The Company of Four, set up at the Lyric Hammersmith in 1945 to stage high-quality experimental work and to provide jobs for actors returning from the forces. It did much fine work including Peter Brook's productions of *The Brothers Karamazov*, Sartre's *Men Without Shadows* and *The Respectable Prostitute* and a sensational American play about witchcraft, *Dark of the Moon*. But it was hard to see much that was experimental about revues like *Tuppence Coloured* or a 1950 piece called *Man of the World*, written by C. E. Webber, in which Kenneth Tynan directed a young Diana Dors clad only in pyjama tops.

You can make a plausible case both for and against the Tennent empire. In an era of austerity, it gave London audiences big stars, high production values, the best imports from Paris (Anouilh, Sartre and Cocteau) and New York (the sensationally popular *Oklahoma!* as well as Miller and Williams). It backed living writers such as Noël Coward, Terence Rattigan, Christopher Fry and John Whiting. It also helped promote, even if it didn't actually discover, future stars such as Richard Burton, Paul Scofield, Dirk Bogarde and Claire Bloom. Without it, post-war London theatre would have been a duller, drabber place. Yet 'the firm' controlled at least twenty-five per cent of available West End theatres and reflected the personal predilections of its boss. Charles Duff, in a not unsympathetic portrait of Beaumont in *The Lost Summer*, claims that 'the dichotomy of his homosexuality and the need to be part of the Establishment dictated his taste . . . he liked to be surrounded by Respectability because it was a defence against being found out.' It's a shrewd psycho-sexual point in that it suggests the sumptuous dressiness and high star-quotient of a typical Tennent production was an elaborate form of disguise and guaranteed protection against exposure. John Osborne made a similar point in more caustic terms when in *Almost A Gentleman* he described Binkie Beaumont as the 'Scargill of the iron-lilac Stage Establishment. Feared and fawned upon by gonged actors, famous playwrights and even the Arts Council of which he later became a member, Binkie dominated theatrical fashion for as long as I could remember.' Although the common allegation that Beaumont ran a gay mafia from which heterosexual talent was excluded is hard to substantiate, there is little doubt that he did operate a velvet tyranny in which those who crossed or displeased him were cast into outer darkness.

But the principal argument against Beaumont is that, by running an empire-building commercial organisation under the cloak of Arts Council endorsement and 'educational' aspiration, he helped to devalue the lofty ideals he used as a protective shield. The 'educational' label was a particularly shifty device; as became apparent when Beaumont's legal adviser, F. A. S. Gwatkin, and his accountant, Willie Gillespie, were summoned to appear before a Select Committee on Estimates at the House of Commons in December 1949 to answer specific questions about the non-profit companies. Doubts were raised about the presentation of Daphne du Maurier's *September Tide*, starring Gertrude Lawrence, under the banner of Tennent Productions. Since the play was a wispy Cornish romance about a woman who goes to bed with her daughter's husband, it was not immediately easy to discern its educational value. Gwatkin's response that seeing Gertrude Lawrence perform on stage was an education in itself, comparable to that of watching Sarah Bernhardt, was mere flim-flam. Far more destructive, however, was the blatant hypocrisy of presenting Tennessee Williams' *A Streetcar Named Desire* at the Aldwych in October 1949 as a non-profit venture. Today few would question the educative power of Williams' masterpiece. But in the puritanically prurient climate of 1949 many people, irked by Beaumont's tax-avoiding bluff, turned their attack onto Williams' play itself. Logan Gourlay in the *Sunday Express*, speaking for the English in one of their periodic fits of morality, all too typically condemned the play as 'the progress of a prostitute, the flight of a nymphomaniac, the ravings of a sexual neurotic'.

Beaumont, while flirting with the Idealists, was at heart a theatrical Pragmatist. But it seems sadly ironic that he brought the idea of 'educational' theatre into disrepute at a time when a genuinely educational organisation like George Devine's Young Vic company was struggling to survive. And although the star-fucking Maynard Keynes – 'not a man for wandering minstrels and amateur theatricals', as Sir Kenneth Clark once wryly noted – believed that the Arts Council would benefit from association with Tennent's West End glamour, all the relationship did was to cloud public perceptions of what the Council really stood for. In 1951 the Council formally severed its connections with Tennent Productions. But it had given Beaumont precisely what he needed: official sanction for his ethically dubious policy of presenting palpably commercial plays under a non-profit banner.

What one can't deny is Beaumont's skill in recruiting living writers to his cause; and of all his associations few were more mutually profitable than that with Noël Coward. *Blithe Spirit* opened at the Piccadilly in 1941 and ran well into peacetime, notching up a staggering 1,997 performances. *Private Lives* was revived in 1944 and clocked up 716 performances. And *Present Laughter*, with Coward himself as the exquisitely beleaguered Gary Essendine, had a brief wartime run in 1943 and then a much longer, post-war Haymarket revival in 1947. Even Beaumont didn't have the chutzpah to present these under the 'educational' banner of Tennent Productions. But they were highly profitable ventures that belonged to Coward's heyday and obliquely revealed his own private preoccupations. As the hero of *Blithe Spirit*, spooked by the ghosts of his two wives, finally tiptoes away from the chaos, he clearly embodies Coward's own dream of a life of work and travel unhampered by binding relationships.

Coward's Peter Pan-like fear of maturity, which was his creative mainspring, was to prove his undoing, however, in the post-war world; and, although he enjoyed periodic success particularly as a cabaret performer, he never recaptured the careless rapture of earlier days. You only have to read his frank and revealing *Diaries* to realise that for Coward, forever trapped in the privileged celebrity of youth, the Second World War was a private and political watershed. 'Personally,' he writes on 21 May 1945, 'I think Labour has behaved abominably throughout this war and before it. At least the Conservatives have some sense of leadership and it is idiotic to try and jettison Churchill at this moment.' When the General Election results were declared on 26 July, Coward fumed: 'It is appalling to think that our Allies and enemies can see us chuck out the man who has led us magnificently through these horrible years.' Ever an Empire loyalist, Coward also rages on 9 May 1946 over Attlee's admission that he had overstated Dominion support for the withdrawal of British forces from Egypt: 'Faced with such palpable incompetence and dishonesty, I should have thought that the great majority of the people would realise that the present Government, for which they voted with such enthusiasm, was not very good; but I am afraid that the people of this country are too stupid and complacent to grasp what is happening.'

I suspect that Coward, the supreme example of the anti-Idealist post-war dramatist, never forgave the British for what he saw as their back-stabbing betrayal in electing a Labour government. But, while that was his right as a private citizen, what is significant is the debilitating effect that his hostility to the post-war world had on his creative talent. His revue, *Sigh No More,* presented under Binkie's banner at the Piccadilly in August 1945, visibly patronised the working classes: 'We may find if we swallow the Socialist bait / That a simple head cold is controlled by the State,' sang one particular couple from Battersea Rise. Coward's big post-war musical, *Pacific, 1860* – which reopened the badly bombed Theatre Royal, Drury Lane in December 1946 – was a prodigious flop. But it was *Peace In Our Time*, conceived in Paris during the Liberation and finally staged at the Lyric, Shaftesbury Avenue in July 1947, that truly revealed Coward's bilious antipathy to modern Britain and total failure to understand its changing character.

Demolishing the myth that he was a stylishly apolitical writer, Coward wrote a 'what if?' state-of-the-nation play. What if, asked Coward, Britain had fallen under Nazi occupation in 1940? Would it have suffered the same 'atmosphere of subtle disintegration, lassitude and, above all, suspicion' that he had witnessed first-hand in France? Taking as his setting a Knightsbridge pub filled with an improbable mix of working-class Cockneys, lorry drivers, county ladies and intellectual homosexuals, Coward sets up the situation with a practised skill. There is nothing in the opening scene, which takes place in November 1940, to convey anything out of the ordinary until, as Big Ben strikes nine, the publican's wife remarks: 'It's funny to think they can still hear that all over the world.' As Harold Hobson wrote, 'without that single-line speech we should find it difficult to accept the premise of Mr Coward's play.'

Sadly, what follows is vindictive melodrama. Still smarting from the pre-war condescension of London's literati – Cyril Connolly had once described him as 'an essentially unhappy man who gives one the impression of having seldom really thought or really lived' – Coward makes his chief villain the effete editor of a left-wing weekly who consorts with a pansy Austrian scenic designer and betrays the pub's resistance cell to the Germans. Even more startling is Coward's attack on Britian's moral decay. At one point a plain-speaking pub regular suggests, with heavy historical irony, that it would have been a disaster if we had won the Battle of Britain:

Because we should have got lazy again and blown out with our own glory. We should have been bombed and blitzed and we should have stood up under it – an example to the whole civilised world – and that would have finished us. As it is – in defeat – we still have a chance. There'll be no time in the country for many a long day for class wars and industrial crises and political squabbles. We can be united now – we shall have to be – until we've driven them away, until we're clean again.

It is perfectly possible, as Philip Roth rivetingly proved nearly sixty years later in *The Plot Against America*, to create an alternative history in which fascist triumph acts as an ironic metaphor for present debility. But Coward's play not only lacks Roth's imaginative consistency. It even seems to imply that wartime defeat would have been a damned good thing and prevented the erosion of our basic conservative values: better a brief period of Nazi rule, Coward implies, than a descent into post-war socialism. But what makes the play not just an artistic failure but morally contemptible is Coward's inability to convey the horror of Nazi occupation or to offer, one brief reference aside, any hint as to the likely fate of British Jews. Coward had enthusiastically told Beaumont it was 'my best play yet, dear boy'; but, while it limped along through the glorious summer of 1947, it closed before the end of the year. And one can see why. Coward had fatally misjudged the mood of the new Britain in which, whatever the hardship, there was an unflinching spirit of optimism. As Ian Bancroft, a young Treasury insider, told the historian Peter Hennessy: 'To be young, alive and unwounded was a joyous experience and there was, too, a great deal of hope. There was a great relief at the war being won and coming through alive.' With news, in the summer of 1947, that the Marshall

Plan would come to the aid of Europe's war-devastated economies and with Compton and Edrich blazing away at Lord's, people didn't want to be told that a Nazi victory would have forced us to pull our socks up. 'I have a sick at heart feeling about England,' Coward confessed to his diary on 23 September 1947. And, although he lived long enough to see his reputation revived, Coward's creative demise and internal exile really starts with the unfortunate *Peace In Our Time*.

Inevitably, because he enjoyed wartime success on Shaftesbury Avenue, was associated with the Tennent regime and lived a discreetly homosexual existence, Terence Rattigan is often linked with Noël Coward. They seem to epitomise boulevard theatre at its most sleekly assured in the pre-Royal Court era. But of far greater significance than the similarities are the differences between them. Coward was born into the Teddington middle classes in 1899; Rattigan, born twelve years later, was the privileged son of a career diplomat. Coward was brought up in the hermetic world of theatre; Rattigan went to Harrow and Oxford where, as a radical undergraduate, he was despatched to review Coward's *Cavalcade* at Drury Lane, heading his distinctly chilly review 'No, No, Noël'. And, while Coward was always a sentimental reactionary petrified of change, Rattigan was a perennially elusive figure whose heart was with the social and theatrical Idealists even if his head was with the Pragmatists. Formally, Rattigan was a traditionalist drawn to classical structures and reticent understatement: thematically, he endorsed defiance of convention and society's repressive rules. It's tempting to attribute the division in Rattigan's work to his double life as debonair Albany clubman and camouflaged homosexual; but that kind of compartmentalisation was common to many in the post-war theatrical Establishment. The schism in Rattigan's work seems to correspond to something deeper within his nature: a desire to follow his liberal instincts while appeasing his supposedly conservative audience.

It is that tension that informs Rattigan's post-war work and makes it infinitely richer and more complex than Coward's. In 1947 Rattigan enjoyed a huge success with *The Winslow Boy* which ran for 478 performances at the Lyric, Shaftesbury Avenue. As the gripping story of a young cadet, Ronnie Winslow, who is expelled from the Royal Naval College on a charge of petty theft and finally vindicated after his case has come to open trial, the play was inevitably claimed by the political right: the Attlee-bashing *Daily Mail* saw it as 'Mr Rattigan's tract for these particular times' in that it showed the private citizen triumphing over Whitehall bureacracy. But the play is far subtler than that. What it actually shows is Catherine Winslow, Ronnie's militant sister, making common cause with a political opponent, the icily effective Sir Robert Morton, in pursuit of liberty and justice. In its yearning for an alliance between the polarities of the radical left and Establishment right, the play touches on the unresolved tension within its author.

But the division in Rattigan – who enjoyed intimate friendship with both the Tory MP, Chips Channon, and Anthony Asquith, the son of Britain's last Liberal Prime Minister – was exemplified, aptly enough, in a double bill, produced in 1948, comprising *The Browning Version* and *Harlequinade*. The first, vastly superior play, is the moving story of a retiring, unloved schoolmaster who breaks down when presented by a pupil with a second-hand copy of Browning's translation of *Agamemnon*. But Rattigan's own championship of the underdog is shown in the hero's final speech in which he informs the headmaster that he intends to exercise his right to speak second at the school prize-giving; it is an act of open rebellion by a man who has played all his life by Establishment rules and, as performed by Michael Redgrave on film and Nigel Stock and Paul Eddington in later revivals, always leaves you cheering on the oppressed. But Rattigan's contradictory conservatism emerges in *Harlequinade*, a fitfully amusing piece about the inbred battiness of theatre folk and the absurdity of taking Arts Council-supported Shakespeare to the masses. 'Theatre with a social purpose indeed!' cries the stage manager of the touring troupe run by Arthur Gosport. 'It's a contradiction in terms. Good citizenship and good theatre don't go together. They never have and they never will. All through the ages, from Burbage downwards, the theatre – the true theatre – has consisted of blind, anti-social, self-sufficient, certifiable Gosports.' Having championed defiance of authority in *The Browning Version*, Rattigan tamely panders to popular prejudice in *Harlequinade*.

Rattigan's work took a new turn, however, in *Adventure Story*: an epic play about Alexander the Great, starring Paul Scofield, that opened at the St James's in 1949 and closed after 107 performances. At the time it was regarded as a famous flop: proof that an essentially intimate, domestic writer lacked either the poetic power or psychological penetration to tackle a big historical theme. In fact, the play offers a perfectly coherent account of the way Alexander's initial belief in universal peace turned into a tragic dream of world conquest. Starting with Alexander on his deathbed, asking 'Where did it all go wrong?', it attempts to answer the question by surveying his twelve-year career of military adventurism. But what stops the play being the masterpiece it might have been is a mixture of Rattigan's own emotional reticence and the inhibiting theatrical conventions of the time. The play implies that Alexander's real failure was one of self-knowledge: in particular, a refusal to accept his bisexuality. But, although we see Alexander seeking to disprove his late father's belief that he was an effeminate weakling, Rattigan tiptoes nervously round his theme. In particular, he ducks the historically attested fact of Alexander's heartbroken reaction, echoing that of Homer's Achilles to Patroclus, to the death of his close friend, Hephaestion. Maybe, given the existence of theatrical censorship and the Lord Chamberlain's known horror of explicit homosexuality, it is unfair to castigate Rattigan for failing to come clean. The idea of a hero who puts fame before friendship and who then suffers remorse after the death of his male lover might also have seemed uncomfortably close to home: Rattigan's own celebrity status had cost him an intimate relationship with a young actor, Kenneth Morgan, who coincidentally committed suicide during the final week of the tour of *Adventure Story*. In the end the play lost Binkie Beaumont, who oddly failed to use the 'educational' escape-route in presenting it, his capital investment of eight thousand pounds, which was the most the Tennent management had ever spent on a new play. But, although *Adventure Story* was a flop, it opened up a theme which Rattigan was to explore with more courage and conviction in later work: the need to confront one's true nature.

If any dramatist of the post-war period came close to breaking the coded secrecy that surrounded homosexuality, it was Emlyn Williams in a now-forgotten but astonishing play, *Accolade*. Like Rattigan – for whom he had brilliantly played Sir Robert Morton in *The Winslow Boy* – Williams was Oxford-educated, part of the Tennent empire and a writer who, while working inside a commercial framework, sought to extend its possibilities. The pre-war *Spring, 1600*, revived in 1945, eerily anticipated the plot of the Stoppard-scripted movie, *Shakespeare In Love*. *The Wind of Heaven* (also 1945) boldly posited the idea of the Second Coming taking place in a small Welsh village. But it was Williams' Celtic obsession with doubleness and ambiguity that marked him out as a peculiarly fascinating writer. And that doubleness lay at the heart of *Accolade*, which came close to blowing the cover off the sexual pretence which governed so many lives in the post-war theatrical, literary and political Establishment.

Williams' play is essentially a Jekyll-and-Hyde story about a celebrated, Nobel-prize-winning author, Will Trenting, who, just as he is about to be knighted, is revealed to have a scandalous secret life. We learn that, although happily married with a wife and son, he habitually attends orgies in a Rotherhithe pub and has been photographed having sex with a fourteen-year-old girl under the impression that she is much older. The girl's father, a shabby-genteel novelist, first tries to blackmail Trenting and, when that fails, reports him to the police. The play ends with the mob stoning the disgraced Trenting's house while he accepts that the price of being an established member of society is that one has to conform to its rules. But, while Williams casts the situation in heterosexual terms, it makes infinitely more sense when seen from a homosexual standpoint. It was an open secret in theatrical circles that Williams himself, married with two sons, was bisexual. And the play clearly combines the public figure's fear of exposure with a justification of the creative stimulus of a double life. Trenting, played by Williams himself in Glen Byam Shaw's production, tells his publisher that since the age of sixteen he has been drawn towards promiscuous sex and to people who are 'sordid, raw, impudent': in other words, rough trade. And the publisher, improbably named Thane Lampeter, sees Trenting's night-owl roamings as both an artistic inspiration and a mark of society's hypocrisy. As Lampeter finally tells the writer, two things will help him face his punishment:

> First we all have *one thing we're ashamed of*. All those out there have. Even the judge has, who'll be peering at you over his glasses making you feel like dirt. His secret may be the nastiest of the lot. Only *you* have committed the sin of being found out. The other thing is that, whatever trouble you have got into, you have *lived*. And because you've lived, you've written.

It's a measure of the commercial constrictions of the time, and the power of the Lord Chamberlain, that Williams could not remotely suggest that his hero might have had sex with a fourteen-year-old boy; and the proprieties are duly observed by assigning Trenting to punitive exile in Guernsey. But what is staggering is just how far Williams does go at a time when so many public figures, not least in the theatre, led double lives and were aware of the penalties for indiscretion. Tremors had been caused by the wartime imprisonment first of theatrical photographer Angus McBean, and later of Ivor Novello: in the latter case, for the relatively minor misdemeanour of using rationed petrol for private purposes. Homophobic journalists, led by the *Evening Standard*'s Beverley Baxter, were starting to write innuendo-filled articles questioning the theatre's dominance by congenital bachelors. Even the rising young critical star, Kenneth Tynan, cryptically observed: 'The most startling feature of the current scene is plays by Emlyn Williams, for Emlyn Williams and *about* Emlyn Williams.' *Accolade,* dismissed by some critics as 'dirty' and 'vulgar', ran for a respectable 180 performances at the Aldwych; and, although it finally bows to the moral laws of the day, proves that the post-war West End theatre was not all fluff and frolic. It also suggests that Williams, a Welsh wizard and a sexual pioneer, is long overdue for public revival.

But, looking back at Britain as a whole from 1945 to 1950, one finds an extraordinary mixed picture in which rapid political advance coexisted with the survival of certain pre-war values. A phenomenal amount had been achieved by the Attlee government: the foundation of the Welfare State, full employment, progressive decolonisation, economic recovery, industrial stability. It is a, literally, striking fact that industrial disputes caused the loss of only nine million working days between 1945 and 1950, compared with 178 million in the five years after the First World War. As Labour prepared for a General Election on 23 February 1950 it could point to a nation that had weathered the post-war storms, was healthier and more financially secure and was playing its part in the wider world through organisations such as the OEEC (Organisation of European Economic Cooperation) and NATO. Yet there still existed a strong sense of social polarisation; and nowhere was this more visible than in the education system which, with its division between private and state schools, perpetuated the old class boundaries. I recall this vividly since my father, anxious that I follow in his footsteps, sent me at great sacrifice in 1949 to the fee-paying Warwick School: a traditional public school, run on strict Arnoldian lines, where sport was regarded as of vital character-building importance and 'sound learning' (in the headmaster's own words) was seen as a necessary adjunct. In many ways, it was a good school; but, as the son of a struggling junior accountant, I was very much aware of being surrounded by the scions of prosperous Midland farmers, landowners and business executives. Even the presence, in the main school, of a limited number of scholarship boys could not dent the air of privileged exclusivity that left me feeling like a perennial outsider.

If the Attlee government could not in the space of five years achieve the kind of classless society many had dreamed of in 1945, it still succeeded in laying many of the foundations of the post-war world: the 1950 Conservative manifesto may have promised to roll back the frontiers of nationalisation but it accepted the newly enacted Welfare State legislation. But what is revealing is how accurately the theatre reflected the temper of the times. Artists and institutions grasped the need for urgent change. The Arts Council laid down the principle of public subsidy. Olivier, Richardson and Burrell not only elevated the Old Vic into a world-class troupe but realised that it could only prosper if supported by a school and a young company. J. B. Priestley initiated the state-of-the-nation play. And, while Theatre Workshop traversed Britain with adventurous work, regional repertory theatres began to stir into active life. The gradual transformation of what was then called 'provincial' theatre is, in fact, one of the great post-war success stories, graphically told by Charles Landstone, a key Arts Council apparatchik, in his book *Off-Stage*.

Birmingham Rep, long at the forefront of provincial theatre under the benign supervision of Sir Barry Jackson, in the autumn of 1945 engaged a nineteen-year-old director called Peter Brook who staged three remarkable productions: Shaw's *Man and Superman*, Shakespeare's *King John* and Ibsen's *The Lady From The Sea*, the first two featuring a young Paul Scofield as Jack Tanner and the Bastard. Jackson had also in 1945 assumed direction of the Shakespeare Memorial Theatre in nearby Stratford and radically reorganised what had been a somewhat rushed, helter-skelter, five-month festival: one of his shrewdest moves, in fact, was to take Brook and Scofield with him. Brook's Watteauesque *Love's Labour's Lost* of 1946 and his 1947 *Romeo and Juliet*, with its vast empty space and surrounding circlet of miniaturised crenellated walls, quickly became Shakespearean benchmarks. Admittedly excitement on stage wasn't always matched off it: Philip Hope-Wallace in an article in *Penguin New Writing* in 1947 caught the mood of the times well when he complained of Stratford's meagre hospitality and said that 'the chances are that at the end of the performance you will be decanted into pouring rain sans light, food, transport or even a cup of cocoa'. But all over the country provincial theatre came to life, with Arts Council aid. The Bristol Old Vic reopened the beautiful Georgian Theatre Royal in February 1946 with a company that included Pamela Brown, Yvonne Mitchell, William Devlin and Kenneth Connor. Salisbury Arts Theatre, under Barbara Burnham and subsequently Denis Carey and Peter Potter, achieved exemplary standards while touring each production to towns in the surrounding area. And in Scotland the Citizens' Theatre, Glasgow, founded by dramatist James Bridie, took over a disused variety house in the heart of the Gorbals, and opened in September 1945 with J. B. Priestley's *Johnson over Jordan*. Tatty weekly reps still survived; but the move to a fortnightly and three-weekly system was actively encouraged, mini-touring circuits were created in the Midlands and the South-West and the result was an audience that, according to Landstone, was 'at least thirty per cent larger than that of the nineteen-thirties'.

Change was in the air; yet some areas of theatre remained obstinately impervious. H. M. Tennent Ltd, as we have seen, kept the star system afloat and manipulated the tax system to its advantage. Ownership of the bricks and mortar in Shaftesbury Avenue, and in many of the big touring theatres, was dominated by the conservative Prince Littler Consolidated Trust. And, although individual dramatists like Fry, Eliot, Rattigan and Williams stretched the boundaries of commercial possibility, many other writers were content to work within their confines. Since the truly popular plays of any period are the ones that tend to get omitted from histories of drama, it is worth recalling some of the big crowd-pleasers of the Forties. The daddy of them all was R. F. Delderfield's *Worm's Eye View*, starring Ronald Shiner, which opened at the Whitehall Theatre in December 1945 and ran for an initial five hundred performances: after a brief interruption, it resumed in 1947 to clock up a record-busting further 1,745 performances. Since it dealt farcically with life in a North Country RAF billet, it clearly tapped into a perverse nostalgia for the deprivations of wartime. In contrast, Ivor Novello's *Perchance To Dream*, which opened at the London Hippodrome in April 1945 and ran for 1,022 performances, was a perfumed musical romance set in the aristocratic retreat of Huntersmoon: its most famous song, 'We'll Gather Lilacs', was on the lips of everyone – well, almost everyone – in the late Forties and neatly

44

encapsulated the show's note of wistful escapism. Meanwhile William Douglas Home's *The Chiltern Hundreds*, which opened at the Vaudeville in 1947 and ran for an impressive 651 performances, perfectly caught a reactionary mood that was the very antithesis of Priestley's *An Inspector Calls*. Set in a feudal castle belonging to Viscount Lister, the play begins with the assembled household listening over the radio to the long tale of Conservative defeats at the 1945 Election. 'Poor Mrs Churchill,' sighs the Countess, clearly echoing the sentiments of many in the audience. But the play's central joke depends upon a subsequent by-election in which the Labour Viscount is defeated by his Conservative butler whose biggest laugh comes when he declares, 'I always understand that finance is uppermost in the mind of every Labour member.' For Douglas Home it was a double whammy: attacking titled renegades who betray their class and endorsing salt-of-the-earth servants who preserve the ancient standards.

Only a prig would deny people the right to escapism or fail to see that, after a long and gruelling war, audiences were hungry for laughter, lightness and gaiety. But when you survey British theatre in the Forties you feel that the tensions within the national psyche were being enacted on the nation's stages. In London, in particular, you see a constant battle between nostalgia and progress. Stop the clock at any moment in the West End – say the early months of 1948 – and you find a host of entertainments that would have been equally at home in the pre-war world: a Lonsdale comedy starring Jack Buchanan and Coral Browne, a Ben Travers farce with Ralph Lynn and Robertson Hare, a courtroom thriller with Basil Radford, an intimate revue with Joyce Grenfell and Max Adrian. Yet in the same period you have Shakespeare and Shaw at the New, a black American company in *Anna Lucasta* at His Majesty's, an adventurous play about sex in a boys' public school at the Fortune, an anti-war play at the St James's and Pirandello's *As You Desire Me* at the Embassy. Constantly derided as a barren theatrical desert, the first five years of the Attlee government were in fact a period of turbulent activity: one in which the Idealists and the Pragmatists were locked in permanent opposition while sometimes adroitly stealing each other's clothes. The big question, as Britain entered on a new decade and Labour went to the country on an optimistic slogan of 'Let Us Win Through Together', was which faction would come to dominate the theatre of the future.

II

1950–55
Safety First

In fact, the Pragmatists were very much in the ascendant in the first half of the Fifties. Although the theatre wasn't exactly dull – how could it be with Peter Brook directorially dominating the West End, Ionesco and Beckett emerging at the Arts and Olivier hitting the Shakespearean heights at Stratford? – it lacked the crusading idealism that sustained it in the immediate post-war years. Where, people reasonably asked, were the new playwrights? What happened to the visionary idea of a National Theatre? And what, if anything, did theatre have to say about a world shadowed by the Cold War and the nuclear arms race?

When President Truman in January 1950 gave the go-ahead for a crash research programme into the hydrogen bomb, he not only lifted the peacetime conflict with the Soviet bloc onto a new plateau: he also helped to create a widespread, and entirely plausible, belief that the end of the world might happen within decades, if not years. The climate of fear created by the bomb eventually began to permeate the culture at large. But, looking back at the British theatre of the early Fifties, one notices the way intimations of disquiet and unease took time to emerge and then often came from abroad. The classical theatre was strong. Good new plays spasmodically appeared. But, as the country itself gradually moved from a hunger for radical change to a desire for incremental improvement, the theatre seemed to be affected by the nation's rightward drift.

The political landscape was certainly shifting. In the February 1950 General Election, Labour, although getting 46.1 per cent of the popular vote, ended up with a slender majority of six. It survived precariously over the next eighteen months in an atmosphere of international crises and internal feuding. The relationship with America had been badly damaged in January 1950 when Dr Klaus Fuchs, head of theoretical physics at the atomic energy base at Harwell, was revealed to be a Soviet spy: Congress, in fact, demanded that Britain be trusted with no more atomic secrets. But the Anglo-American relationship was quickly repaired when Communist North Korea invaded that country's South in June 1950. It was instantly agreed by the Cabinet that a British military detachment be sent to fight alongside the Americans to confirm our position as 'first in the queue' at Washington: an argument we were to hear, couched in Blairite language, over half a century later at the time of the illegal invasion of Iraq. Pressure from America on Britain to re-arm massively, in the light of the Cold War, also had a direct impact on domestic politics. Sir Stafford Cripps had already infuriated the Labour left by sacrificing sacred socialist principles to the demands of the defence budget. But, when Cripps retired as Chancellor in October 1950 to be succeeded by Hugh Gaitskell, Labour succumbed to one of its periods of bloodthirsty tribal warfare. Matters came to a head in April 1951 over Gaitskell's proposed NHS charges for dental and ophthalmic treatment: the resignation of Aneurin Bevan as Health Minister was quickly followed by that of Harold Wilson at the Board of Trade and John Freeman at the Ministry of Supply, ushering in a left–right factionalism that was to haunt the party for decades.

The deep divisions in the country at large were also highlighted by the one undoubted coup of Labour's last year of office: the 1951 Festival of Britain. The idea of a festival celebrating British artistic achievement and scientific and technical innovation had been mooted by Herbert Morrison as far back as 1947. It was a bold, brave concept intended not only to echo the Great Exhibition of 1851 but also to bring a bit of colour and fun to a war-weary nation. As soon as the idea was launched, it was ridiculed by Churchill, the Tory opposition and large sections of the press as an expensive frivolity. Nevertheless it went triumphantly, if sometimes haphazardly, ahead: the main site for the Festival was on London's newly developed South Bank but there was also a funfair in Battersea Park and a swathe of local events up and down the country.

But, if the Festival had great symbolic significance in showing that the state had a role to play in sponsoring communal pleasure, it also exposed a deep cultural divide in British life: one that Michael Frayn famously described in *The Age of Austerity* as a confrontation between the Herbivores and the Carnivores:

In fact Festival Britain was the Britain of the radical middle-classes – the do-gooders; the readers of the *News Chronicle*, the *Guardian*

47

and the *Observer*; the signers of petitions; the backbone of the BBC. In short, the Herbivores, or gentle ruminants, who look out from the lush pastures which are their natural station in life with eyes full of sorrow for less fortunate creatures, guiltily conscious of their advantages, though not usually ceasing to eat the grass. And in making the Festival they earned the contempt of the Carnivores – the readers of the *Daily Express*; the Evelyn Waughs; the cast of the Directory of Directors – the members of the upper and middle classes who believed that if God had not wished them to prey on all smaller and weaker creatures without scruple he would not have made them as they are . . . For a decade, sanctioned by the exigencies of war and its aftermath, the Herbivores had dominated the scene. By 1951 the regime which supported them was exhausted and the Carnivores were ready to take over.

Predictably the Carnivores loathed the Festival. The Skylon, which loomed over the South Bank site like a luminous exclamation mark, was likened to the British economy in that it had 'no visible means of support': a joke later repeated, with suitable variations, about the Millennium Dome conceived by Herbert Morrison's grandson, Peter Mandelson. The Beaverbook press attacked the Festival as a monumental waste of eleven million pounds of public money. Noël Coward sent up the whole project in a song, ironically entilted 'Don't Make Fun Of The Festival', written for *The Lyric Revue*. But the Festival drew eight and a half million people to the South Bank and Battersea Pleasure Gardens. As an eleven-year-old kid, taken by my parents, I was one of them and remember to this day the jostling excitement of Ralph Tubbs' Dome of Discovery and the eccentric whimsicality of the Emett Railway in Battersea. 'People making for the South Bank', wrote the *Manchester Guardian*'s London correspondent, 'begin to smile as they come close to it.' And, from a more privileged vantage point, Harold Nicolson in his *Diaries* described the main exhibition as the most intelligent he had ever visited, adding, 'I have never seen people so cheered up or amused, in spite of a fine drizzle of rain and a Scotch mist.' It's significant that both writers seize on the liberating sense of pleasure provided by the Festival. But it was to prove something of a triumphant last hurrah both for the Herbivores and the Attlee government. A month after the closing ceremony the country went to the polls in October 1951 and returned the Conservatives with 321 seats as against 295 for Labour and six for the Liberals. As a child, I was at first confused by and then resentful of the injustice that enabled Labour to lose the election while winning a majority of the popular vote. I also never recovered from hearing a detested fellow pupil at school storm into our classroom deliriously shouting, as the result was declared, 'We're in!' His arrogant assumption that we were all little Conservatives determined my politics for life.

Although the Festival of Britain was a glorious swansong for Labour, one can't in truth say it did much for theatre: of the extra grant of £400,000 received by the Arts Council for the Festival only £55,000 went to drama. And it says much about the temper of the times that the chief beneficiary was Shakespeare. Everywhere you looked in 1951 – not just at the Old Vic and Stratford-on-Avon but in the West End and around the regions – it was a bonanza year for the Bard. And it was a process that continued throughout the Fifties, leading Stratford-on-Avon's Shakespeare Memorial Theatre, first under Anthony Quayle and then Glen Byam Shaw, to new and glorious heights. But the downside of all this was cogently argued by J. B. Priestley in an essay written in 1955 for a collection of reviews by the renowned Bardolater, Ivor Brown. Priestley's essay, entitled 'The Case Against Shakespeare', argued that the Elizabethan dramatist was 'the greatest blackleg in the business' in that no management had to pay him royalties; that he consistently seduced the top acting talent; and that he appealed to the inherently conservative instinct of British playgoers who preferred him to contemporary playwrights. 'But,' as Priestley forcefully claimed, 'a nation's drama cannot be fully alive unless it is being continually created.' Shakespeare, in short, was driving the living writer out of business.

Not only that: there was a critical bias against anything that deviated from accepted Shakespearean conventions and a comparable endorsement of the tried and true. The Oliviers were hailed for their appearance in *Antony and Cleopatra*, coupled with Shaw's *Caesar and Cleopatra*, at the St James's; only a cheeky young upstart called Kenneth Tynan, then doubling as actor and critic, had the nerve to suggest that Sir Laurence was scaling down his formidable, blow-lamp ebullience to accommodate the more miniaturist skills of Vivien Leigh. Tynan went on wickedly to claim that Olivier was putting his talent into his work and his genius into his wife. Peter Brook's Festival of

49

Britain production of *The Winter's Tale* at the Phoenix, with Gielgud as Leontes, was also praised for its sobriety and austerity: the one visual coup came when the stage rained snow, as in one of those shaken Victorian glass toys, as Time turned the clock forward sixteen years. But when Alec Guinness took an original approach to *Hamlet* at the New he suffered one of the most humiliating flops of his career. Admittedly the first night was a fiasco in which the New Theatre's lighting board malfunctioned so that court scenes were shrouded in obscurity and the battlement scenes played in a blaze of light: actually not such a bad idea. But Guinness was crucified for playing down the 'sweet Prince' side of Hamlet's nature and emphasising his casual cruelty: something that actors of a later generation would do instinctively. The production was also attacked for the exuberant oddity of its casting: especially that of the ubiquitous Kenneth Tynan, as First Player. Beverley Baxter in the *Evening Standard* suggested that Tynan was quite dreadful and 'would not get a chance in a village hall unless he were related to the vicar'. Tynan's wittily elegant reply, in which he claimed that his performance was only slightly less than mediocre and that 'I do not actually exit through scenery or wave at friends in the audience,' attracted the attention of the *Standard*'s editor and led to his being employed first as a feature writer and then as drama critic. Later he turned his attention to Orson Welles's unorthodox Othello at the St James's in a *Standard* review that appeared under the heading of 'Citizen Coon': a pun that, happily, would not be considered acceptable today.

But, with hindsight, it was the much-abused Hamlet and Othello of Guinness and Welles that one would most like to have seen. And I regret that, although living only eight miles from Stratford-on-Avon, I never caught the tetralogy of Shakespeare's histories that, along with *The Tempest*, packed out the Shakespeare Memorial Theatre in 1951. At a time when Shakespeare was invariably seen as a star-vehicle, Anthony Quayle conceived the thrilling idea of rehearsing *Richard II*, *Henry IV Parts I and II* and *Henry V* simultaneously and opening them on consecutive nights. This would confirm their status as England's national epic and allow audiences to trace the transition from Richard II's divinely appointed medievalism to Henry's V's pragmatic modernity. In the event Quayle's plan was scuppered by the theatre's ultra-conservative Governors, of whom Binkie Beaumont was notably one, and the productions opened at regular monthly intervals with

The Tempest shoehorned awkwardly into their midst. Nonetheless, the season revealed the kind of conceptual planning that Peter Hall would develop at Stratford in the Sixties. Tanya Moiseiwitsch's permanent set, based on a galleried Elizabethan theatre with the action thrust well forward, also got away from the promiscuous pictorialism of past Stratford productions. And Quayle created a company of formidable strength that included Harry Andrews, Hugh Griffith, Robert Hardy, Alan Badel and Heather Stannard. Michael Redgrave had a particularly astonishing season in which he not only played Richard II, Hotspur, Chorus in *Henry V* and Prospero but also directed *Henry IV Part II*. Ever anxious to build up personal rivalry, one paper ran a headline saying 'Look Out Larry, There's A Redgrave On Your Tail'. But the discovery of the season was a stocky, brooding Celt named Richard Burton who brought to Prince Hal and Henry V a magnetic quietude and sombre authority. There may have been a surfeit of Shakespeare in 1951. However, by its adoption of a visually unified approach, its engagement of a semi-permanent company and its exploration of the histories' political ideas, the Memorial Theatre had erected a signpost to the future: the only sadness was that its Tetralogy, in the familiar, wasteful tradition of British theatre, was no more than a golden memory by year's end.

Shakespeare in the early Fifties was both the glory and the curse of British theatre. His work was synonymous with national identity, a source of subsidy and something the British undoubtedly did rather well; at the same time, as Priestley pointed out and as the 1951 playbills prove, he absorbed much of the top talent. And, even if he didn't exactly keep living writers off the stage, he camouflaged our dismal failure to produce them in sufficient numbers. Shakespeare encouraged, in fact, a dangerous complacency in which people in Festival of Britain year looked around and concluded that, with Olivier, Gielgud and Redgrave all on top form, our theatre was in damned good shape. When you also recall that Peggy Ashcroft played Electra and Donald Wolfit Tamburlaine at the Old Vic, that Giraudoux and Sartre were on view in the West End and that *Kiss Me Kate* and *South Pacific* both opened to triumphant acclaim, it is possible to look back with a certain nostalgia to 1951. But where were the living writers capable of analysing the tensions in British society or the changing mood of the post-war world? The irony is that when one did finally appear in the shape of John Whiting he was greeted with the kind of vituperative incomprehension critics always reserve for the arrival of a major talent.

Whiting was an intriguing figure. Born in 1917 in Salisbury, he was the son of an army captain, trained as an actor at RADA, initially registered in 1939 as a conscientious objector and then changed his mind and joined the anti-aircraft section of the Royal Artillery. That in itself suggests a man in two minds about the war. And Whiting's internal divisions are apparent in the plays he wrote on being demobbed. *No More A-Roving*, penned in 1946 while Whiting was working in provincial rep, was a domestic sex comedy that had echoes of Coward but also anticipated Pinter in its assumption that people use the past as a means of psychological dominance. *Conditions of Agreement*, written the same year but not premiered until 1965, was an altogether weirder piece in which a defunct clown and a sadistic cripple extract gratuitous revenge on a retired grocer. But 1951 was to prove make-or-break year for Whiting. It began promisingly enough with Tennent Productions Ltd putting on a slap-up production of his *A Penny For A Song* at the Haymarket. Alan Webb and Ronald Squire headed the cast, Peter Brook was the director and Rowland Emett, whose crazy trains were to be a feature of the Battersea Funfair and whose drawings regularly adorned the pages of *Punch*, was its designer. And there is indeed something of *Punch*'s elegant whimsy and Ealing Comedy's exuberant eccentricity in Whiting's quintessentially English play: one that deals with a group of bungling Dorset aristocrats preparing to repel an expected Napoleonic invasion in 1804. The English have a strange fondness for upper-class plays set in summer gardens which end elegiacally with someone playing a musical instrument: you have only to think of Shaw's *Heartbreak House*. And, although Whiting's play flopped in 1951, it has since been revived twice by the RSC as well as by the Orange Tree, Richmond and the Oxford Stage Company, and turned into an opera by Richard Rodney Bennett. Actors and directors love its fantasy and charm. But Whiting's own ambivalence about war emerges through the character of Edward Sterne, a blind ex-soldier obsessed by the idea that if only he can reach George III in time he can prevent a further outbreak of military insanity. Whiting's play is partly a nineteenth-century *Dad's Army* about a comically ineffectual Home Guard. Its most haunting image, however, is that of the returning soldier: a potent figure, as we have seen, in post-1945 drama from *The Lady's Not For Burning* onwards, and a reminder, during the Cold War, of the horror felt by many ex-servicemen at the idea of renewed global conflict.

Soldiers also feature strongly in Whiting's *Saint's Day*: a play he wrote between 1946 and 1948, largely as a technical exercise, but which only surfaced in September 1951. It owed its belated appearance to a New Play competition organised by Alec Clunes at the tiny Arts Theatre in Great Newport Street to celebrate the Festival of Britain: significantly there were nearly a thousand entries, suggesting that Fifties Britain wasn't exactly lacking in new work even if most of it was inherently unstageable. Eventually the competition's judges – Clunes, Christopher Fry and Peter Ustinov, who was himself a prolific playwright – whittled the entries down to a select three which shared the £700 prize money and got a production at the Arts. Two of the finalists – Enid Bagnold's *Poor Judas* and C. E. Webber's *Right Side Up* – made little impact. But the judges perceptively gave the top prize to *Saint's Day*, which was duly greeted with critical howls of execration. *The Times* said it was 'of a badness that must be called indescribable' while Harold Hobson in *The Sunday Times* called Whiting's sanity into question; which is strange because the play, in its image of invasive violence, anticipates Harold Pinter's *The Birthday Party*, of which Hobson was to become a passionate champion. In fact the striking feature of *Saint's Day* – which theatre people including Peter Brook, Tyrone Guthrie, Peggy Ashcroft and John Gielgud ardently supported in letters to the press – is that it signals a major shift in the theatrical tectonic plates. Even the best Forties work of Priestley, Rattigan and Williams depended on inherited, pre-war structures. But with *Saint's Day* we are into a new era. Whiting not only creates his own imaginative world but uses his first-hand experience of war to suggest that we are entering an age of violence, anarchy and chaos. Long before the arrival of Pinter and Arden, with whom he has obvious affinities, Whiting envisages the possibility of social disintegration.

Whiting later revealed that the play sprang from a specific wartime memory. He and a group of soldiers were in the wintry Midlands, desperately short of fuel, and so decided to ransack and burn down a derelict Victorian house which contained an extraordinary mural. Both the painting and the act of military destruction haunted Whiting's imagination. So, six years later, he set *Saint's Day* in a rambling, Gothic mansion owned by an eighty-three-year-old poet, Paul Southman:

an angry old man living in splenetic isolation and at war with both the local village and the London literati, whom he has infuriated with a satirical pamphlet provocatively entitled 'The Abolition of Printing'. Southman clearly represents the poet as angry internal exile. However Charles Heberden, a painter married to Southman's grand-daughter Stella, has voluntarily chosen seclusion: overpraised for a London exhibition at the age of fifteen, he has withdrawn from society and is currently working on a vast mural that resembles the one Whiting and his fellow soldiers destroyed. Into this strange, hermetic world comes a smooth metropolitan poet and belletrist, Robert Procathren. He arrives on 25 January – Southman's birthday and the anniversary of the date of St Paul's conversion – to invite the poet to London for a banquet that will mark his reconciliation with the literary Establishment.

It is at this point that violence erupts. Procathren's visit coincides with the break-out from a detention centre of three soldiers who begin looting the village and terrorising the inhabitants. Rashly given a pistol by Southman in order to help the soldiers in their fight against the detested villagers, Procathren accidentally shoots the pregnant Stella. The dandified poet, who has hitherto avoided any form of moral commitment, decides to break the habit of a lifetime and 'run towards the event'. In the play's final act we learn that Procathren has joined the rampaging soldiers in destroying the local rector's store of rare religious books and burning the village. Embracing anarchy, Procathren returns to the decaying manor house with the three soldiers to supervise the execution of both Southman and Charles.

In 1951 Whiting's play was trashed for its obscurity. With hindsight, it is perfectly clear what it is about. The persecution of the artist by a conformist society. The violence that exists under the thin veneer of civilisation. The danger that the brutality sanctioned by war will persist into the peacetime world. But it's not just a play of big ideas. Whiting enters imaginatively into the minds of all the characters. As a struggling writer he identifies with both Paul Southman and Charles Heberden in their opposition to society's values. As a wartime incendiarist, he understands Procathren's shocked awareness of his appetite for destruction. Written as a personal, skill-testing exercise, the play also reveals Whiting's literary and dramatic preferences. There are strong echoes of Euripides in the destructive zeal consequent upon war. Southman's final descent into madness owes something to *King*

Lear. And, both stylistically and intellectually, Whiting was under the pervasive influence of T. S. Eliot. Stella, shocked at Procathren's transfer of loyalty from her moderating self to her militant grandfather, at one point has a speech that sounds like a pure parody of Eliot. It begins with her announcing, 'Careful! We are at the point of deviation' and ends by her declaring, 'We are approaching that point. The moment of the call from another room.' The idea that English society is both hostile to the artist and on the point of break-up was also expressed by Eliot in *Notes Towards A Definition of Culture*, which appeared at roughly the same time Whiting was finishing his play.

You could argue that *Saint's Day* is Whiting's way of exorcising his own demons. I'd also claim, since it's the work of a poet with acute social antennae, that it's the first truly modern post-war play: there's simply no way it could have been written in the Thirties. It conveys Whiting's private, and in his case far from paranoid, anxieties about artistic isolation and public fears about the loss of order and the triumph of mass culture: it is no accident that the burning of the Reverend Giles Aldus's rare, religious books – which Procathren initially came to inspect – is a governing symbol of communal degradation. But Whiting's play also prefigures much of modern British drama in its obsession with random violence (Edward Bond's *Saved*), with the idea of the reclusive artist at war with society (Pinter's *The Birthday Party*) and with the inherent anarchy of the unattached military (Arden's *Serjeant Musgrave's Dance* and Kane's *Blasted*). Whiting also points the way forward in his abandonment of conventional exposition and linear plot in order to explore his ideas through a series of verbal, visual and aural motifs: the play is haunted by textual images of decay, winter and death – 'the maggot in the peacock', as one character Pinterishly calls it – as well as by the physical spectacle of the unfinished mural and the sound of church bells and a Jericho trumpet. Derided in 1951, Whiting's play was quickly seized on by a twenty-two-year-old Peter Hall who directed an undergraduate production at Cambridge the next year and who went on to become Whiting's most persistent advocate. I've also seen impressive revivals by John Harrison at Birmingham Rep, David Thompson at the Theatre Royal, Stratford East and by Sam Walters at the Orange Tree, Richmond. But, although the play has always had an underground reputation among the cognoscenti, Whiting has never received his due. At a time when British theatre was dominated by classics and curtains rose nightly on instantly recognisable worlds, Whiting was the first dramatist to suggest that violence was the defining quality of modern civilisation and to offer an imaginative dislocation of reality. Sadly in 1951 neither critics nor audiences were ready for the experience.

In a sense one can hardly blame them. If you look at the typical West End fare in the late summer and early autumn of 1951 there was little to condition them to the shock of the new. Shaftesbury Avenue was filled with light comedies with titles like *My Wife's Lodger*, *Mary Had A Little*, *The White Sheep of the Family* and *Waggonload Of Monkeys*. Colin Morris's *Reluctant Heroes*, offering an uncritical look at National Service, and Hugh Hastings' *Seagulls over Sorrento*, set on a disused naval fortress in Scapa Flow, were both prodigiously long-running farces appealing to a built-in Britishness and an ongoing fascination with life in the forces. *The Lyric Revue* was praised for harking back to the wartime *Sweet and Low* series at the Ambassadors and for 'the excruciatingly funny sedan chair incident in the second half'. And, as so often, it was left to the American musical, in the shape of *South Pacific* dominated by an ebullient Mary Martin nightly washing that man right outa her hair, to generate a modest excitement. In the culture at large, there was also a feeling that America possessed a buoyant energy that put our own rather staid and conventional products to shame. In fiction, for instance, Britain's answers in 1951 to *The Catcher In The Rye*, *The Ballad of the Sad Cafe* and *From Here to Eternity* were C. P. Snow's exploration of academic back-stabbing in *The Masters* and Anthony Powell's evocation of upper-class adolescent friendships in *A Question of Upbringing*. Only in radio did one find a note of subversive innovation; and that came from a comedy series initially called *Crazy People*, which by the end of 1951 had been re-christened *The Goon Show*. It took time to find its rhythm and become essential listening. But, as figures like Major Denis Bloodnok and the caddish Grytpype-Thynne emerged as comic archetypes, it eventually dawned on people that Milligan, Sellers and Secombe were not just dispensing with the old radio-comedy sketch format: they were also challenging the existing social order. Milligan and Secombe had served in the forces throughout the war and, in the words of John Cleese, 'it was the very clever NCOs making jokes that the officers wouldn't quite have understood.'

The Goon Show was a rare exception, however, in a culture that, after Labour's defeat, became increasingly class-ridden, deferential and aesthetically hidebound. The October election of 1951 restored to power a seventy-seven-year-old Winston Churchill who promised no trailblazing reforms but simply 'several years of quiet, steady administration'. With the exception of the instant privatisation of the steel and road-haulage industries, there was no violent reversal of previous Labour policy. Churchill was primarily anxious that Britain play a key role in international affairs, develop its own independent nuclear programme and gradually put an end to the privations of the post-war period. Identity cards were abolished in 1952. Rationing of clothes, food, petrol and furniture ended in 1954. And Harold Macmillan as Minister of Housing fulfilled an election pledge to build three hundred thousand new houses a year. Labour had laid the foundations of post-war prosperity and introduced the radical idea of universal welfare but much of what John Betjeman called 'dear old, bloody old England' remained obstinately intact. As the historian Peter Vansittart pointed out: 'World convulsions had scarcely perturbed British social rituals: Ascot, the Eton and Harrow match at Lord's, all-amateur Wimbledon, all-male clubs and Oxbridge colleges, the Boat Race, Promenade Concerts, the Cup Final, the grouse moor, the Derby and the Grand National.' Admittedly the annual Gentlemen vs. Players cricket fixture at Lord's began to lose its mystic allure and some kind of frontier was crossed when Len Hutton, a true professional, was appointed England cricket captain in 1952. But in general the Britain of the early Fifties was a place of modest affluence, social stability and unquestioning acceptance of authority.

Nowhere was this more evident than in the extraordinary attitude to the Royal Family. George VI, a shy, nervous man who had worked hard to share the wartime privations of his people, died in February 1952: an event marked, as I recall, by days of black-bordered newspapers and seemingly interminable solemn music on radio. His daughter, Elizabeth, ascended to the throne and was duly crowned in Westminster Abbey on a dank and rainy June day in 1953. Watched on television by millions – though not, I confess, by our mildly bolshie family – the Coronation was undeniably one of those events that revived memories of wartime national cohesion; but it says much about Establishment fears of undue popular access that the solemn moment of anointing, in which the Queen was 'brought into the presence of the living God' by the Archbishop of Canterbury, was deemed too mysterious to be glimpsed by the watching hordes. My own memory of the times, however, is of the way royalty-worship became a new form of secular religion. The Queen's endless peregrinations around the Commonwealth were treated with the reverence once accorded to religious pilgrimages. And in the press no forelock went untugged. Even the normally liberal *News Chronicle*, a favourite paper of the Herbivores, breathlessly said of one royal tour: 'Into this eager void came the world's principal human being.' What Princess Diana was to a later generation, the Queen was to the majority of her subjects in the Fifties: in a way, even more so since Elizabeth Windsor was surrounded by a supposed aura of sanctity. I even recall one particularly nauseous popular song, written by Noel Gay, which inundated the airwaves with the hortatory cry of 'Let's All Be Good Elizabethans'.

In such a climate it would have been unrealistic to expect the theatre to be wildly oppositional or critical of Britain's hierarchical structure; and it seems suitably symbolic that six weeks after the Conservatives' 1951 election victory Noël Coward's unabashedly right-wing *Relative Values* opened at the Savoy to rave reviews from all the papers except the *Daily Mirror* and the *Observer*. Coward always hid behind the mask of being a pure entertainer blessed simply with 'a talent to amuse'. In fact, he was a deeply political writer with a fixed agenda. Having rebuked the British in *Peace In Our Time* for their naive folly in electing a Labour government, he here goes on to celebrate the restoration of traditional values. The plot revolves around the attempts of the aristocratic Countess of Marshwood to scupper the proposed marriage of her son, Nigel, to an arriviste Hollywood movie star: the instrument of revenge lies conveniently to hand in the shape of the Countess's maid, Moxie, who just happens to be the movie star's long-unseen elder sister. So a presumptuous upstart is sent packing by a Kentish blue-blood with the aid of a subservient underclass.

Lest we miss the point, Coward includes a choric figure in the shape of a butler called Crestwell who dispenses supposedly Olympian wisdom in the manner of Barrie's Admirable Crichton and Shaw's Waiter in *You Never Can Tell*. When the Countess, as part of her ruse to outwit the invasive film-star, upgrades Moxie from maid to personal companion, Crestwell describes it as 'a social experiment based on the ancient and inaccurate assumption that, as we are all equal in the eyes of God, we should therefore be equally equal in the eyes of our fellow-creatures. The fact that it doesn't work out like that and never will in no way deters the idealists from pressing on valiantly towards Utopia.' But the propaganda points really come rolling in after the Hollywood upstart has been successfully seen off. Raising a glass to himself and Moxie in celebration of their pre-ordained station in life, Crestwell declares:

> I drink solemnly to you and me in our humble, but on the whole honourable, calling. I drink to her Ladyship and to his Lordship, groaning beneath the weight of privilege but managing to keep their peckers up all the same. Above all, I drink to the final inglorious disintegration of the most unlikely dream that ever troubled the foolish heart of man – Social Equality.

The Savoy audience must have been immensely cheered to hear this so soon after the seventy-seven-year-old and almost gaga Churchill had sent packing a party and prime minister dedicated to precisely that dream. But, in pursuing his right-wing vision, Coward sadly sacrificed the mercurial invention and crystalline wit that characterised his prewar work. 'As Coward's idea of England ossified,' John Lahr wrote in his acute study of the dramatist, 'so too did his antic spirit . . . By the time of *Relative Values* Coward was over fifty and already filled with a sense of the end.' That didn't, however, prevent the play running for 477 performances at the Savoy.

While Coward's latest play was celebrating the country's – or at least southern England's – new conservative ethos, he himself was dazzling audiences as a cabaret performer at London's Café de Paris. But his post-war dramatic decline was emphasised in 1952 with the arrival of *Quadrille*, starring Alfred Lunt and Lynn Fontanne, at the Phoenix. Tynan described it as 'this monstrously overloaded tea-trolley of a play'. I'd say it was more like *Private Lives* with a pronounced paunch and subject to embarrassing bursts of flatulence. In outline, it follows the symmetrical pattern of the earlier play with obstinate fidelity: two middle-aged lovers abscond to the south of France and their respective partners, in pursuing them, find themselves maturely smitten. But, where in *Private Lives* the rejected couple behave as violently and atrociously to each other as the fugitive Elyot and Amanda, here they are simply mildly bickering, senescent lovebirds. Adorned by the Lunts, his massive dignity matching her aristocratic poise, the play clearly possessed enough wan charm to sustain it through 382 performances. But it was slaughtered in the press and suggests that Coward in the Fifties was in danger of becoming a back number content to turn out quilted claptrap for the middle-class faithful.

That the public was capable of taking more when it was offered was proved by the success of Terence Rattigan's *The Deep Blue Sea* which opened at the Duchess Theatre in 1952 and ran for 513 performances: a play in a different league from *Quadrille* and proof that conventional times could still produce brilliant work. What is sad is that Rattigan – who reached his perihelion in the Fifties – came to be indissolubly linked with Coward as one of the obstacles who had to be removed if British theatre was ever to advance. Kenneth Tynan acerbically wrote in 1955: 'Mr Rattigan is the Formosa of the contemporary theatre, occupied by the old guard but geographically inclined towards the progressives.' But while it was true that Rattigan combined commercial acumen with liberal instincts, Tynan's remark was ludicrously unfair. What he overlooked was Rattigan's ability to put a large slice of contemporary England on stage: far from being Coward's natural ally, Rattigan was closer in spirit to John Osborne, of whom he was a natural precursor.

The Deep Blue Sea is a case in point. At the most basic level, this is a play about the inequality of passion: a theme that Osborne was to explore, with scorching intensity, four years later in *Look Back In Anger*. And, given the proprieties of the early Fifties, Rattigan addresses the subject with surprising candour. His heroine, Hester Collyer, is a daughter of the manse who has abandoned her High Court judge husband, Sir William, to live with her test-pilot lover, Freddie Page; but the play's tragedy stems from Freddie's inability to match Hester's sexual and emotional passion. Freddie himself explains the problem, as explicitly as one could wish, to his drinking chum, Jackie:

> Take two people – A and B. A loves B. B doesn't love A or at least not in the same way. He wants to but he just can't. It's not his nature. Now B hasn't asked to be loved. He may be a perfectly ordinary bloke, kind, well-meaning, good friend, perhaps even a good husband if he's allowed to be. But he's not allowed to be – that's my point. Demands are made on him which he just can't fulfil.

But, although the play is a piercing study of what Rattigan himself called 'the illogicality of love', it is also a Fifties *Heartbreak House* that uses a Ladbroke Grove rooming-house to explore the tensions of contemporary England. And what Rattigan addresses very clearly is the repressive, puritan morality of the Fifties and the belief that, for women especially, sex was thought to be as much a procreative and conjugal duty as a positive pleasure. In the same year that Rattigan wrote the play, 1951, Geoffrey Gorer published in *The People* an analysis of current attitudes to marriage, courtship and sex, based on his book *Exploring English Character*. The picture that emerged was one of startling orthodoxy. Half the married women interviewed claimed that they had never seriously thought of marrying anyone other than their husband. A majority of men and women firmly disapproved of sex before marriage.

And only fifty-one per cent of women agreed with the statement that 'women enjoy the physical side of sex just as much as men'. Which implies that nearly half the female population were taught to see sex as either a disagreeable domestic task or a means of begetting children. If this is true, then Rattigan's Hester becomes a doubly remarkable creation: a woman who defies her class by abandoning the comforts of Eaton Square for a dingy lodging house and who defies the expectations of her gender in her passionate need for sex.

The play, however, is not just a study of Hester's dilemma: what Rattigan offers is a comprehensive and accurate portrait of Fifties England. Rattigan, who had been a flight lieutenant in the RAF and had written sympathetically of the force in the play, *Flare Path*, and the movie, *The Way To The Stars*, clearly understood the character of Freddie Page: the Battle of Britain hero who finds himself a displaced person in a skill-oriented post-war world. Fry and Whiting had written, in historical terms, about the bitter disillusionment of the ex-soldier: Rattigan writes, in vividly contemporary terms, about the kind of jaundiced ex-pilot who was to be seen haunting London's afternoon drinking-clubs. As Hester shrewdly says of Freddie, 'his life stopped in 1940. He loved 1940 you know. There were some like that. He's never been really happy since he left the RAF.' In order to escape the suffocating demands of Hester's love, Freddie finally takes a job, for which he is clearly unfitted, as a test-pilot in South America; and it is one of the play's tragic ironies that, while the suicide-prone Hester precariously survives, Freddie goes to almost certain death. If Rattigan's play anticipates *Look Back In Anger* in its portrait of the inequality of passion, it is also possible to see Freddie as a prototype of Susan Traherne in David Hare's 1978 *Plenty*: another state-of-England play about a protagonist who, after a good war, is unable to adjust to peacetime reality.

Each character in Rattigan's play contributes to the picture of Fifties England. Sir William Collyer, Hester's husband, embodies the pathos of the emotionally corseted, upper-class clubman for whom passion is best confined to the pages of his adored Jane Austen and Trollope: a type whom Rattigan, through membership of Surrey golf clubs, knew well and who in the late Fifties was to become Prime Minister in the person of Harold Macmillan. But too little attention has been paid to the play's minor figures. Kurt Miller, the struck-off émigré doctor who doubles as a bookie's runner and hospital volunteer, functions in plot terms as the voice of sanity and as Hester's ultimate saviour. Less noticed is the fact that he is a victim of England's antiquated homosexual laws. His original crime is never stated but the landlady, Mrs Elton, says that 'what he did wasn't – well – the sort of thing people forgive very easily. Ordinary normal people, I mean.' The careful insertion of the word 'normal' suggests that Miller was guilty not of practising illegal abortion but of committing a sexual offence. Asked about her own forgiveness of Miller's supposed sin, Mrs Elton exudes a relaxed tolerance: 'Oh well,' she says, 'I see far too much of life in this place to get upset by that sort of thing. It takes all sorts to make a world after all – doesn't it?'

In contrast to Mrs Elton's working-class good nature is the stuffy, middle-class conformism represented by the household's young married couple, the Welches. Ann is a social snob dismissive of Miller as a bookie's clerk and impressed by Hester's credentials as Lady Collyer. And Philip, who works for the Home Office, is a prissy moralist who lectures Hester on the relative triviality of sex. There's a hilarious moment when Philip confesses to Hester his own extra-marital affair, from which he recuperated in Lyme Regis. He goes on to lecture Hester, after Freddie has abandoned her, as if her passion were simply a virulent form of flu. 'I mean, without trying to be preachy or anything,' he says, 'it is really the spiritual values that count in this life isn't it? I mean the physical side is really awfully unimportant – objectively speaking, don't you think?' A point which Hester answers with admirable stoicism. And, having tricked Philip into revealing Freddie's whereabouts and shocked him by saying that she has no intention of honouring her solemn promise not to resort to emotional blackmail if her lover returns, Hester revealingly remarks: 'You've got exactly the same expression on your face that my father would have had if I'd said that to him. He believed in spiritual values, too, you know – and the pettiness of the physical side.' Within one household, in fact, Rattigan presents us with a cleric's daughter with an unassuageable sexual and emotional passion, a war hero for whom there is no place in the modern world, a disgraced homosexual, two representatives of marital orthodoxy and an instinctively tolerant landlady. Without making it obvious, Rattigan offers a vivid microcosm of Fifties England.

Admittedly few people in 1952 saw the play in those terms: for most people it was a psychological study rather than a national metaphor. But many people found it difficult to come to terms with Rattigan's Hester. Ivor Brown, a hard-headed Aberdonian who one suspects had little knowledge of intemperate passion, incredibly suggested in the *Observer*: 'Perhaps she [Hester] just needs a good slap or a straight talk by a Marriage Guidance Counsellor.' Even the much younger Kenneth Tynan criticised Rattigan for allowing Hester to survive at the end; but, whereas a climactic suicide would have been melodramatic, her decision to go on living without Freddie has a painful Chekhovian reality. The real surprise, however, lies in discovering the identity of Hester's greatest critic. It was none other than the woman who triumphantly played her, Peggy Ashcroft. When I wrote Peggy's biography, she told me that she at first rejected the role because she found Hester cowardly and selfish in attempting suicide because of her lover's neglect. Frith Banbury, the play's director, suggested to me that Peggy's initial wariness had much more to do with the character's disquieting closeness to her own psychological make-up: like Hester, Peggy was a middle-class woman married to a distinguished lawyer and endowed with a highly sexed nature. When I repeated Frith's point in an early draft of the book, Peggy was apopleptically incensed. But, although I toned down the suggestion in later versions, Peggy's vehemence implied that her director had hit the mark. Maybe one reason for Ashcroft's greatness in the role was that she *was*, as they say in the movie posters, Hester Collyer.

To appreciate Rattigan's skill in so effortlessly creating a state-of-England play, you only have to look at the work of his contemporaries. One of the better plays of the period was Rodney Ackland's *The Pink Room* which Rattigan generously helped to finance and which Frith Banbury, straight after *The Deep Blue Sea*, sympathetically directed. But when the play opened at the Lyric Hammersmith in June 1952 it was ferociously attacked by the critics. The most bitter assault came from Harold Hobson, a Christian Scientist always offended by what he saw as displays of moral evil, who scathingly wrote in the *Sunday Times* that 'on Wednesday evening the audience at Hammersmith had the impression of being present, if not at the death of a talent, at least of its very serious illness'. The result was not only that the play closed after four weeks: Ackland, neurotically sensitive to criticism, found his creative instinct blocked for many years. It was only when the play was rewritten as *Absolute Hell* and revived, first by the Orange Tree in 1988 and later by the National Theatre in 1995, that Ackland's reputation was restored.

Because he was so roughly treated by the critics in his own time and because he possessed an attractive maverick talent, there has been a tendency to sanctify Ackland as a lost dramatic genius comparable to Chekhov. Which is pitching it a bit strong. But *The Pink Room* certainly proves Ackland had a talent for creating bilious national metaphors. His setting is a West End drinking den called 'La Vie en Rose' in the summer of 1945, between VE Day and the General Election. And what unites Ackland's characters is their private desperation and flight from public reality. The club's louche proprietress, who's been deserted by her American lover, is terrified of solitude. A once-famous writer is on the skids while his mother drugs herself with romantic fiction and his potential saviour churns out trashy British movies. Most devastating of all is the portrait of a titled parasite who constantly talks of voting Labour without summoning up the energy to do so. She also dreams of working with displaced people but, when confronted by images of the death-camps, signally fails to take the address of the United Nations' Refugee Relief Assocation. By the time Labour's election victory has been declared, the club is officially closed and the ceiling has symbolically caved in. This is Ackland's far-from-fond farewell to a hedonistic, socially irresponsible Little England that viewed life from the bottom of a glass woozily.

Had the play been produced in 1946, shortly after Ackland finished it, it would have caused a storm. It demolishes many of the sentimental myths about the selfless optimism and cohesive purpose of the British people without descending into the melodramatic vulgarities of Coward's *Peace In Our Time*. With unsparing honesty, Ackland shows a section of raffish bohemia that survived the war having apparently learned nothing: his characters are feckless dreamers shrugging off news of the Nazi death-camps and largely ignoring the political earthquake taking place on their doorstep. But by 1952, with the Tories back in power, Ackland's message had lost its topical sting. And, although Ackland depended on Rattigan's financial aid in getting his play staged, he lacked his patron's emotional generosity and technical skill. Rattigan in *The Deep Blue Sea* shows compassion for all his characters while subtly creating a cross-section of English society: Ackland nails the lie that all England rejoiced at Labour's victory but condemns his myopic drifters to outer darkness.

I hesitate to use Rattigan as a stick with which to beat his contemporaries. But he not only had a broader range of sympathy than Ackland. He also possessed a gift for understatement that few in the Fifties could match. You only have to compare *The Deep Blue Sea* to Graham Greene's *The Living Room* which opened at Wyndham's in 1953 and which enjoyed huge success, partly because of Dorothy Tutin's shining performance in the lead role. On the surface, Greene's play has a lot in common with Rattigan's. Both show a heroine driven by desperation to attempt suicide. But where Rattigan's Hester fails, Greene's Rose Pemberton succeeds: more predictably since this is Greeneland and Rose is a twenty-year-old Catholic orphan having an affair with a married psychologist, Michael, and under moral pressure from her batty aunts and priestly uncle. Like Rattigan, Greene also shows a rejected partner turning up to reason with the heroine. And, again like Rattigan, Greene finds metaphorical resonance in a sexual drama. While Rattigan anatomises English repression, Greene explicitly attacks a Catholic Church that, through its doctrinal severity, has narrowed the possibilities for the living. Before patronisingly attacking early Fifties drama for its social irrelevance, we should remember that it was far more open to religious debate than our own secular product.

Much of Greene's play is very good. Rose's crisis is vividly conveyed. The details of her afternoon adultery in a place called Regal Court are rivetingly specific. And when her crippled uncle falls back on the old formulae of the Mass, the Rosary and the Our Lady prayer, Rose responds with downright vigour by crying: 'Don't talk to me about God or the saints. I don't believe in your God who took away your legs and wants to take away Michael.' But, given Rose's lack of faith, her subsequent suicide ultimately seems avoidable; you long for her either to force her shilly-shallying lover into a decision or to begin a new independent life on her own. And, when the lover's wife turns up and begs Rose to abandon him, we get something close to melodrama:

MRS DENNIS: (*hysterically*): When are you going? I know you are planning to go. Don't torture me. Tell me.

ROSE: I don't know.

MRS DENNIS: You're young. You can find any number of men. Please let him alone. (*Spacing her words*). I can't live without him.

(ROSE *watches her hysteria grow. She is trapped and terrified*).

I'll die if he leaves me. I'll kill myself.

ROSE: No. No. You never will.

MRS DENNIS: I will. I know what you're thinking – after that I could marry him.

ROSE: Please.

MRS DENNIS: Go away from him. Please. Go somewhere he won't find you. You're young. You'll get over it. The young always do.

Admittedly Greene is writing about a woman at the end of her tether; but the heightened emotion is all on the surface and expressed in language of curious naturalistic flatness. If you take a comparable scene in *The Deep Blue Sea*, where Hester's husband turns up in a last-ditch attempt to win back his wife who has been deserted by her lover, the powerful emotion lies beneath what is actually said:

COLLYER: I have a faint inkling of how you must be feeling at this moment.

HESTER: (*Turning. Hard and bright*). Oh, I'll get over it I imagine. You're looking very smart. Where have you been?

COLLYER: At home. I had some people in to dinner.

HESTER : Who?

COLLYER: Olive, the Prestons, an American judge and his wife –

HESTER : Was Olive in good form?

COLLYER: Fairly. She said one very funny thing.

HESTER : What was it?

COLLYER: Damn. I've forgotten. Oh yes. I do remember. Now I come to think of it, it's not all that funny. It must have been the way she said it. She told the American judge he had a face like an angry cupid –

HESTER : An angry cupid? I can just hear her.

(*She starts to laugh and continues longer than the joke appears to warrant*).

An angry cupid.

(*The laugh suddenly turns to sobs. She buries her head in the sofa cushion, desperately trying to control her emotion*).

It may be unfair to compare a theatrical debutant like Greene with a practised craftsman like Rattigan. But, when it comes to prising open the human heart, Rattigan uses a scalpel where Greene deploys a crowbar. Rattigan's language is seemingly just as flat and ordinary as Greene's; but he understands that, in moments of crisis, we often express ourselves circuitously. The point is confirmed in the infallibly moving scene where Freddie returns for the last time to collect his suitcase. Instead of the throbbingly hectic exchanges you might expect, Hester says things like 'Had any food?' to which Freddie replies, 'Yes, I had a bite at the Belevedere. What about you?' It is a classic example of the power of subtext, in which the feeling is at odds with what is actually being said. It also reminds us that the paradox of Rattigan's career is that his best effects are achieved by precisely the kind of emotional reticence that he deplores as the English vice.

Rattigan was still capable of bad mistakes; and in 1953 he made two of them. Firstly he allowed a lightweight comedy he had written as a *pièce d'occasion* for Coronation Year, *The Sleeping Prince*, to be taken over by the Oliviers, thereby creating expectations that the play signally failed to fulfil. He also, at the insistence of his publisher, hurriedly wrote a preface to a two-volume edition of his Collected Plays in which he created a mythical, middle-class playgoer called Aunt Edna whom he held to be the backbone of the theatre and the ultimate arbiter of taste. Aunt Edna may be 'a hopeless lowbrow' but what Aunt Edna does not like, no one will ever like. And, while she may enjoy a little teasing and even some bullying, a dramatist must never go so far as to incur her displeasure. Rattigan, bearing his putative playgoer in mind, even came out with the easily disprovable aphorism that 'a play does not fail because it is too good: it fails because it is not good enough'. Written in a slightly ironic, tongue-in-cheek mode, Rattigan's reactionary preface rebounded disastrously. It did a deep disservice to his talent and became a convenient weapon of attack for critics who saw him as no more than a supine servant of popular taste.

That Rattigan was infinitely more than that was proved by his double bill, *Separate Tables*, which opened at the St James's Theatre in September 1954 and ran for 726 performances. Although no one could have foreseen it at the time, the two plays were to be the climax of Rattigan's golden run of success in the West End: only *Ross* in 1960 was to achieve comparable acclaim as Rattigan became a sacrifical victim of the assault on Shaftesbury Avenue gentility. But the irony is that *Separate Tables* is more radical than many of the loudly trumpeted plays that succeeded it. *Table Number Seven*, the second play in the sequence, marks a historical watershed in that it unequivocally puts the case for charity and understanding in dealing with what at the time would have been called 'sexual aberration': it is a milestone not just in the history of queer theatre but in the shifting nature of public tolerance and shows the capacity of art to anticipate legal reform. But *Table By The Window*, although a lesser play, is equally crucial in that it addresses many of the issues that John Osborne was to confront eighteen months later in *Look Back In Anger*. At the height of his fame, Osborne enjoyed an amiable social relationship with Rattigan – the dramatist he had supposedly supplanted – and wrote fondly of him in private letters, even to a critic like myself. And although Osborne dutifully followed the Royal Court party line and claimed to the Rattigan-hating George Devine that he 'had no high opinion of *Separate Tables*', it is scarcely credible that the first of the two plays didn't leave its mark on his imagination.

Table By The Window dramatises the eroticism of class difference: a subject Rattigan knew all about from his own homosexual experiences and which he here tackles with unusual brio. His hero, John Malcolm, is a defiantly working-class Labour ex-minister confronted by his upper-class ex-wife, Anne, in a Bournemouth hotel; and, on meeting her, he finds his old sexual passions fiercely aroused. Rattigan explicitly links sex and violence, portrays marriage as 'a kind of war' and shows his hero torn between equable companionship with the hotel manageress and the love–hate that comes with spiritual intimacy: ideas that originate with Strindberg and were to be developed by Osborne. The hero's insistence on his working-class background, his sanctification of ground-down, victimised mothers and even the violence with which he hurls Anne to the ground were all to find their echo in Jimmy Porter.

In this state-of-the-nation double bill, Rattigan also deals with the political realities of the Fifties in a way that goes far beyond appeasement of Aunt Edna. By 1954 the Tories had been in power for three years. In spite of Churchill's physical and mental unfitness, they had achieved modest success in ending rationing, building a record number of houses and even opening the first comprehensive school. But Rattigan forcefully reminds us that the old class anatagonisms still existed. At one point, the hotel guests contentedly report that they have been watching a Tory spokesman on television who claimed that 'whereas the Socialists were only concerned about cutting the national cake into exactly equal slices, the Conservatives were trying to increase the size of the cake'. Malcolm, who has hitherto concealed his parliamentary background from the guests, blows his top and his cover by revealing that the MP in question is a thundering hypocrite with a string of adulterous liaisons. At a time of simmering industrial unrest, the hotel residents also endorse the Tory MP's view that the currently striking dockers have no sense of national responsibility; to which Malcolm, who hails from Hull, angrily replies that 'there's no body of men in England with more'. Rattigan's hero even addresses the specific economic circumstances of the hotel guests: he distinguishes between the genteel poverty of Lady Matheson, whose husband died before the Civil Service pension scheme came into force, and the cushioned comfort of the bullying Mrs Railton-Bell, who lives off 'a tidy little nest egg' that would be subject to a capital levy under a future Labour government. Doubtless Rattigan was influenced by his own mother's modest existence in a West Kensington hotel. But by setting 'a genuine, live, roaring savage from the slums of Hull' down amidst a group of elderly people dependent on private incomes, Rattigan shows that the class war was still being actively fought in Churchill's Britain.

If *Table By The Window* is primarily about class, *Table Number Seven* is largely about sex; or, more precisely, about Rattigan's belief that people were far more tolerant of homosexuality than either Britain's punitive laws or prurient press acknowledged. And, even if Rattigan dealt with the subject in coded terms, there was considerable bravery in tackling it at all at a time of gathering media hysteria. In the summer of 1953 Lord Montagu of Beaulieu, the writer Peter Wildeblood and an assistant film director, Kenneth Hume, had all been sentenced to prison at Winchester Crown Court on charges of sexual assault. And in the autumn of that year Sir John Gielgud was arrested for importuning and fined £10 by a magistrate at Chelsea Police Court. The combination of a peer of the realm and a legendary theatrical knight both being arrested for homosexual offences excited the popular papers, who feigned moral outrage and indulged in a good deal of homophobic grandstanding. After the Gielgud case, a boycott of theatres where 'actors with queer habits' were playing was suggested in some sections of the press. And the unspeakable John Gordon in the *Sunday Express* argued that homosexuals should be made social lepers: 'It is utterly wrong that men who befoul and corrupt other young men should strut in the public eye, enjoying adulation and applause, however great their genius.'

The ripples from the tide of media indignation even spread to my own public school in Warwick, where the Headmaster convened a special school Assembly to warn us against the dangers of lurking, predatory homosexuals; unable to bring himself to use the precise word, however, he simply referred obliquely to strange gentlemen who were 'out of focus'. The superfluity of such a message in an English boys' school, filled with sexually inquisitive boarders, hardly needs underlining. But it was the reaction amongst the theatrical community to Gielgud's arrest that was rather more revealing. Noël Coward predictably saw the matter entirely from his own egocentric viewpoint. In a passage tactfully excised from his published *Diaries* he wrote: 'Poor, silly, idiotic, foolish, careless John . . . England, my England, has always been full of intolerance and bigotry. Just when things might have started to improve for us all, John goes and does something so utterly careless that it will do us harm for years to come.' Rattigan, although equally wedded to the idea of sexual discretion, was rather more struck by the reaction of audiences in Liverpool who greeted Gielgud's appearance in N. C. Hunter's *A Day By The Sea* with volleys of support. Some years later Rattigan told the *New York Times*: 'He [Gielgud] had enough courage to go on and the audience had enough grace and sympathy to accept him purely as an actor. The acceptance by these very ordinary people of something about which they had little understanding was very moving.'

Rattigan's belief in English tolerance becomes the theme of *Table Number Seven*. In the play 'Major' Pollock, in reality a lieutenant discharged from the services in 1946, is arrested for interfering with women in a Bournemouth cinema. But, when the domineering Mrs

Railton-Bell seeks to have him drummed out, the other guests, including her shy daughter Sibyl, rally to his side. What is hard to believe is that, even in 1954, audiences didn't see that the Major's offence was a metaphor for homosexual importuning. In court the Major's solicitor reportedly calls his client's offence a 'momentary aberration': a standard exculpatory phrase reminiscent of Gielgud's defence at Chelsea Police Court that 'I was very tired and had a few drinks. I was not responsible for my actions.' The language used by the hotel residents, at the kangaroo court convened by Mrs Railton-Bell, is also more compatible with homosexual cottaging than heterosexual groping. A student doctor, refusing to make moral judgements on grounds of ignorance, says that 'the Major presumably understands my form of lovemaking. I should therefore understand his. But I don't.' Mrs Railton-Bell says to her chum Lady Matheson that 'you know perfectly well what you feel about this dreadful vice that's going on all over the country'. And the Major himself, having admitted to Sibyl that he has always been scared of women and that 'I'm made in a certain way and can't change it', explains why he is reluctant to seek sanctuary with a male friend in London: 'Well – you see – it's rather a case of birds of a feather.' Even Aunt Edna, alerted by the plethora of press stories about rampant vice, would surely have got the point.

With hindsight, it is tempting to accuse Rattigan of lack of moral courage in failing openly to address the subject of homosexuality. And, in fact, when *Separate Tables* moved to Broadway Rattigan inserted a whole new speech for Mrs Railton-Bell making perfectly plain the real nature of the Major's offence; a speech that was never performed because of objections from the show's star, the discreetly gay Eric Portman, and the producer, Robert Whitehead. In fact, Portman and Whitehead did the right deed for the wrong reasons. Rattigan's coded approach is not only true to the spirit of the Fifties but to his own talent for obliquity; indeed, when I saw the revised version played at the Royal Exchange, Manchester in 2006, I was struck by how obvious it seemed in comparison to the idea of the closeted Major furtively groping women in afternoon cinemas. But the precise details of the Major's offence matter far less than the charity it provokes. In the final scene the guests, one by one, acknowledge the disgraced Major, the defeated Mrs Railton-Bell ignominiously exits and a decorous silence reigns in the dining room that, according to the stage directions, 'no longer gives any sign of the battle that has just been fought and won between its four, bare walls'. It was a battle that was being fought not just in Rattigan's fictional hotel but all over Britain. A sharp rise in arrests for homosexual offences in the early Fifties occasioned severe doubts about the underhand methods used to secure convictions. Even the Conservative government was rattled and, two months before *Separate Tables* opened, appointed Sir John Wolfenden to chair a committee to examine the laws pertaining to homosexuality and prostitution. It took three years for Wolfenden to report and to recommend relaxation of the law. But, even if one can't claim Rattigan's play had direct social consequences, it movingly reflected a liberal English instinct that found its voice in Wolfenden.

Rattigan's *Separate Tables*, in its two distinct but artfully linked halves, suggests that the England of the mid-Fifties was a curious place: one in which entrenched class antagonisms coexisted with a subterranean tolerance and decency. And it was certainly true both in the theatre and in the culture at large that nostalgia, escapism and a yearning for pre-war certainties went alongside hints of youthful rebellion, social disturbance and increasing criticism of established values. 1954 is a pivotal year in English life in that the country seemed to be looking backwards and forwards simultaneously. Alongside Rattigan's quietly progressive *Separate Tables*, the two greatest theatrical successes of the year were Julian Slade's *Salad Days* and Sandy Wilson's *The Boy Friend*. The former, emanating from Bristol Old Vic, was a lightweight whimsy about a magic piano that sets everybody dancing: the latter, starting at the Players Theatre, was a more sophisticated pastiche of a nineteen-twenties Riviera musical. Both were celebrations of innocence and romance: melodic fairytales for the middle classes. But the impression they gave of a regressive England pining for the happy days of long ago was starkly contradicted by the two most eagerly discussed novels of the year. Kingsley Amis's *Lucky Jim* announced the arrival of a brand-new literary hero: the provincial academic who is the sworn enemy of Establishment culture, has a mocking eye for artistic pseudery and conceals his go-getting nature under a hapless buffoonery. It was rather as if Richmal Crompton's Just William had been let loose in academia. Far darker in tone than the Amis was William Golding's *Lord of the Flies*, which disturbingly suggested that a group of English prep-schoolboys, stranded on a paradisal island, would quickly regress into barbarism and murder. The backward-glancing conservatism of the musicals by

Slade and Wilson – whose Christian names were later appropriated by *Round The Horne* for the camp duo of Jules and Sandy – was also counterpointed by the emergence of Teddy Boys, narcissistic dandies with razors and flick-knives, in south London and seaside resorts. Violence was in the air in 1954; and the threat of it was sufficiently strong to lead to the banning, in the majority of towns, of a Hollywood movie, *The Wild One*, in which Marlon Brando played the black-leathered leader of a motorised adolescent gang who, literally, gets away with murder.

Evidently England in 1954 was not quite the homogeneous, socially stable, blandly contented place the politicians wanted us to believe. And, even if the theatre was still desperately short of new voices, there were healthy signs of simmering discontent with the status quo. Indeed the intriguing thing is that, between the Coronation of Elizabeth II in June 1953 and the second successive Conservative election victory in May 1955, three stubborn, independent visionaries who were to shape the theatre of the next fifty years all put down their distinctive markers: even though they came to view each other with wary suspicion, Joan Littlewood, George Devine and a young Cambridge graduate, Peter Hall, were all simultaneously working for change in ways that would not just rearrange the existing furniture but open up new theatrical rooms.

Joan Littlewood, as we've seen, was already a veteran of pre-war agitprop and post-war populism through her creation of Theatre Workshop. After eight penny-pinching years of slogging round the provinces the company had in 1953 finally taken up permanent residence in a delightfully tatty Victorian theatre in London's E15 ('The place reeked of perfumed disinfectant and cat-piss,' said Littlewood in her memoirs), and had launched an international repertoire, including Shakespeare, Shaw, Molière, Chekhov and Gogol, that would have shamed any putative National Theatre. Even though the company was pitifully financed and often fitfully attended, it slowly began to attract critical attention: not least in January 1955 when it went head-to-head with the Old Vic by staging a *Richard II* to rival one in the Waterloo Road. The Old Vic had the advantage of a melodiously elegiac John Neville, a large cast and a well-lit stage full of coloured pennants and elegant costumes. Theatre Workshop had a calculatedly effeminate Harry H. Corbett in the lead, fourteen actors and a stark John Bury permanent set that allowed one scene to merge swiftly into the next.

David had taken on Goliath; and, while Kenneth Tynan was not alone in questioning Corbett's frenzied campery, many people found a political edge in the Stratford East production lacking in the Old Vic's picturesque pageant.

But the real breakthrough came in May 1955 when Theatre Workshop was invited to take its productions of *Arden of Faversham* and Jonson's *Volpone* to the second annual Paris Drama Festival. The company enjoyed a spectacular triumph, especially with its modern-dress *Volpone* set in an Italy of seedy spivs and parasites and pineapple-laden bicycles. Where British audiences still regarded the classics as sumptuously accoutred star-vehicles, Parisian theatregoers relished the cheek, irreverence and ensemble spirit of these productions. At home the top people who took *The Times* were also alerted to the company's Paris triumph by a glowing report in the paper's arts pages. But such was the poverty of Theatre Workshop that the actors, who were all on four pounds a week, had to transport the sets and costumes for both productions as hand luggage and lacked even the basic fare to get home: only a whip-round by the Festival's organiser, Claude Planson, got them back to Britain. On their return, the company faced the threat of bankruptcy but went on to give the first professional production of a Brecht play in Britain: *Mother Courage* at the Taw and Torridge Festival in Barnstaple, with Joan herself in the title role.

It would seem to have been a perfect combination: Britain's liveliest ensemble with its own doughty figurehead as Brecht's pragmatic survivor. In fact, it was all a bit of a shambles. Littlewood, overstretched by simultaneously directing and acting, decided to recast Avis Bunnage as Courage, but was ill-fatedly forced, by the threat of an authorial injunction, to resume the role twenty-four hours before opening. Brecht's assistant, Carl Weber, who helpfully turned up with the *Modelbuch* of the original production, was also banned from rehearsals. Seeing the resulting mess, even Tynan was driven to conclude that 'discourtesy to a masterpiece borders on insult as if Wagner were to be staged in a school gymnasium'. But the show wasn't just undercooked. Joan, from her pre-war work in Manchester, had long shared many of Brecht's theatrical and political ideals. She was, however, too much of a robust individualist to offer a reverent simulacrum of the Berliner Ensemble production. No matter: what Joan had conclusively established was a new way of working in which collective discipline was cunningly concealed under a facade of improvisatory freedom.

74

'Why is it always the women who resurrect the theatre in England?' asked one of Joan's French admirers, Jean Vilar. Actually, it wasn't always the women. One of the historical ironies of the *Mother Courage* debacle was that it established a link, albeit temporary, between Littlewood and another visionary, and distinctly male-oriented, strand in post-war British theatre: one that Joan herself came to view with increasing hostility. The British rights to *Mother Courage* had been secured by a young Marxist entrepreneur, Oscar Lewenstein; and it was at his suggestion that the production be invited to play at the 1955 Taw and Torridge Festival in Devon. The Festival itself was a local drama-and-music affair keenly supported by the Queen's cousin, Lord Harewood, and largely controlled by Ronald Duncan, the poetic dramatist and opera librettist who had enjoyed a brief post-war vogue with *This Way To The Tomb*. Duncan had a long-term dream: to use Taw and Torridge to establish a management to produce non-commercial plays – a category into which his own easily fitted – and tour them round regional arts festivals with a climactic season in London. It was to be an 'English Stage Society'. And who better to turn to in setting it up than the go-ahead Lewenstein?

At that time Lewenstein was working as manager for Alfred Esdaile, a pioneer of non-stop variety, who had latterly acquired the lease of both the Royal Court and Kingsway Theatres in London. Lewenstein also knew that, while Ronald Duncan was trying to create a new touring company, George Devine and an ambitious young TV producer, Tony Richardson, were both hunting for a London theatre in which to stage the work of unknown and neglected writers. It's a measure of the desperate mid-Fifties hunger for some alternative to the West End that such a disparate group of people – the right-wing Duncan, the liberal Devine and the Marxist Lewenstein – could come together in a common enterprise. But they did precisely that and a council was formed under the chairmanship of Neville Blond, a wealthy Manchester textile magnate. Blond made it a condition of accepting the chairmanship that the council, now calling itself the English Stage Company, had to seek a permanent London base. In a move that was to have historic ramifications, the organisation was thus transformed, in the words of Irving Wardle, 'from a provincial festival service to a continuous metropolitan management'. Blond even had a specific theatre in mind: the derelict Kingsway just off the Aldwych. And so in July 1955 Devine, now the artistic director but with Duncan and Lewenstein still on board, stood in the shell of the Kingsway and formally announced the creation of the ESC. When the cost of renovating the Kingsway proved prohibitive, Esdaile offered the ESC the Royal Court instead. Exactly like Joan Littlewood inspecting the Theatre Royal, Stratford East three years earlier, Devine found a Victorian theatre given over to light entertainment – currently an intimate revue called *From Here and There* – and in a terrible mess. Water was pouring through the roof. You couldn't even touch the switchboard without getting a thousand-volt shock. Nonetheless Devine told Blond: 'It's perfect, Neville. Let's take it.' By November 1955 a deal had been done.

You could hardly have had two more opposite personalities than Joan Littlewood and George Devine. The one a flamboyant romantic for whom text was only one ingredient in a theatrical spectacle: the other an Oxford-educated actor-director who believed in the essential primacy of the writer. And in years to come there was little love lost between either the protagonists or the institutions they came to represent. In her memoirs, Joan Littlewood refers to the Royal Court as 'soft-centred – very middle-class and proper like their leader, the anti-semitic George Devine': a vindictive remark for which there seems no shred of evidence and which would have come as a surprise to Neville Blond and Oscar Lewenstein. For their part, the Court were not above trying to poach some of Stratford East's writers. Jealousy was also fuelled by the Arts Council's differing attitude to the two organisations. While Theatre Workshop was granted a pitiful £500 in 1955–56, the Court was offered £2,500 start-up money and £7,000 in its first full year of operations. But, whatever the ideological, artistic and financial differences between Littlewood and Devine, both had a passionate, quasi-religious commitment to their individual theatres, a remarkable capacity for self-sacrifice and a clear-sighted vision of the future.

While Littlewood was putting down roots at Stratford East and Devine was getting his foot inside the door in Sloane Square, the twenty-four-year-old Peter Hall – ultimately more powerful than either of them – was already pursuing a progressive policy at London's Arts Theatre. Hall's connection with the Arts had begun in August 1953 when Alec Clunes invited him to fill a two-week summer gap with his Cambridge-acclaimed undergraduate production of Pirandello's *Henry IV*. By December the new owner of the Arts, Campbell Williams, had offered Hall the post, at seven pounds a week plus luncheon vouchers, of script-reader and assistant to the incoming director, John Fernald. At the same time Hall, establishing a lifelong pattern of being in two places at once, was allowed to work as a guest director in rep at Oxford, Windsor and Worthing. Intriguingly Hall's early productions at the Arts in 1954 were of Lorca, Goldoni and Gide: a comment on the dearth of good new writing and on Hall's own youthful internationalism. And when, in January 1955, Fernald was appointed principal of RADA, Hall was his obvious successor at the Arts. Like Littlewood and Devine, Hall was impatient with the prevailing conservatism and cosy insularity of current theatre, as he told an interviewer in *The Stage* in February 1955:

> For the most part the British theatre does not take into account the fact that we have had a World War since 1939 and that everything in the world has changed – values, ways of living, ideals, hopes and fears. As I see it, our theatre is far too often pre-war, safe and easygoing in what it offers and lacking in the stimulation that will attract fresh audiences.

Hall articulated the views of many young people at the time: a sense of cultural exclusion and of impatience with the dominance of the old pre-war gang. The irony is that, by being asked to run the Arts at twenty-four, Hall somewhat undermined his thesis about the marginalisation of youth and acquired a position that enabled him to become an instrument of change.

Hall immediately made his presence felt. In March 1955 he shared a Francophile double bill with his predecessor, John Fernald, who directed Andre Obey's *Sacrifice to the Wind* while Hall staged the first-ever Ionesco play to be seen in Britain, *The Lesson*. With the Ionesco Hall introduced not merely a new voice but a new theatrical style: anti-naturalistic, absurdist (though we didn't use the word then) and free from the prevailing liberal humanism. In Ionesco's play a goatish old professor vents his lunacy on a young female pupil. Fired by her inability to master subtraction, he explodes in nihilistic frenzy when she fails to comprehend his gibberish lecture on the 'neo-Spanish languages' and eventually, and symbolically, thrusts a knife into her lower regions. We learn that she is the fortieth victim he has killed that day. And, as the Maid helps him to dispose of the body, another pupil comes eagerly knocking at the door. Hall, however, disavows as apocryphal the story that he thought it would be more credible if the Professor had killed only three or four pupils, and that Ionesco felt this typified the English love of understatement.

You only have to contrast *The Lesson* with benign English plays about the pupil–teacher relationship – such as *The Linden Tree* and *The Browning Version* – to see how radical Ionesco's work was in 1955. Dealing with the sexuality of teaching, the absurdity of language and the dangers of a fact-based pedagogy, it developed its central idea with a ruthless Cartesian logic. It was a shocking, violent and mordantly funny play that, according to Hall, was greeted with 'abuse, laughter and rage'. It was also the first in a series of detonations in the mid-Fifties which were to shake the British theatre to its foundations. Immediately after *The Lesson*, Hall took advantage of the Arts Theatre's club status to stage Julien Green's *South*, which would never have received a licence from the Lord Chamberlain. Set on a Charleston plantation on the eve of the American Civil War, it was a brilliantly atmospheric and nervily tense play about homosexuality which I saw as an Oxford undergraduate three years later and have never come across since. Revealing both his appetite for the inordinate and an interest in Civil War drama, Hall went on in June to direct O'Neill's four-hour *Mourning Becomes Electra*, which wordily transposes Greek drama to the American South: 'the greatest unwritten play of the century', Tynan called it. During lengthy breaks for technical rehearsals of the O'Neill, Hall read a play that had been running in Paris since 1953: one on which the West End producer, Donald Albery, had an option and which had been turned down by many of the leading actors of the day including Ralph Richardson, Alec Guinness and Michael Hordern. Having greatly admired *South*, Albery thought Hall might be just the man to do it at the Arts: it was, of course, *Waiting For Godot*.

To understand the shock and dismay Beckett's play caused when first staged at the Arts in August 1955, one has to remember how different the rituals of theatre-going then were. The National Anthem was played prior to a performance. Velvet curtains majestically rose or parted. And audiences expected to be transported by the dramatist into a world of heightened reality. Beckett, however, simply specifies 'A country road. A tree. Evening', and starts his play with an image of an old tramp – or could it be clown? – vainly trying to remove his boot. Significantly Harold Hobson began his review in the *Sunday Times* by saying that '*Waiting For Godot* has nothing at all to seduce the senses': a reminder of the extent to which in the Fifties we expected artifice, sensuous escape or at least an aestheticised version of the everyday as part of the theatrical contract.

We had also never before seen a play that made the act of waiting itself dramatic. Obviously throughout history dramatists had shown characters in a state of nervous anticipation: they had waited variously for the Ghost in *Hamlet*, for the arrival of Lady Bracknell in *The Importance*, for the west wind in Shaw's *Saint Joan*, for Lefty in Clifford Odets's American political drama. But expectations in those plays were either thwarted or fulfilled. Beckett, however, was the first dramatist to use boredom to create dramatic tension and to show time as an endless vacuum somehow to be filled: a point reinforced by the original French title, *En attendant Godot*. In other words, '*While* waiting for Godot'. The idea of waiting as a dramatic process was something on which other dramatists eventually capitalised: Osborne in *Look Back In Anger*, Stoppard in *Rosencrantz and Guildenstern Are Dead*, Jack Gelber in *The Connection*, David Mamet in *American Buffalo*. In 1955, however, it was a revolutionary concept.

In the past, we'd also assumed a curve or arc to be the natural symbol for dramatic action: in the Aristotelian sense, exposition, development, peripeteia and denouement. Instead of an arc Beckett offers us repetition. But Eric Bentley was not strictly accurate when he wrote in *The New Republic*, at the time of the play's American premiere, that 'two strips of action are laid side by side like railway tracks'. What Beckett offers us is repetition with a difference: parallels with subtle variations. The most famous example occurs in the ending to each of the two acts. The first ends:

ESTRAGON: Well, shall we go?
VLADIMIR: Yes, let's go.

They do not move.

Whereas the second concludes:

VLADIMIR: Well? Shall we go?
ESTRAGON: Yes, let's go.

They do not move.

The differences are minute but dramatically crucial. In the second act there is an interpolated question mark after the word 'Well': something implying greater uncertainty and enforcing a slowing-down of the speech rhythms. Also in the first act the final question is posed by Estragon and in the second by Vladimir: not just a reminder of their

79

indissoluble kinship but a hint, reinforced by Beckett in his own Berlin production where they wore matching halves of a single suit, that Vladimir and Estragon are separate facets of one person. But there are numerous other parallels between the two acts of *Waiting For Godot*, listed by John Fletcher and John Spurling in their book on *Beckett The Playwright*. Gestures, for instance, are echoed with variations. In the first act the two tramps prop up the hapless baggage-handler, Lucky: in the second act they become supportive caryatids to his master, Pozzo. In the first act Pozzo selfishly bellows 'Coat!' to Lucky: in the second Vladimir selflessly spreads his coat around Estragon's shoulders. All this shows that Beckett, haunted by balance and symmetry, was not destroying the well-made play: he was simply redefining it.

If a drama reliant on waiting and repetition was unnerving to a London audience in 1955, so too was Beckett's dramatic use of silence. In Peter Hall's production pauses were lengthened to the point of embarrassment before being broken; they were also sometimes occupied by audible gibes from the audience. Silence was not, of course, a total novelty in theatre. It was present in Chekhov. It was there in the American comedian, Jack Benny, whom Harold Pinter watched and admired at the London Palladium in the early Fifties. And Peter Brook had inserted an agonisingly long pause into his 1950 Stratford production of *Measure for Measure* before Barbara Jefford's Isabella eventually decided to plead for Angelo's life. Beckett's great innovation, however, was to balance speech and silence in an effort to achieve a musical pattern. If you examine the famous antiphonal passage in Act Two of *Godot* beginning 'All the dead voices' – 'They make a noise like wings', you find that no fewer than nine silences are specifically interpolated to achieve a precise aural effect. George Steiner has pointed out parallels with the silent intervals that are integral to musical compositions by Webern and John Cage: also to the apparently empty spaces of white-on-white or black-on-black minimalist paintings. 'This re-evaluation of silence', wrote Steiner in *Language and Silence*, 'is one of the most original, characteristic acts of the modern spirit.' And in Beckett it is used not just to heighten dramatic tension but as a reminder of the cosmic void in which the characters are symbolically placed.

Waiting, repetition, silence: these were the unusual ingredients of *Waiting For Godot*. But what angered and disturbed many people in 1955 was the lack of any discernible message. Plays in that period were supposed to offer diversion or dogma. But along came Beckett with a play that lacked a precise resolution and that allowed the spectator the freedom to deduce his own meaning. Hobson and Tynan alone amongst the daily and Sunday critics seemed to grasp that point. But it is conspicuous how, in the endless follow-up pieces in the weekly and monthly reviews, even the play's strongest advocates felt obliged to define it in religious or ideological terms. The most famous example came in an essay by G. S. Fraser in the *Times Literary Supplement* in February 1956, after the play's transfer to the Criterion, which saw *Godot* as 'a modern morality play on permanent Christian themes'. In the gospel according to Fraser, Vladimir and Estragon represent the fallen state of man but are also static pilgrims seeking religious consolation. Meanwhile Pozzo is an embodiment of Nietzschean pessimism and Lucky of half-baked knowledge and the plain man's belief in scientific progress. 'The Nietzschean and the Liberal hypotheses being put out of court,' argues Fraser, 'the Christian hypothesis is left holding the stage. It is at least a more comprehensive and profound hypothesis, whatever Mr Beckett may personally think of it; and the total effect of his play, therefore, is not to lower but unexpectedly raise our idea of human dignity.'

Fraser certainly had a point. The more often I see or read *Godot*, the more conscious I become of the play's Christian background. There are the quotations from St Augustine ('Do not despair – one of the thieves was saved; do not presume – one of the thieves was damned') and the Bible; the allusions to the Tree of Life and Knowledge; the references to the angels who keep the sheep and goats. Even more importantly, the whole emphasis on stoical endurance reminds one of the Protestant ethos in which Beckett himself was saturated. But a knowledge of the Bible or *Pilgrim's Progress* doesn't automatically make one a Christian; and Fraser goes too far in asserting that *Godot* is a modern morality play. Eric Bentley was nearer the truth when he wrote:

> I take it that Mr Beckett belongs to that extensive group of modern writers who have had a religious upbringing, retain religious impulses and longings but have lost all religious belief . . . People who have seen *Godot* are able to suggest this or that solution – Christian, anti-Christian etcetera – precisely because Beckett has left the door open to them to do so. They are wrong only if they intimate that the author himself passed through the door and closed it behind him.

It is the openness of that door – as well as the emphasis on waiting, repetition and silence – that marks out *Waiting For Godot* as a turning point in modern drama. Sartre's *Huis clos*, which Peter Brook directed in London in 1946, anticipates Beckett's play in its existential pessimism and pervasive irony: at the end, when three people trapped in hell realise that they are to prey on each other for ever, one of them cries 'Eh bien, continuons' (Well, let's go on) without actually moving. But Sartre's obvious message, that we are all desperate characters forever imprisoned with others of our kind, reduces his play to philosophic melodrama. And, in the more ambitious British plays of the post-war era, there is little doubt where the authors stand. Fry in *The Lady's Not For Burning* writes of the redemptive power of love and the daily miracle of existence. Eliot in *The Cocktail Party* and *The Confidential Clerk* celebrates a spiritual elect who are either able to achieve grace through martyrdom or pass through a private door into a world of spiritual fulfilment. Even Whiting's *Saint's Day* – the most progressive play of the pre-Beckett era – ends with an image of life's continuity: as the death-dealing soldiers' apocalyptic trumpet sounds, a young village child performs a life-giving dance. The shock of *Waiting For Godot* lay in the fact that it closed no door and allowed the spectator total interpretative freedom.

There was a revealing essay about it written shortly after its premiere by Ivor Brown in his book *Theatre 1955–56*. Brown, lately supplanted by Kenneth Tynan as drama critic of the *Observer*, was a fiercely rationalist Scot who suspected that *Waiting For Godot* was a hoax; and as proof he cited the various definitions of the play offered to him by its champions. Brown actually lists nine competing points including the ideas 'That it was a superb tragedy: that it was a superb comedy. That two of the characters are facets of the same person: that all the characters are the same person. That it cheerfully lifted the heart and struck resounding notes of hope: that it was a fine piece of pessimism proper to the doomed and dismal world we live in.' For a conservative critic like Brown these contradictions were proof that Beckett's play was meretricious nonsense. What he didn't consider was that these varying interpretations were all simultaneously possible and evidence of *Godot*'s greatness. In the end that was Beckett's most influential achievement. He erupted into a theatre where plays were categorised and pigeon-holed, as in a postal sorting office, and where they were expected, once delivered, to convey a particular message; the job of the critic was to unseal them and, if necessary, decode them for the benefit of future customers. But along came Beckett with a play that was a strange mix of seaside postcard and letter bomb, that had no distinct address and that even existed in two different languages. It was the indefinibility of the play that baffled many people in 1955. In an essentially conservative culture the artist was allowed to fulfil the role of purveyor of harmless pleasure or truth-bearing prophet. What he wasn't supposed to do was muddle up the genres by using the techniques of the music hall to explore spiritual angst. Beckett's achievement was not merely to extend the boundaries of theatre. It was, in a world still based on the sanctity of authority, to democratise the medium: to suggest that the audience, by the power of its concentration and the variety of its interpretation, ultimately creates the play. It was a subversive idea set to reverberate through the ensuing half-century.

III

1955–59

Twelve O'Clock Rock

Waiting For Godot redefined the nature of drama. It also became an even more controversial talking-point on its move to the Criterion Theatre in September 1955. Performances were interrupted by nightly walk-outs and explosions of indignation, much to the consternation of Beckettian aficionados, including a poetry-loving young rep actor, Harold Pinter, who made a special pilgrimage to the Criterion with his then girlfriend, Jill Johnson. But it would be misleading to talk of either *Godot* or Osborne's *Look Back In Anger*, which opened at the Royal Court in May 1956, as ushering in a 'revolution' in British theatre. That implies a forcible and bloody overthrow of the existing order. What actually happened, both in theatre and society, was something more complex: a perceptible shift in the balance of power and a growing tension between an entrenched conservatism and a burgeoning youth culture impatient with old forms and established institutions. The Tories were still in office and many familiar British rituals, from the Boat Race and Royal Ascot to the Last Night of the Proms, remained unchanged; but there is little doubt that the country itself became a more turbulent and violent place. Britain in the late Fifties effectively became Two Nations in which age, even more than class, was the dividing factor. It was also a period in which culture became a weapon of social antagonism.

That the majority of people were largely content with their lot, in spite of global and domestic convulsions, is shown by the electoral figures. In May 1955, the Conservatives were returned to power, under the flakily charismatic Anthony Eden, with a sixty-eight-seat lead over Labour. In October 1959 the Conservatives, now led by Harold Macmillan, actually *increased* their majority to 108. Even allowing for the vagaries of the first-past-the post system, that suggests there was some truth in Macmillan's much-misquoted vaunt that 'most of our people have never had it so good'. And the statistics tend to bear that out. Average weekly earnings rose thirty-four per cent between 1955 and 1960 even though retail prices also rose by fifteen per cent. But the cost of some objects such as small cars decisively fell. In 1955 there were a record three and a half million private cars on the road. By 1959 that had shot up to five and a half million, including the new Mini which cost as little as five hundred pounds. TV sets, washing machines and refrigerators were also within reach of large sections of the population. For many people, my own family included, a culture of austerity was replaced by one of modest affluence.

But material prosperity also brought with it attacks from the left. In 1955 J. B. Priestley identified a new consumerism and a growing commercialism which he termed Admass. 'This', he wrote in the *New Statesman,* 'is my name for the whole system of an increasing productivity plus inflation plus a rising standard of material living plus high-pressure advertising and salesmanship plus mass-communications plus cultural democracy and the creation of the mass-mind.' But Priestley was not alone in his Cassandra-like warnings against the dangers of a consumerist society. On 22 September 1955 the British way of life was permanently altered by the introduction of commercial television, whose first advertisement turned out to be for Gibbs SR toothpaste. Siren voices had long been raised against the advent of commercial television. The Labour Party prophesied a 'national disaster'. University vice-chancellors and leading clergy wrote protestingly to *The Times*. Lord Reith, the effective founder of the BBC, compared the arrival of commercial TV to the introduction to Britain of 'smallpox, bubonic plague and the Black Death' while Sir William Haley, BBC Director-General, warned that 'the good, in the long run, will inescapably be driven out by the bad'.

Haley, a high-minded proponent of public-service broadcasting, was an icon of liberal seriousness. But it is tempting to juxtapose him, as symbols of the polarisation of Britain in the mid-Fifties, with an even bigger cultural figurehead: Bill Haley. Indeed Sir William, when he exchanged the BBC for editorship of *The Times*, was interviewed by one singularly ill-prepared journalist under the baffling impression that he was the chubby American rock-star. Not, you'd have thought, an easy mistake to make after Bill Haley had injected a note of rude sexual vitality into an anodyne local pop scene dominated by romantic balladeers such as Dickie Valentine, David Whitfield, Anne Shelton and Ruby Murray. The sound of Bill Haley and the Comets – and the famous 'Rock Around The Clock' – was first heard in 1955 in the

American movie, *The Blackboard Jungle*. The song itself quickly became, as Peter Lewis notes in *The Fifties*, 'the anthem of dissident youth of all classes'; and when a catchpenny movie of the same title was released in Britain in 1956 it caused mayhem. Riots in a cinema in the Elephant and Castle led to an orgy of vandalism in which two thousand kids took to the streets; and, even in sedate Leamington Spa where I lived, people tore up the seats and danced in the aisles of the Regal Cinema. Silly swot that I was, I was too busy studying for 'A' Levels to go.

Everywhere one looks in the late Fifties, however, one finds division and bifurcation. Age versus youth was the most obvious distinction. But there was also America versus Britain. While the young aped American manners, morals and fashions, there was often a startling gap between transatlantic energy and British reticence. America offered us Elvis – 'a guitar-playing Marlon Brando' – Bill Haley, Jerry Lee Lewis and Chuck Berry: we countered gamely with Tommy Steele and Cliff Richard who posed little visible sexual threat. In the Fifties there was also a widening gap between an inherent middle-class conservatism and a world of protest and dissent: one that found its voice over Suez in 1956, that led to the foundation of the Campaign For Nuclear Disarmament in 1958 and that expressed itself in the plays, novels and films of the Angry Young Men. With Britain becoming ever more economically dependent on imported African and Caribbean labour, the colour of one's skin also became a source of division: something uneasily witnessed in the Notting Hill Race Riots of 1958. And it seems oddly fitting that a fractious decade ended with C. P. Snow launching an attack, in the 1959 Rede lecture at Cambridge, on 'The Two Cultures' that placed scientists and humanists in two separate, exclusive and mutually ignorant camps. No division, of course, is ever absolute. The generations often united in political protest. According to the novelist Colin MacInnes, jazz clubs also brought people together regardless of class, race or gender. But my memory of Britain in the late Fifties is of a series of opposing constituencies. On arriving at Oxford in 1958, for instance, I found there was a vast gulf between the National Service generation and those, like myself, who were wet-behind-the-ears innocents straight from school. Lodging in a Unitarian establishment that contained many refugees from neighbouring New College, I discovered an even more pronounced gap between the working-class scholarship boys, of whom I was one, and an upper-class set who possessed an ease, social assurance and braying lung-power that I both envied and cordially detested.

The divisions that permeated every area of British life help to explain the theatre of the time. Countless official histories have perpetuated the consoling myth that 1956 was a year of 'revolution' in which the Royal Court and Theatre Workshop banished forever the tight-lipped reticence of the well-made play and the smooth snobberies of drawing-room drama. But, while it is absolutely true that 1956 opened the door to a new generation who reflected the escalating turbulence of British society, the myth overlooks two inconvenient facts. The first is that the previous ten years had already witnessed dramatists dissecting the state of the nation and suggesting that we were now living in a fractured, godless and violent world. And not only dramatists: in addition to landmark plays such as *Saint's Day* and *Waiting For Godot*, Peter Brook's 1955 Stratford production of *Titus Andronicus* had, with the aid of Olivier's towering performance, rediscovered a forgotten tragedy and introduced us to the kind of hallucinatory horror outlined by Artaud's Theatre of Cruelty. But the second crucial fact is that the commercial theatre did not simply lie down and die in the face of the Royal Court onslaught in 1956. The English Stage Company in its first year of operations achieved average box-office takings of fifty-six per cent and even that modest figure was boosted by the runaway success of Wycherley's gloriously smutty *The Country Wife* which swiftly transferred to the West End. The most popular plays of the year, in fact, were Enid Bagnold's *The Chalk Garden*, Peter Ustinov's *Romanoff and Juliet*, Noël Coward's *South Sea Bubble* and *Nude With Violin*, Hugh and Margaret Williams' *Plaintiff In A Pretty Hat* and two translated French imports: a Feydeau–Desvallières farce, *Hotel Paradiso*, unforgettably starring Alec Guinness and Irene Worth, and *Gigi*, adapted by Anita Loos from a Colette story and directed by the radical young Turk, Peter Hall. All this suggests not only that theatre reflected the social divisions within Britain but that the commercial citadel was far better fortified than has been admitted; and so, before examining the new drama, it might be worth asking wherein lay the appeal of the old.

In the case of *The Chalk Garden*, which opened at the Haymarket a month before *Look Back In Anger* galvanised the Royal Court, it is not too difficult to guess. This was a slap-up H. M. Tennent production directed by John Gielgud. It also offered the spectacle of Edith

Evans as the eccentrically aristocratic Mrs St Maugham and Peggy Ashcroft as the dumpy governess, and possible murderess, who rescues her employer's granddaughter, Laurel, from her sterile clutches. Bagnold was a fascinating figure: the wife of the head of Reuters and one-time patroness of an artsy salon that included Wells and Kipling. But, although her play argues that Laurel can no more flourish in the stifling world of Mrs St Maugham than plants can prosper in the arid soil of the house's chalk garden, it appealed to a West End audience's built-in snobberies. The play ostensibly condemns Mrs St Maugham's world of licensed privilege: at the same time it revels in her self-conscious phrase-making. Mrs St Maugham says of Laurel that 'by some extraordinary carelessness she was violated in Hyde Park at the age of twelve'; claims that 'privilege and power make selfish people – but gay ones' and that 'irritation is like a rash on the heart'. Even when her butler simply comes in for a coffee tray she can't resist telling him that 'you've a nose for a crisis like a basset for a wild hare'. This is a mixture of small Fry and sub-Wilde: language full of mandarin metaphor and strained simile in which sound takes precedence over sense. One notices Mrs St Maugham's use of the word 'carelessness' to trivialise the matter of her granddaughter's rape and, without being unduly literal, one wonders how a hollow, muscular organ like the heart can be susceptible to a rash. Clearly audiences were mesmerised by hallowed memories of Edith Evans' Lady Bracknell and by the spectacle of Peggy Ashcroft – recently made a Dame – playing a suspected suburban murderess. And not only audiences. Tynan in the *Observer* mysteriously called the play 'the finest artificial comedy to have flowed from an English pen since the death of Congreve': a fatuous remark which knocks on the head the whole Edwardian school of Pinero, Henry Arthur Jones and St John Hankin. If *The Chalk Garden* ran for 658 performances at the Haymarket, it was because it satisfied the conservative instincts of an audience that liked to see stylish people saying supposedly stylish things.

The success of Coward's *South Sea Bubble*, which opened at the Lyric Shaftesbury Avenue in April 1956, and of *Nude With Violin*, which arrived at the Globe in October, is also not hard to explain. For a start there was the still-potent memory of Coward's pre-war reputation. The first play also starred Vivien Leigh and the second John Gielgud. But, even more significantly, both plays tapped into the mood of middle England in the mid-Fifties. While *South Sea Bubble* appealed to imperialist nostalgia, *Nude With Violin* addressed a philistine resentment at the supposed con-trick played on the public by modern art. Neither play was any good; but both showed that Coward still satisfied the West End audience's hunger for reassurance.

Even conservative theatregoers, however, might have flinched at some of the assumptions behind *South Sea Bubble*. Set in Coward's favourite mythical colony of Samolo in the Pacific, it deals with the sexual misadventures of a progressive governor's flighty wife: a figure loosely based on Edwina Mountbatten who had enjoyed affairs with Nehru and the cabaret-singer, Hutch. When the heroine is asked to use her charms on a pro-British local leader and he responds over-enthusiastically, a scandal is averted only by the politician's mildly improper advances being attributed to a nationalist fanatic. But what makes the play so antediluvian is Coward's patronising vision of the Samolans as happy simpletons who shrink from the notion of self-government and his vilification of anyone who seeks to liberate them. Just in case we are in any doubt as to where Coward's sympathies lie, the heroine tells us that the militant nationalist is 'covered in warts and stinks like a badger'. And when the heroine's liberal husband suggests that the Samolans might actually wish to shoulder the responsibility of their own destiny, she puts him firmly in his place:

> They sing from morning till night. They weave away and make the most lovely waste-paper baskets and never stop having scads of entrancing children who swim before they can walk and have enormous melting eyes like saucers. And whenever they feel a bit peckish all they have to do is nip a breadfruit off a tree or snatch a yam out of the ground.

In such paradisal circumstances, who needs self-determination?

Coward's sentimental colonialism – in which jolly natives should be allowed to romp away eternally under beneficent white rule – was clearly tied up with his sexuality. Having built himself a splendid new home at Firefly Hill in Jamaica, he both worked hard and encouraged an atmosphere of laissez-faire loucheness. As his biographer, Philip Hoare, reveals, Coward allowed his houseboy to rob him blind and was not exactly indifferent to the manly charms of the local Jamaicans: many of his paintings, says Hoare, featured 'well-developed Afro-Caribbeans diving naked off jetties or lying about in the sun'. Coward also entertained his fellow amateur painter, Winston Churchill, at Firefly

Hill; and, as recent biographies have shown, Churchill in his final years easily lapsed into a mood of somnolent melancholy, feeling that his career had 'all been for nothing' because of his failure to prevent the liquidation of the British Empire. Coward and Churchill were both, in a way, imperalists out of touch with the movement of history. The irony is that, after Labour had handed self-governing power to India, Burma and Sri Lanka, it was Conservative administrations in the Sixties that granted independence to Ghana and Nigeria in West Africa and to Malaya. It was also Anthony Eden who, as Churchill's Foreign Secretary, agreed in 1954 to the progressive withdrawal of British troops from the Suez Canal Zone, thus ending eighty years of military occupation in Egypt and precipitating the crisis that was ultimately to ruin him. But Churchill and Coward were united in their attachment to the past and dismay at the loss of Empire.

As amateur painters, they also shared similar views on modern art: when Churchill on his retirement as Prime Minister in 1955 was presented with a portrait by Graham Sutherland, the work was quickly hidden and then destroyed on the orders of Lady Churchill. But the Fifties were a volatile time in British art, what with Francis Bacon's tortured visions of Pope Innocent X, John Bratby launching the kitchen-sink school and Reg Butler's prize-winning sculpture, *The Unknown Political Prisoner*, being publicly vandalised by a fellow artist. Coward's response to the disturbing changes in modern art was to write *Nude With Violin*: a creaking satire which, opening in October 1956, exactly coincided with the ructions over Suez and Hungary but ran serenely for eighteen months. Just as Coward had tapped into the West End public's nostalgia for Empire, he also articulated their anti-modernist instincts.

The plot of *Nude With Violin* revolves, very slowly, around the discovery that a famous modern painter, Paul Sorodin, never put brush to canvas in his life. Having taken three acts to reveal that Sorodin's work was painted by other people, Coward then plays his trump card: we learn that Sorodin's posthumously shown masterpiece, which lends the play its title, was the work of his valet's fourteen-year-old son. Coward not only implies that modern art is a gigantic con-trick. The valet's concluding tirade extends the attack to embrace modernism in general:

If the news leaks out that the great Sorodin's masterpieces were painted by a Russian tart, an ex-Jackson girl, a Negro Eleventh

Hour Immersionist and a boy of fourteen, the rot will spread like wildfire. Modern sculpture, music, drama and poetry will shrivel in the holocaust. Tens of thousands of industrious people who today are earning a comfortable livelihood by writing without grammar, composing without harmony and painting without form will be flung into abject poverty or forced really to learn their jobs. Reputations will wither overnight. No one will be spared.

Taken to its logical conclusion, the speech implies that Beckett's plays, Picasso's paintings, Stravinsky's music are all part of a modernist racket in which rogue charlatans are foisted on a gullible public by a conspiracy of critics, wheeler-dealers and entrepreneurs. This was Coward at his most finger-wagging and reactionary. But, in spite of hostile reviews and the prevailing national crisis, the play ran for 511 performances: a fact that puts the Royal Court revolution into perspective and reminds us that Coward still had a loyal West End constituency.

If Coward's plays appealed to the audience's nostalgic yearnings for the British Empire and representational art, other dramatists tickled its built-in snobbery. William Douglas Home's *The Reluctant Debutante*, for instance, ran for two years at the Cambridge Theatre from mid-1955 onwards. Given that the play deals with a harassed mother trying to launch an obstinate daughter into the right social stream and that the climax depends on the revelation that the chief suitor is a disguised duke, it shows that the West End hadn't exactly embraced the new radicalism. Mercifully the play became a period piece when Elizabeth II's suavely conservative royal court, as opposed to George Devine's rudely progressive one, decided in 1958 to put an end to the whole debutante nonsense, following withering public criticisms of the Windsors' antiquated practices from Lord Altrincham and Malcolm Muggeridge. But snob-drama tenaciously survived in the West End, as proved by the opening at the Duchess Theatre of *Plaintiff In A Pretty Hat* in the tumultuous October of 1956. This was the initial salvo of the husband-and-wife team of Hugh and Margaret Williams who for over a decade turned the allegedly extinct form of drawing-room comedy into a profitable light industry. Hugh Williams, father of the poet Hugo, was a stylish comic actor who had appeared in the New York production of *The Cocktail Party*. And as an antidote to the prevailing cult of the Angry Young Man, he and his wife co-authored a series of insidiously popular plays built around the concept of the Sexy Old Duffer. In this case the SOD in question is the supposedly impoverished Earl of Hewlyn. When his vacillating son is threatened with a breach-of-promise suit by a pushy Australian journalist, the old aristo craftily announces that he will marry the girl himself; but what starts out as a cunning legal tactic turns into a downright declaration of love.

One looks back at the play less in anger than in slack-jawed astonishment at the blatancy of its appeal to its audience's prejudices. On the principle that everyone loves a lord, it constantly begs our sympathy for the financial plight of the landed gentry. Thus our withers are wrung for the Earl of Hewlyn who has been obliged to let his ancestral Welsh seat for six months a year, sell fifteen thousand acres of land to pay death duties and even provide an indoor lav for a female tenant. Given, however, that he is slumming it in a Belgravia mews, keeps a butler and drinks vast quantities of pink champagne, his financial distress seems decidedly relative. Even more startling, since the play was co-authored by Mrs Williams, is its sexual chauvinism. Lecturing the upstart Aussie for pursuing her breach-of-promise case, Hewlyn tartly announces: 'But don't you see that this precious equality, this great twentieth-century emancipation of women which your sex has so relentlessly pursued, and so unfortunately achieved, is knocked cock-eyed when something like this happens because you immediately start shouting for privilege again.' After a tell-tale phrase like 'so unfortunately achieved' you might expect her to tell him where to stick his earldom. Instead the Oz journo seems sexually intrigued by the old dinosaur, even when he lectures her on her supposed control-freakery and claims, 'Believe me, no husband's going to put up with an everlasting succession of crushing matrimonal defeats without ending up a wife beater.' At this point you want her to throttle him; but, reader, she marries him! Indeed the play's final message is that even a tough Australian careerist cannot resist the charm and wiliness of a priapic aristo played, of course, by Williams himself. Combining authorial vanity with a preening misogyny that makes *The Taming Of The Shrew* look positively lily-livered, *Plaintiff In A Pretty Hat* deserves regular, symbolic revival if only to remind us of the values endorsed by Shaftesbury Avenue, and by implication much of middle England, in 1956.

Far from experiencing an overnight revolution in 1956, the British theatre, like society itself, split into opposing camps. The old guard, sensing an external challenge and a shift in attitudes, became ever more protective of its territory and assertive of its values: the West End went on pumping out right-wing propaganda and peddling cosy reassurance. At the same time, a radical generation, principally though not exclusively young, acquired a new militancy and authority. And, in the pivotal year of 1956, two events occurred which in the short term exposed these cultural divisions and in the long term genuinely changed the British theatre. Chronologically, the first event was the establishment of the English Stage Company at the Royal Court in April. The second was the visit of the Berliner Ensemble to the Palace Theatre in August, two weeks after the death of the company's founder, Bertolt Brecht. What is intriguing is how closely the two occurrences were linked.

In September 1955 George Devine, the ESC's director-designate, had paid a crucial visit to Berlin. He was there in a dual capacity as actor and director. He was playing Gloucester in his own hugely controversial Stratford production of *King Lear*, futuristically designed by Isamu Noguchi, and Dogberry in a famous Gielgud-directed *Much Ado About Nothing*. During a meeting, over beer and sausages, between Brecht, Helene Weigel, Devine and Peggy Ashcroft, it was agreed that Ashcroft should play the dual leads in *The Good Woman of Setzuan* at the Royal Court the following year. Brecht even advised his young Ensemble actors to go and see Gielgud and Ashcroft in *Much Ado*; though quite what they made of such a high camp, dressily decorative piece of British Shakespeare is not recorded. But Devine was able to see the Ensemble at work in *The Caucasian Chalk Circle* and recorded his glowing impressions in the April 1956 edition of *Encore*: a campaigning theatrical magazine that justly styled itself 'the voice of vital theatre' and symbolised the new militancy. Conservative playgoers leafed through *Theatre World*: progressive ones subscribed to *Encore*. In his article, Devine was struck by the beauty and simplicity of the Ensemble decor, the polish of the productions and the honesty of the acting: the plain, thick-legged Grusha would, he said, never be employed by any theatre in England, 'at least not as a heroine'. But Devine was at his most eloquent in describing the production of *The Chalk Circle*:

> There is a scene in which twenty peasants are gradually convulsed with laughter. The detail of observation and execution of this scene

was entirely remarkable and it must have been achieved with much time and care: one peasant in the front started laughing, the mirth rippled gradually and then overcame all twenty of them.

Devine contrasted this carefully rehearsed approach with the hit-and-miss methods of British theatre and ended up bowled over by Brecht's achievement of a 'poetic reality'.

Significantly, Devine says little about the play's political content: what impressed him was the company's style and methodology. And when the Berliner Ensemble visited the Palace Theatre in August 1956 with *The Caucasian Chalk Circle*, *Mother Courage* and *Trumpets and Drums*, it was the same story. British theatre practitioners, who hardly spoke a word of German and were not granted the benefit of surtitles, seized avidly on the acting, the decor, the lighting and the austere purity of the productions. For a generation reared on star casting, short rehearsal periods, the encrustations of naturalism and the frayed maintenance of theatrical illusion, the visit of the Berliner Ensemble provided a profound stylistic shock: one that was to permeate the British theatre, and even rival media, over the coming decades. The word 'Brechtian' became an instant theatrical shorthand for a cool presentational method; less attention was paid to Brecht's political beliefs and to his own form of personalised Marxism with its stress on individual survival.

The critics, again speaking little German, were warily sceptical about the plays the Ensemble brought to London: 'I do not believe', wrote the Francophile Harold Hobson, 'that there is any more illumination in *Mother Courage* than there is in *Uncle Tom's Cabin*.' But even Hobson was impressed by the acting. Tynan, who had already seen the Ensemble at the 1955 Paris Festival, where he promptly announced to his wife 'I'm a Marxist', came out in the *Observer* with all flags flying; but even he focused mainly on the actors, who 'look shockingly like people, real, potato-faced people such as one might meet in a bus-queue', and on the unforgettable nature of Brecht's stage pictures which, rather than than begging for applause, possessed 'the durable beauty of use'.

It is hard to exaggerate the impact of the Ensemble visit on our own theatre workers in that hot August of 1956. Peter Hall, who had done his RAF National Service in Germany, was hit amidships. 'Every British theatre person I knew', he wrote in his autobiography, 'was in awe of the talent of the Ensemble and particularly of the weight and richness of the middle-aged actors playing the small parts.' And the Berliner Ensemble, along with the Moscow Art Theatre, Jean Vilar's Theatre National Populaire and the Barrault–Renaud Company, was to shape Hall's vision of creating a permanent company in Britain. But no one has caught better than William Gaskill the adrenalin buzz created by the Ensemble's visit, which, he says, changed his life. In *A Sense of Direction* he writes:

> The first production we saw was *The Caucasian Chalk Circle* which was impressive and very beautiful to look at. In the interval I met John Dexter for the first time. He was already working at the Court. But it was *Courage* that blew our minds. When the half-curtain whizzed back and we saw Helene Weigel smiling up at the sky, Angelika Hurwicz blowing into her harmonica and the cart pulled against the revolve by a sweaty, piggy-eyed Ekkehard Schall and tiny, timid Heinz Schubert, we knew this was it.

Gaskill went on to become Britain's foremost Brechtian director. He applied Ensemble principles assiduously – and sometimes with excessive fidelity – to his work for the Royal Court, the RSC and eventually the National Theatre: indeed Gaskill's first production for Olivier's new-found company in 1963 was Farquhar's *The Recruiting Officer* precisely because it was the source of Brecht's *Trumpets and Drums*. Design was also permanently influenced by the Ensemble's visit: the fastidious spareness of Jocelyn Herbert and the metallic, quasi-industrial functionalism of John Bury were two examples of the Brechtian legacy. Even the visible lighting rigs and swooping cameras that marked BBC TV's *That Was The Week That Was* in the early Sixties showed how Brecht could be accommodated to the small screen. And Brecht's notion of Epic Theatre – with its emphasis on discrete narrative, its use of theatrical montage, its appeal to reason rather than to feelings – had a huge effect on British dramaturgy. Edward Bond admitted that of all the influences on him in the late Fifties 'perhaps the most important single event was the visit of the Berliner Ensemble'. And, when asked if there was any modern play he would like to have written, John Arden succinctly replied, '*Mother Courage*.' Actors too engaged in endless discussion about the famous Alienation-effect: John Gielgud, the high priest of British acting, found Helene Weigel's Mother Courage superb and the whole thing 'so stimulating and exquisitely rehearsed and executed that it was a great inspiration'. The West End old guard may have gone on much as before. But British theatre was stirred from its complacency by that momentous Ensemble visit and the ripples spread steadily outwards: even to the Midlands where, taking up *Encore*'s offer of copies of the Ensemble programmes, I found myself entranced by the designs of Caspar Neher and Teo Otto, which bore no relation to the painted canvas sets that dominated English theatre at the time.

I suspect that the 1956 visit by the Berliner Ensemble had as far-reaching an impact on British theatre as the creation of the English Stage Company. In so far as aesthetic principles won out over Marxist politics, it was, however, an impact that influenced style more than content. For proof you only have to look at the early history of the ESC. It took over the Royal Court six months before the Ensemble even arrived in London; yet its founding principles and ideals owed a huge amount to Devine's own Berlin trip and travellers' tales from abroad. George Devine, in fact, envisaged a Royal Court that would house an eclectic international programme, be based on a permanent company playing in rep and use spare, rigorously beautiful design. Intriguingly, the discovery of brand-new dramatists was relatively low-down on the agenda of both Devine and his flamboyant aide-de-camp, Tony Richardson. Their intention was to bring a breath of Brechtian fresh air into the dusty parochialism of British theatre; and it is significant that, even before they set up shop, they happily leased the Royal Court to Oscar Lewenstein in February 1956 to stage *The Threepenny Opera* which, in spite of the poor singing voice of Bill Owen's Macheath, still achieved a brief transfer to the West End.

The ESC's devotion to the Brechtian style – as opposed to its political content – was shown by Devine's opening production of Angus Wilson's *The Mulberry Bush* in April 1956. The play itself, by an admired novelist, was a thoroughly decent middle-class play: one set in an Oxbridge college where the liberal Warden and his wife are departing to make way for their thrusting successors. In that sense, it was strongly reminiscent of Priestley's *The Linden Tree*. But, where Priestley had passionately defended Herbivore values, Wilson sardonically exposed their flaws – especially the fondness of do-gooding intellectuals, like the departing Padleys, for elevating idealistic abstractions above fallible people. In spite of the play's naturalistic texture, however, Devine was determined to give the play a visibly

Brechtian 'feel'. Doors and windows stood in isolation from each other without any adjoining flats and in the second act a huge mulberry tree occupied centre stage. As Gaskill remarked, 'the play cried out for conventional treatment and no way could George or anyone else turn it into an epic piece.' For the ESC's second production, Arthur Miller's *The Crucible*, the Brechtian design of bare boards and a wooden-frame ceiling suspended on chains accorded with the play's content. But again it was a sign of the disregard for Brechtian politics that Devine cut the character of the old farmer, Giles Corey, who lends the play not just a good deal of emotional weight but also its vital economic perspective.

There was, however, nothing remotely Brechtian, either in style or content, about the third play of the season, John Osborne's *Look Back in Anger*, which opened on 8 May 1956. This is a date that has acquired its own unstoppable historical momentum. It is acknowledged in virtually every post-war account of British theatre as the dawn of a new era and the start of a revolution; and, when the Royal Court celebrated its fiftieth anniversary in 2006, 8 May became the pivotal point of the festivities. You can see why: Osborne's play undoubtedly energised a generation and stimulated hitherto quiescent dramatists to put pen to paper. But, although *Look Back In Anger* caused an initial stir in May 1956, it didn't provoke riots in the streets, lead to the instant collapse of West End theatre or even cause an immediate stampede at the box office. It was only when Lord Harewood introduced an eighteen-minute extract from the play on BBC Television that a sluggish box office suddenly took off. It's also part of the legend that the play was mercilessly savaged by the daily critics and saved only by Tynan and Hobson in the Sundays. In fact, although there were obtuse reviews in *The Times*, *Mail* and *Standard*, John Barber in the *Daily Express*, Philip Hope-Wallace in the *Manchester Guardian* and, most especially, Derek Granger in the *Financial Times* ('its influence should go far beyond such an eccentric and isolated one-man turn as *Waiting For Godot*') all recognised Osborne's bilious, needling talent. The notices were, in fact, what is politely known as mixed. If the play attracted a good deal of attention in 1956, it was less because of the drama critics than because of the BBC extract, the twenty-seven-year-old author's gift for publicity and the ability of truffle-hunting Fleet Street hacks to sniff out a cultural trend.

People noticed that Kingsley Amis in *Lucky Jim* and *That Uncertain Feeling* had overturned the polite conventions of English fiction and introduced a new kind of mildly subversive anti-hero. In the same month as *Look Back In Anger* was premiered, Colin Wilson's *The Outsider* was published and extravagantly acclaimed for its portrait of the alienation felt by men of genius down the ages: a line that apparently reached its culmination in the book's precocious twenty-five-year-old author. Suddenly a movement, that of the Angry Young Man, was born. But, although neither the theatre-loathing Amis nor the library-haunting Wilson had anything remotely in common with Osborne, the idea that Britain was seething with Angry Young Men quickly became a self-fulfilling prophecy. A phrase famously tossed off by the Royal Court's press officer, George Fearon, to describe the supposedly aggressive Osborne – 'Oh, he's just an angry young man,' he told the showbiz hacks – quickly entered the language and became an established fact. Articles, radio and TV programmes chewed over this supposedly new phenomenon. Eventually a book of essays, *Declaration*, appeared, outlining the credos of the young angries. And, at the centre of the furore, lay Osborne's incendiary play. When I finally got to London to see it in one of its recurrent revivals in August 1957, I remember standing on the steps of the Royal Court and watching people coming out of the first-house Saturday performance to see if they had been visibly changed by the experience. Naive perhaps; but a measure of the extent to which Osborne's play, even if it didn't revolutionise British theatre overnight, gradually acquired the glamour of myth and became a set text for the young.

What makes *Look Back In Anger* a durable work of art, as well as a social phenomenon, is its ability to change its meaning according to the temper of the times: something it has in common with *Hamlet*. Inevitably, it was first seen as a cry of political protest with Jimmy Porter acting as the ventriloquial Osborne's mouthpiece. Tynan set the tone for this interpretation by claiming that:

> *Look Back In Anger* presents post-war youth as it really is . . . All the qualities are there, qualities one had despaired of ever seeing on the stage – the drift towards anarchy, the instinctive leftishness, the automatic rejection of 'official' attitudes, the surrealist sense of humour (Jimmy describes a pansy friend as 'a female Emily Brontë'), the casual promiscuity, the sense of lacking a crusade worth

fighting for and, underlying all these, the determination that no one who dies shall go unmourned.

And, if Osborne became a role model for young writers, Jimmy himself quickly became a dramatic archetype to be copied and emulated. Kenneth Haigh, who created the role, once told me that Tynan asked him if he would teach him how to play the trumpet just like Jimmy; patiently, Haigh had to explain to the disappointed critic that he was simply miming to an offstage trumpeter. But the bravura intensity Haigh brought to the character encouraged the idea that the play was purely a series of vituperative solo arias. And that led to the inevitable question. What, countless articles enquired, was Jimmy so angry *about*? Was it, as Jimmy himself implied, about the lack of idealistic causes in the age of the H-bomb? Was it about the fact that the Welfare State had not been accompanied by the promised millennium of socialist brotherhood? Or was his anger prompted by the way power in Britain was exercised by a self-perpetuating coterie which Henry Fairlie had identified, in a famous *Spectator* article of 1954, as the Establishment?

No one seemed to know the answer. But maybe they were asking the wrong question. At the time the play was seized on as a political rallying cry and part of the war between youth and age that dominated the Fifties. The young felt that 'Jimmy spoke for our generation'. The elderly dismissed him as a noisy young pup, with even the progressive J. B. Priestley concluding, 'that young man was rotten with self-pity.' What is striking, however, is the way everyone felt compelled to take a moral stance on the character: as a latter-day Hamlet, a rebel without a cause or a whining, egotistical monster. That last view was scorchingly articulated by the middle-aged Kenneth Allsop in his book, *The Angry Decade*. As a TV presenter and literary man, Allsop seemed especially to resent the theatre's power to create a dynamic and resonant anti-hero. 'When', wrote Allsop, 'you detachedly list Jimmy's cardinal characteristics, sadism, self-righteousness, hysteria, sentimentality, viciousness, immaturity and coldness, they seemed like a quick summary of the type of character who would have found instant employment in Belsen.' Whatever Jimmy's flaws, I find it hard to imagine him ushering Jews into the gas-chamber.

With hindsight, however, it is possible to see that *Look Back In Anger* was always much more than a cry of rage: what it offered then, and still does, is an astonishingly wide-ranging picture of the divisions within Fifties England. In that sense, it's a genuine state-of-the-nation play. Reason and progress are fighting the Anglican church's endorsement of nuclear weapons as well as the mass hysteria induced by Billy Graham's evangelical rallies at Earls Court. We tend to forget that evangelicals have always used religion as an arm of politics; and Graham alarmed as many as he converted with his Cold War vision of 'a great sinister anti-Christian movement masterminded by Satan that has declared war upon the Christian God!' But Osborne's play is also about the cultural division between tabloid and broadsheet Sunday papers. The latter, according to Jimmy, are filled with columns on the English novel usually written half in French while the former are full of sexual scandal and revelations about 'grotesque and evil practices going on in the Midlands'. Again, neither claim is an exaggeration. The *Sunday Times*'s two chief book reviewers, Raymond Mortimer and Cyril Connolly, were both passionate Francophiles. As for the less salubrious Sundays, I had an aunt in Leamington Spa who every week would surreptitiously pass on her copy of the *News of the World* to her respectable solicitor employer as if it were a porno mag. But Osborne paints a comprehensive picture of an England riddled with schism: a place where redbrick universities are in conflict with Oxbridge, where jazz confronts Third Programme classicism, where church bells antagonise the secular spirit, where hetero and homo view each other with mutual suspicion and where class is an abiding determinant. The play, in fact, is built around a series of carefully structured class antitheses. Working-class Jimmy against upper-middle-class Alison. Cliff against Helena. The unseen proletarian Ma Tanner against Jimmy's father-in-law, Colonel Redfern. But the ultimate irony is that both Jimmy and Colonel Redfern are displaced persons hopelessly out of sympathy with monochrome mid-Fifties England. Alison even links the two of them by telling her father, 'You're hurt because everything is changed. Jimmy is hurt because everything is the same.' Alison is half right: the colonialist Colonel grieves over an Edwardian paradise now irretrievably lost whereas Jimmy is an angry romantic nostalgic for a world he never knew.

First Osborne's play was seen as a cry of political despair. Then as a social document. More recently, as in Gregory Hersov's 1999 National Theatre production pairing Michael Sheen and Emma Fielding, it has come to be played as a Strindbergian domestic battle. None of these readings is mutually exclusive: indeed the power of the play lies in its ability to frame the sex war and the class war against a panorama of England. But at its heart lies a furious domestic battle in which Jimmy's weapon is rhetoric while Alison's is silence. Feminists tend crisply to dismiss Osborne's play as misogynistic: I'd say it's about a contest of equals. Far from being a supine punchbag, Alison deploys her taciturnity with provocative skill. And the clues are all there in the text. Left alone with Cliff, Alison recalls a recent remark of Jimmy's that he couldn't remember what it was like to be young: 'I pretended not to be listening,' says Alison, 'because I knew that would hurt him, I suppose.' Later she tells her friend, Helena, that 'I still can't bring myself to feel the way he [Jimmy] does about things.' And, as a tough Roedean cookie, she's quite capable of flooring Jimmy with remarks like *'Oh, don't try and take his suffering away from him – he'd be lost without it.'* The italics are mine because, with that remark, Alison scores an absolute bull's-eye; for at the heart of Jimmy Porter – and I suspect of Osborne himself – is a belief in the authentic validity of pain. What finally restores Alison to Jimmy and secures an uneasy domestic truce is that, by losing their child, she has experienced a physical abasement he can understand. 'I'm in the fire and I'm burning and all I want is to die,' she cries in the closing moments. The barriers have crumbled and Jimmy and Alison are able to face a bleak future based on shared suffering. The fact that Osborne sees this as a cathartic conclusion persuades me that he was always a rebel rather than a revolutionary: a Byronic romantic rather than a political activist with a clearly defined agenda.

But *Look Back*'s most durable impact on the British theatre lay in its freewheeling, inclusive and blazingly intemperate language: this is where it really liberated the next generation. In his introduction to the 1993 Faber edition Osborne talks of his despair, as a young actor, at trying to learn Somerset Maugham's dialogue: 'Maugham's language', he writes, 'was dead, elusively inert, wobbly like some synthetic rubber substance.' His own play is a riposte to the mechanical glibness of the Maugham school but also to the technicolour artifice of the postwar verse drama of Christopher Fry and Ronald Duncan. What Osborne does in *Look Back* is forge a distinctive prose style but also one that borrows from sources as diverse as Max Miller, Terence Rattigan, Mills and Boon, D. H. Lawrence and Shakespeare.

The rhythm of the halls permeates the entire play: the constant vocal repetitions ('Well, she can talk can't she? You can talk, can't you?'), the Sandy Powell catchphrases ('Can you 'ear me, mother?'), the double-act trick of using one's partner as a butt ('My wife – that's the one on the tom-toms beside me'), all have the gamey whiff of Fifties Variety. And, while Osborne was in later years billed as the man who supplanted Rattigan, he was not above harnessing his predecessor's talent for obliquity. There's a classic instance in the play's first act. Alison hesitantly announces, while Cliff is bandaging an arm damaged in one of Jimmy's rough-house games, that she is pregnant. This is followed, after a suitable pause, by Cliff's line, 'I'll need some scissors.' The indirect response and the physical action of crossing to the dressing table both give Cliff time to digest information that will alter not only Jimmy and Alison's marriage but his own role as a buffer-state: it's a sequence straight out of the Rattigan handbook. But, alongside the passages of quiet understatement, Osborne deploys the verbal lushness of romantic fiction ('He looked so young and frail, in spite of the tired line around his mouth'), harps on key words such as 'fire' and 'blood' with Bunyanesque frequency and reveals a deeply Lawrentian side in Jimmy's sexual candour and fear of vaginal obliteration: 'Oh, it's not that she hasn't her own kind of passion. She has the passion of a python. She just devours me whole every time, as if I were some over-large rabbit.' Osborne himself once remarked: 'I thought *Look Back In Anger* was a formal, rather old-fashioned play: I think that it broke out by its use of language.' And he was dead right. In its blend of realism and rhetoric, its comic fury and its merry eclecticism, Osborne's language re-established the vitality of English dramatic prose and reminded us that its author was a rebel with a sense of the past.

Look Back In Anger turned Osborne into a public figure, enfranchised and stimulated young dramatists throughout Britain and became a cultural talking-point. And a further sign the ground was slowly beginning to shift came with the opening of Brendan Behan's *The Quare Fellow* at the Theatre Royal, Stratford East on 24 May. The writer was an ebullient Irishman who had served eight years in prison for his IRA activities, and his play made direct use of his experience. Set in a Dublin prison in the twenty-four hours before the execution of an inmate, Behan's play bristled with native wit. Beneath the gallows humour, however, there was a Swiftian anger at the ritualised barbarity of capital punishment; also a republican disgust at the fact that the official hangman of the Irish Free State was an imported Englishman. Behan in no way sentimentalised the prisoners: he showed them snatching food from the condemned man's last meal and describing the execution in the racy terms of a Grand National commentary. But what Behan brought out, in language of sparkling eloquence, was the inhumanity of capital punishment. At one point an inmate recalled the occasion on which the Prison Board told the wrong man he had been reprieved. This brought to mind an overwhelming passage in Boswell's *Journals* when one of his clients, an alleged sheep-stealer reconciled to death, is given a fourteen-day stay of execution. As Boswell records, 'it was striking to see a man who had been quite composed when he thought his execution certain become so weak and agitated by a respite.' Like Boswell, Behan exposed the appalling consequences of official incompetence. But his main target, at a time when capital punishment was still on the statute book in both Westminster and Dublin, was public collusion in the grisly formalities of state murder: something that could not have escaped a first-night audience overflowing with recognised leaders of the Republican movement. It was, by all accounts, a pretty tumultuous premiere, at whose curtain call Behan claimed that 'Miss Littlewood's company has performed a better play than I wrote.' While Behan owed much to Littlewood's extra-textual inspiration, which included marching the actors round the theatre's roof as if they were prisoners on exercise, he had also written a play that led Bernard Levin to call him 'the most exciting new talent to enrich our theatre since the war'. Behan did not live long enough nor possess sufficient self-discipline to fulfil such expectations; nor did *The Quare Fellow* enjoy much of a run on its West End transfer. But it helped to regenerate theatrical language and proved that things were stirring in officially neglected Stratford East as well as in the more generously subsidised Sloane Square.

One thing was clear by the mid-Fifties: the generational, class and cultural divisions that had been bubbling away for some time in British society were at last beginning to find their expression on the public stage. *Waiting For Godot, Look Back In Anger, The Quare Fellow* and the Berliner Ensemble were addressing one audience: the plays of Enid Bagnold, Noël Coward and Hugh and Margaret Williams quite another. And, if any single event exposed the tensions within the society itself, it was the 1956 Suez crisis: a genuinely momentous affair that led to massive demonstrations and protests, that ultimately brought down the Prime Minister and that had uncanny reverberations nearly half a century later in the Iraq war. As with Iraq, what shocked people was the British government's mixture of militarism and mendacity. The crisis began in 1956 when the Egyptian leader, Colonel Nasser, illegally nationalised the Suez Canal Company, of which Britain owned forty-four per cent, giving him command of crucial oil supplies from the Gulf en route to Europe. The British and French response was to jettison international diplomacy and take the law into their own hands. 'Like Wild West sheriffs restoring order', in the words of Peter Vansittart, they secretly encouraged Israeli forces, led by one Colonel Ariel Sharon, to attack Egypt as a cover for their own military intervention. But, although allied aircraft bombed Cairo and Egyptian airfields in October 1956, Eden's tactics led to dissension within the Cabinet and strenuous opposition from military personnel: 'The Prime Minister has gone bananas,' the Chief of the Air Staff candidly informed his team. World opinion also quickly rallied against an act of 'illegal aggression', and British paratroops who, by 7 November, had penetrated twenty-five miles into the Canal Zone, were humiliatingly forced by the UN to halt military action in return for the creation of an international peacekeeping force. By that time world attention had already shifted to another crisis: the Soviet invasion of Hungary on 5 November, when tanks rolled into Budapest to suppress the liberal reforms of Imre Nagy. In the succinct words of historian Christopher Lee, 'Britain and France had attempted to assert their rights over what they regarded as their territory and failed. The Soviet Union did the same thing and succeeded.'

What is hard to convey now is the intensity of the passion aroused by the Suez debacle. On the one hand, it bred a kind of gung-ho, saloon-bar, imperialist nostalgia. Living, as I did, in Anthony Eden's parliamentary constituency of Warwick and Leamington, I heard loud, jingoistic voices raised on all sides arguing that we should have gone through with the Egyptian invasion and, in the cant phrase of the time, 'finished them off'. Against that, there was a growing moral outrage at the government's breach of international law and downright deception that came to a head in an anti-war demonstration in Trafalgar Square on Sunday, 4 November: one that led to fierce battles between mounted police and protesters. On that same Sunday David

Astor wrote a blistering leader in the *Observer* which called for Eden's resignation and argued, 'We had not realised our government was capable of such folly and such crookedness. In the eyes of the world, the British and the French government have acted, not as policemen, but as gangsters.' Harold Nicolson, whose son Nigel was eventually to lose his safe Bournemouth seat over his opposition to the invasion, also has a telling entry in his diaries for that day recording the resignation of Anthony Nutting, Minister of State for Foreign Affairs: 'Nutting knew everything and has yet decided that it is evil. The central fact remains that Eden has deliberately ignored the recommendation passed by the overwhelming majority of the United Nations Assembly. This is a breach of law.' In one way, it was very like the invasion of Iraq in 2003: routine comparisons of Colonel Nasser to Hitler, government disregard for international protocol, a wave of liberal revulsion and mass protests by ordinary citizens. But in other respects Suez was very different from the later debacle. Where Britain and the US were allies over Iraq, Suez ruptured Anglo-American relations and led to President Eisenhower supporting UN threats of oil sanctions against Britain and France. Suez, even more than Iraq, also exposed the deep fissures in British society and seemed to signal the twilight of Britain's lingering imperialist dream. 'The Last Post', in Peter Vansittart's eloquent phrase, 'had sounded on its great-power status.' That is why Suez was a watershed in the life of the nation. It marked the end of one era and the start of another, in which the quest for a new identity would become a source of endless debate while acting as an inspiration to writers.

For John Osborne the nature and character of England – rather than of Britain as a whole – was already an ungovernable obsession. And by a happy chance, one evening in October 1956, just before the Suez storm broke, Osborne took himself off on his own to see Max Miller performing at the Chelsea Palace. What particularly intrigued him was a down-the-bill act offering an impersonation of Charles Laughton as Quasimodo. As Osborne recorded in his memoirs: 'A smoky green light swirled over the stage and an awesome banality prevailed for some theatrical seconds, the drama and poetry, the belt and braces of music hall holding up epic.' It's a rather confused sentence but it evokes both the tat and the faded glory of music hall; and it was that combination, rather than a commission from Laurence Olivier or the influence of Bertolt Brecht, that provided the emotional trigger for

Osborne's new play. But, writing the play during the upheavals of 1956, Osborne found that the technical problem of depicting the world of twice-nightly variety was solved by treating the music hall as a metaphor for England itself. It was a perfect symbiosis which made *The Entertainer*, as it came to be called, not only a resonant play for its own times, but also an astonishing historical record and a work of lasting influence.

What Osborne instinctively grasped was the inherent theatricality of Suez: a crisis characterised by lies and evasions and leading to the downfall of its protagonist, Anthony Eden, who resigned in January 1957. In his memoirs Osborne talks of the exaggerated 'theatrical' responses to the Suez crisis. He also descibes how 'the Korean War had come and gone like a number two touring company: this one would run on well into the foreseeable future'. But Osborne, like a true artist, also saw that there was some symbiotic link between the last futile gesture of imperialism and the declining music halls. All these halls had been built in the heyday of Victorian and Edwardian expansionism, as signified by their triumphalist names: the Chiswick *Empire*, the Hackney *Empire*, the Glasgow *Empire*, the Liverpool *Empire*. And in the play the very theatre itself becomes a symbol of a country living off memories of past grandeur and forced to confront its current global impotence. As Osborne's comedian hero, Archie Rice, says in his final routine: 'Don't clap too hard, we're all in a very old building.' But the theatre is not just a metaphor in *The Entertainer*: it permeates the whole text. In one little-remarked passage Archie asks his grandfather, Billy: 'Are you one of those who don't like the Prime Minister? I think I've grown rather fond of him. I think it was after he went to the West Indies to get Noël Coward to write a play for him.' The irony is that, after the Suez debacle, Anthony Eden did indeed retreat to Coward's adopted home in Jamaica to convalesce; and Coward, who had once been quite close to Eden, referred to him at the time of his resignation as 'a tragic figure who had been cast in a star part well above his capacities'. What both Osborne and Coward successfully pin down is the matinee-idol element, combining good looks, flaky egotism and capricious temper, lurking within Anthony Eden: it is rather as if the country had been run by Coward's Gary Essendine during its greatest post-war crisis. By tapping into the world of music-hall in *The Entertainer*, Osborne also pointed the way for other writers. *Look Back In Anger* had liberated theatrical language.

The Entertainer set the generation of playwrights who succeeded Osborne – Peter Nichols, Joe Orton, Peter Barnes, Charles Wood and the rest – on the track of popular culture and the rackety vitality of the halls. In the words of Ronald Bryden in the *Observer*, 'Osborne showed the way to a drama which could image the nation to itself, not just the inhabitants of drawing rooms to the inhabitants of drawing rooms.'

But what makes *The Entertainer* a great play is the way it precisely captures what Osborne in his memoirs calls 'the muddle of feeling about Suez and Hungary'. It's as if the battles being played out at the time on the English streets, in the saloon bars and in the leader columns find their echo inside Osborne's own divided soul. He laments the decline of the music hall and the common culture it represented: at the same time he's dismayed at the pointless waste of life in an imperialist adventure. He respects the dignity and grace of grandfather Billy Rice: he also understands the political imperative that drives Archie's daughter, Jean, to protest in Trafalgar Square. And nowhere is Osborne's ambivalence more clearly registered than in his portrait of Archie Rice. Archie is a third-rate comic who tells dreadful jokes with a mechanical, dead-behind-the-eyes ennui and who leeringly plays on his sexual ambiguity. Privately, he's also a shit prepared to abandon his sad, sozzled wife to keep his wretched little nude revue alive and ready to kill off his father to stave off bankruptcy and imprisonment. Yet, exactly as with Jimmy Porter, Osborne displays a complex compassion towards his hero. Osborne acknowledges the stoicism that enables Archie to die twice nightly in front of unsympathetic audiences: he also understands the animal instinct that, at home, drives Archie to keep the party going to camouflage the news about his son, Mick, being taken hostage at Suez. And, even if Archie has little talent himself, he recognises its stigmata in others: in particular, the defiant passion he once heard in a black singer in a bar on the American–Canadian border. 'If I'd done one thing as good as that in my whole life,' he says, 'I'd have been all right.'

Osborne's ambivalence about Archie was brilliantly brought out in Olivier's dazzling performance: the great actor always had something, as he confessed, of the pub entertainer about him. Yet what is astonishing is how close the ESC's Council came, in a fit of deluded puritanism, to rejecting both the play itself and a major casting coup. In the end, it was only Lord Harewood's casting vote at a specially convened

Council meeting that saved the day. Which is just as well since Olivier's commitment to Osborne's play was a decisive moment in post-war British theatre: one with huge implications both for the Royal Court and Olivier himself. It signalled the Establishment's recognition that the theatrical centre of gravity was gradually shifting from the West End to Sloane Square. And, where Olivier audaciously led, his compeers, including Gielgud, Richardson and Guinness, eventually followed. *The Entertainer* not only showed Britain's greatest actor allying himself with the country's most vibrant young writer: it also led to a sense of personal renewal in that before long Olivier had divorced Vivien Leigh to marry the Royal Court's rising star, Joan Plowright, who was to play Jean in the West End transfer. Olivier's Archie was, in every sense, a daring departure into unknown territory, yet it strangely echoed the emotional trajectory of his sensational Stratford Macbeth two years earlier. In both performances what we saw was a figure of outward bravura yielding to a soul-wrenching despair before finally subsiding into weary emptiness. Out of many great moments in Olivier's Macbeth I especially recall the soaring vocal arc on the phrase 'troops of friends', when the cornered king lists the consolations of age which he knows he cannot look to have. And there was a comparable moment in *The Entertainer* where, after the revelation that Mick has been killed, Archie starts to sing the blues before emotionally and physically collapsing. The play's director, Tony Richardson, describes it as 'the single most thrilling moment I've had in theatre'. For Osborne too the moment was a revelation, as he recalled in *Almost A Gentleman*:

> One Saturday run-through about mid-day, he [Olivier] sprang his first realized version of the scene in which Archie sings the blues and crumples slowly down the side of the proscenium arch. The spring sunshine and the noise of the Sloane Square traffic poured through the open door. A dozen of us watched, astounded. Vivien [Leigh] turned her head towards me. She was weeping. I immediately thought of the chill inflection in Olivier's Archie voice. 'I wish women wouldn't cry. I wish they wouldn't . . .'

That open door of the Royal Court on a spring Saturday morning is a potent symbol; for what Osborne himself had done was to open a metaphorical theatrical door and allow a wildly divergent range of

dramatists to come tumbling through. They did not all fit the stereotype of the Angry Young Man. Nigel Dennis, who wrote *Cards of Identity* and the gaily blasphemous *The Making of Moo*, was a middle-aged
novelist and literary critic who was something of an anarchic conservative. N. F. Simpson (popularly known as 'Wally' after the Duchess of
Windsor) was a gaunt Battersea schoolmaster with a gift for surreal
comedy which he revealed in *A Resounding Tinkle*. And, if they were
varied in age and background, not all the writers immediately flocked
to Sloane Square: shocks to the theatrical system were registered in
Stratford East, Hammersmith and even Coventry.

In the turbulent period that followed Osborne's advent, several things
became apparent. One was that violence was a theme that preoccupied
a large number of writers; and the reasons for this were social, political
and cultural. For a start Britain in the mid-Fifties was a society where
the old restraints were breaking down. Teddy Boys were on the ram-
page. Street battles were not uncommon. Crimes by offenders under
twenty-one sensationally doubled in the period from 1955 to 1959. The
government itself, in sanctioning military action over Suez, also helped
to legitimise violent protest: the clashes between demonstrators and
police in Trafalgar Square were of an ugliness not seen in Britain since
the Thirties. Punitive military responses by British troops to outbreaks
of terrorism in Cyprus, Kenya and central Africa were also widely reported back home and fuelled a corresponding anger. And one shouldn't
underestimate the power of popular entertainment in shaping public
attitudes: violence had always been a staple part of the movies but it
acquired a new edge in the era of Marlon Brando and James Dean as
films now seemed to be on the side of the rebel and against established
authority. Theatre absorbed and reflected this growing culture of violence. And, as new writers emerged, they brought with them a vibrant
theatrical diction: one that abandoned the clipped exchanges of naturalism and the formal constraints of metre and rhyme to explore the music
and muscularity of prose. In a sense the liberation of language was a
necessary by-product of the preoccupation with violence. Both were
symbols of a world in which inherited disciplines and structures were
automatically suspect; and the two movements converged in some of the
excitingly idiosyncratic dramatists who emerged in Osborne's wake,
including Ann Jellicoe, Harold Pinter and John Arden.

Violence and verbal vivacity certainly informed the work of Ann Jellicoe. Described by William Gaskill as 'warm, breezy and sometimes

bossy', Jellicoe was an actress, director and writer who shared third prize with N. F. Simpson in the 1957 *Observer* Play Competition for a piece called *The Sport of My Mad Mother*. When it was put on at the Court in February 1958, *Sport* – as it quickly became known – lasted a mere fourteen performances and played to twenty-three per cent at the box office. Yet it was a pioneering play that combined an instinct for the increasing anarchy of the streets with jazzy verbal acrobatics; and what Jellicoe caught was the conflict between a raw, edgy gang ethos and a traditional liberal belief in justice and order. On the one hand, her play presents a gang of teenage Teds whose leader is a pregnant, powerful earth mother called Greta. Speaking up for the pacific virtues is a young American called Dean who is harassed by Greta's gang even to the point of being wrapped like a mummy in newspapers and Sellotape. When his plea for love and truth goes unheard, Dean himself succumbs to violence, like Procathren in *Saint's Day*, only to be flicked contemptuously aside by Greta, who dismisses him as 'a wisp of will, a thread of pride, a sigh of thought'. Jellicoe's ultimate point is that violence may be inherent in both society and humanity but that the life principle, embodied by the prodigiously fertile Greta, is even stronger.

This is a play that bypasses rational analysis to express itself through exultant language. Throwing off the shackles of naturalistic restraint, Jellicoe creates a razzle-dazzle prose that simply cries out to be spoken. 'Anyone'll do anything for her,' says one of Greta's adoring female acolytes. 'She'll have Solly caper down Blackpool pier with no clothes on and bash a copper with a Pepsi-Cola bottle.' Before Pinter had become a household name, Jellicoe also finds a wild poetry and strange music in demotic speech. At one point, she has her characters rhythmically chant the instructions to be found on the back of a home-perm packet:

DEAN: Take a section the size of a curler
DODO: Thoroughly saturate with the lotion
PATTY: Fold an end paper over and under
FAK: Wind it firmly to the root of the hair

DEAN: Again

DEAN: Take a section the size of a curler
DODO: Thoroughly saturate with the lotion

PATTY: Fold an end paper over and over
FAK: Wind it firmly to the root of the hair

Take a section
Saturate
Fold a paper
Wind it firm

This reminds me of T. S. Eliot's vision of a drama of modern life, 'perhaps with certain things in it accompanied by drum beats'; and Jellicoe takes Eliot at his word by having the stage action accompanied by a choric figure called Steve who makes use of drum, motor horn, triangle and cymbals. Jellicoe also echoes the syncopated rhythms of Eliot's dramatic fragment, *Sweeney Agonistes*, which begins:

– How about Pereira?
– What about Pereira? I don't care.

Compare Jellicoe's

– What about me? What about me?
– What about you? This about you.

But, while Jellicoe is obviously indebted to Eliot, she goes much further than him both in exhibiting violence on stage and in treating birth, copulation and death as demonstrable events rather than abstract concepts.

It's also significant that, at a time when women's voices were virtually unheard in the British theatre, Jellicoe's play preceded by a few months the Theatre Royal Stratford East's production of the nineteen-year-old Shelagh Delaney's *A Taste of Honey*: a more naturalistic play but one which, in Joan Littlewood's production, also made extensive use of onstage music. Jellicoe's play, however, is infinitely more radical than Delaney's in its linguistic verve and its celebration of the life-giving female principle. Jellicoe's enigmatic title came from a Hindu hymn claiming that 'all creation is the sport of my mad mother Kali'. And, appropriately, the play ends with Greta, in the throes of parturition, going behind a sheet and proclaiming, 'Rails, rules, laws, guides, promises, terms, guarantees, conventions, traditions: into the pot with the whole bloody lot. Birth! Birth! That's the thing! Oh, I shall have hundreds of children, millions of hundreds and hundreds of millions.' Jellicoe herself may not have been quite that fertile; but the groundbreaking nature of her achievement has been overlooked. She invaded the predominantly male club of British dramaturgy and cleared a path for succeeding generations of women dramatists. Not only that: in her combination of explicit violence and verbal experiment she anticipated a whole generation of later Royal Court writers including Sarah Kane, Jez Butterworth and Mark Ravenhill.

Jellicoe's unsung play not only preceded Shelagh Delaney's far-more-famous work by three months. It also came before Harold Pinter's *The Birthday Party*, which opened at the Lyric Hammersmith in the middle of May 1958. Like Jellicoe's play, Pinter's was a resounding flop: his lasted for a mere eight performances as against Jellicoe's eighteen. Both plays were critically slaughtered: only Hobson stood up for Pinter as Tynan had done for Jellicoe. And both plays were explorations of violence that introduced rare poetic voices. The difference was that, where Jellicoe abandoned the security blanket of linear plot, Pinter worked within the formal traditions of the rep thriller: not surprising when you consider that this struggling young actor had spent much of the Fifties slogging round the weekly reps appearing in such stock fare as *The Uninvited Guest* (as a runaway ex-mental patient), *The Whole Truth* (as an insidious killer) and *Dead On Nine* (as a 'husky Canadian'). Pinter brought to the craft of playwriting an actor's know-how, a carefully honed poetic gift and the instinctive outsider's resentment of social conformity.

Violence, which permeated the culture in the Fifties, is central to *The Birthday Party*: a play in which Stanley, a truculent lodger in a grotty seaside boarding house, is first terrorised and then carted away by two mysterious strangers. Pinter does not shirk either physical or psychological pain: this is a play that includes knees in the groin, sadistic interrogation, near-rape and finally the reduction of the hero to a gibbering wreck. But, unlike *The Sport of My Mad Mother*, Pinter's violence stems from personal memories and has a political purpose. Born in Hackney in 1930 into a working-class family of Ashkenazic Jews, whose ancestors had fled the Polish pogroms, Pinter grew up in a world with an inherited memory of suffering. As a child of the Blitz, Pinter also saw bombs falling from the skies, houses obliterated, neighbours killed. And, as a teenager in the East End of the Forties, Pinter and his predominantly Jewish mates knew what it was like to be threatened by roving gangs of Fascist thugs: in one well-documented incident, Pinter found himself encircled by six youths with broken milk bottles and bike chains at a corner of Dalston Lane and escaped serious injury only by a hair's breadth. What angered Pinter and his friends, however, was the injustice of a society in which fascism, supposedly defeated in war, was tolerated in peacetime in the name of free speech. And that resentment of society's hypocrisy was a major factor in Pinter's decision to reject his National Service call-up papers and to register as a conscientious objector: something that, at the time, carried with it the threat of imprisonment.

All this, along with literary memories of Hemingway's *The Killers* and Kafka's *The Trial*, feeds into *The Birthday Party*. But Pinter is also writing about something both specific to the times and universally applicable: the need to resist social, political and religious pressures. Pinter doesn't make large symbolic statements; nor does he suggest that Stanley's chief tormentors, Goldberg and McCann, are representative of all Judaism and Catholicism. But their identity is not lightly chosen. Between them they embody the world's two most autocratic religions and persecuted races. And, having established them as agents of oppression, Pinter finally shows them as victims of the culture they represent. But what is unusual about *The Birthday Party* is that Pinter expressed his feelings about the play's meaning in a letter to its first director, Peter Wood, just before rehearsals began:

> We've agreed: the hierarchy, The Establishment, the arbiters, the socio-religious monsters arrive to effect censure and alteration upon a member of the club who has discarded responsibility (that word again) towards himself and others. He does possess, however, for my money, a certain fibre – he fights for his life. It doesn't last long, this fight. His core being a quagmire of delusion, his mind a tenuous fuse box, he collapses under the weight of their accusation – an accusation compounded of the shit-stained strictures of centuries of 'tradition'.

That last phrase is highly significant: it suggests that Pinter, much more than Osborne, was a genuinely angry young man fighting against the weight of the past. It also makes it clear that *The Birthday Party* was not, as critics assumed, a derivative piece of Ionesco Absurdism or a Hitchcock movie with the last reel missing. It was always intended as a cry of protest: something instinctively recognised by a generation of Oxbridge undergraduates, including John Tydeman and John Drummond, who revelled in the play in the course of its pre-London tour. After Stanley has had his glasses smashed and his tongue maimed and has been dressed in a conformist suit, he still emits inarticulate cries of rage. And as he is led off to rejoin the organisation, his landlord Petey says 'Stan, don't let them tell you what to do': something Pinter now calls 'one of the most important lines I've ever written'. Like *Saint's Day*, Pinter's play deals with the pressures on the aggressive outsider to play by society's rules. Where Whiting's Paul Southman ends up hanged, Pinter's Stanley is finally disabled but resistant, suggesting some grit in the human spirit that defies total submission. It is this unyielding quality, this note of bloody-minded defiance, that marks out Pinter's play and says a lot about the character of the man himself.

Most of the emerging writers in the late Fifties, whatever their backgrounds, were fascinated by societal violence and the thrill of words. Few more so than John Arden. Like Ann Jellicoe, Arden was a product of the Royal Court and an active member of its Writers' Group, which formed a nursery of talent and met regularly in Lower Mall, Hammersmith. And, like Harold Pinter, Arden was born in 1930 and intrigued by the politics of violence and the possibilities of language. But Arden's background was more traditionally middle-class than that of either Pinter or Jellicoe. Arden's father managed a glass-making factory in Barnsley, his mother was a primary-school teacher and he himself, after boarding school in Sedbergh and two years' National Service, went on to study architecture at Cambridge and Edinburgh. While working as an architectural assistant in London, Arden wrote a play for BBC radio – a vital outlet for young writers in the Fifties – which attracted the attention of George Devine and led the Court to stage Arden's *The Waters of Babylon* as a Sunday-night 'production without decor' in 1957.

Despite Arden's architectural training, his first play was a somewhat jerry-built affair. But what blows one away is its Jonsonian vitality and uncanny social antennae. Proving that dramatists often sense what is going on long before anyone else, Arden anticipates many of the issues that were to become headline news in the Sixties. The plot revolves around a Polish immigrant, Krank, who attempts to rig a municipal lottery in order to pay off a blackmailing fellow Pole. Krank, who crams eighty mixed-race immigrants into a single lodging house and runs a call-girl racket, seems a prototype of Peter Rachman: an immigrant villain who cashed in on the London property boom, was involved in Soho vice rings and who later became the model for the protagonist of Peter Flannery's play, *Singer*. Arden also prefigures the civic corruption and public profiteering that in the Sixties led to the imprisonment of architect John Poulson and Newcastle Labour boss, T. Dan Smith. And, even before the next decade's revelations about the sexual activities of John Profumo and Lords Boothby, Lambton and Jellicoe, Arden pins down the involvement of right-wing politicians with prostitutes and gangsters. But the really big issue that Arden grasps – in a way that no other dramatist of the time did – was that the London of the late Fifties was less a melting-pot than a place of sim-mering racial tension in which Commonwealth, Irish and East Euro-pean immigrants lived uneasily alongside the Anglo-Saxon majority. Eleven months after Arden's play, in September 1958, violent race rioting broke out in Notting Hill directed against the local West Indi-an population. And the xenophobia that was to be a sickening feature of British life for the next fifty years is unerringly captured by Arden. At one point a crypto-fascist Hyde Park orator, Henry Ginger, cries 'There are untold thousands of criminal foreigners in this country – they are being let in by the British government, a monstrous threat to our liberty, a threat to our freedom, to all our freedoms.' At which point you seem to hear the hysterical voice – and this in 1957 – of a modern tabloid leader-writer or craven politician ratcheting up the immigration debate for short-term electoral gain.

Arden shared Pinter and Jellicoe's ability to translate a concern with society's endemic violence into vigorously poetic prose. What made him disturbing was his blank refusal to offer moral guidelines and his knack of giving all his characters a comparable vitality. You see that clearly in *Live Like Pigs* (1958) which sets an anarchic family of sturdy beggars next to a respectable, petty-bourgeois household. Critics back in the Fifties were puzzled by Arden's play: where was the balance of sympathy supposed to lie? But the question seems almost irrelevant in the face of the ribald, riotous, O'Caseyesque language. At one point Rosie, daughter of a tyrannical vagrant, recalls her mother's memories of her dad as a young man. After a hard day's working and drinking he'd 'likely fight a pair o' men into a canal dock, knock a copper over after – then home like a traction engine and revel her three times down to Rio without he'd even take off his boots'. If *Live Like Pigs* left peo-ple bewildered, that was even more true of Arden's undoubted master-piece, *Serjeant Musgrave's Dance* (1959), which emptied the Royal

Court like a dose of salts, and infuriated critics. With the benefit of hindsight, however, it's not so difficult to see what Arden was up to: using the historic past as a metaphor for the present. Although set in Victorian England, his play was clearly fuelled by a rage at the residue of the British colonial inheritance. The Fifties was a particularly troubled time for the British abroad. Guerrilla wars raged in Malaya and Kenya, leading, in the latter case, to the loss of ten thousand African and European lives. And in Cyprus the British were accused of stoking the conflict between the majority Greek and minority Turkish populations on a divide-and-rule basis. It was, in fact, a particularly horrifying incident in Cyprus that prompted *Serjeant Musgrave's Dance*. A British soldier's wife had been shot by terrorists in Famagusta in October 1958. In retaliation some of the military went wild and five innocent people, including a little girl, were shot in the resultant round-up.

That was not the only source for *Serjeant Musgrave's Dance*. As a Cambridge student, Arden had been overwhelmed by Peter Hall's undergraduate production of Whiting's seminal *Saint's Day*. He was also influenced by a 1954 Civil War Hollywood Western, *The Raid*. And, as a highly visual writer, Arden was attracted by the picture of military redcoats seen against a cold, grey, wintry background: proof that plays often start from images as well as ideas. Embodying this particular colour contrast, Arden shows a group of soldiers, back from a Victorian colonial war, arriving in a bleak, strike-bound Northern mining town. Ostensibly they are on a recruiting mission. Eventually it becomes apparent that their leader, the maniacal Musgrave, wants to rub the noses of the local civilians in the nature of the slaughter being carried out in their name. After training his Gatling gun on the town's worthies and executing a wild dance, Musgrave is overpowered and executed. But, as he awaits death, Musgrave claims that he imported war to the town in order to try and end it. 'To end it by its own rules,' says one of his fellow soldiers, 'no bloody good . . . You can't cure the pox by further whoring.'

Arden's message now seems perfectly clear. But, as he told me over forty years after the play's premiere, audiences and critics were confused by the fact that there was no leading character with whom they could identify:

You can't latch on to Serjeant Musgrave, because he doesn't announce what he's trying to do; and when he does commit an action, there's something crazily wrong with it. What people would have expected is that Musgrave be signalled either as a dangerous lunatic who had to be stopped or as a hero who had to be defeated but who would go down in glory. My story ricochets between those two pillars.

It is precisely that moral ambivalence that now makes *Serjeant Musgrave* seem a great play: one that stands up to repeated viewing and was memorably revived by Sean Holmes in 2004 for the Oxford Stage Company. Its warnings about the horrors of cyclical violence and its image of the madness that follows military occupation have also given it a continuing relevance to situations ranging from Northern Ireland to Vietnam and Iraq. The reaction to *Serjeant Musgrave* in 1959, however, shows just how much people at the time still hungered for moral signposts and a clear-cut authorial viewpoint. Like *Saint's Day*, *The Sport of My Mad Mother* and *The Birthday Party*, Arden's play was ritually abused by the critics. 'Baffling, sprawling and pretentious,' wrote Cecil Wilson in the *Daily Mail*. 'An inordinately long-winded and rather foolish play,' intoned *The Times*. Only Philip Hope-Wallace in the *Manchester Guardian*, invoking O'Casey and Buchner, rallied to its defence. But, in spite of Lindsay Anderson's brilliant production and Ian Bannen's demonic performance as Musgrave, the play achieved only twenty-one per cent sales at the Court box office. Simply because there was a fantastic explosion of new writing in the late Fifties doesn't mean there was a revolution either in critical acumen or audience habits.

Even the Royal Court itself wasn't quite the hotbed of political radicalism that people retrospectively imagine. When, for instance, it uncovered in Arnold Wesker a genuinely working-class writer who had briefly belonged to the Young Communist League and a Zionist Youth Movement, its initial reaction was to send him, quite literally, to Coventry. Like Pinter, Wesker was born into an East End family of Jewish immigrants and had a garment-worker father. Wesker had also knocked about the world a bit: he'd been a furniture-maker and plumber's mate, done National Service in the RAF, worked on the Norfolk land and spent nine months as a pastry cook in Paris. But, although he'd planned to go to the London School of Film Technique, he was diverted into theatre by the all-important *Observer* play competition – for which he entered *The Kitchen* – and by the success of *Look Back In Anger*. Wesker would seem, in fact, to have been just the kind of working-class intellectual whom the Court was designed to discover.

In reality, Wesker's work took a long time to gain acceptance at its natural home. Neither George Devine nor Tony Richardson warmed to *Chicken Soup With Barley* when they read it in 1958. Astonishing when you look at the play's social and historical scope: spanning the period from 1936 to 1956, it charts the disintegration of the East End Kahn family against the background of a collapsing communist ideology. Mosley's Black Shirts and the Cable Street riots, the post-war Attlee government, the Soviet invasion of Hungary: all provide a rich political context for a work in which the state-of-the-nation intersects with the crumbling condition of the Kahns. And the final scene in which the young Ronnie, returning from Paris shattered by the march of the Soviet tanks into Budapest, confronts his mother's unwavering faith in communism, is a superb piece of writing. Intellectually, Wesker sides with Ronnie: emotionally, with his mother – which gives the scene real tension. But the Royal Court management passed on the play and sent it to Bryan Bailey who was running the Belgrade, Coventry: the first civic theatre to be built in Britain since the war. Later in 1958 Wesker's *Roots* underwent a similarly circuitous journey. Again it was a first-rate play whose heroine, Beatie Bryant, returns to her Norfolk roots and parrots the ideas of her London boyfriend before exhilaratingly learning to think and speak for herself. But Devine and Richardson myopically and absurdly suggested that Wesker should write a new third act in which the London lover, the self-same Ronnie of the previous play, should finally appear. Fortunately Wesker had his champions at the Court including Lindsay Anderson, Peggy Ashcroft and, crucially, John Dexter who became Wesker's skilled directorial interpreter. Dexter's productions of *Chicken Soup With Barley* and *Roots* both came from Coventry to the Court and in 1960 *I'm Talking About Jerusalem* was added to form the complete 'Wesker Trilogy'. I'll give the work more consideration in the next chapter; but what is extraordinary is the Court's dilatoriness in realising they had discovered a genuine poetic realist.

That prompts an inevitable question: what, by the end of the Fifties, had the Royal Court actually achieved? Going back to its original aims, it had failed to establish a permanent company working in a rotating repertory system. And it had scant success in discovering untapped dramatic talent in British novelists. It is also romantic to imagine that it had changed the British theatre overnight: the old West End power bases remained intact and even at the Court itself the most popular works, aside from *Look Back In Anger* and *The Entertainer*, were by Wycherley (*The Country Wife*), Aristophanes (*Lysistrata*), Ibsen (*Rosmersholm*) and Feydeau/Coward (*Look After Lulu*). You only have to look at the box-office records to realise that there was still no loyal, regular audience in London for new writing. What the Court *had* done was promote a bewilderingly kaleidoscopic array of new dramatists: apart from those mentioned, Alun Owen, Willis Hall, Donald Howarth and Christopher Logue all had work produced at the Court in its first three years. The Court was also the first public theatre to recognise that Fifties Britain was slowly becoming a multi-racial society. Barry Reckord's *Flesh To A Tiger*, starring Cleo Laine, became in 1958 the first West Indian play to be professionally staged in Britain and it was quickly followed by Errol John's *Moon On A Rainbow Shawl*, which won the *Observer* play competition: at a time when the black and Asian population of Britain was officially listed at 180,000, and growing rapidly, the Court was in the forefront of recog-nising social change.

But arguably the Royal Court's most signal achievement was aes-thetic. Heavily influenced by the Berliner Ensemble, it sought to ban-ish the decorative prettiness and 'rococo effeminacy', to use Eric Bentley's phrase, of West End design. Dan Rebellato in his fascinating book, *1956 And All That*, makes much of the ironic contrast between the Court's heterosexual agenda and the fact that the majority of its directors, with the robust exception of George Devine, were openly or discreetly gay. Even so, designers such as Jocelyn Herbert, Stephen Doncaster, Sean Kenny and the trio known as Motley were engaged in a sustained war on West End camp. In William Gaskill and John Dex-ter, the Court also discovered two hugely exciting young directors whose talent for realising an author's text was matched by a strong visual puritanism. It was the unostentatious spareness of their produc-tions that was so impressive. And when you consider that Gaskill and Dexter were headhunted by Olivier for his new National Theatre com-pany in the early Sixties, and that they brought with them a whole generation of actors including Joan Plowright, Robert Stephens, Colin Blakely and Frank Finlay, you realise how the influence of the Royal

Court gradually spread far beyond Sloane Square. We always celebrate the Royal Court as a writers' theatre and there is no doubt that
it greatly extended the range of British drama. But, in so doing, it also
banished frippery and fuss from design and gave rich opportunities to
a talented cadre of regional actors. Even if the Royal Court didn't revolutionise British theatre, it certainly infiltrated it; and, without its
pioneering example, the National Theatre would never have achieved
the early success it did.

In the late Fifties, however, John Osborne was very much the public
face – to some the unacceptable public face – of the Royal Court.
Today there is a tendency to claim that of the two seminal works that
emerged in the mid-Fifties – *Waiting For Godot* and *Look Back In
Anger* – it was the former that had the more profound and long-lasting
influence. But it seems idle to play them off against each other as if art
were a competitive, two-horse race. Osborne and Beckett were both
major writers who represented two vital, necessary strands in modern
drama: the realistic and the poetic. And, although they may seem
polar opposites, the two dramatists have more in common than is at
first apparent. John Heilpern reveals in his excellent biography of
Osborne, *A Patriot For Us,* that Osborne not only admired Beckett's
work 'but related to the dark, heroic soul of the man'. Both were also
haunted by a Protestant inheritance which they could neither totally
discard nor fully endorse. Both, in their most famous plays, also
attempted to dramatise the dilemma of waiting: Jimmy Porter suffers
just as much as Vladimir and Estragon from the futility of inaction
and the idea of hope endlessly deferred. But where Beckett, although
privately companionable, shunned the limelight, Osborne sought to
compensate for his own private guilt and inadequacy by courting it.
He was ceaselessly interviewed and profiled on TV and in the press.
He churned out good knocking-copy for the papers himself. He was
also the star turn in *Declaration:* that influential book of essays assembled by Tom Maschler in 1957 from a motley batch of young dis-
senters including Kenneth Tynan, Lindsay Anderson, John Wain and
Colin Wilson. No unifying philosophy emerged from the book but
Osborne confirmed his gift for memorable phrase-making. He lashed
out at royalty ('a gold filling in a mouthful of decay'), at religion
(referring to 'the spiritual spiel of the wide boys of the Church') and,
above all, at Fleet Street, for its tawdry trivia and jingoistic tub-
thumping – 'It's our H-Bomb!' the *Daily Express* had trumpeted in

response to Britain's first nuclear test which, according to Osborne, was 'the most debased, criminal swindle in British history'. But if Osborne was riding high in the late Fifties, nemesis lay around the corner in the shape of a musical, *The World of Paul Slickey*, written by Osborne with Christopher Whelen as composer, Hugh Casson as designer and Kenneth MacMillan as choreographer. Not even this rich array of talent could turn an eccentric ragbag into a coherent satire; but the disproportionately savage response to a failed musical proved the extent to which Britain was still two nations.

Osborne's starting point was a country-house comedy, *Love In A Myth*, that he had written in 1955 while waiting for *Look Back In Anger* to be staged. Onto this throwback to his old days in rep, sensibly turned down by George Devine and Tony Richardson, Osborne proceeded to graft an acidic attack on Fleet Street gossip columnists. This spiralled into scattergun satire aimed randomly at the mendacity and lechery of the upper classes, the trendiness of hip priests, the sentimentality of pop singers (accused of 'emptying the slop buckets of modern love into a microphone') and High Tory bloodthirstiness. The most interesting part, given Osborne's continuing fascination with sexual ambivalence, was the final lyric hymn to the idea of gender-switching: 'You could swap your pretty bras / For a moustache with handlebars / And be a woman at the weekend and a man all the week.' Admittedly behind the show lay an intuitive awareness that the country was, in the words of Anthony Sampson, 'in the throes of a public relations takeover', and that the mass media required the constant manufacture of ever more, instantly disposable celebrities. But, if Osborne had a prophetic insight into the way Britain was going, he paid a heavy price for it. Even before the show opened, the whispering campaign against it had begun. Gossip writers, led by the *Daily Mail*'s Paul Tanfield, were despatched to the out-of-town try-out in Bournemouth to stick the boot in. And the opening night at the Palace Theatre on 5 May 1959 produced something akin to a riot. Booing broke out in the gallery halfway through the show, provoked by lines like 'God in Heaven, it's like a pantomime' and, at the curtain calls, the cacophony continued for two minutes non-stop. According to Heilpern, 'In a gloating last hurrah from the old guard, Coward – and more surprisingly Gielgud – were on their feet booing with the rest.' Adrienne Corri, one of the show's stars, retaliated to the storm of abuse with three V-signs to the gallery and an audible cry of 'Go fuck yourselves.' Osborne himself, hastily exiting through the main foyer, was pursued down Charing Cross Road by an angry mob of theatre-goers shouting 'Tripe' and 'Bloody rubbish' before hopping into a taxi and heading for the relative safety of his Chelsea home. Next day the notices put the final nail in the coffin. For sheer hypocrisy it was hard to beat Cecil Wilson in – yet again – the *Daily Mail* who, having pre-viously attacked the 'repetitiousness' and 'laborious shock tactics' of *Look Back In Anger*, now accused Osborne of betraying his earlier brilliance with a 'sniggering, schoolboyish show'. The vindictive hoo-ha went on for weeks with everyone offering their twopenn'orth of opinion. Perhaps the nastiest piece of all came from Kenneth Allsop – in which paper I'll leave you to guess – who insultingly linked Osborne, Kingsley Amis and John Braine with the one-hit wonders of the pop industry and saw them as part of 'the new age of folk-heroes and youth whisking to the pinnacle riding a guitar and a gimmick'.

That neatly encapsulates the way *Paul Slickey* was elevated from a resounding flop into an instrument of generational revenge. Charles Marowitz, an articulate American director-critic who was to have a decisive influence on the London fringe, got it right when he wrote some months later in *Encore*:

The great point about *Paul Slickey* is not that it is badly hashed, anti-musical comedy but that it is a weapon, naively provided by *the* angry young man himself, with which a fed-up British bourgeoisie can clobber the surly, intellectual movement that has been razzing it since the end of the war.

All those who hated everything associated with contemporary youth – Bill Haley, *Lucky Jim*, raucous Ban-the-Bomb marchers, the Royal Court, Royalty-bashers and the infernal, ubiquitous Angries – could vent their spleen on Osborne's mixed-up musical. *The World of Paul Slickey* may have been a rotten show, although curiously enough one I'd love to have seen, but it also became a potent symbol: a red rag to the defenders of John Bull. What was revealing, however, was the hysterical reaction to it. It wasn't enough that the show be labelled a big floperoo. It was savaged with a vindictive glee that showed anger wasn't the exclusive privilege of the under-thirties. And there was something about the intemperate abuse it provoked that proved that Britain in the late Fifties was made up of mutually hostile groups glar-ing at each other across a cultural chasm.

IV

1960–63

The Ground Shifts

In the early Sixties the chasm widened. If the previous decade was marked by generational division and conflict, the Sixties saw the young not merely rattling and shaking the culture but increasingly taking charge. Youth, which had been knocking at the door in the previous decade, finally attained the commanding heights in theatre, film, television, pop and fashion. A twenty-nine-year-old Peter Hall became one of the two most powerful men in British theatre while a group of recent Oxbridge graduates put a comic bomb under the Edinburgh International Festival. British movies awoke from their periodic slumber to address social issues and to make international stars out of young actors like Albert Finney, Peter O'Toole and Richard Harris. David Frost, who had graduated from Cambridge only in 1961, instantly became the most familiar face on British television: it was even said tartly, by Kitty Muggeridge, that 'he rose without trace'. The Beatles and the Rolling Stones more markedly, but equally swiftly, leapt from obscurity to become pop icons. Mary Quant, who had opened a small boutique in Chelsea in 1955, had become the head of a multi-million-dollar international business by 1962. Wherever you looked there was a hunger for new names, new voices, new ideas. But the early Sixties wasn't just about the rise of media celebrities. If any one event helped to change the country as a whole, it was the phasing out of National Service in 1960. As the historian Christopher Lee has remarked:

> This single factor changed the appearance, ambitions and attitudes of a whole generation. Until the Sixties every young man who left school knew that he would have to go into one of the three services, probably the army, and by the time National Service was finished, 5.3 million teenagers would have learned to stand straight with their shoulders back . . . In the Sixties the first teenagers since 1938

crossed into adult life at their own pace and in their own style. Collectively, they were able to question every frailty of authority and laugh openly at it.

It was that disintegration of automatic deference, and the growing gap between the governors and the governed, that characterised the early Sixties.

The irony was that, while Britain as a society was rapidly changing, the old guard was still in power: the Tories had been re-elected in 1959 with a thumping three-figure majority over Labour and were still led by the grouse-shooting, benignly patrician, deeply Edwardian Harold Macmillan. Easily mockable though he was, Macmillan was a by no means contemptible politician: as a minister in the Fifties, he had initiated a massive house-building programme and in 1960 he made a famously prophetic speech in Cape Town announcing that 'the wind of change is blowing through this continent and, whether we like it or not, this growth of national consciousness is a political fact'. But, for all his liberal instincts, Macmillan came to seem a tragically out-of-touch figure presiding over a country, and even a Cabinet, of which he had little understanding. Part of the problem lay in the arthritic nature of the country's political power structures. Anthony Sampson's *The Anatomy of Britain*, published in 1962, examined a number of key institutions and found them to be run by a male hierarchy of top people who all shared the same public-school, Oxbridge background. And Sampson's point was reinforced by the Robbins Report on Higher Education in 1963 which argued that the root cause of the post-war economic malaise lay in the failure to promote advanced learning for anyone other than a small, public-school elite. The new talentocracy may have taken over the arts and media; but government and the Civil Service were still in the grip of antiquated systems readily symbolised by a Cabinet that contained more Old Etonians than women.

For all the brave talk of de-colonisation in Africa, Britain also appeared increasingly impotent on the world stage, as if clinging on desperately to its Great Power status. In a speech at West Point in December 1962 Dean Acheson, the former US Secretary of State, condemned British delusions about both the Commonwealth and the Anglo-American special relationship and pointed out that Britain 'has lost an empire and not yet found a role'. It was a cruelly accurate phrase that was to reverberate down the decades; and it was that search for a role that was to define much of Britain's political life and, in a paradoxical way, to act as an artistic stimulus. Out of our quest for a new post-imperial identity came an abundance of plays, films and novels: not knowing who we were, or quite where we were going, proved to be as big a creative goad as the national self-assurance that prevailed during the first Elizabethan age. But the accuracy of Acheson's observation was proved in late December 1962 at a vital summit conference between Macmillan and America's dynamic new President, J. F. Kennedy, at Nassau in the Bahamas. It was a conference at which America grudgingly agreed to maintain the polite fiction of British nuclear independence through the deployment of Polaris missiles on British submarines. Our own right-wing press certainly saw our dependence on America as something of a national humiliation. But what sticks in my mind is a story that the young Kennedy allegedly shocked Macmillan by revealing that he suffered severe headaches if he didn't have sex on a daily basis and asked the older man's counsel; it was not, at the time, thought to be a problem on which Macmillan could offer much practical advice. If Britain, however, was a largely impotent satellite of the United States, it was at the same time a pariah in Europe. Shortly after the Nassau agreements, General de Gaulle in January 1963 exercised his decisive veto over Britain's application to join the European Econonic Community; ironically, the same month saw the death of the Labour leader, Hugh Gaitskell, who had once claimed in a spirit of defiant nationalism that membership of the EEC would threaten British sovereignty and wind up 'a thousand years of history'.

While Britain became an increasingly marginal player on the world stage, it also suffered extraordinary domestic upheavals. And the abiding impression was of an Establishment that appeared totally out of touch with the world most people inhabited. This was famously revealed in the *Lady Chatterley's Lover* trial at the Old Bailey in 1960 when a jury decided that D. H. Lawrence's long-banned novel was no longer obscene. The much-quoted turning point in the trial came when one of the prosecution's barristers, Mervyn Griffiths-Jones, having described thirteen passages of sexual intercourse between Lady Chatterley and Mellors, asked the jury, 'Is it a book you would wish your wife or your servants to read?'; only later was it felt that the numerous academics who had been summoned by the defence to claim that Lawrence's book was some kind of masterpiece were as detached from reality as Mr Griffiths-Jones. But the truly devastating sign of an out-of-touch ruling elite came with the so-called 'Profumo scandal' of 1963. It's astonishing to think how titillated we all were at the time by what was a sad and sorry escapade. We lapped up all the details of the affair between the Secretary of State for War, John Profumo, and a high-class prostitute, Christine Keeler. We got highly excited by the idea, revealed by an osteopath called Stephen Ward who later committed suicide, that Ms Keeler may have shared state secrets with a Soviet military intelligence officer. We even believed stories that a high-placed minister may have been 'The Man In The Iron Mask' who appeared in the nude at orgiastic Belgravia parties: when the late Duchess of Argyll was revealed to be a key player in these multiple sex romps, the comedian Tommy Trinder cheekily suggested on television that 'perhaps, instead of marrying the Duke of Argyll, she should have married Plymouth Argyle.' That confirmed the extent to which the ruling Establishment had become a public laughing stock. But, as the revelations tumbled out, Macmillan appeared an increasingly isolated figure, both deceived by Profumo and blithely unaware of other ministerial sexual shenanigans. At the same time as the Profumo affair erupted, a judicial inquiry into the case of an Admiralty clerk who had been entrapped by the KGB at a homosexual party accused ministers of ultimate responsibility. When in September 1963 the Denning Report criticised the Prime Minister and the Cabinet for failing to be more open about the Profumo affair, it was clear that the game was up. An air of sleaze and incompetence surrounded the Macmillan government; and in October 1963 Macmillan resigned, on grounds of ill health, only to be replaced by the 14th Earl of Home, who renounced his title to become plain Sir Alec Douglas-Home. He was a nice enough, cricket-loving man – and brother of a West End playwright – but a sitting target for the new Labour leader, Harold Wilson, who combined economic nous with a popular, cheeky-chappie appeal. Douglas-Home certainly wasn't the 'cretin' that Bernard Levin intemperately called him on television. But he seemed badly miscast as leader of the sexually permissive, culturally expansive, technologically progressive, youth-oriented country that Britain was rapidly becoming.

That shake-up of British life had started in the Fifties and had been expressed in rock 'n' roll, the Royal Court, Theatre Workshop, *Waiting For Godot, Lucky Jim, The Outsider*, the Free Cinema movement, *Declaration*, the deification of American actors like Brando and Dean.

But, in theatre as in politics, the old guard did not surrender overnight: London theatre was still dominated by quilted divertissements even if the shrewdest of all the West End managers, Donald Albery, invited a number of shows from Stratford East – including *Make Me An Offer*, *Fings Ain't Wot They Used To Be* and *The Hostage* – into his commercial domain. But it was only with the new decade that one began to see real signs of radical change. And, if any one event marked a genuine cultural turning point, it was not the first night of *Look Back In Anger* in May 1956: it was the slightly shambolic opening performance of a late-night revue at the Lyceum Theatre, Edinburgh on 22 August 1960. It was called, significantly, *Beyond The Fringe*; and it was a blatant attempt by the director of the Edinburgh Festival, Robert Ponsonby, to cash in on the popularity of Oxbridge student revues. But the show – which famously united Cambridge's Jonathan Miller and Peter Cook with Oxford's Alan Bennett and Dudley Moore – didn't simply bottle and preserve a pervasive irreverence. Although not openly didactic, it exposed the widening gulf between the generations, helped change our attitude towards authority for ever and made satire in Britain a practical possibility. Having gone up to Edinburgh as a student critic, I was one of the relatively few people present at that momentous first performance and remember coming away not just aching with laughter but sensing that the ground had genuinely shifted. All the talk in Edinburgh that week – at a time when the International Festival still held sway over a modestly sized Fringe – was of this subversive quartet. And at a midweek press conference in the gloomy crypt of the Freemasons Hall, I recall asking members of the *Beyond The Fringe* gang precisely what they were attacking. 'Complacency,' said Peter Cook. But in taking on smug Prime Ministers, the Second World War myth-makers, head-in-the-sand Civil Defence experts, mandarin Third Programme voices, God-evading vicars, racist landladies, arrogant trade unionists, role-playing homosexuals and barnacled Old Vic Shakespeareans, *Beyond The Fringe* put a large slice of contemporary Britain on stage and spoke to and for a generation in a way that not even John Osborne could match. The show was not only witty in itself: it launched a whole era of snook-cocking disrespect and became a force for social change.

It is a measure of *Beyond The Fringe*'s iconoclasm that Peter Cook's parody of Harold Macmillan – much expanded and developed in the show's long London run at the Fortune Theatre – was the first time a living Prime Minister had been lampooned on the twentieth-century British stage. But what gave Cook's impersonation such force was its impression of Macmillan as an Edwardian patrician out of touch with the modern world. Catching the embarrassed awkwardness of Macmillan's TV manner, Cook would periodically reach out to poke a languid finger at a nearby globe to indicate the Prime Minister's vaunted world travels on our behalf. And at our expense. After Kennedy's inauguration in January 1961 Cook added a crucial passage that ran:

> I then went on to America and there I had talks with the young, vigorous President of that great country . . . We talked of many things including Great Britain's position in the world as some kind of honest broker. I agreed with him when he said that no nation could be more honest and he agreed with me when I chaffed him and said that no nation could be broker.

The laugh lies in the line's painful truth and adoption of a nineteenth-century Bismarckian concept; but it is the brilliant use of the word 'chaffed' that pins down precisely the gulf in class, age and temperament between the Prime Minister and the President. Cook also caught Macmillan's tone of blithe condescension. Macmillan was in the habit of donning tweeds for the Glorious Twelfth – the start of the grouse-shooting season – and adopting the cloth-capped persona of a Scottish crofter. So Cook had Macmillan at one point take from his pocket a letter of complaint from an elderly Mrs McFarlane of Fife. After solemnly reading it out – 'Dear Prime Minister, I am an old-age pensioner in Fife, living on a fixed income of some two pounds, seven shillings a week. What do you of the Conservative Party propose to do about it?' – Cook tore it to pieces. But the killer punch came as Cook, continuing to address the fictive Mrs McFarlane, spoke 'as one Scottish old age pensioner to another': there was something in that phrase that harpooned the Macmillanesque hauteur beneath the false intimacy. No governments fell as a result of *Beyond The Fringe*; but what Cook did, long before the Profumo scandal erupted, was to replace the cartoon image of 'SuperMac' with an enduring portrait of the Prime Minister as an absurd relic from a bygone age: a Beerbohm Tree in the age of television.

Significantly the satirical element in *Beyond The Fringe* was much sharpened between its Edinburgh and London openings: it became more barbed, less playful. One item that caused massive offence to an older generation – indeed I remember much huffing and puffing in the

Fortune bar in the interval – was 'The Aftermyth of War': a necessary puncturing of Pinewood nostalgia about the Second World War. Alan Bennett, adopting the pipe-smoking, tin-legged persona of Douglas Bader, reminisced at one point: 'I could see Tunbridge Wells, and the sun glinting on the river, and I remembered that last weekend I'd spent with Celia in the summer of '39 and her playing the piano in the cool of the evening.' Even better was the vignette of the hapless pilot, Perkins, instructed to pop over to Bremen, take a shufti and not come back: 'We need a futile gesture at this stage,' he was told. 'It'll raise the whole tone of the war.' This may seem harmless enough now; but, at a time when British movies like *Reach For The Sky* and *The Wooden Horse* sanctified the cameraderie of war, such satire was socially necessary. And, with the nuclear threat a living reality that haunted people's lives, Peter Cook's lecture to Civil Defence volunteers exposed the absurdity of proposed countermeasures: 'Now,' said Cook at his loftiest, 'we shall receive four minutes' warning of any impending nuclear attack. Some people have said "Oh my goodness me – four minutes? – that is not a very long time!" Well I would remind those doubters that some people in this great country of ours can run a mile in four minutes.' As in his Macmillan sketch, Cook unerringly caught the tone of Establishment condescension that was a particular irritant to a younger generation.

And it was primarily to the young that this matchless revue appealed.

One reason why comedy is more immediately subversive than drama is that it can be quickly parroted and imitated; and, shortly after it opened at the Fortune, *Beyond The Fringe* was issued as an LP which allowed aficionados to regurgitate its best items at parties with nerdish, trainspotter accuracy. Like *The Goon Show* in the Fifties and *Monty Python* in the Seventies, the show became an unofficial set text. As Christopher Hitchens told Humphrey Carpenter, it also became difficult for school authorities to stamp out the *Beyond The Fringe* cult since it came with the imprimatur of the Edinburgh Festival; 'But,' added Hitchens, 'somehow the boys who found it funny and could do all the scenes from memory were just those boys who always set a bad example.' The show's impact, however, extended far beyond samizdat boarding-school and student reproduction: if the corduroyed dream of the mid-Fifties had been to graduate into an Angry Young Man, now in the early Sixties it was to join the ranks of the emergent satirists.

Blessed, at the time, were the piss-takers. In October 1961, just over a year after the debut of *Beyond The Fringe*, Peter Cook opened The Establishment Club in Soho: with its mix of blasphemy, lavatorial humour and topical gibes at Macmillan, Douglas-Home and Rab Butler, its political position was defined by Kenneth Tynan as one of 'radical anarchism'. And, as with *Beyond The Fringe*, its regular performers – including John Bird, John Fortune, Eleanor Bron (all ex-Cambridge) and John Wells (ex-Oxford) – were graduates of the older universities and shared the same privileged background as their political targets. Three weeks after the launch of The Establishment came the first edition of a magazine called *Private Eye*: again largely the work of recent Oxbridge graduates, although this time with the addition of a rotund ex-Salopian cartoonist called William Rushton. Even though it eventually came to be criticised for its public-school tone, latent anti-Semitism and sublime disregard for factual accuracy, it reinforced the idea of *Beyond The Fringe* that anyone in public life was fair game for attack. Its early issues in 1961 included Uncle Mac (a convergence of the PM and the presenter of BBC Radio's *Children's Hour*) explaining to children how to make 'a simple, old-fashioned atom bomb', a joke piece elevating Liberal leader Jo Grimond into Bore of the Week and a very funny interview by critic Harold Throbson with a rambling anecdotal actor called Sir John Feelgood. By the summer of 1962 the magazine's circulation had shot up from an initial three hundred to around fifteen thousand, confirming that there was a sizeable market in Britain for licensed mockery.

It was as if the lid had come off the pressure cooker: everywhere you looked Coward's 'talent to amuse' was replaced by a talent to abuse. Television, the most parasitical of all mediums, followed the stage and journalism by launching *That Was the Week That Was* in the autumn of 1962: this was satire for a mass audience and it is hard to exaggerate the impact it had. At the time I was living in Lincoln where I worked for the local rep company. As the relatively fortunate owner of a TV set, I soon found that my tiny flat over a sad café was packed late on Saturday nights with actors who would rush round as soon as their curtain fell: not to have seen the programme was to be excluded from all manner of conversations over the next week. And, although it made hypnotic television, I was struck by how much it depended on theatre for its effect. Its liveness gave it a dramatic unpredictability. Each week, for instance, Bernard Levin would confront an angry group respresenting some vested interest which led to a verbal punch-up: on one occasion Levin was even bopped over the head by the husband of an actress he had abused in his *Daily Express* theatre column. The use of the studio's naked back wall and the sight of cameras prowling around like purposeful Martians was pure Brecht. And virtually everyone involved in the show had a theatrical pedigree. Ned Sherrin, its prime mover, had a parallel career as a creator of stage musicals with his partner, Caryl Brahms. David Frost, the show's presenter, was a Cambridge Footlights graduate. Performers like Millicent Martin, Roy Kinnear and Lance Percival came from the world of West End musicals. And the vast team of writers included not only several theatre critics (Herbert Kretzmer, David Nathan, Kenneth Tynan) but playwrights (Keith Waterhouse, Willis Hall, Peter Shaffer, Alan Plater, Jack Rosenthal) and actors: the most controversial and best-written of all *TW3* sketches, a 'Consumer Guide to Religion', was the dazzling work of two jobbing thespians, Charles Lewsen and Robert Gillespie. The success of *TW3* – apart from its fortunate timing in coinciding with the decay of the Macmillan government – lay in the fact that it was pure Saturday-night theatre.

That perennially ailing patient, British cinema, also began to shed its polite middle-class image, again with a good deal of help from the theatre. Out of the partnership between Tony Richardson and John Osborne at the Royal Court sprang Woodfall Films, named after the Chelsea street in which Osborne happened to be living with Mary Ure at the end of the Fifties. Woodfall's successes included the film versions of *Look Back In Anger*, *The Entertainer* and *A Taste of Honey*, all directed by Richardson. Karel Reisz and Richardson, respectively, directed *Saturday Night and Sunday Morning* and *The Loneliness Of The Long Distance Runner*, both based on works by Alan Sillitoe. And in 1963 came the biggest money-spinner of them all, *Tom Jones*, written by Osborne, directed by Richardson and so stuffed with Sloane Square alumni as to resemble, in the words of Philip French, 'a Royal Court home movie'. When you add to them *This Sporting Life*, which launched a memorable partnership between David Storey as writer and Lindsay Anderson as director, several things become apparent. The first is that all these films, even including *Tom Jones*, feature a protagonist at odds with the status quo. Jimmy Porter and Archie Rice, fairly obviously. But Arthur Seaton in *Saturday Night and Sunday Morning* expresses his philosophy as 'Don't let the bastards grind you down. What I'm out for is a good time; all the rest is propaganda.' In *The Loneliness Of The Long Distance Runner* the hero is a Borstal Boy who deliberately loses a race against a public-school team in defiance of the reformist values of the paternalist governor. And *This Sporting Life* features an inarticulate Rugby League footballer at odds with the world and unable to express his affection for an embittered widow. But the second key fact is that the leads in many of these films were played by working-class actors who had emerged from the theatre and who were to become role models for a new generation. I'd first noticed Albert Finney at Birmingham Rep in the late Fifties where he combined a heavyweight physical presence, unusual in a young actor, with an impish sense of mischief: both came into play in his aggressively truculent Arthur Seaton and his sexily sportive Tom Jones. Tom Courtenay, fresh out of RADA, attracted instant attention as a hollow-eyed, faintly cadaverous Konstantin in the otherwise conventional production of *The Seagull* that preceded *Beyond The Fringe* at the Edinburgh Lyceum in August 1960: what Courtenay brought to the screen in *The Loneliness of the Long Distance Runner* was the gangling outsiderishness of the compulsive non-joiner. And Richard Harris, who'd worked briefly with Joan Littlewood at Theatre Workshop, filled the screen with his muscular pugnaciousness in the Anderson–Storey masterpiece. Even the actor who was to eclipse them all in international popularity, Sean Connery, putting down his marker as James Bond in 1962's *Dr No*, had been playing in Pirandello and Euripides at Oxford Playhouse a few years earlier. Without the British theatre, there simply wouldn't have been a Sixties revival of British cinema.

What characterised the Richardson–Reisz–Anderson school of movies was sexual candour, respect for the texture and pattern of working-class life and a truculent individualism. And that individualism was even more marked in popular music and fashion where a new generation embraced its own sounds and styles rather than simply receiving what the old order handed down to it. Out of the Cavern Club in Liverpool, which I signally failed to visit during a brief, disastrous spell working on the local *Post* and *Echo*, emerged the Beatles who in October 1962 first entered the charts with 'Love Me Do'. A year later a far more anarchic, subversive group – the Rolling Stones, led by a strangely androgynous ex-LSE student called Mick Jagger – began making regular appearances at the Craw-Daddy Club in Richmond. In fashion too there was a sense of the old order rapidly changing with Glasgow's John Stephen pitching camp in Carnaby Street, with Mary Quant, having already conquered the King's Road, opening a second Bazaar in Knightsbridge in 1961 and with the mini-skirt everywhere riding blissfully high. Long associated with the sturdy tweed and the furled umbrella, England suddenly became chic and cheerful in the bravery of its apparel. 'London', as Mary Quant said, 'led the way in changing the focus of fashion from the Establishment to the young.' Of course, not everything that happened in the early Sixties was of equal weight or value; but it was clear that there was an identifiable youth culture and a new spirit of liberation – helped by the marketing of the contraceptive pill from 1961 – that was totally out of synch with a society in which capital punishment remained on the statute books, abortion was still illegal and homosexual acts were punishable by law.

Far from being insulated from this process of rapid change, the theatre was very much part of it: even in the higher classical regions. In 1960 the most sensational production of the year was Franco Zeffirelli's Old Vic *Romeo and Juliet*: not the usual staid exploration of passion but an electrifyingly realistic, youthfully cast recreation of a bustling, brawling Renaissance Verona in which Judi Dench's Juliet and John Stride's Romeo were so desperately smitten that they maintained tactile, finger-tip contact until the very last second of their balcony-scene parting. Equally unforgettable was Alec McCowen's Mercutio: wounded by a chance stroke, he leaned against a pillar sourly joking until sliding down to his shockingly unforeseen, unintended death. In that same year, the twenty-nine-year-old Peter Hall formally took charge at Stratford-upon-Avon and set about turning a star-laden, six-month Shakespeare festival into a monumental, year-round operation built around a permanent company, a London base and contemporary work from home and abroad. Looking back, it is difficult to realise just how radical Hall's dream was at the time; or indeed how much opposition there was to the creation of what became officially known in March 1961 as the Royal Shakespeare Company.

That opposition took many forms. Not all actors were enthralled by Hall's robust attacks on contemporary verse-speaking and his desire to rid it of both Victorian sentimentality and slovenly naturalism: 'His remarks', the Old Vic's John Neville told an Oxford student audience in 1960, 'would be laughable if they weren't so bloody insulting.' West

End managers were also dismayed at Hall's plans to invade their patch. Binkie Beaumont, who resigned from the Stratford board of governors in 1960, did everything possible to block the RSC's move into the West End, correctly seeing it as the first stage in the dissolution of his own empire. The Stratford company's first application for a lease on the Aldwych was also abruptly rejected by Prince Littler, head of the giant Stoll Moss Empires chain. He gave way only when Hall, using his inbuilt strategic skill, let it be known that he might do a deal with his brother and deadly rival, Emile Littler, and take over the Cambridge Theatre instead: at that point the Aldwych became magically available. But if West End managers were alarmed, proponents of a National Theatre were also panicked by the prospect of an expansionist Stratford company offering classical and contemporary work in London. In April 1959 a meeting was held between representatives of the Joint Council of the National Theatre and the Old Vic on the one side and of the Shakespeare Memorial Theatre – as it still was – on the other. Significantly it took place at Notley Abbey: the baronial home of Laurence Olivier, who had already been sounded out by Oliver Lyttelton, chairman of the Joint Council, as a future director of the NT. On the table was a proposal that Stratford should be incorporated into the National Theatre scheme: an idea which Hall, then Stratford's director-designate, and his chairman, Sir Fordham Flower, instinctively rejected.

That in itself says a good deal not just about Peter Hall but about his creation of what eventually became known as the RSC. Its survival in those precarious early years was based on a combination of artistic vision and political pragmatism. The vision, which Hall had outlined to Sir Fordham Flower in a Leningrad hotel in the winter of 1958, was based on a belief that permanence and continuity were vital for the performance of Shakespeare and that a classic tradition could only be kept alive if it were accompanied by new work. It was a distillation of everything Hall had seen and learned as a young man: his memories of the Olivier–Richardson seasons at the New, his experiences in post-war Germany, his sightings of the Berliner Ensemble and Jean Vilar's Théâtre National Populaire. But Hall also had the political skills to make his vision a reality. You see this in his persuasive handling of Sir Fordham Flower, one of the numerous father-figures to thread their way through Hall's career. Hall was also the first post-war theatre director to understand the value of publicity: where Binkie Beaumont employed a press rep, Vivienne Byerley, to skilfully ration press information and shield himself from the public gaze, Hall argued that 'in the fight to establish the company, we *had* to be in the newspapers every day of the week if possible'. But Hall's political skills were most apparent in his ceaseless quest for public subsidy. As Colin Chambers notes in *Inside The Royal Shakespeare Company*, Hall took a calculated gamble: 'Stratford would have to become bankrupt in order to receive state aid but it would go bankrupt by supporting the vastly expanded work of the new company.' The risk paid off; but it was a damned close-run thing. In effect, Hall created the RSC out of the reserves built up by Quayle and Byam Shaw in the Fifties. But he then found himself in the midst of a complex political chess game in which advocates of the proposed National Theatre argued that there was no room for another big institution. Hall had to preserve the integrity, and London presence, of the RSC without seeming to damage the embryonic National Theatre. He did this partly by orchestrating a brilliant press campaign in 1962 masterminded by head of press John Goodwin, which argued that the Aldwych would have to close if public subsidy was not forthcoming. After a series of tortuous negotiations, the RSC was told by the Arts Council in October that year that it would receive £47,000 in 1963/64. It was half what the RSC claimed it needed. It also created an historic imbalance with NT funding that has never been fully corrected; but at least Hall ensured that the idea of twin national companies was accepted, however grudgingly, by the arts Establishment.

To praise Hall's political skills is not to belittle him as an artist. Indeed it was his fascination with the politics and the dynamics of power that led the RSC towards one of its defining early triumphs: *The Wars of the Roses* at Stratford in 1963. But it took time for Peter Hall to achieve his declared aim of transforming an ad hoc Stratford company into a glittering ensemble on the European model. The opening Stratford season in 1960 boasted a knockdown stellar performance from Peter O'Toole as a blazingly romantic Shylock; but the difficulties of maintaining a company in a freelance industry were emphasised when O'Toole announced in November that he had landed the movie role of Lawrence of Arabia and would not be available to play Henry II in a projected Aldwych production of Anouilh's *Becket*. And although in that first season there was fine work from such established Shakespeareans as Peggy Ashcroft (Kate in *The Taming of the Shrew*, Paulina in *The Winter's Tale*) and

Dorothy Tutin (Portia, Viola and Cressida), the attempt to incorporate actors from diverse traditions did not immediately pay off. With Denholm Elliott from British cinema and Shaftesbury Avenue, Jack McGowran from the Dublin Abbey and the world of Samuel Beckett and Frances Cuka from Joan Littlewood's Stratford East, the 1960 Stratford company still looked like a scratch team rather than a real ensemble. If any one performer embodied Hall's ideal of a witty, intelligent approach to verse-speaking, in which the actor illuminated the sense while observing the form, it was Eric Porter. He was a notable Malvolio and Leontes; but my abiding memory is of seeing him play Ulysses in *Troilus and Cressida* before a packed Saturday-night house who gave him a spontaneous exit-round after his delivery of the inordinately complex speech beginning 'Time hath, my lord, a wallet at his back'. It was Porter's ability to explicate Shakespeare, through a skilful use of vocal antithesis and manual expressiveness, that made him not only the quintessential Hall actor but also the best verse-speaker on the British stage.

For all the ups and downs of its early seasons, the RSC quickly established one vital point: the huge gain of blending Shakespeare and contemporary work. Large-cast historical plays at the Aldwych, including John Whiting's *The Devils* and Jean Anouilh's *Becket,* were accompanied by a remarkable seven-play season at the Arts Theatre in 1962 which yielded two works that indicated the direction in which British theatre was heading: towards the ever-greater exploration and understanding of violence. David Rudkin's *Afore Night Come* was an astonishing play about the ritual murder of an Irish itinerant in a Worcestershire pear orchard. I'll return to it later in the context of the 'tramp' plays that suddenly mushroomed in the early Sixties; but what is significant is that it heralded the abiding Sixties fascination with Theatre of Cruelty. Less remembered is a play by Fred Watson, *Infanticide In The House of Fred Ginger,* directed by William Gaskill: one scene in which a shy babysitter and two psychopathic Teds murder a crying baby eerily anticipated Bond's *Saved* and marked a new level in what was permissible in terms of staged violence. Sadly, the Arts season was a one-off event abruptly curtailed by the RSC's cash crisis. But what was extraordinary about the company was its ability to triumph over adversity: indeed it came of age, artistically, in the autumn of 1962 when its very future hung in the balance. When Peter Brook's scheduled Stratford production of *King Lear* was delayed by the illness of Paul Scofield, the gap was hastily filled by Clifford Williams' interim version of *The Comedy of Errors*. Rehearsed in three weeks, it was simply staged on three raked platforms and began with the whole cast marching downstage clad in uniformly grey costumes; only as the action proceeded, with Ian Richardson and Alec McCowen as the memorably alarmed Antipholi, were touches of colour added. But it was Kenneth Tynan who alone grasped the significance of the achievement:

> *The Comedy of Errors* is unmistakeably an RSC production. The statement is momentous; it means that Peter Hall's troupe has developed, uniquely in Britain, a classical style of its own. How is it to be recognised? By solid Brechtian settings that emphasise wood and metal instead of paint and canvas; and by cogent deliberate verse-speaking that discards melodic cadenzas in favour of meaning and motivation.

The irony is that it took a fill-in production by the RSC's staff director to show that, after nearly three years of expansive empire-building and hectic politicking, the company had at last achieved a house style.

The defining production of those early years was undoubtedly *The Wars of the Roses*: an epic trilogy in which the three parts of *Henry VI* were conflated by John Barton into two plays and followed by *Richard III*. Why exactly did this work so catch the public imagination in 1963? Partly it had to do with the project's Wagnerian scale: Hall introduced the idea, commonplace now but unheard-of then, of playing the complete cycle on selected Saturdays in an orgiastic theatrical marathon. This was theatre as Big Event. *The Wars of the Roses* was also a company triumph that showed the RSC's ability to embrace both veterans and relative newcomers. The Tynan-fostered notion of Peggy Ashcroft as an essentially genteel actress, forever betrayed by her Kensington vowels, was banished by her magnificent Margaret of Anjou: in the course of a day you saw her move from sexy, light-footed princess to battle-hardened warrior daubing the Duke of York's face with the blood of his murdered son to bedraggled, revenge-obsessed old crone. At the other end of the scale, a young, Leamington-born actor called David Warner, briefly seen in the RSC's Arts Theatre season, astonished as the ineffectual Henry VI: out of one of Shakespeare's least promising heroes Warner created a gawky, gently spoken figure radiating a spiritual beneficence that called to mind Dostoevsky's Prince Mishkin or even Jesus Christ. But the company also had immense weight in the middle ranks with Donald Sinden as the crown-hungry York and Brewster Mason as the treacherous Warwick: both, bearing six-foot long, two-handed swords by the pummel, terrifying embodiments of secular power. These giant swords were the brainchild of John Bury, late of Theatre Workshop, who set the whole action in a harsh metallic world dominated by iron-clad lock-gates and a diamond-shaped council table that rose from the floor for the fractious Westminster scenes. This was worlds away from the painterly, decorative design, steeped in post-war romanticism, familiar in Fifties Stratford; even the sound of Bury's giant swords abrasively scraping the raked stage surface, made of steel treated in an acid bath, haunts the memory.

All this helps to explain why *The Wars of the Roses* was an instant hit. But, at a deeper level, it seemed in touch with the spirit of the times in a way that is rare in Shakespearean production. For a start it reflected the work of a number of theorists fashionable in the early Sixties. The fascination with ritual violence stemmed from Artaud's *The Theatre and Its Double*: a seminal text first published in 1938 which influenced a whole generation of practitioners from Jean-Louis Barrault and Peter Brook to the Living Theatre's Julian and Judith Beck and which gave popular currency to the phrase 'Theatre of Cruelty'. The idea of history as a brutal elemental force 'like hail, storm, hurricane, birth and death', rather than a Hegelian grand mechanism, derived from the Polish critic, Jan Kott, whose *Shakespeare Our Contemporary* had greatly influenced Peter Brook's *King Lear*. But the biggest influence, I suspect, was the idea of the Austrian ethologist, Konrad Lorenz, that human aggression can be understood in largely animalistic terms. Peter Hall, in a programme note, endorses this vision by talking of men hunting in packs and of the way 'the man who kills the beast becomes the king and must kill his rivals to remain king'. Intriguingly Lorenz's ethological view of human behaviour was later popularised by the American writer, Robert Ardrey, whose play about Hungary, *Shadow of Heroes*, Hall had directed in 1958. But *The Wars of the Roses* was much more than a collage of fashionable ideas: it coincided, in the most extraordinary way, with the national mood in 1963. Its chauvinist portrait of the perfidious French reminded us that earlier in the year General de Gaulle had personally vetoed British membership of the EEC. Its cynicism about power-politics coincided with a year of Tory disarray in which Macmillan's resignation was followed by an unseemly back-stabbing scramble for the premiership. Even its reminder that authority was no protection against sudden, merciless extinction coincided with the tragic assassination of President Kennedy in November 1963. *The Wars of the Roses* was not just brilliant theatre offering a rediscovery of a neglected part of the canon: it was an expression of the zeitgeist and an exploration of power by a company whose own survival depended on astute political manoeuvring. The only sadness is that the very success of *The Wars of the Roses* has overshadowed its remarkable sequel: the 1964 Stratford season in which the trilogy became the climax of a seven-play history cycle co-directed by Hall, Barton and Clifford Williams, taking us from *Richard II* to *Richard III*. Seeing the plays in succession during a single week, I was struck by the creative tension between the Kott-inspired notion of history as an irrational force and Shakespeare's own grand design showing the corrosive effects of Bolingbroke's act of usurpation in the very first play. The RSC cycle acknowledged the traditional Tillyard view of the plays as the story of a curse lifted only by the establishment of the Tudor succession: at the same time they reminded us that these plays existed in the historic present.

The Wars of the Roses offered conclusive proof that Peter Hall had finally created a de facto national company out of a Shakespearean summer festival; and his success only served to highlight the tortuous nature of the progress towards a National Theatre. The genesis of the latter is a long and wearisome story chiefly of interest to specialists. But the key fact is that the Attlee government's idealistic promise in 1948 of a million pounds towards a suitable building had got bogged down in the classic British vices of inertia and committee-itis. A foundation stone laid by the Queen on the South Bank in 1951 and promptly forgotten became a melancholy symbol of official inaction. Even intense lobbying in the early Sixties by Lord Chandos (chairman of the Joint Council for the National Theatre), Lord Cottesloe (newly appointed chairman of the Arts Council) and Lord Esher (Olivier's old nemesis from the post-war Old Vic) had little effect: three lords a-leaping could not conjure up a theatre. In March 1961 Selwyn Lloyd, Chancellor of the Exchequer, told the Commons that the government would not release the promised money towards the building of the National:

instead it would offer an extra £450,000 to help regional theatre. In the end, it was the Labour-led London County Council, under Sir Isaac Hayward, that broke the logjam by promising to provide £1.3 million towards the building of the National if the government honoured its own long-standing commitment. The only snag was that it was still envisaged that any future National would incorporate the Old Vic, Stratford and Sadler's Wells Opera Company. After much argy-bargy, the last two formally pulled out of the scheme and in July 1962 Selwyn Lloyd finally gave the green light to a National Theatre existing as a separate entity to be built on a 1.2-acre site next to Waterloo Bridge. In August Olivier – by then in the midst of his first season running the Chichester Festival Theatre – was formally appointed as the National's director. It was agreed that the National Theatre Company would take over the Old Vic in August 1963 (in the end it turned out to be October) pending completion of the new South Bank building by the mid-Sixties (it finally opened in March 1976). The whole saga, dating back to 1848, was one of delays, infighting, muddle and incompetence. But at least by the autumn of 1963 the twin national companies were both up and running: a structure was in place that was to shape British theatre over future decades and that was to mark a decisive shift in the balance of power away from the commercial sector. At the time both the National and the RSC were the focus of theatrical idealism and youthful optimism: only later did they come to be seen as grant-consuming behemoths and icons of Establishment power. But, by emerging in the early Sixties, they became part of a vibrant culture celebrating youth, enterprise and vitality. They didn't merely express the times. In many significant ways, they also helped to change them.

It may seem perverse to claim a National Theatre headed by a fifty-six-year-old Laurence Olivier, with his instinctive patriotism and actor-manager paternalism, as part of a changing, youth-oriented culture. But much of Olivier's success in the early years at the National lay in surrounding himself with radical young talent. Many older actors who had fought alongside Olivier at his cinematic Agincourt or been part of the post-war Old Vic applied to join the National only to be rejected as decisively as Falstaff by the newly crowned Prince Hal. Olivier not only had a young wife – the thirty-three-year-old Joan Plowright – who was a pillar of the new company. He plucked John Dexter, Wesker's champion, and William Gaskill, Britain's foremost

Brechtian, from the Royal Court. His appointment of Kenneth Tynan as Literary Manager – the equivalent of the continental dramaturg and a wholly new concept in British theatre – also sent out a strong signal. Tynan had famously written to Olivier, after making disparaging comments about his first Chichester season in 1962, recommending himself for the post. Olivier's own recollection is that he was flabbergasted by Tynan's sauce and was ready to write a withering reply. But it was Joan Plowright who saw that Tynan's audacious presence would counter any fears that Olivier's National would be fuddy-duddy or old-fashioned. Advocating Tynan's appointment, she told her husband: 'They would look at you with a new eye. The younger generation would rejoice.'

In reality, Tynan's appointment created its own tensions within the organisation. In an intriguing interview with Charles Marowitz in *Encore* in July 1963, Tynan talked of the possibility of building up a repertoire of forty-nine productions over a five- or six-year period: an idea dating back to Granville Barker that was a wholly impractical notion on an initial subsidy of £130,000 and in a building with the Old Vic's limited storage space. More significantly, Tynan discounted the idea that the National should have as recognisable an approach as that of the Berliner Ensemble, claiming 'I don't think it is any part of the aim or ambition of a National Theatre to have a style as rigidly prefabricated as that': sentiments with which neither Gaskill nor Dexter would have agreed. Tynan also later seriously fell out with George Devine when the latter was invited to direct Beckett's *Play*: as the NT's house critic, Tynan sent off a series of memos urging that, in contravention of Beckett's own instructions, the piece be played at a more easily comprehensible speed, arguing, 'We are not putting on *Play* to satisfy Beckett alone.' Devine sent an understandably angry response and Olivier put Tynan firmly in his place in a long, admonitory letter in which he wrote, 'I like having you with me, apart from it rather tickling me to have you with me, but you can be too fucking tactless for words.'

But, whatever the artistic tensions within the NT, there was a palpable buzz about its early productions. It also emerged at a fortuitous moment. In the very month in which the Tory party took a retrograde step through the elevation of Sir Alec Douglas-Home to the leadership through backstairs intrigue, a state-aided National Theatre Company began operation; it seemed, like so much happening in the arts at that time, to point the way towards a more dynamic future and to suggest that the nation's energy resided with its creators rather than its politicians. And, even if the inaugural production of *Hamlet* with Peter O'Toole was a wretched disappointment, order was soon restored with importations from Chichester of Dexter's rigorous *Saint Joan* and Olivier's legendary *Uncle Vanya*. This last was a great production that captured the play's essence without suffocating it in false 'atmosphere'. It also boasted, alongside Olivier's own sleekly narcissistic Astrov, a truly overwhelming Vanya from Michael Redgrave. In Redgrave's Vanya you saw both a tremulous victim of a lifetime's emotional repression and the wasted potential of a Chekhovian might-have-been: as Redgrave and Olivier took their joint curtain call, linked hands held triumphantly aloft, we were not to know that this was to symbolise the end of their artistic amity. But if any one production defined the new company it was Gaskill's version of Farquhar's *The Recruiting Officer* which opened in December 1963. At the time the words 'Restoration Comedy' were generally taken as an excuse for dandy-mincing display and fan-fluttering camp. Gaskill banished all that by reminding us that Farquhar had written a provincial comedy set in Shrewsbury in 1706 and dealing with the realities of recruitment: when Robert Stephens's Plume and Colin Blakely's Kite manipulated two locals into joining the army, you felt you were watching a timeless process in which the military cunningly exploits popular nationalist sentiment. René Allio's designs, based on the red-brick Queen Anne buildings of Amersham's main street, also combined practicality with Brechtian beauty. And, by the use of rehearsal-room improvisation, Gaskill welded a diverse bunch of actors – including Olivier himself, Maggie Smith, Max Adrian, and Lynn Redgrave – into a genuine team. Gaskill's triumph was quickly followed by Dexter's reclamation of another regional classic in Harold Brighouse's *Hobson's Choice*: a production swathed in affectionate detail and boasting a magisterial performance from Michael Redgrave as the tyrannical patriarch who here became a Lancastrian Lear.

Any lingering notion that the National would turn into a Waterloo Road version of the Berliner Ensemble was, however, a pipe dream. For a start it lacked the advantage, which the RSC enjoyed, of its own house dramatist. It was also run by an actor of genius who, while encouraging new talent, could not help but effortlessly dominate. And in Tynan as Literary Manager it possessed the ultimate star-fucker.

What the National offered in its initial season was not a simulacrum of the Berliner Ensemble but something more characteristically British: an eclectic mix of ten productions, ranging from Shakespeare and Shaw to Beckett and Frisch, that was both pragmatic and pluralist. There were no new British plays in that first season, no realisation that one function of a National Theatre was to debate or embody the state of the nation: the only black face seen on the Old Vic stage was that of a heavily made-up Laurence Olivier as a vain, imperious Othello endowed with the emotional force of a tornado. But that first season had achieved much. It had made the idea of a National Theatre a practical reality. It had brought on a wide range of young actors including Frank Finlay, Robert Stephens, Colin Blakely, Derek Jacobi and Lynn Redgrave. It had reclaimed two regional classics in the Farquhar and Brighouse productions. Not least it had improved all-round standards of presentation: as someone working in provincial rep in Lincoln at the time, I remember being impressed on a first visit by the informative, compact richness of the programmes. A seemingly trivial matter; but, after years of putting up with the West End's flimsy, over-priced cast lists, supplemented by vivacious advertisements for gas boards, it was a reminder that a National Theatre existed to provide a public service rather than to maximise profits.

If the National was slow to stage a contemporary British play, it eventually made spectacular amends with Peter Shaffer's *The Royal Hunt of The Sun*: a work that it presented first at the Chichester Festival Theatre and then at the Old Vic. The astonishing thing was that Shaffer, previously known for his skilled five-finger exercises in domestic naturalism, here launched into epic mode with an historical play about the Spanish conquest of Peru. The story goes that Shaffer, while staying at Binkie Beaumont's country cottage one weekend, overheard Binkie's partner, John Perry, outlining the play to him in graphic detail. As Perry described the Spanish army marching over the Andes, the battle scenes, the blood sacrifices, the multifarious scene changes, there was a horrified pause before an incredulous Binkie whispered, 'She's *mad*' ; although Shaffer himself, in substantiating the story, denies the use of the female pronoun. In reality, Shaffer was anything but mad, as John Dexter's lavish Chichester production and Robert Stephens's sensational performance as the Inca king, Atahualpa, subsequently proved. In addition to pursuing his own obsessive theme of

the limits of rationalism and the power of divinity, Shaffer had also
cottoned on to the fact that in the early Sixties there was an extraordinary revival of the historical epic. Plays like Robert Bolt's *A Man For
All Seasons* (1960), John Osborne's *Luther* (1961) and John Whiting's
The Devils (1961) all ransacked history for some clue to the dilemmas
of modern man; and the fascinating question is why, at a time when
contemporary Britain was changing at such a giddying pace, so many
dramatists used the past as a metaphor for the present.

Harold Hobson in his introduction to Bolt and Whiting's work in
Penguin's *New English Dramatists: 6* argued that the momentous
nature of world affairs in the Sixties meant that dramatists were
obliged to raise their eyes beyond domestic events. In the past, said
Hobson, it was possible for private people to live private lives: Jane
Austen's heroes and heroines could go about their business without
reference to the rise and fall of Napoleon or the madness of George III.
Now such detachment was unfeasible:

> A slight miscalculation in places as widely separated from each
> other and as far from us as Cuba, Berlin or Laos could at any
> moment result in our own personal annihilation. We cannot there-
> fore divorce our attention from world affairs. The continuance of
> our existence depends on them. This consciousness is bred into the
> bone of all serious writers today.

Hobson had a point. The survival of mankind was a major issue. And
the early Sixties saw a number of earth-shaking events. The disastrous
'Bay of Pigs' fiasco in which CIA-backed Cuban exiles attempted to
invade their homeland. The rise of the Berlin Wall. The eyeball-to-eyeball
confrontation between Khrushchev and Kennedy over the erection of
Soviet medium-range missiles in Cuba: an event that seemingly
brought the world to the brink of nuclear war. But the fact was that
the history plays of Bolt, Osborne and Whiting pre-dated those particular global crises. In so far as the three writers had a common
theme, it was the conflict between the individual and the established
institutions of Church and State. But why should so many dramatists
have looked to the past for their inspiration in the early Sixties?

One obvious answer was the pervasive influence of Brecht. Even if
British dramatists rejected his Marxist message, they were seduced by
his form: in particular, his abandonment of Aristotelian revelation in
favour of an epic structure in which each scene became an individual

unit. The result may have been bastardised Brecht but there is little doubt that, after the seminal visit by the Berliner Ensemble in 1956, British dramatists were more likely to use *Galileo* than *Ghosts* as a model. It is also highly probable that Bolt and Osborne's active support of CND explained why they were compulsively drawn to defiant heroes; but then so too was Whiting who was temperamentally conservative. If three leading British dramatists, more or less simultaneously, wrote plays about intransigent, spiritually driven protagonists, it was because of a shared disillusion with the moral vacancy of the times. The Sixties saw rapid gains in social liberation and material comfort for the majority of citizens. But it was also a period when identity was increasingly related to acquisition; and it was against that kind of steady erosion of the self that dramatists were starting to rebel.

Bolt says as much in his eloquent introduction to *A Man For All Seasons* in 1960. He paints a vivid, Sartre-like picture of the existential helplessness of modern man. 'We no longer have,' writes Bolt, 'as past societies have had, any picture of Individual Man (Stoic Philosopher, Christian Religious, Rational Gentleman) by which to recognise ourselves and against which to measure ourselves; we are anything. But if anything, then nothing and it is not everyone who can live with that.' Bolt then brings the argument closer to home by describing the difficulties of living in a modern western democracy where the individual is defined only by his wants and needs. He continues:

> The individual who tries to plot his position by reference to our society finds no fixed point but only the vaunted absence of them, 'freedom' and 'opportunity'; freedom for what, opportunity to do what is nowhere indicated. The only positive he is given is 'get and spend' ('get and spend – if you can' from the Right, 'get and spend – you deserve it' from the Left) and he did not need society to tell him that. In other words, we are thrown back by our society upon ourselves at our lowest, that is at our least satisfactory to ourselves.

This, it becomes clear, is what drew Bolt to the subject of Sir Thomas More. In contrast to our own world where man has simply become a loose congregation of appetites played on by politicians, More possessed an 'adamantine sense of his own self' and a great capacity for life. Not only that. He trusted in forces greater than the solitary individual: the efficacy of the law and the Church of Christ ruled from Heaven. As an ex-communist himself, Bolt seems to be almost pining for a world of fixed values and lost certainties.

Although popular with audiences, *A Man For All Seasons* was critically attacked in 1960 as commercialised Brecht and, in particular, as a more pallid version of *Galileo*. 'Bolt looks at history exclusively through the eyes of his saintly hero – Brecht's vision is broader: he looks at Galileo through the eyes of history,' wrote Tynan. But a more fruitful comparison would be with Arthur Miller's *The Crucible*, dating from 1953 and part of the Royal Court's opening season. Like Miller, Bolt uses history as a metaphor for the present. He also deals with a hero who believes that a compromised life in which he sacrifices his 'name' – his essential core of integrity – is not worth living. And if one is looking for influences, one can't ignore the prototypical *Sir Thomas More*, written in 1592 by Anthony Munday and later revised by a syndicate possibly including Shakespeare. But where that, for fear of censorship, skates over More's opposition to the Act of Succession, Bolt makes it abundantly clear why More cannot sign an Act that would acknowledge the King's precedence over secular law and divine authority as manifested in the Pope. In fact, Bolt's play passes the acid test for all works of history. It successfully brings the past to life. At the same time, its portrait of a man blessed with an intransigent selfhood and sanctioned by higher forces offers its own ironic comment on the vacillating present. If audiences flocked to the Globe Theatre in 1960 it was partly because of the iron gracefulness of Paul Scofield's performance. It was also because they responded keenly to Bolt's portrait of a principled hero.

The play even offered a prophetic comment on Bolt's own fluctuating sense of identity. In September 1961, as part the Committee of 100 which extended anti-nuclear protest to acts of civil disobedience, Bolt was arrested along with a third of the Committee's membership and charged with incitement to commit a breach of the peace. After two days in Brixton, Bolt was transferred to Drake Hall Open Prison in the Staffordshire countryside. At the time, however, he was working on the screenplay for *Lawrence of Arabia* for the Hollywood tycoon, Sam Spiegel. A furious Spiegel told Bolt that his act of conscience was jeopardising the whole movie and causing a hundred people to go without pay. After a fortnight in prison, Bolt signed an agreement to keep the peace and was driven away in Spiegel's Rolls Royce to a celebratory lunch at London's Berkeley Hotel. Only then did Bolt realise he had been conned and that shooting on the movie had ceased while the director, David Lean, sought new locations. Bolt called it 'the most shameful moment of my life' and said that 'for six months I found it very hard to look in the mirror'. He salvaged his self-respect by donating the money he had earned from his premature release to Centre 42, a missionary arts organisation run by his fellow protester, Arnold Wesker. But Bolt's misguided sacrifice of conscience to commercial imperatives sheds retrospective light on his envious admiration of Sir Thomas More's spiritual tenacity.

If there is any fault in Bolt's portrayal of More, it is that it is almost too hero-worshipping: in particular it omits the scatalogical venom that enabled More to say of the radical religious reformer, Martin Luther, that he farts anathema, that someone should piss and shit into his mouth and that he was filled with excrement. More even suggested that Luther celebrated Mass '*super foricam*' (upon the toilet). But if Bolt was naturally hesitant about reproducing More's excretory language in an H. M. Tennent production, John Osborne had no such inhibition about echoing his own hero's faecal attraction in *Luther*, which opened at the Royal Court in 1961 before moving into the West End. What is extraordinary is that Osborne and Bolt, both of whom were arrested in the mass anti-nuclear protest in Trafalgar Square in September 1961, should independently have conceived quasi-Brechtian plays about a rebellious individual's defiance of authority. The link goes even further: as Peter Ackroyd shrewdly points out in his biography of Sir Thomas More, Luther (1483–1546) and More (1487–1535), while on opposite sides of the religious divide, had a good deal in common. Both were juvenile ascetics who later rejected the monastic life. Both, by their fanatical piety, took late medieval Catholicism to its limits. But, whatever the hidden links between More and Luther, Bolt and Osborne take radically different attitudes to their heroes. If More was an idealised version of the man Bolt would like to have been, Luther is much closer to the individual Osborne actually was.

In the second volume of his autobiography, *Almost A Gentleman*, Osborne refers to the 'nag of disquiet' with which he was born; and, in choosing the architect of the Protestant Reformation as his hero, Osborne finds a magnified echo of his own implacable resistance to all forms of imposed authority. Osborne's battles with school-masters, commercial managers, critics and the Lord Chamberlain may seem puny in comparison with Luther's conflict with the

Catholic Church and ultimate excommunication. But if one asks why Osborne, after two acclaimed contemporary plays and a flop musical, suddenly in the early Sixties writes about a zealous religious reformer, the answer must be for deep-seated personal and political reasons. Central to the thinking of the historical Martin Luther was the idea of justification by faith rather than by good works. On the personal level, that chimed exactly with Osborne's own passionate belief in the primacy of stubborn visionaries over *bien pensant* liberals. Politically, Luther's defiance of the Catholic hierarchy also became a metaphor for Osborne's own hatred of the British Establishment: specifically its endorsement of nuclear weapons and the 'balance of terror' at a time of escalating Cold War. Between the trimphant opening of *Luther* at the Royal Court in July 1961, with a brawnily powerful Albert Finney, and its autumn transfer to the West End Osborne wrote a celebrated 'Letter to my Fellow Countrymen': a missive that appeared in a small left-wing newspaper, *Tribune*, but soon achieved massive circulation. At a time when leading Tory and Labour politicians, with popular approval, backed the independent nuclear deterrent, Osborne lashed out at our supine representatives:

> My hatred for you is almost the only constant satisfaction you have left me. My favourite fantasy is four minutes or so of non-commercial viewing as you fry in your democratically elected hot seats in Westminster, preferably with your condoning democratic constituents. There is murder in my brain and I carry a knife in my heart for every one of you. Macmillan, and you, Gaitskell, you particularly.

Even the tone of the letter echoes the rasping rhetoric of Martin Luther.

But what makes *Luther* a fine, passionately felt play is Osborne's ability to discover in his hero's intestinal struggles a metaphor for the creative process. In 1517 Luther famously nailed to the church door at Wittenberg his ninety-five theses on Catholic indulgences, and Osborne expressess his hero's religious revelation in a magnificent sermon filled with bowel-churning language:

> It came to me while I was in my tower, what they call the monk's sweathouse, the jakes, the john or whatever you're pleased to call it. I was struggling with the text I've given you: 'For therein is the

righteousness of God revealed, from faith to faith; as it is written, the just shall live by faith.' And seated there, my head down, on that privy just as I was when I was a little boy, I couldn't reach down to my breath for the sickness in my bowels, as I seemed to sense beneath me a large rat, a heavy, wet, plague rat slashing at my privates with its death's teeth.

This not only expresses, in vigorously dramatic terms, the finding of the psychiatrist Erik. H. Erikson: that 'a revelation is always associated with a repudiation', and that there was a direct link between Luther's bowel movements and his illumination by the Holy Spirit. It also articulates Osborne's conviction that there is a parallel between faith and creativity. Intriguingly Osborne got into spiritual shape for the play by spending a week as the guest of an Anglican monastic community at Mirfield in West Yorkshire run by the bonily ascetic future bishop, Trevor Huddleston; though, with typical asperity, Osborne described other Mirfield pilgrims as kitschy incense queens and Walsingham Matildas. But there was clearly a strong autobiographical element to *Luther* in which faith, like art, is never achieved without physical struggle. And Osborne later acknowledged the strong personal drive behind the play by admitting that the role of Staupitz, Vicar-General of the Augustinian Order and Luther's pastoral mentor, was a tribute to George Devine who first played the part at the Court. According to Osborne, when Devine received the long-delayed text he even spoke in suitably Lutheran terms:

He lifted his arms aloft and cast a fine growl. 'By God, boysie, you've done it! You've done it again!' I never saw him so thoroughly satisfied and joyful, like a man acquitted by a torn jury. 'I always say to them: it may take time and a lot of sweat but when Johnny finally does bring one out, he really *shits* it out.'

In 1961 Osborne's *Luther* had many admirers. His fellow dramatist, John Whiting, however, was not one of them. He began his review in the *London Magazine* by telling his readers what he thought of the historical Martin Luther: 'This disgusting peasant, filthy in word, mind and body, a kind of human sewer, did more harm to Western Europe than any other man.' Whiting went on to say that, although Osborne's play had been widely praised, 'I've yet to meet anybody who likes it.' And he laid the blame for that squarely at the door of the director, Tony Richardson, and his 'criminally mishandled' production. One can only hope that Mr Whiting was not piqued by the fact that his own play, *The Devils*, which opened five months before *Luther* in a spectacular RSC production at the Aldwych, enjoyed only moderate success. For the truth is that, although *Luther* is a far better work than *The Devils*, the two plays have a good deal in common. Both feature defiant protagonists. Both celebrate the courage born of faith. And both, in an age of accelerating secularism, seek to understand religious experience.

Whiting's play tells the historical story of Urban Grandier: a sensual young seventeenth-century priest falsely accused of diabolical possession by a group of Ursuline nuns, led by the erotically obsessed Sister Jeanne. But, although brutally tortured, Grandier refuses to confess to sorcery and goes to the stake. As historical drama, the play lacks the gift for dialectic Shaw brought to *Saint Joan* and the rancid eloquence of Osborne's *Luther*. What it does possess is a blatant theatricality: one scene where a royal emissary exposes the nuns' hysterical claims by showing a box, supposedly containing the blood of Christ, to be totally empty was as exciting as anything London had seen since the days of Lyceum melodrama. Where Whiting's play coincides with Bolt's and Osborne's, however, is in its celebration of the triumph of the individual spirit over the claims of Church and State. Under the threat of torture, Grandier cries, 'My conscience forbids me to put my name to something which is untrue': a resonant line with strong echoes of John Proctor in *The Crucible*. And when, at the end, the vacillating Governor and Chief Magistrate of Loudon say that, as rational men, they should be taking a stand against hysteria and prejudice, Whiting is clearly attacking the ineffectual liberalism of both the seventeenth and twentieth centuries. Like his colleagues, Whiting uses the past to explain the present; and what he shows is a yearning for a spiritual fortitude and a sense of self unlikely to be found in a modern materialistic society. If dramatists increasingly turned to history in the Sixties, it was partly for pragmatic reasons. New spaces and new companies, quite simply, made epic plays possible. But it was also because past martyrs, prepared to sacrifice everything for the integrity of their beliefs, acquired in Macmillan's Britain an unexpectedly heroic lustre.

What is significant about so much Sixties drama is its total rejection of the values of the time. In many respects, there was a lot for which to be grateful. Wages were rising at double the rate of prices. The number of registered unemployed rarely reached two per cent. Consumer spending was on the increase. But, as so often in the post-war period, dramatists were obsessed with the negative aspects of material advance: in particular, the spread of consumerist conformism, the erosion of individual identity, the threat of a prevailing blandness. While Bolt, Osborne and Whiting looked to history for examples of principled opposition, another group of dramatists was obsessively concerned with a very different form of social resistance to prevailing values: that provided by dossers, derelicts and drop-outs. Harold Pinter in *The Caretaker* and David Rudkin in *Afore Night Come* both wrote plays about testy vagrants. Edward Bond's *The Pope's Wedding*, James Saunders' *Next Time I'll Sing To You* and Henry Livings' television play, *Jim All Alone*, tackled the difficult subject of the total recluse. One reason for this sudden interest in outsiders was the publication in 1960 of Raleigh Trevelyan's *A Hermit Disclosed*, which told the haunting story of a real-life Essex solitary, Alexander James Mason. And Beckett had shown in *Waiting For Godot* that vagrants could become dramatic exemplars of the human predicament. But the Sixties preoccupation with outcasts was also a potent reminder of the fact that not everyone was caught up in the rising tide of affluence: there were people who fell outside the provisions of the Welfare State and, either by accident or design, had no place in the new consumerist Britain.

Not that Pinter's *The Caretaker* was conceived as social criticism. The play, which had its triumphant premiere at the Arts Theatre in April 1960 and almost overnight elevated its author to star status, originated in Pinter's own experience of living in a cramped Chiswick High Road flat in the late Fifties, where he encountered an intrusive vagrant, a kindly housekeeper and his mysterious brother. At the time Charles Marowitz dubbed the play 'a kind of masterpiece' and predicted that it would 'suffer the terrible consequences which critics inflict on all such works'. And so it has proved. Over the years it's been variously interpreted as a political power struggle, a religious allegory, a Freudian drama, an ethological battle, a study in interlocking pipe dreams and much else besides. But what is revealing is how it ties in with the Sixties concern about the nature of identity. Robert Bolt had written poignantly about the anchorless nature of modern man. And, while Bolt went back to history to discover a hero with an obstinate sense of self, Pinter looked around him to create in Davies/Jenkins a rudderless protagonist: a man who has no certifiable name, no definable past, and is even excluded from the kind of invisible fraternal bond that links his host, Aston, with his fly-by-night landlord, Mick, the original man in the white van. Pinter had been fascinated by derelicts from an early age, and had even spent a vital year of his youth playing truant from RADA and bumming around London; as he later showed with Spooner in *No Man's Land*, he remained haunted by characters of no fixed spiritual abode. And that is one clue to *The Caretaker*. The penalty of vagrancy, implies Pinter, is that you constantly adapt to shifting circumstances. Davies's repeated reference to going to Sidcup to get his papers is not a running gag but a reminder that his ascertainable identity lies elsewhere; and he shapes himself according to the needs of the moment. 'I've eaten my dinner off the best of plates,' he improbably announces at one point. Later he appropriates Aston's experience of coping with demanding females who want to look at his body. And when Mick enquires whether Davies was ever in the colonies, he promptly replies, 'I was over there. I was one of the first over there.' Davies can be whatever you want him to be: Lord Muck, Don Juan, Gordon of Khartoum. And Donald Pleasence, wolfishly aggressive and cringingly defensive by turns, captured in that famous first performance all of Davies's chameleon qualities. There were many reasons why *The Caretaker* became an instant hit in 1960. But one of them was that Pinter understood something highly relevant at a time when identity was increasingly equated with possessions: that the price of social exclusion is a steady erosion of the self.

Like Pinter, David Rudkin in *Afore Night Come* takes a genuine tramp as his hero. Given that the play was written for my own Oxford college drama society before being picked up for the RSC's season at the Arts, I can vouch for the fact that Rudkin had fallen under the spell of Pinter: he was haunted, like many of us, by Joan Kemp Welch's ITV version of *The Birthday Party* and had seen *The Caretaker* at the Arts. But Rudkin had also spent the summer vacation in 1960 working in a Midlands pear orchard very similar to the one described in the play. On top of that he combined a passion for Hitchcock with a precocious knowledge of Genet and Artaud. Quite how Rudkin, who came from a guilt-haunted religious family in the Birmingham suburbs, had stumbled upon Artaud's *The Theatre and Its Double* I don't know; but

Artaud's notion that theatre should furnish the spectators with 'the truthful precipitates of dreams' left its imprint on his imagination. Yet, for all its influences, *Afore Night Come* is defiantly Rudkin's own work in its obsession with childlessness, sexual ambiguity and the violence beneath the crust of everyday life.

On one level, it is very much a work play. The setting is an orchard in a rural pocket of the Black Country and much of the fascination in performance lies in seeing pears being picked, stacked, stowed in boxes and eventually shipped off to Doncaster. But, having effortlessly established the joshing banter of the rural regulars, Rudkin introduces his wild card in Roche: an itinerant, talkative, work-shy Irishman with dark glasses and a mysterious teacloth draped over his head. And what Rudkin shows is how Roche, as the archetypal outsider, becomes the focus for the group's prejudice, hatred and violence. For a start, Roche is old: 'You'm not a student, you'm bloody fifty.' His Irishness also releases a flood of racial bile: 'You'm a dirty-looking sod. All you Irish'm filthy dirty.' But it is Roche's claim to be a poet, leading to his being derisively dubbed 'Shakespeare', that causes most offence:

> Natter, natter. They bloody rile me, talkers. What were it he kept on saying? Irish Gaelic the language of bloody kings. I said to him 'Ho Ho' I said, 'Shakespeare, I bloody caught you there count of there baint no kings no more.' Saving on the pack of cards, like; know what I mean?

Roche symbolises everything the workers and their foreman instinctively fear and distrust: an aged Celtic poet who has the gift of tongues and claims to be in touch with supernatural forces. And at the end, in a burst of controlled savagery, Roche is decapitated and marked with the sign of the cross.

The Pinter influence is sufficiently strong for the actors in the original RSC production to have dubbed the play 'The Peartaker'. The sound of a crop-dusting helicopter overhead inescapably reminds one of *North By Northwest*. But the play's power lies in its blend of workaday reality and Artaudesque ritual. Rudkin draws on atavistic memories of a still unsolved rural witchcraft murder which took place in Warwickshire in 1945. At the same time he pins down the ferocious hatred of outsiders which, while not peculiar to the English heartland, seems peculiarly intense there: Rudkin's aged Irish hobo stands for all the alien cultures regarded with uncomprehending fear by people in the West Midlands. I well remember the panic that ensued at the arrival of the first wave of Asian workers in Leamington Spa in the early Sixties; and, only six years after Rudkin's play, Enoch Powell was to make a notorious speech in Birmingham about the dangers of unchecked immigration that invoked an image of 'the River Tiber foaming with much blood'. Rudkin's play had a direct influence on theatre in that it sparked a passionate interest in Artaud's Theatre of Cruelty. But it was also an important social phenomenon in so far as it was one of the first plays to pin down that hatred of otherness that was to become a disfiguring feature of British life.

Rudkin and Pinter were not alone, however, in discovering in the outcast a permanently arresting symbol. Edward Bond in his extraordinary first play, *The Pope's Wedding*, given a one-off Sunday-night production at the Royal Court in 1962, uses a hermit as a means of criticising both the surrounding society and the idea of seclusion as a seductive option. Bond's hero, Scopey, is a north Essex village boy who finds himself magnetically drawn to the seventy-five-year-old Alen, who lives in a remote run-down shack amidst a mounting clutter of newspapers and empty tins. Bond, who was evacuated to Cornwall and East Anglia as a child, paints a vivid picture of the aimless boredom of rural life where most of the local lads, when not boozing or chasing girls, work for a feudal farmer. But Bond also suggests there is something dangerous about Scopey's obsession with the alienated Alen: he eventually abandons his job and his flirty, faithless wife to look after the old man before killing him and assuming both his greatcoat and his identity. 'The pope's wedding', said Bond, 'is an impossible ceremony. Scopey's asking for an invitation to something that isn't going to happen, that *can't* happen.' Three years before *Saved*, Bond offers a persuasive picture of a coldly materialist, exploitative society that dismally fails its young. At the same time he demolishes, in language of blunt, elliptical poetry, the illusion that total withdrawal from society provides its own freedom.

To each dramatist, however, his own hermit. For Bond isolation is no solution to society's evils. For James Saunders in *Next Time I'll Sing To You*, which started its life at the Questors, Ealing in 1962 before moving to the Arts and the West End, seclusion becomes a defining image of the human condition. Saunders, who enjoyed great success on BBC radio and spasmodically in the commercial theatre, was a playfully philosophical writer heavily influenced by Pirandello and Beckett. Unlike Bond, he also openly acknowledges that the starting point for his play was the hermit of Great Canfield, Alexander James Mason. We learn that at the age of forty-eight, after rejection by a girl twenty-five years his junior, Mason barricaded himself in a hut for the rest of his life surviving on the food left each day by his brother. But Saunders is less interested in the stark facts than in what they signify. At one point the actor playing the hermit undergoes a Pirandellian transformation in which he seems to become the character. At another, Saunders uses Mason's shadowy history to ask whether, since he went unseen for so long, he could in any real sense be said to exist: a philosophical idea later explored in more depth by Frayn, Stoppard and Terry Johnson. But, principally, Saunders sees the hermit as a universal symbol. And the point is rammed home in a Beckettian speech by the play's authorial figure, Rudge, played at Ealing by the future dramatist, Peter Whelan:

> We are locked in ourselves as he [the hermit] was. We live our lives in a little dungeon as he did. Only for most of the time we forget about it. We have other things to do. We nod, touch hands, gesticulate, dance the ritual dance. But he, you see, had no such pretence. His environment was not a cloak but a reflection – a cell, a prison where he dwelt alone, always alone.

Saunders' writing has shafts of wit and lovely lyrical passages, but one feels it is faintly perverse, and even condescending, to treat an Essex hermit as a representative of all humanity. Behind the play also seemed to lurk what Charles Marowitz called 'a pious negation of the mundane'. Quibble as one may over individual plays, the startling fact is that in the early Sixties, when more people than ever before were in work and Britain was enjoying an affluence unseen since the war, dramatists increasingly turned their attention to people living on the margins of society. You can attribute it, if you wish, to the influence of Beckett. But for me it is confirmation of the truth of Robert Bolt's point in his introduction to A Man For All Seasons: that the more the individual is identified by his material wants and needs, the more he loses his sense of identity.

The helplessness of modern man. The erosion of self. The need for a faith that transcends materialism. These were the recurrent themes of the early Sixties. And dramatists dealt with them in diverse ways. Bolt, Osborne and Whiting tackled them by invoking examples of unyielding integrity from the historic past; Pinter, Rudkin, Bond and Saunders by exploring the dilemma of the derelict or the temperamental outsider. But there was a third strand of drama that was openly political and that took a wide-ranging, satirical look at contemporary Britain and its recent past. It was a time when writers bracingly experimented with form and sought new ways to express their criticism of society; and you see this most clearly in the work of Arnold Wesker, John Arden and the directorial genius, Joan Littlewood. Between them they reminded us of theatre's oppositional role and its capacity to raise questions.

Wesker, for all his failure to appeal instantly to George Devine and Tony Richardson, had already made his mark with the first two thirds of his projected trilogy charting the disintegration of an East End Jewish family, the Kahns, and the collapse of the communist dream. *Chicken Soup With Barley* (1958) was an impressive hindsight saga with a strong emotional climax and *Roots* (1959), showing its heroine liberated from her overbearing intellectual mentor, the unseen Ronnie Kahn, was like an East End version of Shaw's *Pygmalion*. But it was with the final play in the sequence, *I'm Talking About Jerusalem* (1960), that Wesker's purpose became clear: not merely to show communism as the light that failed but to suggest that the post-war Attlee government had foolishly squandered any possibility of creating the new Jerusalem. Not only that: Labour had betrayed its core principles by its endorsement of the nuclear deterrent. One could take issue with many of Wesker's arguments. In showing Ronnie's sister, Ada, and her husband, Dave, retreating to Norfolk and seeing their dream of creating their own furniture business collapse, Wesker implies that socialism is somehow at fault. You could just as easily see Dave and Ada as precursors of the Thatcherite belief in the power of small businesses rather than as inheritors of the William Morris romantic ideal. But, even if one questions Wesker's analysis, his play is one of the first seriously to attack the compromises of the post-war Labour government. And there is no doubting the passion of Ronnie – who clearly speaks for Wesker – in his final assault on the Attlee years: 'They sang the Red Flag in Parliament and then started building atom bombs. Lunatics! Raving lunatics! And a whole generation of us laid down our arms and retreated into ourselves, a whole generation.' Wesker's point is clear: that disillusion leads ultimately to disengagement and impotent solitude.

Much as I admire parts of the *Trilogy*, Wesker generalises wildly from his own experience: whatever the disappointments and setbacks, whatever the failures of the Attlee years, the battle to achieve democratic socialism in Britain was something to be applauded rather than condemned. For my money, there was more subversive subtlety in Wesker's next play, *Chips With Everything*, which opened at the Royal Court in 1962 in another dazzling John Dexter production and which enjoyed simultaneous premieres at Sheffield Playhouse and the Glasgow Citizens'. Wesker's theme was the nature of the class system in Britain: specifically, the means by which a minor act of rebellion by Pip Thompson, a general's son who rejects officer training during National Service, is effectively squashed by his superiors. We see Pip goading his fellow recruits into cultural insurgency at a NAAFI party. He even leads them on a nocturnal raid on a coke store. But the officers are simply biding their time. In the silkily repeated mantra of the Pilot Officer: 'It goes right through us, Thompson. Nothing you can do will change that. We listen but we do not hear, we befriend but do not touch you, we applaud but do not act – to tolerate is to ignore.'

What is astonishing about Wesker is how accurately and intuitively he anticipates many of the arguments of the German-American social philosopher, Herbert Marcuse. In his book, *One-Dimensional Man*, not published in the US till 1964, Marcuse argued that capitalism cunningly anaesthetises the oppressed by manipulating the means of communication so as to stiumulate trivial, material desires: exactly Ronnie's point of view, as voiced through Beatie, in *Roots*. Marcuse's concept of 'repressive tolerance', by which a ruling elite sanctions ineffectual protest, also lay at the heart of *Chips With Everything*. The play's excitement resides as well in its genuine ambivalence. In performance, audiences invariably thrill to the spectacle of awkward, stumbling conscripts being turned into disciplined airmen. And the coke-store raid, which Wesker precisely choreographs in his stage directions, belying the old canard that he owed everything to Dexter's direction, is a tremendous piece of visual theatre. Even the final passing-out parade, in which hitherto uncoordinated individuals march and present arms with total precision, achieves a kind of ironic triumph. We admire the transformation that has been achieved while being reminded that the price you pay for corporate discipline is social conformity and the perpetuation of hierarchy. As so often, contradictory emotions are proof that a piece of political theatre has genuinely worked.

One of Wesker's unsung achievements was gradually to free political theatre from the conventions of naturalism. And the same was true of John Arden who likewise chipped away at the old traditions. In 1963 Arden wrote a big, noisy musical play for the Chichester Festival Theatre, *The Workhouse Donkey*, which he described as a 'vulgar melodrama'; and what was astonishing was Arden's success in jettisoning both the monochrome realism of conventional political drama and the synthetic sugariness of the showbiz musical. Arden's theme was civic corruption; and its embodiment was Charlie Butterthwaite, self-styled 'Napoleon of the North', who made an earlier appearance in *Waters of Babylon* and who ran a Yorkshire industrial town as if it were his private fiefdom. On one level, Arden's play was a Jonsonian social document. Charlie's burglary of the town-hall safe was based on a similar incident in Arden's native Barnsley. The ruination of the sea-green incorruptible Chief Constable, Feng, derived from recent events in Nottingham and the downfall of a police chief splendidly named Athelstan Popkess. And the exposure of a garish clip-joint, owned by a Conservative alderman and offering svelte hostesses to rich clients, had obvious resonances in the year of Profumo's disgrace. This was a provincial England many of us recognised and knew: when I worked, briefly, in Liverpool in the early Sixties I was astonished at the way the local Labour chieftain, Jack Braddock, although personally above reproach, seemed to have the city in the palm of his hand. But Arden's skill lay in mixing social accuracy with unsentimental uplift as characters burst into song out of joyous necessity. In attempting to unionise the Copacabana Club's showgirls, Charlie first announces that 'they're sweet and jetting little wildflies and they deserve our firm attention' before ebulliently singing:

> When I was a young man in my prime
> Hoor ray Santy Anna
> I knocked them yeller gals two at a time
> All on the plains of Mexico.

Watching Frank Finlay's charismatic, disgraced Charlie tipsily transported out of the theatre at the end by his chanting supporters was also to feel, optimistically, that a different kind of theatre was possible: one that combined topical commentary with Dionysiac spectacle. But, although Arden's play was a genuinely liberating experience written in a heightened poetic prose that flamed and soared, it always seemed a bit of an outsider in Chichester: the Sussex audience, as I recall, reacted coolly to the moment when electorate, police and politicians drew up together in defiance of southern England ('We stand all alone to the north of the Trent'). This was a Northern or Midlands play; and its true successors lay in the work undertaken by David Hare and Howard Brenton at Nottingham Playhouse in exploring the sleaze and skulduggery of English provincial life.

But political theatre was changing in the early Sixties. It was going beyond didacticism and dialectic to embrace music, spectacle and song; and one of the most famous and resonant examples was *Oh, What A Lovely War*, produced at the Theatre Royal, Stratford East in 1963. Created by Joan Littlewood, the show was prompted by a Charles Chilton radio series based on the songs of the First World War. But, even though Littlewood transformed a radio anthology into a sensuous satire, she was not the first person to cast a jaundiced eye on that particular war. The poetry of Siegfried Sassoon and Wilfred Owen had famously caught the horror of war with compassionate realism. In Noël Coward's 1931 *Cavalcade* at Drury Lane sentimental recruiting songs led to an image of gassed soldiers trudging over a ramp of duckboards. And Robert Graves in *Goodbye To All That* and Alan Clark in *The Donkeys* had written, with controlled fury, of the appalling human cost of Haig's policy of attrition. But Littlewood's production was the first work of art to see the war almost entirely from the perspective of ordinary soldiers. By its long-running success, both at Stratford East and in the West End, it also helped to sway hearts and minds and induce a pervasive horror at the political and military prosecution of the war. Joan Littlewood recalls in her autobiography that the show 'awakened race memory in our audiences. At the end of each performance people would come on stage bringing memories and mementoes, even lines of dialogue, which sometimes turned up in the show.' And among those credited in the programme were Bert Sweet, who kept the café in Angel Lane next door to the theatre and who supplied his own first-hand reminiscences of life in the trenches. The show was a form of Remembrance Play that helped to launch the oral history movement, and at the same time a piece of radical political theatre: one that attacked all those collectively responsible for the deaths of ten million people.

Littlewood's achievement was not only to arouse our anger and pity but to enlarge the stylistic possibilities of theatre; and she did this in two specific ways. One was by a news panel that ran above the stage and provided the stark information that counterpointed the nostalgia induced by the songs themselves. It was impossible to read a statistic like 'Battle of the Somme Ends . . . Total Loss . . . 1,322,000 Men . . . Gain, Nil' without one's gorge rising. The other brilliantly ironic idea was to clothe the actors in white satin pierrot costumes, redolent of an Edwardian concert party, and add on the military externals as required. For Littlewood the costumes made a political point: 'War is only for clowns.' But the effect, in performance, was to create a world of extraordinary visual elegance and style that contrasted with the horrors being recounted. The whole show, in fact, was built around a series of interlaced oppositions. Military fact against melodic charm. Trench warfare against silken beauty. Lyrics against tunes. At one unforgettable moment, while a harmonium played 'Onward Christian Soldiers', the rankers entered a church singing to the familiar hymn tune:

> Forward Joe Soap's Army, marching without fear
> With our old commander safely in the rear
> He boasts and skites from morn till night
> And thinks he's very brave
> But the men who really did the job
> Are dead and in the grave.

It was as the last words were sung that the statistics about the Somme appeared on the news panel; which sums up, as well as anything, Littlewood's genius for tapping into a maelstrom of contradictory emotions in a way that is unique to theatre.

For all these achievements, not everyone felt cheered by the new movements in theatre of the early Sixties. Charles Marowitz used the columns of *Encore* in autumn 1963 to describe theatre as 'a moribund art-form. It reminds me of that historical truism about empires appearing most confident just before they are due to collapse.' And what Marowitz lamented, in particular, was the absence in England of a laboratory or studio theatre that would peer intently into its own nature to discover something about its own chemistry: exactly the kind of theatre that Peter Brook and Marowitz himself were shortly to set up in a LAMDA experiment that appeared under the generic, Artaudesque title of 'Theatre of Cruelty'. But, whatever the gaps in

British theatre, something of great importance happened in the early Sixties. The creation of the Royal Shakespeare Company and a National Theatre in embryo at the Old Vic represented a major shift away from the haphazard chaos of commercialism towards the coherence of subsidy. And, even if they emerged towards the end of a long period of Conservative rule, these companies embodied many of the values laid down in the post-war Attlee years. In their choice of personnel, they also represented aspects of the sceptical, questioning culture of the Sixties. But theatre in the early Sixties didn't merely reflect the society around it. At its best, it became a means of shifting outlooks and attitudes. The quartet who wrote and performed *Beyond The Fringe* weren't just Oxbridge smart-arses but exceptional talents whose irreverence towards authority was aped and imitated by the impressionable young. *Oh, What A Lovely War* wasn't simply a polemical revue. It was a means of rearranging consciousness so that warmongering appeals to our patriotic instinct could never again be met with blind, unquestioning obedience. Even a Shakespearean reconstruction such as *The Wars of the Roses* jolted us into a heightened awareness of both the addictiveness and brutality of power. Britain, in the early Sixties, was a very different country from the austere, disciplined, deeply hierarchical place it had been in the immediate post-war years. There was greater prosperity, less deference, and a cynicism about those placed in command of our destiny that the Tory sex scandals of 1963 certainly did nothing to lessen. Far from being an innocent bystander, theatre was making its own contribution to the accelerating process of change and growing distrust of the governing Establishment. What was clear was that, after thirteen years in power, the Conservative Party had reached exhaustion point and was on the verge of intellectual collapse. Having helped to destroy the old order, would theatre have the guts and initiative to assist in the creation of the new?

1964–70

Theatre of Opposition

In October 1964 a Labour government achieved power, for the first time in thirteen years, with a precarious majority of four. And a new national mood was established almost the second a victorious Harold Wilson stepped off a train at Euston Station on election night to be asked by the BBC's Anthony Howard what he felt like: 'I feel like a pint,' was Wilson's chirpy response. After eighteen months, in which Labour initiated a good deal of domestic reform, another election was called in 1966 in which Labour increased its overall majority to ninety-seven. It remained in power until June 1970 when, with the economy looking sound, the opinion polls highly favourable and the Conservatives apparently lurching insanely toward pre-Keynesian, free-market economics, Labour sleepwalked into an election which it proceeded to lose. But those six years of Labour government, which it is now fashionable to deride, achieved a great deal and helped to create a more liberal, tolerant and equitable Britain. They were also good years for the theatre. In retrospect, the period from 1964 to 1970 looks like a golden age: an equivalent to the first Elizabethan era in which a wealth of new writing was accompanied by a prodigious amount of theatre building and a quest for new expressive forms. Yet productivity did not mean political passivity. Just as the theatre had helped to expose the moral decay and geriatric incompetence of the Tory government in its final years, so now it turned its sights on the Wilson administration for its alleged failure to achieve radical change, its subservience to America over the Vietnam war and its transformation of Britain into a glitzy showbiz society. If we learned anything in the Sixties it was that the theatre had acquired a decisive new role: that of a more-or-less permanent opposition to whichever party was in power.

Ironically, during its six years in office the Labour government achieved many reforms that either benefited the theatre greatly or

echoed its liberal sympathies. One of Wilson's most inspired appoint-
ments was that of Jennie Lee – Aneurin Bevan's widow – as Minister
for the Arts. Working closely with the ubiquitous Pooh-Bah-like figure
of Lord Goodman as Chairman of the Arts Council, Lee oversaw an
exponential rise in the Council's budget from £3.2 million in 1964 to
£9 million in 1970. I even recall Wilson boasting, admittedly during a
campaign speech in 1966 in Lee's Govan constituency, of Labour's
passionate commitment to the arts. For the theatre, it was not only
revenue funding that rose. New buildings also popped up all over the
country. In fact, there were more spectacular erections than in an old-
style Windmill Theatre audience. Brighton and Leatherhead in the
south, Exeter in the west, Worcester in the Midlands, Leeds, Sheffield,
Bolton, Chester and Newcastle in the north and Stirling in Scotland all
acquired gleaming new playhouses. A new theatre became a badge of
civic pride even if questions about its future funding were often eva-
sively shelved. But Labour's most crucial gesture was its endorsement
of the Theatres Act of 1968 which finally abolished the power of the
Lord Chamberlain to license theatre productions. Over 230 years of
stifling state power was ended at a stroke: no longer would writers and
directors have to go cap in hand to argue the toss over deleted exple-
tives, intimations of sexual intercourse, references to the Deity or the
representation of living persons on stage. Although Nicholas de Jongh
argues in *Politics, Prudery and Perversions* that Wilson was personally nervous about giving the stage the freedom to ridicule public figures
such as the Queen, the Prime Minister and foreign heads of state, the
evidence produced by a select parliamentary committee was overwhelming: the Lord Chamberlain's arbitrary powers had become an
anachronistic absurdity in an age of free speech.

As private citizens, most people in the theatre welcomed the rush of
liberal reforms that Labour either sanctioned or initiated in the course
of six hectic years. In 1965 the veteran left-winger, Sidney Silverman,
was given parliamentary time to put through a private member's bill
for the abolition of hanging, initially for a trial period of five years: in
1969 a new Home Secretary, James Callaghan, made the abolition
permanent. Roy Jenkins' benign stewardship at the Home Office from
1965 to 1967 also saw homosexual relations between consenting
adults cease to be a criminal offence: a major piece of legislation that
helped to erode the climate of fear that had, amongst many other ill
effects, threatened the careers of several theatrical luminaries.

Women's groups welcomed the legalisation of abortion: the result of a private member's bill in 1967 promoted by the young Liberal, David Steel. And the passage of the Race Relations Act in 1965, and the subsequent creation of the Race Relations Board, at least addressed – if it did not end – the odious practice of racial discrimination. Those who accuse the Wilson government of betraying its radical principles ignore the myriad ways in which it made Britain a more tolerant and civilised society.

But Britain changed in many ways in the Sixties. A defining moment arrived, early on in the Wilson years, with the death of Winston Churchill in January 1965. And Churchill's momentous state funeral, in which the coffin was transported on a gun carriage from the Palace of Westminster to St Paul's Cathedral through the crowded, leaden-skied streets, led to a rush of metaphors. The funeral was seen as the eclipse of national heroism, an act of mourning for the imperial past, the final act in Britain's greatness. Bernard Levin in *The Pendulum Years* saw it as the moment when national unity and faith in great men, which Churchill represented, departed once and for all, and when Britain shook off its past and confronted an uncomfortable future. All symbolism aside, the funeral itself was a highly theatrical occasion as the *Observer*'s Patrick O'Donovan realised:

> The coffin moved, huge and red with the Union flag, past the hotels and steamy restaurants and the newspaper offices and pubs, surrounded by this extraordinary silence, not of grief but of respect. In fact the City was stopped and was turned into a theatre and it was all performed as a drama that all men understand.

The sense of theatricality was compounded by the fact that, for those watching the funeral on ITV, the commentary was delivered by Laurence Olivier. Meanwhile on BBC we heard the sonorous tones of another actor, Tom Fleming. Churchill's funeral was both magnificent theatre and a historical watershed: something quickly grasped at the time. Tom Stoppard, then an obscure young journalist, chose Churchill's funeral as the backdrop for the macabre farce of his first novel, *Lord Malquist and Mr Moon*, published in 1966. But, far from defacing a national monument, Stoppard implicitly endorsed Lord Malquist's point that history was 'a drama directed by great men' and that the post-Churchill era would be random, chaotic and even possibly violent. Other writers were less charitable to the departed colossus: in the years to come Charles Wood, Joe Orton and Howard Brenton would see Churchill as an aggressive warmonger, a comic icon or a symbol of political repression.

Change was in the air well before the Churchill funeral: irreverence, mockery, subversion of tradition were all around us in the early Sixties. But in the post-Churchillian world there was an increasing sense that all public life was an arena for performance. The fashion-conscious young strutted along Chelsea's King's Road on a Saturday afternoon in all their peacock finery as if taking part in a theatrical costume parade. The verbal and visual arts both aspired to the condition of theatre: Allen Ginsberg read his extravagant poem, 'Howl!', to a packed Albert Hall while the ICA exhibited a huge plastic tube which visitors entered and walked about inside as if they themselves were on show. Television also benefited from its palpable actuality. It was on a live late-night chat-show in 1965 that Kenneth Tynan (who else?) became the first person to say 'fuck' on British television, while two years later Mick Jagger, given a suspended sentence following a charge of illegal possession of amphetamines, was helicoptered into a Sussex garden to be solemnly interviewed by the editor of The Times and senior churchmen. Even the huge anti-Vietnam war demo that took place in Grosvenor Square in October 1968, while motivated by political passion, acquired theatrical overtones. Tariq Ali, one of its prime movers, explained that he was summoned the day before by members of the Redgrave family to ensure that Vanessa Redgrave was duly protected in the melee. It also seemed fitting that Mick Jagger, who had been on the demo, wrote 'Street Fighting Man' to express his disappointment at the marchers' lack of battle-readiness. Politics was quickly absorbed into pop culture; and, although the pervasive image of the metropolitan Sixties is that of a druggy hedonism, far more significant was the way society itself turned into a performance arena. As the actress-heroine of John Osborne's Time Present, written in 1968, claims: 'You're all in Show Business now. Everybody. Books, politics, journalism, you're all banging the drum, all performers now.'

If society itself was becoming a theatrical spectacle, where did that leave the theatre? What was its role in the newly liberated High Sixties? As a community, theatre benefited greatly from Labour's infusion of cash and its liberalising laws. Truculent dramatists and discontented companies, however, increasingly saw theatre as a vehicle of protest and became even more ferociously oppositional than they had been during thirteen years of Conservative government. It was to become a repeated pattern in the rare interludes of twentieth-century Labour rule and one easily explained. From the Conservatives little is expected in the way of social progress, whereas Labour is always judged by an imaginary radical Utopia which it regularly fails to build. Labour achieved much in the Sixties: social liberalisation, the creation of the Open University, the final dismantling of empire, increased public spending on schools and hospitals. But incremental reform is not enough: Labour is always expected to build the new Jerusalem within six months of taking office and is always castigated for failing.

Admittedly in the Sixties there were some grounds for a growing disenchantment with the Labour administration. 1967 was a particular *annus horribilis*: one that saw devaluation of the pound, the second veto by General de Gaulle of our application to join the EEC, a standoff with the Rhodesian leader, Ian Smith, whose white minority government had unilaterally declared independence. 1968 brought with it a massive sterling crisis and student uprisings in Paris (*les événements*), which spread the prospect of revolution throughout Europe and which fed into violent anti-Vietnam protests in America and Britain itself. Those who had warmly welcomed Wilson's advent in 1964 turned on him in the late Sixties for his subscription to American foreign policy and its prosecution of an unwinnable guerrilla war; it was only in the light of history, and in particular, Tony Blair's military zeal over Iraq, that Wilson came to be praised for his honourable resistance to pressure from President Johnson to send British troops to the combat zone.

If some of the sheen came off the Wilson government in its later years, it was in part because of events beyond its control. Everywhere you looked there was a rejection of imposed authority. Student demos and sit-ins were the order of the day, not just in such familiar battle-grounds as the London School of Economics but also in the staid quadrangles of Oxford and Cambridge colleges. Soft drugs were freely used, even though the government rejected the Wootton committee's recommendation that cannabis should be legalised. Revolutionary figures such as Bolivia's Che Guevara, Germany's Daniel Cohn-Bendit ('Danny the Red') and Britain's Tariq Ali became popular icons. The High Sixties, as historian Arthur Marwick labelled the period, was an era of agitational fervour and revolutionary optimism; and, even if much of the idealism on display eventually ran into the ground, it had a huge effect on the culture. And not least on the British theatre. The late Sixties saw an explosion of offbeat, countercultural metropolitan activity that came to be institutionalised as 'the fringe'; much of it started, intriguingly, by bearded, renegade Americans. Jim Haynes, who back in 1963 had created the sixty-seat Traverse Theatre in Edinburgh, now launched the amiably chaotic Arts Lab in a dingy cellar in Drury Lane. Charles Marowitz, aided by Thelma Holt, created the influential Open Space off the Tottenham Court Road. And Ed Berman, a zany visionary and astute self-publicist, spearheaded the new lunchtime theatre movement in Baywsater's Ambiance Theatre, where one cheerfully munched one's sandwiches while watching various forms of sexual congress. But one of the most significant moves came in 1969 when the Royal Court opened the Theatre Upstairs in a tiny room, previously a private club, at the top of the building: the first time a mainstream theatre recognised the need for an ancillary studio space, thus paving the way for a proliferation of 'black-box' theatres. The Sixties was a period of ferment in which everything suddenly seemed possible. Theatre, it was widely assumed, not only had a duty to scrutinise and question the political status quo. It also had an obligation to experiment with new forms and to examine its reasons for existence.

One person who strongly believed in theatre's self-questioning quality was Peter Brook; and, by following the trajectory of his career from 1964 to the end of the decade, one gets a good idea of the way theatre of the period was engaged simultaneously in a passionate social critique and a search for new forms. As an associate director of the RSC with a ground-breaking *King Lear* to his credit, Brook could easily have become part of the Stratford assembly line. Instead he embarked on a series of experiments that were to reorient his life and career and lead to some of the most startling productions of the decade. And at the centre of Brook's thinking was Antonin Artaud, whose subversive manifesto, *The Theatre and its Double*, had been published in France in 1938. Jean-Louis Barrault once called it 'far and away the most important thing that has been written about theatre in the 20th century'. For a rationalist English critic like Laurence Kitchin, who wrote extensively for *The Times*, it was 'the bible of sick theatre'. Artaud's imagination, claimed Kitchin, 'is cluttered with the shopworn cliches of romanticism': the Noble Savage fallacy, the cult of orientalism, the belief in narcotics. But although much of Artaud's doctrine, such as the dismissal of classical drama as bourgeois conformism, is perverse and nonsensical, it appealed very directly to the irrationalism of the Sixties. At a time when language was in question, Artaud attacked 'the subjugation of the theatre to the text'. He called for the dissolution of the old duality between author and director, to be replaced 'by a sort of unique Creator upon whom will devolve the double responsibility of the spectacle and the plot'. And he envisaged a theatre that would embody the spectators' dreams, 'in which his taste for crime, his erotic obsessions, his savagery, his chimeras, his utopian sense of life and matter, even his cannibalism pour out on a level not counterfeit and illusory but interior'. Dissatisfied with existing theatrical forms and aware that he had explored the limits of his own versatility, Brook found in Artaud exactly the imaginative stimulus he needed; but he combined his explorations of Artaud with his own highly developed sense of English pragmatism.

Anxious to conduct experiments with a hand-picked group of actors, Brook was given complete freedom by Peter Hall at the RSC to carry out an eight-week research project with no obligation to provide a public performance: something previously unheard of in the productivity-based British theatre. But, believing that even an experimental project needs to be tested in front of an audience, Brook eventually staged a 'work in progress' entitled 'Theatre of Cruelty' at the London Academy of Music and Dramatic Art (LAMDA) in January 1964. In later years, Brook described it to me as the turning point in his career: the moment when he became fascinated as much by the process as the product and began to use theatre to investigate form. It is characteristic of Brook, however, that he needed to expose his findings to the public gaze, and the resulting show became rather like a surrealist revue. It comprised, in a kaleidoscopically shifting programme, two versions of Artaud's own *Spurt of Blood*, a short play by John Arden and Margaretta D'Arcy, a wordless version of a short story by Alain Robbe-Grillet and a twenty-minute collage on *Hamlet* by Brook's co-director, Charles Marowitz. But the item that captured people's imagination was a piece devised by Brook himself, *The Public Bath*, that subliminally linked Christine Keeler and Jackie Kennedy. It started with Glenda Jackson appearing dressed in the standard gear of a high-class tart, complete with tight black dress and high-heeled shoes. Jackson then did an antiseptic strip and was placed in a tin bath where she was washed and dressed before emerging in rough, shapeless clothes. As she knelt patiently beside the bath, imaginatively transformed into a coffin, she seemed to become the mourning widow of the US President. As Michael Kustow, Brook's biographer, put it: 'The audience was left with the sight of a grieving woman, the Madonna and the Whore, exposed to "the public bath" – the bath of voyeurism, sexual fantasy, vicarious emotion – a curdle of emotions repeated nearly half a century later when Princess Diana died.' Even an Artaudesque experiment with form was thus turned by Brook into a piece of social criticism.

Having assembled what he once described to me as 'this little experimental group', Brook was determined to hold on to it. Out of the 'Theatre of Cruelty' season stemmed a trial run of the first twelve scenes of Genet's *The Screens*, staged privately in the Donmar Rehearsal Rooms in Covent Garden. Again Brook was able to combine formal experiment with moral investigation, in that Genet's play is an assault on the barbarity of French colonialism. But, when two representatives of the Lord Chamberlain came to see it, their intemperate reaction ('open and sadistic enjoyment of filth and cruelty') made it clear that the play would never be publicly licensed. So, at the suggestion of the BBC's Martin Esslin, Brook turned his attention to a German play by Peter Weiss accurately known as *The Persecution and Assassination of Marat as Performed by the Inmates of the Asylum of Charenton under the Direction of the Marquis de Sade*. 'Have you seen the play?' a colleague whispered to Alan Brien as the house lights went down on the first night at the Aldwych in August 1964. 'No,' replied Brien, 'but I've read the title.'

Brook's production of what became popularly known as *The Marat/Sade* was a crucial event in the culture of the mid-Sixties. For a start Weiss's text articulated a standard, dialectical debate of the time: one between a Utopian (Marat), who believed that society can only be changed by violent revolution, and a sexual visionary (Sade), who argued that the world could be transformed through individuals using their unrestricted imaginations to unlock the 'cells of the inner self'. Brook's rehearsal techniques, in which the actors explored the paintings of Bruegel, Bosch and Goya, held meetings with psychoanalysts and paid visits to mental hospitals, required the performers to 'find the madmen in themselves': Brook was asking his actors not so much to impersonate as to embody sundry forms of insanity. Out of this he created an extraordinary theatrical spectacle that explored different levels of reality. We, the audience, were watching spectators at a Charenton asylum in 1808 who were themselves voyeuristically observing the inmates re-enacting the murder of Marat (Clive Revill) by Charlotte Corday (Glenda Jackson) as conceived and staged by Sade (Patrick Magee). At the end our own role came into question as the inmates, having run riot in an orgy of rape and violence, were brought under control by a whistle-blowing stage manager and then turned towards us and ironically mimed our applause. Brook turned Weiss's dialectical drama, which reached no fixed conclusion, into a dislocating Artaudesque spectacle. But a sharp reminder of the residual conservatism of the West End Establishment came shortly after the production opened in the late summer of 1964. Emile Littler, a governor of the RSC, commercial producer Keith Prowse, owner of London's largest ticket agency, and Peter Cadbury, a right-wing moralist, used *The Marat/Sade* as a prime vehicle with which to attack Peter Hall for putting on 'dirty plays' at the Aldwych. From one angle, it was a typical British silly-season story. But although the row eventually died down after Littler resigned as an RSC governor and privately apologised, it had wider theatrical and social reverberations. It revealed the continuing opposition to the RSC's presence in London. It re-ignited the debate about theatrical censorship. It was also a reminder that, even in the progressive Sixties, there were still those who resented what they saw as the destruction of traditional values. The chairman of the RSC, Sir Fordham Flower, found that his office was deluged with letters supportive of Littler's views about 'dirty plays', even if few of the correspondents had seen the work they condemned. Indeed their vehemence was reminiscent of that of Mary Whitehouse and her National Viewers' and Listeners' Association, which eagerly monitored the airwaves. *Lady Chatterley* was no longer banned. The BBC, under its enlightened Director-General Hugh Carleton Greene, promoted topical satire and agitational drama. And sexual intercourse, as Philip Larkin later ironically reminded us, 'began in ninety sixty-three'. But the 'dirty plays' row, although pumped up by the press, showed that Britain was still a divided nation in which large sectors of the population were wary of the new artistic freedoms.

Undeterred, Peter Brook continued his own investigations into the nature of theatre. Early in 1965 he gave a series of lectures, at the invitation of Granada TV's Sidney Bernstein, which resulted in a book called *The Empty Space*: still a well-thumbed bible for students and theatre practitioners all over the world for its enlightening analysis of Deadly, Rough, Holy and Immediate Theatre. As Michael Kustow shrewdly claims, 'With its touchstone of Shakespeare and the Elizabethan, *The Empty Space* is very English but in its dialectic and search for universals, it is very French.' To put it another way, the genius of Brook's book lay in its mixture of the pragmatic and the visionary. To argue, for instance, that what remains behind after a great performance is an ineradicable central image was a statement of a basic truth. But to suggest that theatre contains within itself a metaphor for spiritual renewal, that it is always on the move and that its special virtue is that 'the slate is wiped clean all the time', was to offer an inspirational vision of theatre as a medium in a state of perpetual revolution.

In a sense, Brook was rationalising from his own experience: all his work in the Sixties, and well beyond, sought to escape deadly repetition and use theatre for a process of moral and formal investigation. And *The Investigation* was, in fact, the title of the Peter Weiss documentary-play, based on concentration-camp trials recently concluded in Frankfurt, to which Brook next turned his attention. But although Brook and David Jones gave a late-night public reading of Weiss's play at the Aldwych in October 1965, Brook was still searching for other ways to engage with public issues; and at the time none was bigger than the Vietnam War. It was President Kennedy who in 1961 had first committed military 'advisers' to Vietnam to combat what Americans saw as the domino effect of Asian Communism. By 1964 the US had fifteen thousand troops in Vietnam. After an attack on an American destroyer in the Gulf of Tonkin, the authenticity of which was later questioned, the numbers steadily escalated, and by 1965 Lyndon Johnson was irrevocably committed to a hopeless and unwinnable war. It was a war greeted with hostility, bewilderment and a sense of impotent anguish in Britain: even the Prime Minister's vain attempts at peacemaking had been met by Walt Rostow, President Johnson's special adviser, with a dismissive 'We don't give a damn about Wilson'.

For Brook it was vital that the theatre test itself against the big public issue of the day. Once again Peter Hall, to his credit, sanctioned a fourteen-week rehearsal period for an experimental process that would start without a script but would ideally lead to a mainstage RSC production: the result, *US*, finally opened at the Aldwych in October 1966 and, whatever its detractors may have claimed, was historically informative, theatrically gripping and a goad to the liberal conscience. The first half, jointly created by Adrian Mitchell, Geoffrey Reeves, Albert Hunt and composer Richard Peaslee, used many of the techniques of pop culture to offer a kaleidosopic history of Vietnam and of America's fatal intervention in the war between North and South: the climax was an American bombing raid, recreated with ear-shattering sound and the descent of a thirty-six-foot-high puppet from the proscenium arch. But the second half, both more meditative and more provocative, began with a dialogue about what could be done in the way of demonstration against the war. This reached its climax in a speech, written by Denis Cannan and memorably delivered by Glenda Jackson, which argued that only by experiencing our own Vietnam could we begin to understand the horrors of war:

> I would like to smell the running bowels of fear over the English Sunday morning smell of gin and roasting joint and hyacinth. I would like to see an English dog playing on an English lawn with part of a burned hand. I would like to see a gas grenade go off at an English flower show and nice English ladies crawling in each other's sick. And all this I would like to be photographed and filmed so that someone a long way off, safe in his chair, could watch us in our indignity.

The speech greatly antagonised Mitchell and Hunt, both of whom threatened to dissociate themselves from the production: their argument was that they wanted to stop the war altogether rather than transpose it to Britain and that the speech allowed a *bien pensant*, middle-class Aldwych audience to wallow in its own futility. The speech nonetheless stayed in and, far more than the symbolic burning of a paper butterfly that ended the evening, acted as an imaginative wake-up call to those still unable to conceive of the horrors of war. It was shock tactics if you like. But the speech achieved through language what Sarah Kane's *Blasted*, thirty years later, attempted through visceral imagery: it delivered a blow to the solar plexus and aroused an English audience from its habitual state of moral detachment. Inevitably *US* attracted fierce opposition from both right and left. An MP from South Antrim demanded the withholding of RSC funds on the grounds that the show was 'full of poisonous anti-American propaganda'. Meanwhile Kenneth Tynan, who was trying to persuade the National to mount a production about the Cuban missile crisis, sour-grapishly attacked the show as 'ignorant and tepid' and Charles Marowitz, Brook's quondam collaborator, lambasted its 'failure to elucidate and give a positive lead'. But what did they want? *US* could hardly be expected to stop the Vietnam war, provide a blueprint for action or modify the British government's attitude of passive support for the Johnson administration. What the show did do, very powerfully and emotionally, was contextualise the war, heighten public consciousness, and make it more rather than less likely that an individual spectator would be spurred to some form of protest. At the very least, *US* showed that theatre was a politically relevant medium: one that could challenge the hegemony of TV and newspapers by confronting the big moral topic of the day.

All Brook's productions in the Sixties, however, raised crucial questions. How does theatre tackle burning contemporary issues? Does text still enjoy its old aristocratic supremacy? How is the role of the actor changing? And, with his production of Seneca's *Oedipus* for the National Theatre at the Old Vic in 1968, Brook raised yet another key question: is ritual magic possible in a secular society? I'm not sure he answered the question. But *Oedipus* was undeniably virtuosic. For a start Ted Hughes's translation of Seneca's play had a rich poetic immediacy. The production also yielded unforgettable sights and sounds. As we entered the theatre a huge gold cube revolved centre-stage while actors were strapped to the Old Vic's columns like caryatids: an effect somewhat disconcerting to Sir Ralph Richardson who, going in search of cast information, claimed the programme-sellers were all lashed to pillars. As the action progressed the chorus, scattered throughout the theatre, became an orchestra of wind instruments driving the tragedy forwards. The blinding of Oedipus was mimetically suggested by John Gielgud, tense and ramrod-backed, placing two patches of black over his eyes: a far cry from the howling animalistic realism of Olivier in the Sophoclean *Oedipus Rex* twenty-three years before. At Jocasta's suicide, Irene Worth lowered herself onto a sharp spike while emitting deep rhythmic groans. And the carnivalesque release that followed classical tragedy was evoked by the eruption of a carriage bearing a fifteen-foot-high gold phallus and the sound of a jazz band brassily rendering 'Yes, we have no bananas'. Brook's initial idea was that cast and audience should join together in a wild, orgiastic version of 'God Save The Queen': this was firmly vetoed by Olivier but, tricked into accepting

Brook's alternative, he claimed that 'Peter had dealt a shrewder blow to my *amour propre* than he could have known'.

Stripping classical tragedy of its false accretions, Brook's production got down to the square root of suffering. It was also an important stage in his quest for greater simplicity. But, for all its brilliance, there seemed something self-conscious about the attempt to revive the ambience of antique tragedy and satyr play in the Waterloo Road. As Ronald Bryden wrote in the *Observer*, 'It's impossible to believe that Brook seriously supposes his production can work as a ritual. It is ritualistic, using rite as an ornament.' And Martin Esslin made a similar point in *Plays and Players*: 'Is ritual possible for sceptics, unbelievers? I doubt it very much. The only sphere of primeval awe and primitive emotion left to twentieth century mass man is sex. That is why all ritualistic theatre nowadays has to veer towards sexual shocks and images.' Brook had certainly posed a question that was to haunt succeeding generations of theatre-makers: how do you recreate the rituals of the past for a modern spectator? Peter Hall, in his future productions of Greek classics, would opt for masks and archaeological verisimilitude. Mark Rylance, in his ten-year span at Shakespeare's Globe (1995–2005), would follow even the most sombre tragedy with a rumbustious Elizabethan jig. But ritual is something that stems either from genuine religious beliefs or shared social customs: since, on the whole, we lack those today, any attempt to recreate the ceremonial aspect of theatre inevitably seems a matter of directorial choice. Brook's *Oedipus* wasn't an authentic rite: more a radical attempt to find a new way of doing classical tragedy.

Brook in the Sixties was like an introspective magician: aware of his own formidable powers but constantly asking to what use they should be put and what function theatre possessed. Given his own Prospero-like self-questioning, it was not surprising that when Brook was invited by Jean-Louis Barrault to stage a Shakespeare play for Paris's annual Théâtre des Nations, he chose *The Tempest*; except, crucially, Brook said that he'd prefer not to do a finished production but to use the play as the basis for an international workshop drawing together actors from Britain, France and Japan. Then *les événements*, involving student-led street demonstrations against the government, erupted in Paris in May 1968 and Brook was forced to shift his research process to London: a reminder that even someone who believes the theatre should be in a state of perpetual revolution finds it difficult to cope with constant political upheaval. But eventually *The Tempest* was exposed to public inspection at the Roundhouse in Chalk Farm and the result was a fascinating piece of collage Shakespeare. Also one that left behind many resonant images: a kimono-clad Yoshi Oida restoring a group of stricken bodies to life as Miranda distantly chanted the 'brave new world' speech, and Barry Stanton's burly Caliban emerging from Sycorax's thighs and learning from Prospero the language that brought him closer to enslavement. By exploring the fusion of word and image, Brook was unconsciously preparing the ground for what, two years later, would become one of the most celebrated Shakespeare productions of modern times: his Stratford *Midsummer Night's Dream*. By working with a multi-national cast, Brook was also prefiguring his later Paris researches. But what made Brook such a significant figure in the Sixties was his ability to keep asking subversively awkward questions. What is theatre for? What meaning does it have for a modern audience? How can it reflect the form and pressure of the time? Brook was not simply interested in blind-alley experiment: he always wanted to engage with the audience and confront major moral issues such as Vietnam and the Holocaust. Behind his sophisticated showmanship there also lay a childlike inquisitiveness about the way things worked. I've seen Brook in many situations, including radio and TV studios, asking naive, practical questions about day-to-day mechanical operations that everyone else took for granted. Part of Brook's genius has been to retain that same spirit of inquiry about his own chosen medium. And, if he symbolised a crucial aspect of the Sixties, it was because he took nothing on trust and posed fundamental questions about theatre and society at large.

The one frustrating aspect of Brook's Sixties work was his lack of engagement with living British dramatists: the man who had worked with Fry, Eliot, Whiting and Cannan in the Fifties directed only one solo-authored text by a British playwright in the Sixties and that was *La Danse de Sergent Musgrave* in Paris in 1963. Brook, in effect, turned his back on a whole generation of British writers, all of whom, like him, were questioning established values. As society itself turned into a form of showbiz spectacle, it was left to dramatists to anatomise Britain and to question its sexual, political and moral standards, to delve into issues of class and race and to ask whether a Labour government had really instituted fundamental change. Good and interesting novels were written in the Sixties by the likes of Anthony Burgess, Margaret Drabble, Angela Carter, Doris Lessing, William Trevor, John Fowles and Angus Wilson along with the old respected firm of Evelyn Waugh, Anthony Powell and C. P. Snow. British cinema, too, showed sparks of liveliness with Joseph Losey's *Accident*, Lindsay Anderson's *If*, Ken Loach's *Kes*, John Schlesinger's *Darling*, Ken Russell's *Women in Love*. And TV drama acquired a new urgency with *Cathy Come Home*, innovative both for dealing with an important social topic – homelessness – and for being shot almost entirely in real locations. Film and television undoubtedly reflected the mood of the times. But theatre had a greater capacity to act as society's permanent house critic and to produce work of lasting literary value; and, at a time when the supremacy of text was subjected to rigorous Artaudesque inquiry, it was cheering to find a whole new generation of dramatists confirming the vitality of language. Somewhat arbitrarily one can divide them into three categories: Disturbers of the Peace, Anatomists of Albion and Contemporary Classicists. These are rough-and-ready divisions that obviously overlap. But the nice paradox of the High Sixties is that increased subsidy led to an explosion of dissent, and that subvention proved no barrier to subversion.

One genuine disturber of the peace was actually a highly commercial dramatist, Joe Orton, whose shockingly brief biography has turned him into a period icon. Born into a working-class Leicester family in 1933, Orton studied acting at RADA where he met his partner Kenneth Halliwell. He was later imprisoned for six months for stealing and defacing library books and enjoyed instant fame with *Entertaining Mr Sloane* (1964) and *Loot* (1965) before being brutally murdered in August 1967 by the unsuccessful Halliwell. But Orton's fame was, if anything, enhanced by the posthumously noisy production of *What The Butler Saw* (1969), by the publication of his sensational *Diaries* (1986) and the transformation of his life into a highly successful film, *Prick Up Your Ears* (1987). In a sense Orton was an archetypal child of the Sixties in that he moved from utter obscurity to scandalous fame in four short years. Through his success he was able to hobnob with the Beatles, put in charmingly mendacious appearances on chat-shows and indulge his sexual appetites in north London 'cottages' and trips to Morocco, where the young local populace was duly colonised. Ronald Bryden wittily dubbed him 'the Oscar Wilde of Welfare State gentility' and John Lahr has claimed that

Orton's plays 'caught the era's psychopathic mood, that restless pursuit of sensation whose manic frivolity announced a refusal to suffer'.

It is tempting to see Orton's sudden spurt of fame and appalling, bloody death as some kind of paradigm of Sixties life or moralistic metaphor. But the mundane truth is that Orton simply seemed unaware of the looming domestic disaster or the marginalised Halliwell's breakdown: as Peter Ackroyd said in reviewing the *Diaries*, 'it is a terrible irony that Orton could invent the grotesque or the macabre without recognising it when it was in front of his nose.' What really makes Orton a quintessential Sixties writer is his combination of a relentless cynicism about authority with an impudently formal style. Orton's world is one in which all power corrupts, all institutions are contaminated and avarice, greed, lust and hypocrisy are the driving forces in human life. But, even though I find the absence of any implied moral positive limiting, I am always tickled by the fastidious elegance of his language.

Language is the key; and Harold Hobson got it exactly right when he compared *Entertaining Mr Sloane* in 1964 to Jane Austen's *Northanger Abbey*. The sustained joke in both lies in the contrast between the Gothic strangeness of the subject and the formal gravity of the style. Set in a solitary house in the middle of a rubbish dump, Orton's play shows the stalking of the eponymous lodger's cock by his landlady, Kath, and of his arse by her businessman brother, Ed. The subversiveness lies in Orton's vision of sex as a bargaining chip and of life as a series of tactical erotic manouevres. But the humour derives from the characters' ability to mask their desires under periphrastic camouflage or stately verbal rhythms. 'Until I was fifteen I was more familiar with Africa than my own body,' announces the nymphomaniac Kath. And Sloane, invoking a previous encounter with an enthusiast for the adolescent male body, tells the voracious Ed, 'If you were to make the same demands, I'd answer loudly in the affirmative.' But Orton went much further in *Loot*, which extended the boundaries of farce by taking it out of the bedroom and into the funeral parlour: this is Feydeau with fangs or Ben Travers rewritten by a social anarchist. The action hinges on the stolen loot being stashed in a coffin while the displaced corpse is bundled around the stage. The physical mayhem, however, simply becomes a platform for an attack on the hypocrisies of mourning, the fake pieties of the Catholic Church and the venal brutality of the British police: Orton's manic Inspector Truscott actually uses one of the lines of Detective Sergeant Harold Challenor, who in 1965 was suspended from the force for his brutally unsavoury methods, when he cries, 'You're fucking nicked, my old beauty.' But, even in topical satire, Orton remains a consummate stylist. At one point Truscott proudly announces that he is the man who once tracked down the limbless girl killer. 'Who', someone enquires aghast, 'would kill a limbless girl?' 'She', replies Truscott, 'was the killer.' It is the application of such poker-faced verbal precision to a play about corpse-switching, serial killing and police brutality that gives *Loot* its perennial appeal.

The irony is that Orton's most radically satirical play and the one most in tune with fashionable Sixties thinking, *What The Butler Saw*, had the roughest ride in the theatre. Disastrously, and posthumously, produced at the Queen's Theatre in 1969, it prompted a display of mob hostility from the gallery unknown since the heady days of Osborne's *The World Of Paul Slickey*. Orton's offence was to have written a Royal Court play for a West End audience; and, by subverting stock responses to sex, insanity and Winston Churchill, Orton duly offended the commercial theatre's beleaguered moralists. For a start Orton questioned the whole notion of gender classification. Fair enough, you'd have thought, at a time of increasing androgyny when even a verifiable hetero like Mick Jagger performed at a Hyde Park rock concert wearing a dress; but too much for a West End audience still wedded to the idea of the manly man and the womanly woman. By setting his farce in a psychiatric clinic, Orton was also popularising ideas that R. D. Laing had explored in *The Divided Self* (1959) and *Sanity, Madness and the Family* (1964): especially the notion that doctors were all too ready to collude with families in labelling as 'mad' any brand of social nonconformity, and that the dividing line between madness and sanity was increasingly blurred. At one point Orton's psychiatric hero, Dr Prentice, announces, 'I've been too long among the mad to know what sanity is': a very Laingian line but, again, too much for a West End audience. But the final insult was a running gag involving the penis from an exploding statue of Winston Churchill which had become embedded in an old lady's body. Surveying the outsize member, a government inspector filled with wartime memories cries: 'How much more inspiring if, in those dark days, we'd seen what we see now. Instead we had to be content with a cigar – the symbol falling far short, as all realise, of the object itself.' The phallic finale put the kibosh on a premiere that had been punctuated with pre-mature ejaculations from the gallery of 'Rubbish', 'Filth' and 'Shame'. Orton's play was partly the victim of a poor production by Robert Chetwyn that, by casting Ralph Richardson as the visiting inspector, aroused false expectations. But its rowdy reception was also a salutary reminder that plays could still shock. The award-strewn and highly profitable *Entertaining Mr Sloane* and *Loot* (for which the film rights alone earned Orton £100,000) had suggested that subversion was in danger of becoming the new orthodoxy. *What The Butler Saw* proved that, even in the permissive Sixties, you could still disturb the public peace by joking, in elegantly Firbankian language, about sex, sanity and the size of Churchill's cock.

Orton's antic spirit may have stirred things up even when he was in his grave. But it was violence, which had rumbled through the previous decade, that became, even more than sex, the defining artistic issue of the Sixties. In 1964 the ICA, ever alive to current trends, staged an important exhibition on Violence in Society, Nature and Art: one sentence that leaps out of the catalogue claims that 'anthropologists will demonstrate that both sane and insane expressions of violence are culturally determined'. And that was precisely the issue raised by one of the key plays of the decade, which not only shifted the boundaries of taste but also triggered a series of events that led to a change in the law. The dramatist was Edward Bond and the play was *Saved*: one of those rare works of art, like Stravinsky's *The Rite of Spring* or Picasso's *Les Demoiselles d'Avignon*, that can be said to have rearranged the cultural landscape. Like most such landmarks, it was also brusquely savaged on its first appearance. In particular a scene of infanticide, in which a sleeping baby is stoned to death in its pram by a gang of youths in a south London park, caused revulsion and outrage when the play was produced at the Royal Court in 1965. W. A. Darlington in the *Daily Telegraph* announced that 'my only emotion was cold disgust at being asked to sit through such a scene'. The more analytical Irving Wardle in *The Times* concluded a hostile notice by arguing that the play, having failed to illuminate violence, 'amounts to a systematic degradation of the human animal'. J. W. Lambert in the *Sunday Times* widened the attack on Bond to include plays by other authors such as *Afore Night Come* and *The Marat/Sade*, concluding that 'we are being offered not a keenly understanding, and therefore implicitly compassionate, study of deprived and unfortunate people but a concocted opportunity for vicarious beastliness'. Ronald Bryden in the *Observer* was one of the few critics to grasp Bond's purpose, describing *Saved* as honest and accurate, 'presenting its violence not as some neo-Gothic testimony to the cruel absurdity of the universe and human nature but as a social deformity crying for correction'.

This is what absolves Bond of the charge of crude sensationalism. In *The Pope's Wedding* he showed how a life of quasi-feudal deprivation leads to morbid fascination with the outcast. In *Saved* he takes the argument a stage further by suggesting that violence is culturally determined rather than the product of a built-in biological programme. You could argue that Bond fails to pay sufficient attention to the idea of individual moral responsibility; but his play is a major contribution to the debate about violence by suggesting that it stems from a class-based, capitalist society that depends for its very existence on a semi-skilled, half-educated workforce saturated in images of aggression. 'Violence', as Bond later said, 'will only stop when we live in a just society in which all people are equal in all significant respects.' But Bond was writing a play rather than a Marxist thesis; and what makes *Saved* dramatically remarkable is the concrete way in which he shows physical action devoid of emotional resonance. Language, in Bond's world, is also reduced to a blunt, affectless instrument.

This is apparent in the very first scene when Len, Bond's anti-hero, is invited back by Pam to her parents' home for one purpose only: a straightforward fuck to be achieved with a minimum of verbal or physical foreplay. Words are simply rough counters used to convey the most basic needs or feelings. Even Len's question, 'Wass yer name?' is answered by Pam with 'Yer ain' arf nosey', as if genital contact precludes ordinary conversation. But Bond shows how society is simply becoming a series of atomised selves in the third scene where Len meets his mates in a south London park. One of them, Pete, has killed a kid in a road accident but, to him, the dead boy is simply an aggravating nuisance whose funeral causes him to lose a morning's pay. Another youth, Barry, openly boasts of the many blokes he has killed: 'Mor'n you had hot dinners. In the jungle. Shooting up the yeller-niggers. An' cut 'em after with the ol' pig-sticker.' This may be bravado; but it's a reminder of the dubious legacy of a system that trained National Service conscripts to view the enemy as dehumanised objects.

What Bond depicts, in language that deliberately lacks the literary camouflage that enables us to term Pinter's demotic speech 'poetic', is a world shorn of imaginative empathy. You see this in scene iv of *Saved*: 'the scene in which the real crime is committed', according to the play's director, William Gaskill. Len is now installed in Pam's home where the family eat, bicker and watch telly, totally ignoring the wailing cries of Pam's baby offstage. But what shows Bond is a born dramatist is his gift for creating meaningful action: in this case, the festering, silent hatred between Pam's parents is caught through a simple gesture. The scene starts with Mary, Pam's mother, entering the darkened room where Harry, the father, morosely sits. Mary switches on the light. After she exits, Harry defiantly turns the light off again. Mary re-enters and puts the light back on. No word is spoken: everything is contained in the Brechtian 'gestus'. Pam then enters in her slip and makes up her face, while watching the telly, in order to go out to meet her lover, Fred. Mary listlessly joins her in front of the box. Len solidly eats. Meanwhile, the offstage cries of Pam's baby grow into screams of rage and pitiful whimpers. Pam's only response is to turn the telly up even louder. This is what Gaskill rightly calls 'the crime of the lack of love'. And, when Mary briefly remonstrates about the baby's cries, Pam says, 'I thought the cat was stuck up the chimney': the most heartless line in the whole play. It's an astonishing scene filled with quiet despair at a society that can create such stony indifference; and Len, who doesn't lift a finger to help the crying baby, is just as culpable as the narcissistic Pam or her silently quarrelling parents.

But it was scene vi – the baby-stoning scene – that caused outrage in 1965. And, as I remember, it was stomach-churningly horrific to watch. When you analyse the scene, what is striking is the way Bond contextualises the violence. It actually starts with a long exchange between the baby's father, Fred, who is out fishing, and Len, who has been reduced to the role of impotent voyeur in the Pam–Fred relationship: what the dialogue conveys is the male dehumanisation of women ('Get that any time,' says Fred), and the reduction of sex to a casual transaction ('No, it's all a giggle, ain't it,' says Len). The crisis itself is triggered when Pam arrives with the baby and abandons the pram in the park in protest at Fred's desertion of her. As Len and Fred's mates casually assemble, Bond shows how the violence builds slowly out of a mixture of aimlessness, bravado and moral blankess. First the pram is used as a battering-ram in a game between Pete and Barry. Then the gang peer at the baby as if it were an inanimate object devoid of feeling. They pull its hair, pinch it, pull its nappy off, spit at its crotch and

punch it. 'Looks like a yeller-nigger,' says one of them, echoing an earlier line: one that equates the baby with the objectified enemy that soldiers are trained by society to kill. Eventually the violence escalates to
the point where, in a state of hysterical emulation, the gang start to
hurl stones into the pram. As the park bell rings, they rush off in blind
panic, leaving Pam, on her return, to push off the pram, oblivious to
the fact that her baby is dead. It's a terrifying scene, unmatched in
British drama until the advent of Sarah Kane's *Blasted*. But its power
lies in Bond's awareness both of the accelerating, competitive rhythm
of group violence and of the fact that insane cruelty is a cultural phenomenon. King Lear asks 'What cause in nature makes these hard
hearts?' For Bond the answer lies in nurture rather than nature: in a
society that brutalises by example, that treats violence as escapist
entertainment and that fails to nourish the hearts, minds or spirits of
its disaffected young.

But Bond's play is not without hope: indeed, he himself once called
it 'almost irresponsibly optimistic'. In this sense, the pivotal character
is Len. He moves from emotional obsessive to helpless voyeur and
Oedipal figure, attempting to seduce his surrogate mother, Mary, and
maim his substitute father, Harry. But within Len, suggests Bond, there
is some spark of irreducible decency: just as Brecht argues that survival in an imperfect world is some kind of triumph, so Bond shows
how virtue requires peculiar tenacity in a capitalist society. All this is
made clear in the virtually wordless final scene in the living room.
Harry studiously does the football pools: the poor man's ultimate
escapist dream. Mary and Pam sit on the sofa vacantly reading the
Radio Times: the magazine whose loss, earlier on, drove Pam into a
greater state of agitation than the death of her baby. Len, meanwhile,
quietly mends the chair that was damaged in the earlier ruckus with
Harry. It is also Len who utters the scene's single sentence, 'Fetch me
'ammer,' and who by the end has mended the chair. As Bond himself
wrote: 'The play ends in a silent social stalemate but if the spectator
thinks this is pessimistic this is because he has not learned to clutch at
straws. Clutching at straws is the only realistic thing to do.' That is
why the title, *Saved*, is crucial: it implies that the situation is at least
remediable, even if a capitalist society has, in Bond's words, 'made
violence a cheap consumer commodity', and linguistic impoverish-
ment has led to moral vacancy. Change society and you change the
human animal.

Saved was a landmark play in many ways. It proved that the kind of violence accepted without demur in classical drama could be applied to a contemporary issue. It showed that inarticulate characters were as worthy of dramatic attention as anyone else. It also exposed the absurdity of theatrical censorship and helped to promote its demise. Unsurprisingly C. D. Heriot, in his initial Reader's Report to the Lord Chamberlain, Lord Cobbold, took against Bond's play: he insisted on fifty-four textual changes and went on to claim that it was 'a revolting amateur play by one of those dramatists who write as it comes to them out of a heightened image of their experience. It is about a bunch of brainless, ape-like yobs with so little individuality that it is difficult to distinguish between them.' Warming to his theme he went on to state, 'It does seem that the taste of Messrs Devine and Richardson has gone rancid – though with all the public money at their disposal, I don't suppose anybody cares.' It was an oddly revealing rant that clearly exposed both the aesthetic arrogance and the built-in bias against the jumped-up johnnies of subsidised theatre within the Lord Chamberlain's office: it was as if the theatre were being censored by Disgusted of Tunbridge Wells. Bond's stoic refusal to countenance textual cuts meant, however, that the play could be presented only as a club production for members of the English Stage Society. Lord Cobbold saw this as the thin end of a very nasty wedge and determined to make *Saved* a test case. So, during the run of the show, William Gaskill was charged under the Theatres Act of 1843 – along with Greville Poke, the ESC secretary, and Alfred Esdaile, the theatre licensee – with presenting a play 'for hire' before it had been licensed by the Lord Chamberlain. Eventually, on 14 February 1966, Gaskill was summoned before a stipendiary magistrate; and, despite eloquent speeches by Laurence Olivier and Lord Harewood, the Royal Court was found technically guilty and its representatives were fined a nominal £50. But, although this seemed serious at the time, its main effect was to expose the ludicrous English hypocrisy whereby, on payment of a token sum to join a fictive theatre club, audiences supposedly became immune to moral corruption. The ensuing uproar prompted the creation of a Joint Parliamentary Committee on Censorship which early in 1967 advocated the abolition of the 1843 Act. Final credit, however, belongs to a campaigning Labour MP, George Strauss, who brought a private member's bill before the Commons which was given a fair wind by the new Home Secretary, James Callaghan, and which became law in September 1968.

Even in his death throes Cobbold wasn't quite finished with either Bond or the Royal Court. Confronted early in 1968 by the script of Bond's *Early Morning* – in which Queen Victoria enjoys a lesbian relationship with Florence Nightingale, Albert and Disraeli are involved in a murderous coup d'état and the dramatis personae all end up in a cannibalistic heaven – Cobbold struck out like a wounded scorpion. He not only refused Bond's play a licence. He also tried to ban any club performances for members of the English Stage Society. Undeterred, the Court staged a private performance on 31 March 1968, dutifully attended by police officers and members of the Vice Squad. Against the wishes of the licensee, Alfred Esdaile, they staged another performance the following Sunday afternoon, calling it a 'dress rehearsal'. I well remember being instructed to attend as a junior critic on *The Times*. I recall the furtive thrill of being ushered in through a side door of the theatre in order to maintain the elaborate charade that this was a not-for-hire performance: I also remember the less appetising sight of William Gaskill surrounded in the foyer afterwards by mackintoshed police officers as if he were a common criminal. Sadly, the play itself proved a damp squib offering a blunt and over-calculated metaphor for the iniquities of Victorian imperialism and our own ravenously consumerist society. But bad plays as well as good have the right to public performance; and Bond, in both *Saved* and *Early Morning*, proved himself not only a genuine disturber of the peace but a dramatist who expanded the limits of the possible and exposed theatrical censorship as an archaic protection racket. For that, as well as for his considerable body of plays, he has earned his place in history.

A contemporary of Edward Bond's who also deserves his niche in the history books is Charles Wood; for it was Wood who, in *Dingo* in 1967, went further than any dramatist before in calling into question both Winston Churchill's mythic greatness and the motives for fighting the Second World War. Although born in 1932, Wood wrote about military life from first-hand experience, having spent five years as a professional soldier with the 17th/21st Lancers before becoming a scenic artist with Theatre Workshop. Aside from such diversions as the 1965 Beatles film, *Help*, nearly all Wood's work for theatre, film and television has been concerned with military life: both its romantic myths and historical aura. As Tony Howard and John Stokes point out in their book, *Acts of War*, 'For Wood the army is a source of poetry as well as madness, a place where moral values are defined as well as breached.' But it was in *Dingo* that Wood went for broke by calling into question not just the conduct but even the necessity of the Second World War. Commissioned by the National Theatre, the play was quietly dropped after being refused a licence by the Lord Chamberlain. But it eventually received its premiere at the Bristol Arts Centre in May 1967 before moving to the Royal Court where it was presented under the hypocritical masquerade of a club performance. Although relatively little seen, it left its mark on a whole generation of young dramatists and was ultimately far more disturbing than Rolf Hochhuth's *Soldiers*, which suggested that Churchill had connived in the murder of the Polish leader, General Sikorski.

Wood's *Dingo* is a savage, surreal, impressionistic play, set in the desert and a POW camp, that demolishes a whole series of myths about war. Dingo himself, one of two Desert Rats caught in a dusty foxhole, says that 'the thing about fighting in the desert is that it is a clean war': a lie that is quickly nailed by the agonising screams of a man burning to death inside a tank. Wood also punctures the notion that the Second World War was fought for lofty idealistic reasons. As the charred remains of Chalky are retrieved from the tank, his friend Tanky claims that he died well:

TANKY: He died to rid the world of evil – what about the concentration camps?
DINGO: We don't know about those yet.
TANKY: What about the Jews?
DINGO: We don't know about the Jews yet.
TANKY: He died for spiritual purpose.
DINGO: I heard him. Gott mit uns.
TANKY: He died for . . . he died anyway.
DINGO: Yes he died. He died because he couldn't get out.

But Wood's greatest venom is reserved for Churchill. He is seen as a war criminal who sanctioned the second battle of Alamein not out of military necessity but in order to impress the Americans and bolster home morale. His notorious claim that 'no Socialist system can be established without some form of political police' is greeted with derision by the war-sick troops. And Dingo, in a swipe at the enduring myth of British decency, finally blames Churchill for having taken away his sorrow and capacity for feeling: 'That's what I blame the bastard for more than anything, chopping off, more like wearing away, rubbing down my compassion to not a thing, it is nothing.' No one could claim that *Dingo* was a fair-minded or impartial study of the Second World War. Although full of brilliant images, it was also verbally diffuse. But, as Ronald Bryden wrote in the *Observer*: 'I suspect it may be one of those milestones at which a younger generation overthrows the tastes and beliefs of an elder one.'

Like Charles Wood, Peter Barnes was a nonconformist writer who emerged in the Sixties with disruptive intent. But, where Wood was permanently haunted by the aftermyth of war, Barnes was appalled by Britain's obstinate attachment to the hereditary principle and what he saw as the unchanging nature of our class-ridden, deferential society. The great thing about Barnes, who died in 2004, was his mixture of a carnivalesque instinct with exuberant scholarship; significantly, his parents ran amusement stalls at Clacton-on-Sea while he himself was a passionate devotee of Ben Jonson. And the two sides of Barnes's nature came together in the hilarious *The Ruling Class*, which opened at Nottingham Playhouse in 1968 before moving to the West End. It was a sign of the expansive times, and of Stuart Burge's adventurousness, that a play involving twenty-four characters and multiple set changes could be premiered in a regional playhouse. Even more striking was the play's subversive gaiety. In the the first act the 14th Earl of Gurney believes he is the New Testament God and is classified as mad. 'How do you know you are God?' he is asked at one point. 'Simple,' he replies. 'When I pray to Him I find I'm talking to myself.' In the second act the Earl espouses Old Testament ideas of punishment and revenge and believes he is living in Victorian England: as a result he is regarded as sane and becomes a pillar of the House of Lords. Barnes's point is that, for all our supposed radicalism, we still inhabit an ancestor-worshipping world where embedded Tory values dominate. At one moment, two upper-class ladies ask the Earl to open their fête. He can talk, they tell him, about whatever he likes: 'Hanging. Immigration. The Stranglehold of the Unions. Anything . . . so long as it isn't political.' But, even if his message is pessimistic, Barnes's play displays a freewheeling theatrical inventiveness: the mad Earl believes he is married to Dumas's Marguerite Gautier and at one point an actress is hired, Pirandello-like, to play the role and enters singing the drinking song from *La Traviata*. Barnes was always something of a maverick outsider whose work was championed by a select handful of admirers including Burge and Terry Hands; but at his best, as in *The Ruling Class*, he questioned stock notions about the new Britain and proved that you could lift the spirits while also disturbing the peace.

Obviously Orton, Bond, Wood and Barnes were not simply concerned with disrupting the spectacle: they were all, in their different ways, social commentators. But alongside them was another group of writers – including John Osborne, Peter Nichols, Alan Bennett and David Storey – whom I would dub 'anatomists of Albion', if only because they were primarily preoccupied with using theatre as a metaphor for the nation as a whole. And the nation in the High Sixties offered so many contradictory facets that it provided rich pickings for dramatists. Optimists could point to much that was good about Britain. England's triumph in the 1966 World Cup made at least one section of the United Kingdom very happy. Pop culture, spearheaded by the Beatles and the Rolling Stones, was riding high. *Time* magazine lavishly endorsed 'Swinging London'. And a combination of factors – including the availability of the Pill and the new liberal laws on homosexuality and abortion – meant that sexuality had been freed from its traditional puritan restraints. At the same time, pessimists could argue that the Labour government had lost its reputation for competence and was living on borrowed time. Even as England won the World Cup, there was a six-month freeze on pay and dividends followed by public-expenditure cuts and higher taxes. Travellers abroad faced a £50 currency limit on foreign holidays. 1967 saw the devaluation of the pound and further austerity measures. And, behind everything, lay the shadow of Vietnam. In Sixties Britain psychic liberation was accompanied by economic anxiety and political anger. But if any one phrase can ever be said to pin down a particular period, it was one used by the art historian Edward Lucie-Smith. 'This', he wrote, 'is the first age which has erected the enjoyment of the moment into a moral imperative.' For some, that was a sign of liberating freedom: for others, one of spiritual decay.

Inevitably, dramatists were drawn into anatomising the times; and for one in particular, John Osborne, it was almost a temperamental compulsion. The received media myth about Osborne is that, like novelists such as Kingsley Amis and John Braine, he moved from left to right in the Sixties and forfeited his right to speak for liberal England. And it is perfectly true that he started the decade as a member of the

Committee of 100 and ended it as a fierce critic of mass protest. But the basic fact about Osborne is that he had always been a congenital outsider marching to his own distinctive rhythm and more than half in love, as *Look Back In Anger* and *The Entertainer* showed, with a vanished Edwardian dream of grace, nobility and style. Osborne was an emotional aristocrat who had the bad luck to be born in Fulham. And what happened in the Sixties was that he found new targets for his disdain. In the Fifties Osborne had aimed his silver bullets at a geriatric Tory Establishment, a petrified class system, royalty-worship and an impotent religion. In the Sixties, after Labour came to power, he attacked what he saw as the infatuation with showbiz, the slavering obeisance to youth, the modish intellectual orthodoxy of Wilson's Britain. The oppositional stance was much the same: it was simply the political backdrop that had shifted.

The signs were already there in *Inadmissible Evidence*, which opened at the Royal Court in September 1964, a month before Labour came to power. But although the play was full of blistering rhetoric and boasted a superlative performance from Nicol Williamson as its self-lacerating hero, it never achieved the rich metaphorical resonance of Osborne's earlier work. Ronald Bryden once described Osborne's hero, Bill Maitland, as 'a kind of Willy Loman in striped English serge'; but, whereas Miller's salesman embodies the corruption of the original American dream, it was hard to see Osborne's disintegrating solicitor as anything other than a special case. As a study in paranoia and physical breakdown, the play was spellbinding: it took an effort of will, however, to view Maitland's collapse as a symbol of Britain's inability to cope with the world. The voluptuously theatrical *A Patriot For Me* (1965), set in the Habsburg Empire between 1890 and the eve of the First World War, was, in many ways, a more intriguing play: written before the liberalisation of our own laws, it showed a homosexual Viennese officer coming agonisingly out of the closet. As Tynan, no longer close to Osborne, wrote in defence of the play, in reply to a vicious attack by Mary McCarthy in the *Observer*: 'For the first time in Western drama, we are asked to identify with a queer not because he is charming or tragic or a genius but simply because he is queer.' But Osborne returned to his preordained role of anatomising Britain in two plays for the Royal Court in the summer of 1968. They were presented under the joint heading 'For The Meantime': an indication of Osborne's progressive disenchantment with the Sixties. As drama, they were also wildly divergent:

Time Present was verbose and dramatically lax while *The Hotel in Amsterdam* was precise and hauntingly rueful.

In form and structure, *The Hotel in Amsterdam* is a blend of private drama and social satire. Three couples, variously involved in the film business, simply take themselves off for a fugitive weekend in Amsterdam to escape the tentacular reach of the monster producer, KL. But, in an *Observer* interview with Tynan, Osborne rejected the idea that the play was a closed metaphor since in Sixties Britain everyone was contaminated by show-business:

> Dockers are interviewed in the streets and writing a play about show-biz people isn't the kind of 'in' experience that it used to be. At one time theatrical folk only spoke to other theatrical folk but today social contacts are much freer. We're all in show-biz now.

What Osborne picked up on was the way in which long before the proliferation of 'reality' television, everyone in Britain seemed to be self-consciously playing a role. Politicians had always been performers, but union bosses, teachers, policemen, nurses were now expected to be ready to articulate their views in front of a camera or microphone. For some of us this was a healthy extension of democracy; for Osborne it was an unhealthy intimation of a society where everyone was competing for their fifteen minutes of fame. But the virtue of *The Hotel in Amsterdam* is that its screenwriter hero, Laurie, is both Osborne's spokesman and a tragically self-questioning figure: Chekhov's Trigorin shifted, as it were, to the modern world. When Laurie launches an attack on the squishy softness of hippiedom – 'All those sleepy-eyed young mice squealing love, love' – he expresses Osborne's loathing for contemporary England. But Laurie also conveys the nag of disquiet that attacks many supposedly successful people in mid-life. When Annie, his secret love, tells Laurie that at least he produces the goods, he cries: 'But what goods I ask myself: can anything manufactured out of this chaos and rapacious timidity and scolding carry-on really be the goods?' And when Laurie goes on to criticise his own work for its lack of 'precision, design, logical detail, cunning formality', you feel Osborne is discreetly admitting that, by the exemplary standards of great art, his own work falls short. As both Anthony Page's original production with Paul Scofield and Robin Lefevre's superb 2003 revival at the Donmar Warehouse with Tom Hollander showed, this is a play in which Osborne bares his soul while anatomising Albion.

But Osborne was not alone in mixing autobiography and an ungovernable obsession with England. In 1953 he had appeared in rep at Frinton-on-Sea with a young actor called Peter Nichols. They had performed together in Agatha Christie thrillers and the famous Philip King farce, *See How They Run*, in which Osborne played a character called The Intruder. As Nichols delightedly told Osborne's biographer, John Heilpern: 'That's exactly what he was. He came into English society as The Intruder and put a bomb under the whole bloody thing.' In the late Eighties Nichols and Osborne, both disenchanted with the London theatrical scene, even became neighbours in rural Shropshire. But, although Nichols claims they were never spiritually that close, they had certain things in common. Both ruthlessly excavated their own lives as a source of drama. Both were fascinated by the music hall. And both were obsessed by the state of England, which seemed to arouse in them a mixture of temperamental loyalty and cordial loathing.

There was, however, one obvious difference. Osborne tended, with a few exceptions, to be formally conservative, taking his models from the past: the three-act rep play, Brecht, Chekhov. Nichols, however, was always searching for new forms. And in the introduction to the Methuen edition of the 1967 play that put him firmly on the map, *A Day In The Death of Joe Egg*, Nichols offers an incisive history of naturalism. Above all, he shows how a nineteenth-century theatrical form found its perfect expression in twentieth-century television; and for much of the Sixties Nichols turned out highly skilled pieces for the box which exploited television's gift for keyhole realism. But, in a pregnant phrase, Nichols describes naturalism as 'a purgative reform that became an inflexible genre': in short, a movement pioneered by geniuses such as Ibsen and Chekhov and lesser talents such as Becque and Hauptmann turned into the stale conventions of the standard West End play. And, after several straightforward realistic drafts of *Joe Egg*, Nichols realised that the problem it presented was not how to live with a handicapped child. It was how to describe that life 'in a way that will prevent a sudden stampede to the exit doors'. Nichols' solution was to break down the illusionist fourth wall and engage the audience directly. As Nichols himself says, '*Joe Egg* is a play about a play'; and, heavily influenced by the frontal technique of the music hall, he played a vital part in the stealthy erosion of naturalism that is part of modern British drama.

Joe Egg was formally experimental. It also brought to the stage a subject unfamiliar to most of us but which Nichols and his wife, Thelma, knew at first hand: the difficulties of bringing up a child with a damaged cerebral cortex. So when we see Bri and Sheila endowing their daughter with a fictive identity and indulging in endless role-playing, we feel Nichols is being both true to life and solving a dramatic problem. The play has been justly acclaimed for its lack of mawkishness. Less attention has been paid to another crucial fact: that it offers a vivid, microcosmic portrait of a morally confused England. Religion, for instance, is a subject that runs right through the play. Bri rejects its consolations, seeing God as 'a sort of manic-depressive rugby footballer'. At the same time he has, like so many of us, a residual memory of faith that makes him appalled at the Christmas image of a neon-lit Jesus placed on top of Bristol's electricity showroom. The chairbound Joe Egg also exposes our ethical uncertainty about euthanasia. Bri loves Joe deeply but believes she'd be better off dead: his friend, Freddie, is a moral absolutist who argues 'Thou shalt not kill' – except, as Bri caustically interjects, 'when it shall come to pass that thy trade routes shall be endangered'. Joe, in Nichols' hands, also becomes a symbol for our constant evasion of reality: Freddie's wife can't stand anything Non Physically Attractive while Bri's mum uses the child as a means of attacking her daughter-in-law's supposedly tainted genes. Nichols' play touches us at many levels. It is palpably a play about marriage and the stresses of bringing up a handicapped child. But it is also about the new materialist England: a country that has no common belief system, no coherent attitude to life and death and no real religion. In the absence of God, it is driven to put its trust in jargon-spouting medical professionals conspiring against the laity.

Nichols' ability to experiment with form while taking the nation's temperature was confirmed by his follow-up play, the aptly titled *The National Health*. Commissioned by the National Theatre, it opened at the Old Vic in 1969 and became a huge hit in spite of severe opposition from that interfering busybody, Lord Chandos, who tried to use his power as Chairman to persuade Olivier to cancel it. Olivier, who had his own doubts, mercifully stuck with the play, for what it showed was Nichols' gift for extracting a national metaphor from personal experience. Nichols himself had suffered a collapsing right lung, which gave him extensive experience of hospitals. Out of that came an image of a crumbling Victorian Gothic ward as a microcosm of modern

Britain: a place where excessive respect was paid to autocratic, godlike experts while a decaying infrastructure was kept going by ill-paid, immigrant underlings. Nichols clearly believed strongly, in a post-war Labourite way, in socialised medicine: what he was lamenting was the way our public services were lapsing into decrepitude. But the play was anything but a tract. It was filled with parodic soap-opera interludes, in which adoring Sisters fell for crusty old Scots surgeons straight out of *Dr Finlay's Casebook*. Glamorised fiction thus became a counterpoint to run-down reality. And linking the two worlds was the ward orderly, Barnet: as played by Jim Dale in Michael Blakemore's superb production, he became a campy modern Thersites ushering the patients towards death and exposing the bent nature of the healing arts. This was the National doing what it does best: putting its considerable resources towards a public examination of the nation's health.

Like Osborne, Nichols was severely critical of modern England. Both also drew heavily on traditional music-hall techniques as if to indicate their disaffection with contemporary life. As yet another anatomist of Albion, Alan Bennett was more poetically equivocal than either Osborne or Nichols. Suspicious of tradition but historically intrigued by it, welcoming social justice but wary of the new materialism, Bennett seemed to have a foot in both camps: sometimes even a touch of camp in both feet. As the bright child of working-class parents who had made his way, via National Service, from a Leeds grammar school to Oxford, Bennett was an archetypal product of Butskellite post-war Britain. But, although he had made his name in *Beyond The Fringe*, it was possible even there to detect a secret reverence for his targets: especially Church of England vicars and wartime sentimentalists. And Bennett's own brand of satiric nostalgia was the wellspring of *Forty Years On*, which reached the Apollo Theatre in October 1968 and which, with Gielgud and Bennett himself in the cast, quickly became a gold-plated hit. Set in a minor public school on the South Downs, symbolically named Albion House, it combined literary parody with silky innuendo and showed that Bennett's attitude to a vanished England was a highly complex one: residual affection for its grace and civility was combined with acrid awareness of its snobbery and injustice.

What only one critic noted in 1968, however, was the radical form of *Forty Years On*. To some, it looked like an extended revue or post-

graduate ragbag. In *Plays and Players*, however, Martin Esslin cleverly spotted its structural similarities to Peter Weiss's *The Marat/Sade*.
Both showed history naively presented by the inmates of an institution. Both used song as a source of narration and exploited the equivocal position of the audience as enforced spectators of a
play-within-a-play. And both presented a conflict between opposing
world-views: in Bennett's case, the Headmaster represents the old conservative Britain while his successor-designate embodies the contemporary desire for change. Like Weiss in his confrontation of political
and personal revolution, Bennett also seemed capable of empathising
with diametrically opposed points of view. Bennett's play-within-a-
play, 'Speak For England, Arthur', was described as 'a memoir of two
nice people in a world we have lost'. And as we watched the two
beleaguered Bloomsburyites, loosely based on Harold Nicolson and
Vita Sackville-West, crouching in the basement of Claridges during the
Second World War, we felt Bennett's sympathy for their stoicism and
his detestation of Thirties appeasers like Neville Chamberlain and the
Times editor, Geoffrey Dawson. But, in the sketches that made up the
bulk of the evening, we also saw Bennett's fascination with the dis-
torting nature of memory and his lethal ability to puncture Anglo-
Saxon attitudes through parody. The finest example came in his
treatment of the Edward VIII–Mrs Simpson scandal in terms of a
Buchan or Sapper adventure story. It didn't just catch the tone of voice
of the whole 'snobbery with violence' school: it also pinned down its
strange misogyny. 'Women had never much come my way and I knew
as much about their ways as I knew about the Chinese language,' is
authentic Buchan. 'Women are queer cattle at the best of times but
she's like no other woman I have known,' is pure Bennett. Apart from
the fact that Bennett's parody is more elegantly phrased, it would be
hard to tell the difference.

Bennett is both a caustic observer of a vanished, class-bound England and yet someone who has the northern scholarship boy's secret
envy of it. That emerges clearly in the play's final speeches, which offer
a communal threnody for a lost world. 'We have become', says the
Headmaster, 'a battery people, a people of under-privileged hearts fed
on pap in darkness, bred out of all taste and season to savour the
shoddy splendours of the new civility. The hedges come down from
the silent fields. The lease is out on the corner site. A butterfly is an
event.' When delivered by John Gielgud the lines had an elegiac beauty

and seductiveness. Yet we are in danger of being deceived by their mel-
lifluousness. It would be perfectly possible to paint an alternative
vision of Sixties Britain in which more people than ever before had
access to what Matthew Arnold called 'the best that has been thought
and said'. Cheap paperbacks, the Third Programme, the National and
the RSC, the Open University, even BBC TV on a good day all testified
to a culturally enriched Britain: a few months after Bennett's play
opened, Kenneth Clark's thirteen-part series, *Civilisation*, made
Europe's artistic heritage available to a mass audience in a way that
had never happened before. And if, as the Headmaster claims, 'the
crowd has found its way into the secret garden,' then one is tempted
to reply, 'So much the better.' But Bennett's virtue is that he sees the
value of tradition and of abstract ideals like chivalry and duty while
retaining his innate scepticism. He concludes his published journal for
Forty Years On on Armistice Day 1968, which marked the fiftieth
anniversary of the end of the First World War. 'I listen to the ceremony on the radio,' he writes, 'and, as I type this, I hear the guns rumbling across the Park for the start of the Two Minutes' Silence. I find
the ceremony ridiculous and hypocritical and yet it brings a lump to
my throat. Why? I suppose that is what the play is trying to resolve.'
But it is precisely because the contradiction in Bennett is unresolvable
that *Forty Years On* remains one of the most durable – as well as one
of the funniest – state-of-the-nation plays.

Differences of temperament and taste, however, determine the way
England is depicted on stage – as you can see by contrasting the work
of Alan Bennett and David Storey. In terms of background, the two
men have a good deal in common. Bennett, the son of a Co-op butcher, was born in Leeds in 1933; Storey, the son of a miner, was born in
Wakefield in 1934. But while Bennett progressed to Oxford and the
world of stage and TV satire, Storey at one point combined life as a
London art student with playing professional Rugby League. While
Bennett reveals the verbal brilliance and parodic skill of a latter-day
Max Beerbohm, Storey conceives his plays in visual terms. Even in
outlook the two men are very different. Storey, forever haunted by his
origins, once told me that he regularly put in a solid eight hours at his
writing desk in imitation of the rhythm of the working-class day.
Meanwhile Bennett, although himself an assiduous worker, once
wrote a TV sketch unforgettably satirising the 'professional' northern-
er with a literary bent. I'm sure he didn't have Storey in mind, but one

recalls Bennett's staunchly proletarian writer posing in front of picturesque slag-heaps and claiming that, just as his father was a miner and his mother was a miner, so he too was 'a miner writer'.

But Storey is every bit as preoccupied by the nature of England as Bennett. He began his literary career as a novelist with *This Sporting Life*, *Flight Into Camden* and *Radcliffe*: works that explored the division between body and spirit, and even good and evil, in powerful Lawrentian terms. It was at the suggestion of Lindsay Anderson, who filmed his first novel, that Storey turned to drama, with *The Restoration of Arnold Middleton* (1966), dealing with a schoolmaster's mental disintegration. After that came *In Celebration* (1969), boasting mesmerising performances from Alan Bates and Brian Cox, which used a North Country family reunion to explore long-buried guilts. But it was with *The Contractor*, also staged at the Royal Court in 1969, that Storey showed his instinctive mastery of theatre and his ability to create resonant visual metaphors. Drawing on his own teenage experience of working for a tent contractor, Storey made something poetic, beautiful and mysterious out of an event as simple as the erection and dismantling of a wedding marquee. Harold Hobson said the play was as exquisite as Keats's 'Ode on a Grecian Urn'. And it is true the play prompted all kinds of thoughts about human transience and artistic durability. But Storey is also an unsentimental realist whose play was rooted in a close observation of class, family and work.

What is so brilliant about the play is Storey's ability to offer a comprehensive picture of English life without making us aware of the fact. Character and circumstance are revealed through action. Or sometimes inaction. Ewbank, the Yorkshire contractor of the title, who uses one of his own firm's thirty-five marquees to celebrate his daughter's wedding, is a tough, paternalist boss filled with a gnawing discontent: something that vividly emerged in Bill Owen's performance. Ewbank constantly interferes with the process of erecting the tent as if to prove to everyone that he was once a manual worker. He has an awkward relationship with his educated son and no time at all for his future son-in-law: 'a bloody aristocrat, so refined if it wasn't for his britches he'd be invisible'. He also employs local drifters and deadbeats, as if to exorcise his guilt about his wealth. If Ewbank is sharply characterised, so too are his casual labourers. There's the taciturn foreman who's been jailed for embezzlement, the surly sidekick soured by his wife's desertion, the stammering halfwit with the inordinate appetite, the two Irishmen who acknowledge they are 'the debris of society'. Like Rudkin in *Afore Night Come* and Wesker in *The Kitchen*, Storey both dramatises work and reflects the hierarchies within a group of labourers. Tent-poles have to be inserted, ropes fastened, sheets of canvas laced together: a reminder that Auden was hopelessly wrong when he wrote, in *The Dyer's Hand*, that 'work cannot be represented on stage because it ceases to be work if the time it takes is foreshortened'. But Storey also uses the stage with painterly imagination. There's a shocking contrast between the immaculate tent at the end of the second act – with its polished floor, muslin drapery and floral decorations – and the image that confronts us at the start of the post-nuptial third act. Now the drapery is torn, wrought-iron tables have been overturned, bottles are scattered everywhere along with napkins, streamers and paper wrapping. It is a picture of riotous disorder; and you are left wondering in what way the unseen party guests are superior to the deadbeat workmen who have at least created an object of elegance and beauty. But Storey refuses the easy options of the moralist. Instead he allows the spectator to find in the play whatever he or she wants: a metaphor for the decline and fall of capitalism, the passing away of the British Empire, the evanescence of artistic creation. For me, however, the greatness of Storey's drama rests in its honest and poetic portrait of the class system in action.

Class is a recurrent theme of Sixties drama: a reminder that, even in a decade that saw the rise of a youthocracy and a much greater social mobility, the old structures hadn't greatly changed. And education provides a perfect example. As Anthony Sampson points out, 'The Sixties in Britain were the decade of the degree; at the end of it there were twice as many students as at the beginning.' But Sampson also observes that, for all the spread of higher education and the opening of new universities, Oxbridge retained its hold over government, Civil Service and the media: by 1970 it provided twenty-six of the thirty Permanent Secretaries, 250 of the 630 Members of Parliament. In theatre too it dominated the upper levels of the National Theatre, the RSC, the Royal Court. Only playwrights reflected something of the diversity of British life; and one source of the vitality of Sixties drama was the breadth of experience its writers encompassed. Just think of the dramatists so far mentioned. Edward Bond had worked as a labourer. Charles Wood had been a professional soldier. Peter Barnes, after National Service, worked for the London County Council. Peter Nichols had been a schoolteacher and, like Osborne and Orton, an actor. David Storey had played Rugby League and done a variety of manual jobs. This was the last generation of dramatists, Alan Bennett excepted, for whom playwriting emerged from experience of work rather than being a post-university career choice. I'm not prejudiced against graduate playwrights. But these Sixties writers, because of their background, possessed an unsentimental view of physical labour and a direct experience of the dynamics of class that fed directly into their work. It certainly helps to explain why they were disturbers of the peace or obsessive analysts of the national mood.

Alongside these, there was another group of writers who pursued their own private vision within a relatively traditional framework: Harold Pinter, Tom Stoppard, Christopher Hampton and Alan Ayckbourn, whom I would dub, for want of a better term, Contemporary Classicists. All such categories are bare approximations to reality; and I wouldn't deny that these four writers all had disruptive qualities and a keen political instinct. Pinter, in particular, had a lot in common with his immediate contemporaries in that he had worked as waiter, doorman, dishwasher, snow-shoveller, dance-hall bouncer and actor, was alive to the existence of a deprived underclass and, by risking imprisonment as a conscientious objector, had revealed his profound hatred of any imposed authority. But, although Pinter's early plays such as *The Birthday Party* and *The Dumb Waiter* are implicitly political, I wouldn't classify him as a state-of-the-nation dramatist. Pinter's genius is for exploring the politics of personal relationships and for excavating his own sense of life's precariousness in a way that connected with a wider audience. What is especially fascinating about Pinter in the Sixties is the way he moves from the dream-like realism of *The Homecoming* to the spare, lapidary, poetic drama of *Landscape* and *Silence*, which offer Beckettian images of separation and solitude.

The Homecoming remains, to this day, a seminal text of the Sixties and one with a uniquely disturbing power, stemming from its equivocal portrait of its heroine, Ruth. Having returned with her expatriate husband to his north London working-class family, Ruth famously rejects marriage, children and a comfortable campus existence to stay with her in-laws, apparently as breadwinning whore and surrogate mother. For over forty years now people have been crying, like Judge Brack at the end of *Hedda Gabler*, 'People don't do such things!' Even some of Pinter's closest friends suspect there is an element of male fantasy in Ruth. As Simon Gray once told me, British academics don't on the whole marry whores: 'unless', he mischievously added, 'they're very lucky.' But all this begs several questions. The most obvious is whether Ruth actually is a whore or simply a shrewd operator who, by the end of the play, has swapped her manipulative prick of a husband and her role as a trophy wife for the animal vitality of life with her in-laws. I also see another possibility: that Ruth is a multi-dimensional figure who manages simultaneously to be, to her deluded in-laws, an idealised mixture of madonna-and-whore and, in her own imagination, a seeker of freedom and liberation. Admittedly Pinter was writing five years before the publication in 1970 of Germaine Greer's *The Female Eunuch*, which helped to define and mobilise the British feminist movement. But, with an artist's intuition, Pinter pins down a female yearning for self-determination that was certainly growing in the Sixties and of which Ruth is a feisty and freewheeling example. Rather than a reactionary work about a woman who accepts prostitution in preference to marriage, *The Homecoming* thus becomes a play about a heroine who exercises sexual, social and economic choice: that is certainly how Ruth has emerged to me in the successive performances of Vivien Merchant, Gemma Jones, Cherie Lunghi, Lindsay Duncan and Lia Williams. I'm also reminded of a nineteen-twenties short story by Elizabeth Bowen – a writer whom Pinter later adapted for the screen in *The Heat of the Day* – called *Joining Charles*. In Bowen's story an upper middle-class woman, about to join her banker husband in France, realises that she hates him and much prefers to be with her in-laws. Trapped by the class and social conventions of her time, Bowen's heroine rejects 'this fullness, this intimacy and queer seclusion of family life' to go back to her detested husband. Pinter's Ruth, in the progressive spirit of the Sixties, makes the opposite decision, suggesting that personal liberation starts with individual choice and enthusiastic acceptance of one's sexuality.

The Homecoming was directed by Peter Hall for the RSC in 1965 with a fastidious attention to detail normally reserved in Britain for Shakespeare, Ibsen or Chekhov: indeed its select team of actors had just emerged from a season playing the histories in Stratford. But it was followed by an exceptionally long Pinter pause. Hampered, I sus-

pect, by the tensions in his own domestic life and by a growing dissatisfaction with the impedimenta of naturalism, he wrote nothing for
the stage until *Landscape* and *Silence* appeared as an RSC double bill
in 1969. In the intervening years Pinter was busy with film and television. But the break in style and tone between *The Homecoming* and
the later plays is remarkable. Gone are exits and entrances, doors and
windows and the kind of loaded banter, mixing aggression and
defence, that had become Pinter's trademark. In *Landscape* a married
couple called Duff and Beth sit on either side of a kitchen table: intimate but separate, they recall a Beckett line from *Ohio Impromptu*,
'Alone together so much shared.' *Silence*, strangely unrevived, shows
three atomised characters locked into their memories and invoking
lost love, with a mixture of poignancy and stoicism. At the time, critics tended to see Pinter's move towards a more distilled, poetic drama
as a retreat: only later, as Pinter increasingly used it to embrace political themes, would it come to be seen as a liberation.

Obviously Beckett's magic minimalism was a big influence on Pinter: especially a work like *Play* which showed you could explore your
characters' emotional past while keeping them physically confined,
even to the point of placing them in funeral urns. Beckett had an even
greater impact on Tom Stoppard, who started the decade as a journalist on the *Bristol Evening World* and ended it as one of Britain's most
celebrated dramatists: witty, articulate, endlessly interviewable. I first
came across him in 1966 when I was commissioned by Philip French
at the BBC to give an eight-minute Third Programme talk on a couple
of his early radio plays: *The Dissolution of Dominic Boot*, in which
the hero runs up an escalating taxi fare, and *If You're Glad I'll Be
Frank*, in which time is seen to be both a philosophical concept and an
arbitrary invention. But it was *Rosencrantz and Guildenstern Are
Dead*, famously picked up by the National Theatre after its Edinburgh
Fringe success, that made Stoppard's name. It was a play that could
hardly have been written without *Waiting for Godot*. As Stoppard
admiringly said of Beckett's play, 'It redefined the minima of theatrical
experience. Up to then you had to have X; suddenly you had X minus
one.' But where Beckett's Vladimir and Estragon are driven by panic
to fill the endless void, Stoppard's twin heroes remain voluble puppets
dancing remorselessly to their author's tune. For all its dependence on
Hamlet, Stoppard's play also ignores the fact that Shakespeare's characters are not bewildered nonentities but figures with a defined social

role, as the prince's former chums now complicit in Claudius's internal espionage. It was the play that made Stoppard's reputation. Yet I infinitely prefer his 1968 one-act comedy, *The Real Inspector Hound* – a marvellous Fabergé egg of a play, which gains with every viewing. By showing two critics drawn into the world of a Christie-ish who-dunnit, Stoppard successfully lampoons critical pretension and the creaky country-house thriller while evoking the universal fear of slipping out of ordered experience into chaos.

What was intriguing about Stoppard was that he emerged at a time when dramatists were increasingly defined by their subjective angst or their political anxiety; yet he seemed to have no particular axe to grind. In later years, in fact, he admitted that his favourite line in modern drama was, 'I'm a man of no convictions. At least I think I am,' from Christopher Hampton's *The Philanthropist*. Which is interesting since, although they were born nine years apart (Stoppard in 1937, Hampton in 1946), the two dramatists have a certain amount in common. Both spent much of their childhood in outposts of the old Empire – Stoppard in Singapore and India, Hampton in Egypt – leading them to view British life with a certain clinical objectivity. Both allow us to deduce their political attitudes from their work rather than displaying them overtly. And both are classicists in a generation of romantics. After a rare undergraduate excursion into semi-autobiographical drama with *When Did You Last See My Mother?*, Hampton put down his marker with *Total Eclipse*, first produced at the Royal Court in 1968. This was a cool, beautifully written play about artistic frenzy and destructive passion: one that charted, with objective truth and emotional understanding, Verlaine's obsessive love for Rimbaud. And once again it proved Auden wrong about theatre. He claimed that the dramatist would sooner or later substitute the artist-genius for the man-of-action as dramatic hero; but, said Auden, 'a sensible dramatist would immediately realise that a direct treatment would be bound to fail', on the grounds that creativity cannot be shown. But Hampton falls into no such trap. He never shows his poetic subjects in the throes of creative agony in the manner of a Hollywood biopic. At the same time, he says a lot about the erratic nature of genius. Rimbaud is savagely intolerant while Verlaine is pathetically obsessive. Rimbaud draws his sword on an incompetent poet while Verlaine actually shoots his lover. Rimbaud enjoys a rash, fierce blaze of riot while Verlaine ends up publicly acclaimed but wanly dissolute. I am reminded of J. B. Priestley's description of Rimbaud as a combination of 'the intellectual and the tough' and of Verlaine as 'the drunk murmuring magical regrets at three in the morning'. But the chief impression left by Hampton's play is of the dramatist himself as a rational, Apollonian writer coolly observing a world of Dionysiac excess.

I would add Alan Ayckbourn to my quartet of contemporary classicists on the grounds that his early work was driven by the joy and discipline of craft rather than the imperative of romantic self-revelation. Like Pinter, Ayckbourn learned his craft as an actor and stage manager working in weekly rep. In 1957 he also came under the magnetic spell of Stephen Joseph when he appeared in a season at the Scarborough Library's in-the-round theatre: an event that was to shape Ayckbourn's subsequent life and career. It was, in fact, Joseph who, when Ayckbourn complained about the lightweight role he was playing, urged him to write something of his own. And, after some conventional early plays, Ayckbourn came up in 1964 with a highly original piece called *Mr Whatnot*: a play that pitched a silent piano-tuner into a country house, and drew on the techniques of early Chaplin and Jacques Tati long before 'visual' and 'physical' theatre became specialised ghettos. Then in 1967 Ayckbourn achieved national recognition with *Relatively Speaking* (originally entitled *Meet My Father*), which had a long run at the Duke of York's with a star cast including Michael Hordern, Celia Johnson, Richard Briers and Jennifer Hilary. Ayckbourn's play looked deceptively simple: it depended on a man airily mistaking his girlfriend's middle-aged lover and the lover's wife for her parents. Indeed it was sufficiently traditional to gain the kid-gloved imprimatur of Noël Coward. But, under the bland routines of Sunday-morning suburbia, the play showed, with considerable wit and skill, a middle-class marriage falling inexorably apart. We had not expected this: a return to classical comedy at a time when the nation was engulfed in a spiralling economic crisis. Ayckbourn's special genius for pushing traditional comedy into new territory was highlighted by his next major play, *How The Other Half Loves*, which premiered in Scarborough in July 1969 and came to London a year later. This is the play where Ayckbourn experiments with space and time by physically entwining two households unlike in dignity. But Ayckbourn's technical legerdemain – comparable to anything in Goldoni's *The Servant of Two Masters* – was not an end in itself: it was a means of exploring the impact of class, income and education on sexual behaviour. As time went by, it would become even clearer that Ayckbourn was infinitely more than a supplier of ami-able divertissements. Initially marked down as one of the light brigade, not to be spoken of seriously in the same breath as Osborne, Pinter or Bond, he was eventually recognised as both a contemporary classicist and a shrewd social commentator with a gift for anatomising a rapidly changing Albion.

Change. That is the word that sums up both society and theatre in the Sixties. Everything seemed to be in ferment. Towards the end of the decade there was a clear sense that, alongside the emergence of a canonical generation of new dramatists, a different kind of theatre was also appearing: one that had its origins in American and Euro-pean experiment and was more fluid in form and less anchored in text than conventional theatre. Historically, the most important event of the time was the demise of theatrical censorship in 1968. Those who imagined that the theatre would, as a result, be flooded with unbridled displays of filth were surprised or disappointed, according to taste. What actually happened was that, immediately after the passage of the Theatres Act, we got a chance to see *Hair* at the Shaftesbury Theatre in 1968. Lord Cobbold, the Lord Chamberlain, had actually banned three versions of the Jerome Ragni–James Rado–Galt MacDermot musical in the last months of his office. One of his readers had also reported: 'It extols dirt, anti-Establishment views, homosexuality, free love, drug-taking and it inveighs against patriotism.' Apart from the gratuitous mention of dirt, that was a not inaccurate description of *Hair*: it was a joyous celebration of American countercultural values and an attack on the political-military nexus. As Charles Marowitz noted, 'Without Vietnam and the American repugnance to that war, the show would never have come into being. It is almost entirely nour-ished by the current hatred of what its "senior citizens" have allowed America to become.' But what Tom O'Horgan's dazzling production also did was absorb many of the anti-illusionist techniques of groups like La Mama and the Living Theatre and deploy them in a piece of popular musical entertainment. It brought hippie values and visual shock tactics into the commercial theatre: seeing it for a second time in Los Angeles, after its London opening, I've rarely felt a greater sense of communion between actors and audience. This was truly a tribal musical and, if you want to understand what the late Sixties was like, you only have to listen to the original cast's recording.

Hair not only conquered London: it was also a potent reminder of how indebted our alternative theatre was to America for its expression of anti-Establishment values – a stark contrast to the rooted British-ness of our mainstream writers. As I've noted, it was the presence in London of American renegades such as Charles Marowitz and Ed Berman that opened up the possibilities of a new kind of off-West End theatre. Marowitz at the Open Space in Tottenham Court offered an eclectic programme that ranged from Shakespearean collages to transatlantic plays such as John Herbert's *Fortune and Men's Eyes*, dealing with gay sex in a prison reformatory. Ed Berman was even more of a wild card, who operated on a variety of fronts. He set up the Ambiance Lunch-Hour Theatre Club in Bayswater, created Dogg's Troupe to do plays and street improvisations and involved local chil-dren in Chalk Farm and Notting Hill in communal projects. Berman was a radical spirit who understood theatre's social potential long before it was fashionable, enlisting the active support of Tom Stop-pard in the process. Lacking a strong experimental tradition of our own, we constantly looked to America for guidance. Visitors to our shores in the late Sixties included New York's Bread and Puppet Thea-tre and Paper Bag Players and, most famously, the Living Theatre cre-ated by Julian Beck and Judith Malina. They came to the Roundhouse in 1969 with a sequence of shows – including *Frankenstein*, *Paradise Now* and *Antigone* – that varied wildly in quality but introduced us to the delights of elaborate physical spectacle, communal nudity and invasion of the audience's privacy and space. Much of what Living Theatre did eventually turned into the cliches of avant-garde theatre; but the company spawned work all over the globe and nourished the spirit of revolution, even if it failed to accomplish it.

Continental European influences also fed into British work. Artaud's theories became an unofficial bible. Grotowski's concept of Poor Theatre was constantly invoked, even if some of us resisted its air of puritan elitism: I have a vivid memory of being transported to Lon-don's East End, in a blacked-out bus in which we were asked to deposit our worldly possessions, to see his Laboratory Theatre stage Calderón's *The Constant Prince* in a production that seemed rather to relish, as well as demonstrate, expertly choreographed sadism. Far more to my taste was Jean-Louis Barrault's *Rabelais*, which came to the Old Vic in 1969: while embracing many of the ideas of Artaud, Grotowski, Living Theatre and La Mama, it put them to the service of a great literary text. But the mixture of international experiment and the rejection of official culture certainly left its mark on British theatre in the late Sixties. Everywhere you looked itinerant new companies seemed to be springing up. Portable Theatre, founded by Tony Bicat and David Hare; the Pip Simmons Theatre Group; the People Show; Freehold, founded by another anglicised American, Nancy Meckler; John Fox's Welfare State in Leeds; Albert Hunt's Bradford College of Art Group; the Brighton Combination on the south coast. Some of these groups survived. Some disappeared. But it was a sign of the changing times that even the traditionally conservative Arts Council set up a sub-committee (later called the New Activities Committee) to offer a modest £15,000 to seed new projects.

To put it simply, there was an air of turbulence about the late Sixties which clearly witnessed the burgeoning of an alternative theatrical culture. Much of the work may have been ephemeral and silly: 'getting the guests', in imitation of Living Theatre, became something of a fetish and I recall the horror of sitting in the Arts Lab in Drury Lane while a plastic sheet was thrown over the audience's heads. Even in the emerging fringe, as well as in mainstream theatre, there were also vast gaps. Looking back, it is astonishing how thinly the experience of both women and ethnic minorities was represented: to all intents and purposes, British theatre was still a white, male-dominated club. Yet it both reflected and contributed to the sense of flux that characterised a momentous decade. Examine the work of the period and you get a sharp sense of the political scepticism, youthful disaffection, sexual freedom and spiritual questioning that were part of the times. There is also little doubt that British theatre at the end of the decade was infinitely richer than when it had begun. It combined a corps of first-class dramatists, unequalled in scope since the first Elizabethan age, with a new generation of theatre-makers anxious to subvert the primacy of text. As the Sixties revelled to a conclusion, there was certainly an abundance of high-flying energy around. Was it, however – like even the best parties – destined to come to an end leaving behind only a handful of sensory memories and a throbbing hangover?

VI

1970–74

Blasted Heath

In fact, the prospects didn't seem too bad as we edged into a new decade. With the Wilson government having weathered the worst of its economic troubles, it looked as if we were in for a period of artistic expansiveness and continuing social reform. Roy Jenkins, an excellent Chancellor of the Exchequer, had transformed the financial situation. By 1970 government income exceeded expenditure by over five per cent of Gross Domestic Product. Northern Ireland was still a potential flashpoint, with the British army now responsible for security, but Jim Callaghan had some success in keeping the lid on possible trouble. And the formal abolition of capital punishment in December 1969 was a reminder of Labour's liberal domestic record. So when Wilson called a General Election for June 1970, we serenely anticipated a decade of continuing progress. And that was part of the trouble. There was a complacency about Wilson's belief that Labour had now become the natural party of government. Not even the revelation of a temporary balance-of-payments deficit or England's shock defeat by West Germany in the World Cup during the election campaign dented Labour confidence. So it came as a rude shock to the pundits, the pollsters and the dangerously smug Wilson when the Conservatives, under Edward Heath, romped home in the 1970 election with 330 seats to Labour's 280. It remains one of the great post-war electoral upsets, and a result that would leave Labour with permanent mental scars. It also marked the end of liberalising Sixties reform and signalled that the party was officially over.

Vilifying the Seventies is temptingly easy. Nick Tiratsoo, in a balanced, cogent essay in *The Folio History of England*, argues that 'Thatcherites have endlessly blackened the period in order to make the achievements of the Eighties seem more dramatic'. He goes on to point out that Neanderthal management attitudes were as much responsible for the wave of Seventies strikes as union militancy, that Britain was by no means unique in experiencing a falling growth rate and rising unemployment and that, even in a time of recession, the middle classes quietly prospered. Yet, when all is said and done, Heath's Seventies was a period of continuing crisis marked by industrial chaos, social division and international instability. A month after the election the dockers staged their first national strike since 1926. The miners also went on strike in 1972 and 1974. In the first case, a state of emergency was declared. In the second instance, partly because of a simultaneous train-drivers' strike and soaring petrol prices, the nation was put on a three-day week. Factories and offices simply shut down. Domestic electricity supplies were curtailed. And, in a move that really hit the nation where it hurts, BBC and ITV were forced to go off the air at ten-thirty at night. It was almost incredible: largely through Heath's intransigence and refusal to negotiate with the striking miners, Britain was reduced in the early months of 1974 to conditions that recalled the worst deprivations of wartime.

In fact, during Heath's premiership everything seemed to fall apart. Inflation and unemployment rose. Crimes of violence soared. And the situation in Northern Ireland rapidly deteriorated. The most shocking incident came in January 1972 when British paratroopers opened fire on peaceful demonstrators in Londonderry, killing thirteen people. Over three decades later the event was still the subject of a second, exhaustive official enquiry: one that, incidentally, produced a remarkable piece of verbatim theatre at the Tricycle Theatre. What was immediately clear, however, was that 'Bloody Sunday' escalated the tension in Northern Ireland and led, directly or otherwise, to a wave of IRA bomb attacks in London, Guildford and Birmingham in the early Seventies. To be fair to Heath, he was also the victim of international events. America's unqualified support for Israel in the Yom Kippur War provoked the Gulf states into increasing oil prices by seventy per cent in December 1973: an action that added more than four hundred million pounds to the UK's oil import bill and caused the government to introduce petrol rationing and a speed limit of fifty miles per hour. It is also fair to acknowledge that the good side of Heath's obduracy was seen in his dedicated Europeanism, which led to Britain's formal admission to the EEC, along with Ireland and Denmark, in January 1973; but even that was a red rag to many left-wingers, who saw it as a symbol of Britain's alignment with the European capitalist club. Even if Heath could claim success over

Europe, he showed a reckless naivety in going to the country in February 1974, at the height of the miners' strike, on a manifesto asking 'Who governs Britain?' As the historian Peter Clarke has noted: 'The Government found its immediate case on coal falling apart, day by day . . . It was not, however, the small print which sealed Heath's fate but the big picture: a hapless Government, hamstrung in the darkness of another three-day week, presiding over double-figure inflation.' In the event, Labour was narrowly returned as the largest party, with 301 seats to the Conservatives' 296, with fourteen Liberals and twenty-three others. Wilson was precariously back in power; and even a second General Election in October 1974 left Labour with a tenuous overall majority of only four over Conservatives, Liberals and the various minority groups. It was hardly a ringing popular mandate or a recipe for stable government; and it helped to perpetuate the mood of crisis that seemed to permeate every aspect of British life during the decade. It was as if the optimistic dream that sustained the Sixties had abruptly ended and the country had awakened to a new and unpalatable reality.

Life, of course, went on: the sun still rose in the morning and set in the evening, the seasons passed and many individuals, if they were lucky enough to be in work, led happy and fulfilled lives. I was certainly one of the fortunate ones. In October 1971 I was invited by Peter Preston to become drama critic of the *Guardian* which was the start of a durable professional marriage. I was also blessed with a supportive partner and a young daughter who had been born at the time of the 1969 moon landings and whom we wisely resisted calling Luna. My chief personal memory of the Seventies is one of ceaseless activity as I covered a profusion of first nights, travelled widely and presented various arts programmes on radio and television. Yet, even though I was doing my dream job and leading a life of relative comfort, I still remember the stab of anxiety created by the temper of the times. What kind of world was our daughter being born into? How could one justify one's own privileged existence at a time of increasing hardship? And, while dramatic criticism was personally fulfilling, was it making any useful contribution to society? My only answer to a nagging puritan conscience was to work remorselessly hard and to encourage, perhaps indiscriminately, dramatists who addressed the political issues of the time.

Although I had been writing about theatre since 1965, what

principally struck me when I became a full-time critic was how stag-
nant the commercial theatre had become: all the real life and energy
seemed to be in the subsidised institutions and the burgeoning fringe.
And a survey of the playbills for the autumn of 1971 confirms that
impression. Virtually all the good plays in the West End – including
Osborne's *West of Suez*, Nichols' *Forget-Me-Not-Lane*, Ayckbourn's
How The Other Half Loves, Hampton's *The Philanthropist* and
Sartre's *Kean* – had their origins in subsidised theatre: the sole exception was Simon Gray's *Butley*. Equally striking is the prevalence of sex
comedies and farces whose titles embodied, in characteristically
British fashion, some urgent, nannying imperative: *Don't Start Without Me*, *Don't Just Lie There, Say Something*, *Move Over Mrs
Markham*. Even an American comedy by Larry Gelbart was abruptly
entitled *Jump!!* – as if two exclamation marks miraculously doubled
the excitement. But sex was clearly a major selling point since the West
End boasted not one but two erotic revues: the Tynan-fostered *Oh!
Calcutta!* and an American import, *The Dirtiest Show In Town*, neither of which left one profoundly stirred. I suspect that romping rud-
ery and prospective nudity, rather than a profound love of medieval
literature, also accounted for the fact that *Canterbury Tales* was in its
fourth year at the Phoenix and that *Abelard and Heloise* was standing
up well at Wyndham's. And, as a reminder of the fact that racial
enlightenment had not yet spread to popular entertainment, the Black
and White Minstrels were still strutting their blandly offensive stuff at
the Victoria Palace. Even superannuated actors, and playgoers, were
catered for, with William Douglas Home's *The Jockey Club Stakes* at
the Vaudeville. The West End was still there; but it seemed increasingly irrelevant to a Britain where unemployment was touching the million mark and where internment without trial had been introduced in
Northern Ireland.

The West End of the early Seventies was like some once-great empire
living off memories of its former glories. Where in the past it had dominated the surrounding terrain and colonised satellite kingdoms, it was
now dependent on imported product to sustain its home base. Sometimes that bought-in product was first-rate; and, if the West End justified its existence, it was with a show like Stephen Sondheim's *Company*
that arrived from Broadway in January 1972. This remains one of the
red-letter nights of my theatregoing life. Here was a musical that
touched on serious themes: commitment, friendship and the contest

between the dignity of solitude and the need for permanent relationships. It also boasted the wittiest lyrics heard in any American musical since the heyday of Cole Porter: its portrait of marriage in 'The Little Things You Do Together' ('It's things like using force together, shouting till you're hoarse together, getting a divorce together') remains timelessly true. And, although Sondheim is often patronised as a composer, his songs both acknowledged Broadway's past and were individually memorable. Harold Prince's production, with streamlined Boris Aronson sets that evoked the vertiginous restlessness of Manhattan life, was also a perfect expression of the score. This was the musical doing something it all too rarely did: interpreting life and, at the same time, enhancing it. It was also a musical that made up for the grisly tune-and-toe shows that invaded the West End in the early Seventies: shows like *Pippin* and *Popkiss*, *Gone With The Wind* and *I and Albert*, which resonated with all the excitement of a damp fart.

Company aside, my other golden memories of commercial theatre in the early Seventies are of prodigious solo performers. The London Palladium still housed nightly Variety and brought us both Ethel Merman and Jack Benny. The former was not quite the leather-lung'd, diamante-frocked, ambulatory brass band one had been led to expect. True, she had volume; but she also had the gift, shared by all great singers, of making the lyrics of a song tell. 'They're writing songs of love but *not* for me', with its oblique emphasis on the negative, sticks in my mind as an example of her ability to convey sadness as well as celebration. As for Jack Benny, then in his late seventies, I was obviously impressed by the famous timing and the ability to make silence eloquent: something that had a lasting impact on a young Harold Pinter when he saw Benny in a previous Palladium incarnation. But I was equally struck by Benny's sophisticated camp and physical economy. Chekhov once wrote that 'when a man spends the least possible number of movements over some definite action that is grace': words that seemed to apply to the minimalist Benny. At the opposite extreme was the English comedian, Max Wall, who enjoyed a spectacular comeback, after several years in the wilderness of clubland, in a revue called *Cockie* at the Vaudeville. Wall was brought up in the rubber-limbed tradition of the eccentric comedian and still appeared even in his late sixties as the wild-eyed, lank-haired Professor Wallofski, who resembled a mixture of Grock and Frankenstein's Monster. But Wall's debt to a Continental style of grotesque physicality was allied to a deeply

English delight in the oddities of language that harked back to Dan Leno and even, in literary terms, to Dickens. There was also about Wall an air of lugubrious desperation: 'If they sawed a woman in half,' he lamented, 'I'd get the half that eats.' And it was this quality that, in his twilight years, made him a peerless interpreter of Samuel Beckett. But, although the commercial theatre still played host to vintage performers, in dramatic terms the real action was elsewhere: at the RSC, then enjoying a period of progressive expansion under Trevor Nunn; more fitfully at the National Theatre, torn apart by the badly bungled transfer of power from Olivier to Peter Hall; occasionally in the regions, where large new theatres in Birmingham and Sheffield raised equally big questions as to how they were to be financed and filled; and more often on the fringe, where emerging venues included the Almost Free and Soho Poly in central London and the Bush and the Orange Tree in the city's western suburbs. There was a vast amount of fragmented energy and activity in the theatre of the early Seventies and swathes of interesting new writing. But the abiding impression was that the political dreams of the late Sixties had not been fulfilled and that the failure of the hoped-for revolution of 1968 had led to the entrenchment of established authority. British theatre of the early Seventies was intensely political; but the voluminous product was based on disappointment, disillusion and a pervasive sense of despair.

No dramatist was better at analysing that disillusion than Trevor Griffiths; and he was especially important for a variety of reasons. Having been born in 1935 into a Manchester working-class family, Griffiths came relatively late to theatre, which gave him a refreshing intellectual maturity. He had, in fact, worked as a teacher and a further education officer for the BBC, and also spent a lot of time in the New Left movement of the Fifties and Sixties, which brought him into contact with left-wing intellectuals such as Raymond Williams, E. P. Thompson, Stuart Hall and Christopher Hill. Griffiths was also keen to reach as many people as possible through his writing, which is why he exploited the possibilities of television and was often scathingly dismissive of the fringe: 'I am not interested', he once said, 'in talking to thirty-eight university graduates in a cellar in Soho.' His declared aim, as a socialist, was 'strategic penetration' of the citadels of bourgeois culture; and within four years of The Wages of Thin being staged at the Manchester Stables Theatre in 1969, Griffiths was to find his work being produced by the National Theatre and providing Laurence

Olivier with his final theatrical appearance. That was penetration on
the grand scale.

Out of disillusion Griffiths fashioned tremendous drama. He later
recalled:

> I was deeply involved with and deeply affected by the student unrest
> of the Sixties. The detonations set off then put revolutionary trans-
> formation back on the agenda of the society. But by 1970 one could
> see that it was all a failure, it was gone and I was trying to account
> for my feelings. I felt anger and I felt pain and I wanted to make a
> play that said something about it.

The result was *Occupations*, which was first produced at the Manchester Stables in 1970, with Richard Wilson in the lead role, and quickly picked up by the RSC for a London season at The Place in 1971,
with Patrick Stewart and Ben Kingsley. What made Griffiths such a
powerful writer was his ability – strongly influenced by the Communist Party Historians Group, which included Thompson, Hill and Eric
Hobsbawm – to explore the present in terms of the past. Set in Turin
during the factory sit-ins of the nineteen-twenties, *Occupations* was
about contrasting attitudes to revolution; and the action hinged on the
confrontation between a ruthless pragmatist and a Utopian idealist.
The pragmatist was Christo Kabak: a Bulgarian Communist and representative of the Third International. The idealist was Antonio Gramsci: a leader of the Turin insurrections and a cult hero to many of the
revolutionaries of 1968. In the end, Griffiths showed how the Turin
insurrection was defeated in a workers' referendum and how the practical Kabak struck a deal with a Fiat intermediary, one that involved
massive investment by the company in the new Soviet state. But Griffiths left open the question of whether Kabak's actions were historically justified or whether Gramsci was right in suggesting a revolution
not based on love for the people was ultimately sterile. Above all, his
play seemed enormously pertinent to 1968, where a spontaneous student uprising in Paris had been greeted with mistrust both by organised labour and the French Communist Party. It was also highly
relevant to modern Britain where, in September 1970, workers at the
Upper Clyde Shipbuilders took over the shipyards, giving rise to a
wave of similarly optimistic but short-lived factory occupations. Griffiths' achievement was to view the potentialities and pitfalls of radical
action through the prism of history.

In *The Party*, presented by the National Theatre at the Old Vic in December 1973, Griffiths focused more directly on contemporary Britain: in particular, the multiple reasons for the failure of revolution. And, for a young critic like myself, it was a thrilling occasion. It showed Britain's most prominent public stage being used for serious political analysis. With characters being allowed to develop their arguments in twenty-minute speeches, it yielded the most intelligent dramatic dialectic since the demise of Bernard Shaw. And the quality one had always admired in Laurence Olivier – his appetite for risk – was symbolised by his decision to make his farewell to the British stage by playing not, as sentimentalists expected, an elegiac Prospero, but a hard-headed Glaswegian Trotskyite. It came as no great surprise that the majority of British theatre critics, with the honourable exception of Milton Shulman, dismissed the play as a long-winded bore. Rather more disturbing was the fact that so many on the left, from *Tribune* to the *Workers Press*, attacked the play as anti-socialist propaganda; but then the fragmentation and divisiveness of the left, as well as its frequent hypocrisy, was one of Griffiths' central themes.

Griffiths sets the action in the swish South Kensington apartment of a left-wing TV producer, Joe Shawcross, on the night of 10–11 May 1968: a date with its own built-in irony since, while students are clashing with riot police outside the Sorbonne in Paris, a group of London intellectuals are debating radical change. Joe, as we graphically learn from the opening scene, is temporarily afflicted by sexual impotence: an apt metaphor for the political ineffectiveness of both himself and his guests. They have assembled to offer a socialist analysis of modern Britain and to hammer out a plan of action. But they can't even agree what form the evening should take, let alone achieve a concerted view of the potential for revolution. Andrew Ford, a self-important lecturer at the London School of Economics, suggests that Marx's vision of a proletarian revolution has been denied by European history, that the urban working class is no longer a subversive force and that only in the Third World do you find centres of revolutionary struggle. His arguments are then instantly refuted by the Trotskyite John Tagg. Tagg points out the revolutionary potential that exists among students, blacks, women and what he terms 'social deviants'. He goes on to argue the need for a new Revolutionary Party based on discipline, criticism and self-scrutiny. But he sees no chance of it being led by British intellectuals. 'Imagine', he says,' a life without the approval of your peers. Imagine a life without success. The intellectual's problem is not vision, it's commitment. You enjoy biting the hand that feeds you but you'll never bite it off.' After his departure, Malcolm Sloman, an itinerant northern playwright closely based on David Mercer, attacks Tagg's rigidity while endorsing his point about individual careerism and the repressive tolerance of institutions like the BBC's *Wednesday Play*:

> The only thing you're allowed to put into the system is that which can be assimilated and absorbed by it. Joe, this is a society that matured on descriptions of its inequity and injustice. Poverty is one of its best-favoured spectacles. Bad housing, class-divisive schools, plight of the sick and the aged, the alienating indignities of work, the fatuous vacuities of 'leisure' – Jesus God, man, we can't get enough of it.

Griffiths has said that there is a part of him in all the main speeches; yet each speaker brilliantly undercuts his predecessor. Ford's notion of European intellectuals assisting Third World uprisings sounds patronising and implausible once you've heard the hard-headed Tagg. Yet Tagg's adhesion to a past world of hierarchical structures seems dated as soon as you've listened to Sloman. And even Sloman's belief in the 'germ of discontent' that will eventually lead to a mass uprising is undermined by his own boozy anarchy. The final resonant image is of a compromised, solitary impotence as Joe Shawcross, who is forming his own TV company and who lends his brother three hundred quid to start up a business, listens to a lugubrious pop record. Britain, says Griffiths, is a society where protest is sanctioned and absorbed. Which is perfectly true. Yet that doesn't invalidate the need for protest. Nor does it mean that Britain hadn't been changed as a society by a succession of agitational *Wednesday Play*s – most famously Ken Loach's *Cathy Come Home*, from the story by Jeremy Sandford – by the realism of Sixties cinema or by its authority-subverting theatre. It's also fair to ask whether wholesale revolution was ever on the cards in a Welfare State society like Britain, cushioned against the worst excesses of social deprivation. Nevertheless *The Party* – revived by David Hare in a simplified NT Touring production in 1974 and by the RSC in 1984 – is remarkable for the maturity of its political analysis. Griffiths sees Britain as a society where the fragmentation of the left, careerist individualism and the institutional tolerance of organisations like the BBC, and even the National Theatre, militate against radical change; and his play combines elegiac regret for revolutionary failure with an accurate vision of a country that seems temperamentally averse to social upheaval.

Not all dramatists shared Griffiths' disillusion. In the same year that *The Party* played at the Old Vic, John McGrath was busy touring the Highlands of Scotland with a play for 7:84 called *The Cheviot, The Stag and The Black, Black Oil* that clearly struck a chord with local audiences. And it is fascinating to contrast the methods and approaches of the two dramatists. Griffiths was a soberly realistic Mancunian who believed that the best way to achieve a humane socialism lay in strategic penetration of the mass media and the National Theatre; McGrath was an idealistic Liverpudlian who, having co-founded *Z-Cars* for the BBC and written feature films such as *Billion Dollar Brain* and *The Virgin Soldiers*, eventually decided that the mass media were themselves so penetrated by the ruling-class ideology that 'fighting within them is going to drive you mad'. McGrath retained a wary respect for Griffiths; but he felt that even getting a play like *The Party* on at the National was not 'contributing to the creation of a genuinely oppositional theatre'. In 1971 McGrath, turning his back on lucrative film and TV work, founded the 7:84 Theatre Company, whose name alluded to the disturbing fact that a mere seven per cent of the population in Britain owned eighty-four per cent of the wealth. Two years later the company split into Scottish and English branches, and it was the former whom McGrath led on a triumphant Highlands tour with *The Cheviot*.

Which achieved more: *The Party* or *The Cheviot*? Numerically, there was little in it. One played to nine hundred people a night at the Old Vic for around thirty-five performances; the other to over thirty thousand people in a hundred performances that involved the company in seventeen thousand miles of travel. *The Party* reached metropolitan opinion-formers; *The Cheviot* spoke to Scottish audiences who were given a new perspective on their own history. What the two plays illustrate, however, is the divergent approaches of left-wing writers to the crises of the early Seventies. While Griffiths' play was a rigorous dialectical drama that had a continuing afterlife, McGrath's work was a piece of instructive popular entertainment of the kind that Ewan MacColl created for Theatre Workshop in the Forties. Employing the traditional form of a ceilidh, *The Cheviot* was also based on intense research, undertaken by the whole company, into the Highland Clearances. In the early nineteenth century, Highlanders were evicted or forced to emigrate to make way for Cheviot sheep. At the end of the century tenants were again cleared off the land to satisfy the aristocratic appetite for stag-shooting, hunting and fishing. And the show went on to explain how, in the twentieth century, the rights to North Sea oil had been sold off to the multinationals. That was in contrast to Norway, Algeria and Libya, where governments exercised control over shares or profit distribution. In the past opposition to the land Clearances had taken the form of organised militancy. McGrath's message was that 'we too must organise and fight not with stones but politically, with the help of the working-class in the towns, for a government that will control the oil-development for the benefit of everybody'. You could accuse McGrath of reckless optimism in believing that the Scottish people could single-handedly counter the force of the multinationals. Nevertheless in the October 1974 General Election the Scottish Nationalists gained eleven crucial seats at a time when the Labour government had an overall majority of only six. It seems reasonable to infer that a show like *The Cheviot*, later televised by the BBC, played a vital part in reinforcing Scotland's sense of national identity and influencing the popular vote.

Tempting as it is to pit John McGrath against Trevor Griffiths – the instinctive populist against the strategic penetrator of both high and mass culture – the two dramatists had a good deal in common. Both were born in 1935 and had direct experience of grammar school, the BBC, New Left politics and teaching. But in the early Seventies, a new generation began to emerge that was different in all sorts of ways from its immediate predecessors. The new gang, most prominently David Hare and Howard Brenton, had not done National Service (unlike McGrath, who used it as the source for *Events While Guarding The Bofors Gun* in 1966), had little experience of the workaday world and had not been part of any formal radical grouping. They were alienated by what they saw as the failures of the Wilson government and shocked by the collapse of the Paris student uprising : 'May '68', said Brenton in 1975, 'gave me a desperation I still have.' The new gang, however, were as much intrigued by the spectacle of capitalism in crisis as they were dismayed by the failure of Utopian dreams. Brenton graduated from Cambridge in 1965 and Hare in 1968. Hare's tutor had nominally been the Marxist critic, Raymond Williams, and Brenton's the defiantly internationalist George Steiner. However, repudiating their background, both writers rejected the idea of a canonical culture, attacked the conventional proprieties of British theatre, and were gleefully preoccupied by a society they believed to be in a state of terminal decay. Hare and Brenton, while occasionally collaborating, developed their own distinctive voices. But their emergence at roughly the same time signifies a decisive shift in tone in British drama. In the past criticism of society was the fruit not just of reading and research but of knocking about the world in search of a living or doing National Service in former colonial outposts. Now it was the product of a restless intellectual discontent devoid of much in the way of work experience.

Hare's own writing career was driven initially by external necessity rather than inner compulsion. Shortly after leaving Cambridge, he and Tony Bicat set up a touring company, Portable Theatre, that bowled round the country in a van taking drama to the culturally starved. And Hare's ephemeral first two plays – *How Brophy Made Good* and *What Happened To Blake* – were written largely to give the company some much-needed product. Even Hare's more obviously committed work suggested a writer with a sharp, caustic view of the world but better at demolition than construction. *Slag* (1970), which showed three young women setting up a boarding school as a social experiment, was apparently intended as a satire on gesture politics but was worryingly seen by some as an assault on female independence. And *The Great Exhibition* (1972) was a callow piece about an alienated Labour MP for whom socialism was largely a career choice. Although Hare slagged off parliamentary democracy, left-wing careerism, right-wing moral squalor and druggy vacuity with supercilious scorn, the play seemed to have no anchor in reality. Typically, the hero's wife attempted to take over his Sunderland parliamentary seat in six days without a mention of anything so mundane as a selection committee.

Hare seemed to find his voice as much through collaboration as solo work. He joined with six other writers – including Trevor Griffiths – on *Lay By*, which was first shown at the Edinburgh Traverse in 1971 and was a disturbing and sexually graphic account of a rape case on the M4. Even more significant, in view of Hare's later fascination with factual drama and the state of the nation, was *England's Ireland*. This was another joint-authored piece by seven writers – including David Edgar, Howard Brenton and Snoo Wilson – that attempted to show, in 1972, how Northern Ireland had reached its current state of crisis. I

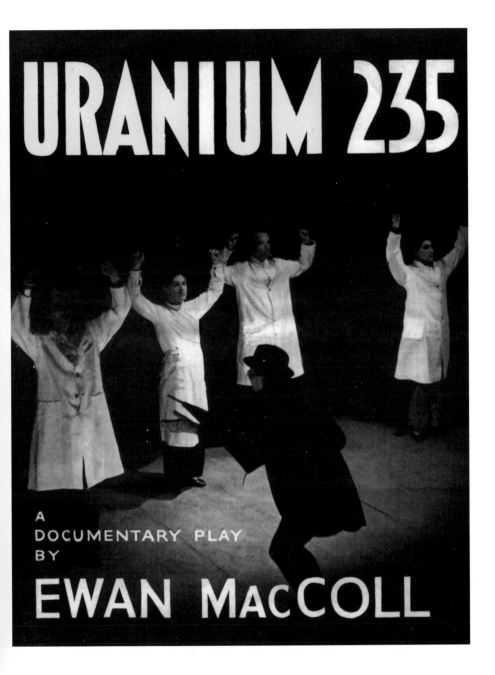

1 Joan Littlewood's Theatre Workshop production of *Uranium 235* which toured the UK from 1946 to 1952

2 Michael Hordern as Paul Southman in John Whiting's seminal *Saint's Day* at the Arts Theatre, 1951
3 Laurence Olivier as Archie Rice in John Osborne's *The Entertainer* at the Royal Court Theatre, 1957

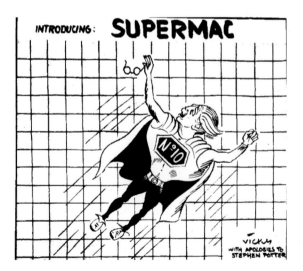

4 Dudley Moore, Alan Bennett, Peter Cook and Jonathan Miller in *Beyond the Fringe* at the Royal Lyceum Theatre, Edinburgh, 1960
5 Vicky's iconic cartoon image of one of *Beyond the Fringe*'s prime targets, Harold Macmillan

6 The baby-stoning scene from Edward Bond's *Saved*, with Tony Selby in the foreground, at the Royal Court Theatre, 1965

7 Laurence Olivier in his farewell stage appearance as John Tagg in Trevor Griffiths's *The Party* at the Old Vic, 1973

Lindsay Duncan (Lady Nijo) and Gwen Taylor (Marlene) in Caryl Churchill's *Top Girls* at the Royal Court Theatre, 1982

Harold Pinter (Deeley) and Liv Ullmann (Anna) in the American tour of Pinter's *Old Times*, 1985–6

JUNE 20, 1983

$1.75

TIME

AFGHANISTAN
Behind the
Lines

MAGGIE
BY A MILE

What It Means
What She'll Do

British Prime Minister
Margaret Thatcher

10 and 11 Two British success stories of the 1980s: Margaret Thatcher, after her first re-election as prime minister, and Andrew Lloyd Webber

JANUARY 18, 1988 $2.00

TIME

Trying to Tame
Wall Street

After the
triumphs
of *Evita*
and *Cats*,
Andrew Lloyd
Webber brings
Phantom
to Broadway

Magician
Of the
Musical

03

12 John Thaw as Labour leader (George Jones) in David Hare's *The Absence of War* in the Olivier at the National Theatre, 1993
13 Fiona Bell (Phyllis), Daisy Maguire and Kathy Rose O'Brien as her daughters (Poppy and Lori), in Lucy Caldwell's *Leaves* at the Royal Court Jerwood Theatre Upstairs, 2007

remember it as a brave, bold, investigative show that tried to address the province's long history of social injustice as well as religious bigotry. How, it asked, could one hope for a return to 'normality' in Northern Ireland when that meant an unemployment rate of forty-three per cent in some areas, a weekly wage of eleven pounds and a situation in which five per cent of the population owned forty-seven per cent of the wealth? But 1972 was the year of Bloody Sunday, of the Aldershot bombing in which seven people were killed and of the establishment of direct rule from Westminster. In the event over fifty theatres turned the play down and, even in London, it was seen only briefly at the Royal Court and the Roundhouse. But Hare himself did much to kickstart the work into existence on the rational grounds that 'theatre *should* cover political subjects' – and, most especially, Northern Ireland.

Hare's earliest plays showed a certain talent to abuse; and my memory of meeting him for an interview in a pub just before *Lay By* is of a faintly raffish head-boy glamour symbolised by the yellow sweater loosely knotted around his neck, suggesting he had just stepped off a Sussex tennis court. Very quickly, however, Hare began to reveal his fascination both with the nature of England and the crisis in capitalism. In 1973 he and Brenton were jointly commissioned by Richard Eyre to write a 'big' play for Nottingham Playhouse. The result was *Brassneck*, which offered an exhilaratingly panoramic satire on England from 1945 to the present through depicting the meteoric ups and downs of a self-seeking Midlands family, the Bagleys. The idea was to create an imagined sequel to Angus Calder's *The People's War*. This was a book that for the Hare–Eyre–Brenton generation became a far more important bible than the works of Marx or Freud. What Hare and Brenton set out to explore in *Brassneck* was 'The People's Peace': 'a peace seen, in our case,' said Hare, 'through the lives of the petty bourgeoisie, builders, solicitors, brewers, politicians, the masonic gang who carve up provincial England'. And what Hare and Brenton vividly caught, in the style of John Arden's *The Workhouse Donkey*, was the maggot-like corruption at the heart of England: the way the high ideals of Attlee and Bevan had been compromised by squalid municipal back-scratching, sordid alliances between political opponents and local Rachmanism. The authors were not afraid to be topical: a dubiously biddable ex-Tory Cabinet minister, ready to offer governmental expertise to private industry at the drop of a cheque, evoked recent memories of Reginald Maudling's involvement with a gaoled Midlands architect, John Poulson. And the play ended with the ultra-theatrical image of the reunited Bagleys, now living off proceeds from strip clubs and the sale of Chinese heroin, raising their glasses in a toast to 'the last days of capitalism', as darkness swallowed them up. In the event, mercantile capitalism was to prove rather more resilient than Hare and Brenton suggested. Even so, the play was a swaggeringly ambitious attempt to present a pageant of post-war England: a cynic's *Cavalcade*, showing how a symbolic family had moved, in a couple of generations, from singing the Red Flag in 1945 to acting as a conduit for the Oriental drug market in the decadent Seventies.

But Hare really came of age as a writer with *Knuckle*, which Michael Codron produced in the West End in March 1974. The play opened, in fact, in the same week that Harold Wilson returned as Prime Minister, to confront an economy brought to its knees by a combination of massive government borrowing (more than £4 billion), soaring oil prices and union militancy. Middling notices, the pervasive economic crisis and a feeling that the West End was not perhaps the ideal place for an assault on bourgeois capitalism led to the play having a relatively short run. But it was an excellently written play that applied the tone of a hard-boiled Ross Macdonald–Raymond Chandler thriller to darkest Guildford and that was, in Hare's own words, 'modestly prophetic'. As he explains, 'It is organised round the two types of capitalism which ten years later were to clash so violently: the paternalistic kind with its old social networks and its spurious moralizing and the new aggressive, shameless variety which would gain such ascendancy in the Eighties.'

Hare's plot revolves around the return of a gun-seller, Curly, to his native Guildford. His aim is to investigate the disappearance of his sister, Sarah, last seen on a beach in Eastbourne. And what Curly uncovers is a murky tale of blackmail, harassment and shady property deals in which an old woman has been dispossessed by a company ultimately financed by his father. Hare's progress as an astute social commentator is evident. In particular, he conveys the shift in England from a smooth, gentlemanly capitalism to the kind of freebooting, classless variety that was to become prevalent under Thatcher: the words 'quiet' and 'loud' resound antithetically throughout the text. But Hare is sharp enough to see that this was not an overnight transition but one that had been taking place since the Sixties. At one point Jenny, the owner of a louche Guildford niterie, invokes the names of John Bloom whose washing-machine empire ignominiously crashed, Harry Hyams who disastrously commissioned Centre Point, the long untenanted office block, and Jack Cotton, a property tycoon responsible for the evisceration of old working-class communities. All embodied what even Edward Heath in 1973 had been driven to call 'the unacceptable and unpleasant face of capitalism'. But in *Knuckle* it is Curly, the amoral arms salesman, who is given the most remarkable speech, about the England he has encountered after a long absence abroad:

> When I got back I found this country was a jampot for swindlers and cons and racketeers. Not just property. Boarding houses and bordellos and nightclubs and crooked charter-flights, private clinics, horse-hair wigs and tin-can motor-cars, venereal cafés with ice-cream made from whale blubber and sausages full of sawdust . . . Money can be harvested like rotten fruit. People are just aching to be fleeced. But those of us who do it must learn the quality of self-control.

That speech conjures up, far better than any journalist could or did, the tacky vulgarity of an unbridled free-market system that was to reach its apogee in the deregulated Eighties. The only danger of Hare's perceptive assault is that it induces a faintly perverse nostalgia for the old-style capitalism practised by Curly's father, Patrick. This is a man who reads Henry James's *The Golden Bowl* and plays the cello at home while in the City he makes money with 'silent indolence'. But, while Patrick attacks 'the wide boys and the profiteers who have sullied our reputation', he is also a first-class hypocrite who simply gets other people to do his dirty work for him and who left his daughter to kill herself. Even allowing for its whiff of ambivalence towards gentlemanly Toryism, *Knuckle* was Hare's graduation ceremony: the work in which he discovered his own voice through the form of a pastiche thriller and in which his own fastidious distaste for the new capitalism clearly emerged.

Knuckle also showed just how different a writer Hare was from his friend and frequent collaborator, Howard Brenton. Both were social commentators who started from the same assumption: that post-war Britain had failed to fulfil the expectations aroused by the 1945 Labour government. But, although Hare had directed Brenton's

Christie in Love for Portable and the two had worked together on *Lay By*, *England's Ireland* and *Brassneck*, they had contrasting outlooks and personalities. Brenton was, and thankfully still is, a large, genial, rumpled teddy bear of a man; Hare is leaner, more prefectorial and capable of delivering devastatingly curt judgements with a nerve-racking smile. Brenton, as Hare later admitted, was always more scornful of social democracy than he himself. Brenton, I feel, always wanted to smash the system; Hare, preoccupied by the question of how you live decently inside a corrupt, capitalist world, wanted to change it from within. Those differences came home to me when I spent a day watching rehearsals at the Royal Court in 1973 for Brenton's *Magnificence*, which was, amongst other things, an attack on English humanism. When I asked Brenton why he was so invincibly hostile to it he replied:

> Because it has become so sullied. Humanist ideas always come from the Right. The humanist line, for instance, is to recognise that there is a class conflict but not to accept the necessity to change it. The truth is that people are in constant pain in the way they live. Violence on the individual level is not the most horrifying thing in our society but rather the violence of a system that permits homelessness and degrading poverty.

That is far closer to the moralistic Marxism of Edward Bond than it is to the revolutionary disillusion of Trevor Griffiths or the stylish radicalism of David Hare.

Griffiths, in fact, once said affectionately of Brenton that 'the trouble with Howard is that he's a bloody Utopianist'. But, in trying to place Brenton amongst the upsurge of post-1968 political writing, I'd say his real gift was for poetic imagery rather than hard-headed analysis: his work has often struck me as the theatrical equivalent of an action painting in which the tactile excitement of applying pigment to the canvas is as important as the finished artefact. And, if one speech lingers in the mind from *Magnificence*, it is that belonging to Jed, a product of the alternative culture who turns into a bungling, bomb-throwing terrorist. In graphic detail, Jed describes being in a cinema watching *The Carpetbaggers* when a drunk threw a bottle at the screen aimed at Carroll Baker's left breast:

> The left tit moved on in an instant, of course. But for the rest of the film there was that bottle-shaped hole. Clung. One blemish on the

screen. But somehow you couldn't watch the film from then. And so thinks . . . the poor bomber. Bomb 'em. Again and again. Right through their silver screen. Disrupt the spectacle. The obscene parade, bring it to a halt! Scatter the dolly girls, let the advertisements bleed.

It is an arresting image that provided Peter Ansorge with a title for a book on the new alternative theatre: *Disrupting The Spectacle*. Ansorge even saw Brenton's play as a critique of fringe theatre in its failure to assist, or accomplish, revolution. But that is to limit its meaning. What it conveys is the contradiction you often find in Brenton's work. It's an attack on acts of random violence written from the vantage point of a romantic anarchist who delights in the momentary disruption of the public charade.

Brenton played his own part in disrupting the spectacle with *The Churchill Play*: a theatrical hand-grenade tossed into the wide-open spaces of Nottingham Playhouse in May 1974 under Richard Eyre's direction. This was very much a play of its time, coming shortly after the three-day week and the miners' strike and coinciding with a renewed outbreak of IRA violence in mainland Britain. Set in an authoritarian 1984 where a Conservative–Labour coalition has created a series of gulags for the detention of terrorists and industrial saboteurs, Brenton's is a nightmarish extrapolation based on the febrile mood of the early Seventies. It also rests on two crucial assumptions. One is that Churchill, far from being a popular hero, was an enemy of the working class who created an illusory sense of liberty. The other is that the internment without trial of Republican political prisoners at Long Kesh created a dangerous precedent that could lead to the mainland detention of social malcontents. Post-war Britain, in Brenton's view, was losing even its distant memory of freedom.

In the short term, there was a measure of both dramatic implausibility and left-wing paranoia about Brenton's dystopian scenario. It beggared belief that a group of political internees would be allowed, even with the connivance of a liberal doctor, to stage a subversive play about Churchill for the benefit of a visiting parliamentary delegation. As an obvious contrast, one has only to think of *The Island*, created by Athol Fugard, John Kani and Winston Ntshona in 1973, in which prisoners on South Africa's Robben Island plausibly got away with staging *Antigone* precisely because it was an uncensorable classic.

Even the arguments aired against Churchill – that he had a syphilitic father, that he despatched troops against the Welsh miners in 1910, that he was pissed out of his mind at the Yalta Conference – lack the force of those in Charles Wood's *Dingo*. Wood caught the authentic, anti-Churchillian bitterness of Second World War survivors; Brenton either simplifies the arguments ('People won the war') or puts them into the mouths of alienated outcasts. What Brenton does have, though, is a fierce poetic intuition about the state of Britain. His play opens with a chilling image of the dead Churchill knocking on his coffin and rising from his catafalque in Westminster Hall: a brilliant reminder of the iconic hold of Churchill on the British psyche that was confirmed by Mrs Thatcher's frequent invocations of the wartime leader during the Falklands War of 1982. And, although Britain hardly degenerated into a gulag-filled police-state, Brenton foresaw the growing conflict between security and liberty. What politician or journalist in 1974 would have dared predict that thirty years later terrorist suspects would be held for three years without trial in a maximum security jail in south London? Or that the House of Lords would fiercely condemn such 'draconian' measures as being incompatible with human-rights laws? Yet that is precisely what happened in 2004 with a Labour government's detention of eleven north African Muslims in Belmarsh jail under the Anti-Terrorism, Crime and Security Act. And, whatever the sensationalist element in Brenton's play, it offered an imaginative vision of a future in which basic human freedoms would be curtailed by the state. As so often, a dramatist saw things that others didn't.

This image of a Britain on the verge of disintegration was one that had great potency in the early Seventies, and it's not hard to understand why. On the one hand, the post-war consensus had broken down as government strove to become ever more authoritarian: the immediate reaction to the crisis in Northern Ireland, for instance, was the imposition of direct rule from Westminster and a policy of internment without trial. At the same time, there was a sense that the Heath administration was impotent and helpless in the face of mounting union militancy. In 1974 the NUM, demanding a thirty to forty per cent pay rise, refused even to negotiate with the government and, at the height of the three-day week, Lord Carrington told parliament that 'We are confronted today by one of the most serious crises in peacetime that any of us can recall.' Terrorism had also become a European phenomenon. Alongside the IRA and the Angry Brigade in Britain, the Red Brigades in Italy and the Red Army Faction in Germany assassinated political and judicial figures. And the attention of the world had been seized by the Black September raid on the Olympic Village near Munich in 1972 when Arab terrorists, demanding the release of Palestinian prisoners, killed eleven members of the Israeli Olympic team. Increased terrorism, of course, meant increased government security; which, in turn, fuelled left-wing fears of declining individual liberty. Wherever you looked there was a sense of incipient chaos in the Seventies which was keenly reflected in the drama of the time.

Even dramatists often thought of as detached from daily political reality were affected by the growing social unease: most notably Christopher Hampton and Tom Stoppard whom I earlier dubbed Contemporary Classicists. Hampton conceived *The Philanthropist* as an inversion of Molière's *The Misanthrope*, believing that, in the current climate of anger, reflex niceness was somehow more offensive than truculent candour. So Hampton came up with the very funny idea of an academic philologist whose compulsive amiability creates havoc: he triggers the death of a budding playwright, outrages an opinionated novelist and successfully alienates both his own fiancée and an easy campus lay. At the Royal Court in 1970, where Hampton was resident dramatist, the play deeply embarrassed the puritanical management because of its instant popular success; and their alarm was not assuaged by its transfer to the West End, where George Cole and Nigel Hawthorne followed in Alec McCowen's dazzling footsteps as the innocently destructive hero. But where Hampton's play shows extraordinary prophetic insight is in its image of public life descending into chaos. At one point, we learn that a retired lieutenant colonel has assassinated the Tory Prime Minister and half the Cabinet in order to save the country from creeping socialism: news that is greeted round an Oxbridge dinner table with donnish indifference. Later we hear of an organisation called Fellowship of Allied Terrorists Against Literature – FATAL – that aims to exterminate twenty-five of the most eminent English writers. Hampton uses this to expose the bumptiousness of a self-regarding novelist, Braham, who is unsure whether to be relieved or insulted that he is not on the list. It is impossible today not to be struck by Hampton's chilling awareness that the proscriptive violence of the times could easily be applied to books and their writers: something eventually realised in the fatwa issued against Salman

Rushdie after the publication of *The Satanic Verses* in 1988.

But Hampton wasn't alone in showing academia as fatally detached from a violent, chaotic and disintegrating society: his admirer, Tom Stoppard, did something very similar in *Jumpers*, which in 1972 gave the Olivier National Theatre regime one of its greatest hits. Over the years *Jumpers* has been viewed from every possible angle. As a play about moral philosophy. As a study in marital anguish. As a pyrotechnical whodunnit. But, while all those approaches are valid, the play is a direct product of the early Seventies and of Stoppard's own concern at the breakdown not just of ethical certainties but of the fabric of society itself. In that sense, it's a political play charting Stoppard's emotionally conservative reaction to the volatility of the times. At the play's centre lies the philosopher-hero, George Moore, wrestling with the existence, or otherwise, of God while his wife, Dotty, copes with the corpse of a murdered logical positivist in her bedroom. Less attention has been paid, however, to the public context, which implies that the world is going to hell in a handcart. The murder of the academic arouses little protest since the victim himself argued that killing is not inherently wrong. Astronauts are squabbling on the surface of the moon; Captain Scott, in an inversion of Antarctic myth, even knocks his subordinate, Oates, to the ground and abandons him to his fate. And at Westminster the Radical-Liberals have seized power. As a result, they have rationalised the Church, appointed an ex-Minister of Agriculture as Archbishop of Canterbury, abolished press freedom and imprisoned property speculators and Masters of Foxhounds. This is not just a jolly joke or an attempt to provide background colour. It is an extension of Stoppard's main argument: that, if you choose to inhabit a moral limbo where absolute values have been eroded and the idea of a beneficent God discredited, then anarchy will prevail.

Looking at the world around him in 1972, Stoppard could well argue there was plenty of empirical evidence to back up his argument: at home, over a million unemployed and the panic of Bloody Sunday; abroad, escalating international terrorism and the start of the Watergate crisis. As Christopher Lee points out in *This Sceptred Isle*: 'It is difficult to find a bright moment in 1972. Even the good news that sixteen people had survived an air crash in the Andes was tempered when it was discovered that the survivors had kept themselves alive by eating the dead.' But, if there was a measure of paranoia on the left about the imminence of a police state, Stoppard's fear that lunar exploration would accelerate the descent into moral chaos now seems exaggerated. George's wife, Dotty, argues that the moon landings will make our moral absolutes look like 'the local customs of another place': a quaintly dated suggestion now that lunar exploration has, largely for economic reasons, become an historical footnote. Dotty also says to George, 'Do you think it is . . . significant that it's impossible to imagine anyone building a church on the moon?' In fact, one of the first actions of the American astronaut, Buzz Aldrin, on landing on the moon was to perform a Communion ceremony with bread and wine. Admittedly, Stoppard showed uncanny foresight in pinning down the radical left's constant preoccupation with fox-hunting. But the real irony of *Jumpers* is that the kind of moral desert Stoppard envisaged was far more visible in the Eighties than in the Seventies. Rising crime, the decay of the nuclear family, the decline of established institutions: all these coincided with Reaganomics and Thatcherism and their subscription to the untrammelled play of market forces. While *Jumpers* still holds the stage for its verbal exuberance and insight into marital anguish, it now looks questionable as social prophecy.

But Stoppard remains a fascinating case: a conscious and meticulous artist who denies the practical efficacy of art. At a time when it was almost mandatory to accept that art could be a means of changing society, Stoppard argued the precise opposite. As he told Janet Watts in a *Guardian* interview in 1973:

> I think that art ought to involve itself in contemporary social and political history as much as anything else but I find it deeply embarrassing when large claims are made for such involvement: when, because art takes notice of something important, it's claimed that art is important. It's not. We are talking about marginalia – the top tiny fraction of the whole edifice.

And that belief was one of the animating ideas behind *Travesties*, Stoppard's intellectual whirligig of a play, which delighted audiences at the Aldwych in 1974. But, looking back, one is tempted to wonder how much of our pleasure stemmed from a true understanding of Stoppard's purpose and how much from John Wood's brilliant performance as Henry Carr. Carr was the play's motor: a minor consular official through whose prismatic memory events in Zurich in 1917, when Lenin, Joyce and the Dadaist Tristan Tzara were all living in the city, were fallibly recalled. What dazzled one in *Travesties* was Wood's labial skill and lightning physical transitions: his switches from the aged, self-deluding Carr, in outsize dressing gown and battered panama, to his sporty, straw-boatered younger self. Wood once told me that his director had evolved an elaborate scheme to cover the age-changes. In the end the actor himself decided to indicate them with nothing more than a change of hat. 'I didn't', says Wood, 'want to do a pyrotechnical thing that drew attention to itself. I wanted to keep the background clear because in Tom's plays the word is all.'

True enough. But, although Stoppard's words are often dazzling, his views on artistic and political revolution are open to question. Throughout *Travesties* Stoppard makes ingenious structural use of *The Importance of Being Earnest*: at one point he even thought of calling his own play *Prism*. Stoppard's argument is that Wilde's play 'is important but says nothing about anything'. In reality, as Eric Bentley has pointed out, an annotated copy of *The Importance* would show such headings as 'death; money and marriage; the nature of style; ideology and economics; beauty and truth; the psychology of philanthropy; the decline of aristocracy; nineteenth-century morals; the class system'. Stoppard also sees Joyce as an exemplar of the artist as magician, whose aim in *Ulysses* is to produce 'a corpse that will dance for some time yet and *leave the world precisely as it finds it*'. The italics are Stoppard's. But it seems perverse to argue that a book which enlarged people's consciousness and extended the possibilities of fiction left the world exactly as it was. Cyril Connolly, in describing what he called the *Ulysses* generation, wrote of 'the enthusiasm which comes to everyone when they discover themselves through a book – a service which Joyce, Proust and Gide have rendered generally to almost all our thinking generation'.

Stoppard saves his heavy artillery, however, for Marx: a false prophet, he suggests through the mouth of Henry Carr, who got it wrong twice over. First, Marx was the victim of a historical accident in that he witnessed capitalism at a stage when he saw its physical enslavement of the proletariat rather than the benefits it brought to industrialised societies. Secondly, Marx assumed that people were 'a sensational kind of material object and would behave predictably in a material world'. Writing fifteen years before the collapse of Soviet Communism, Stoppard could be credited with historical foresight. But the debate about Marx is by no means concluded. Eric Hobsbawm in *Age of Extremes* argues that the breakdown of the USSR exemplifies,

rather than disproves, Marxist analysis: that when the forces of production come into conflict with the ideological superstructure then
social revolution will follow. And even bourgeois historians concede
that, while Marx was wrong about the inevitability of proletarian revolution, he was right about the unchecked development of capitalism.
With multinational corporations superceding the nation state and the
social fabric endangered through the free market, Marx is widely credited with a shrewd understanding of the capitalist dynamic. Even on a
technical level there is something awkward about the way Stoppard
stops the play dead in its tracks so that Cecily can give a ten-minute
lecture expounding Marxist theory: contrast the way Trevor Griffiths
in *The Party* allows political ideas to become both an expression of
character and part of a dialectical debate. Griffiths and Stoppard, perfectly good friends whom I've seen warmly embracing each other, in
fact make an intriguing antithetical pair: Griffiths, the disillusioned
Marxist and formal traditionalist, and Stoppard the formal innovator
with an essentially conservative temperament.

Stoppard may not always be right about Marx. But, at a time of escalating uncertainty and confusion in Britain, he raised a question of
passionate concern to many dramatists. Does art have any direct
social or political impact? Cathy Itzin in *Stages In The Revolution* lists
literally hundreds of political plays from the post-1968 period: they
range from the mature work of writers like Griffths, McGrath, Arden,
Hare, Brenton and Edgar to occasional pieces from Agitprop Street
Players and CAST. The same period also saw an explosion of fringe
theatre with the creation of new venues and companies, many predi-
cated on the belief that they could assist in dismantling the existing
structure of society. Yet, as the revolutionary Sixties turned into the
chaotic Seventies, writers were increasingly asking a number of questions. What, if anything, had changed? Where was the evidence that a
passionately committed and socially exploratory drama had produced
a better world? Had analysis of Britain's ills led in any way to meaningful action? Stoppard in *Travesties* attacks the notion that art has a
utilitarian function and reserves his praise for writers like Joyce and
Wilde who, according to his definition, left the world precisely as they
found it. Edward Bond in *Bingo* approaches the same question from a
different perspective. Bond, a born disturber of the peace, had forced
us in *The Pope's Wedding* and *Saved* to examine the failings of society.

And behind both plays lay an assumption that such failings were remediable either through the moral scrutiny of drama or political action. Now in *Bingo* Bond laments the insufficiency of art and the writer's moral impotence in the face of social cruelty. And Bond's pain is all the more acute in that his protagonist is Shakespeare and his setting is Stratford-upon-Avon in 1615–16. 'Was anything done?' is the question that haunts Bond's Shakespeare at the end of his life. And, although ostensibly about a Shakespeare living out his last days with a detested wife and an emotionally estranged daughter, *Bingo* clearly stems from Bond's own sense of guilt at the helplessness of the writer in a violent, materialistic society.

Bond's play, with its image of a brooding, largely silent Shakespeare who sees his public career as something without value, is immensely moving: both Bob Peck at the Northcott, Exeter in 1973 and John Gielgud at the Royal Court in 1974 brought their own specific gravity to the role. And Bond's play poses a genuinely disturbing question. How could the Shakespeare who exposed the terrifying consequences of cruelty and injustice in *King Lear* have settled down into life as a prosperous Stratford burgher? And how could he have endorsed, by his silence, the brutal land enclosures that were currently threatened? Bond's answer is that he couldn't. That he could only survive by killing in himself the great, humane Shakespeare of the plays. Bond's *Bingo* offers one of the most powerful images of the despairing artist in the dramatic canon. Sitting wanly in his New Place garden, Bond's Shakespeare tells his daughter, Judith, that the one thing he can give her is money – 'but money always turns to hate'. He recalls that in London he had to pass amongst baited bears and sixteeen severed heads on a gate to get to his precious theatre. And, in the fields at Welcombe where the common land from which he drew his rents was threatened with enclosure, he cries: 'Every writer writes in other men's blood. The trivial and the real. There's nothing else to write in. But only a god or devil can write in other men's blood and not ask why they spilt it or what it cost.' Bond's idea that the artist is inevitably implicated in the moral cruelty of his or her society is a dramatically persuasive piece of self-accusation. At the same time, it is dangerous to deduce from that the idea that art itself is powerless. No poem, as Auden famously said, saved a single Jew from the gas-chambers; but art's failure to initiate action does not invalidate its capacity to subvert, question and provoke. *Timon of Athens*, *Saved* and Picasso's *Guernica* did precisely that. And Shakespeare's silence on the subject of land enclosures is a symbol of his human contradiction rather than of art's ineffectualness. *Bingo* is a tremendous play that one longs to see revived. But the logic of Bond's argument, about the impotence of art, is that it would be better for a dramatist to be a political activist than to indulge in the luxury of creativity.

The pessimism Bond expresses in *Bingo* was all too typical of the gloomy Seventies: a period when writers seemed haunted by the failure of art to revolutionise society or to alleviate the threat of social breakdown. And, if you turn from the Contemporary Classicists like Hampton and Stoppard and a Disturber of the Peace like Edward Bond to the Anatomists of Albion, you find a similar sense of pervasive melancholia. Britain underwent something very close to a national nervous breakdown in the early Seventies. The buoyancy of the previous decade gave way to creeping despair as a combination of governmental and managerial incompetence, union militancy, mainland violence and rising oil prices meant that Britain as a society was often failing to function on even the most basic level. Even the freedoms of expression that had been so hard won in the previous decade came under threat from a variety of sources. Mary Whitehouse's National Viewers' and Listeners' Association grew in influence and power. Its sister organisation, the Festival of Light, held a mass rally in Trafalgar Square in 1971. *Oz*, an underground magazine, provoked the longest obscenity trial in Old Bailey history in 1971 for 'Schoolkids', an issue in which a rampant Rupert Bear was seen violently raping an American comic character, Gipsy Granny. Libertarians were as depressed as moral watchdogs were exultant. From an economic, political and cultural standpoint, it was a grim period in English life. And, even though the theatre capitalised on the continuing crisis, it meant that dramatists either reflected the national mood or retreated into private anxiety.

John Osborne, as we have already seen, was out of step with what he saw as the squishy hippiedom and showbiz self-consciousness of the Sixties. But in *West of Suez*, which appeared at the Royal Court and then the Cambridge Theatre in 1971, he took the argument a stage further: the play was both a lament for the decline of western civilisation and a defence of language and the validity of suffering in a barbaric age. Because Osborne's setting was an independent

Caribbean island where a group of British exiles cast aspersions on the indigenous population and the prevailing youth culture, the play was inevitably seen as confirmation of Osborne's swing to the right. But it struck me as neither inherently right-wing nor left-wing: more a cry of anguish about a civilisation that no longer put its trust in reason, in respect for other people's values or in language. It was no accident that three of the characters, including the central figure of Wyatt Gilman, superbly played by Ralph Richardson, were writers. Asked by a local journalist if he still believed that words had any meaning, value or validity, Gilman replied: 'I still cling pathetically to the old bardic belief that "words alone are certain good".' Osborne also deliberately contrasted Gilman's studied eloquence with the incoherent, expletive-filled rage of a fascistic American student. And when Gilman was senselessly killed by a group of island terrorists, we were clearly meant to feel, as John Heilpern says, that 'a moral universe has collapsed along with its culture'. *West of Suez* may have lacked narrative dynamic, and suffered from an overcrowded canvas. It didn't, however, deserve the vitriol it attracted. It proved that for Osborne, ever since *Look Back In Anger*, the time had been out of joint; and that in the neurotically chaotic Seventies the only real sin, in Gilman's words, was 'the incapacity for proper despair'.

If Osborne's response to the times was one of Spenglerian disillusion, that of his fellow national anatomist, Peter Nichols, was a theatrical retreat into private life. He accomplished this with a chirpy resilience in the highly autobiographical *Forget-Me-Not-Lane* which started life at Greenwich Theatre before moving to the West End. Even if the play ultimately argued that we all end up like our parents, it recaptured Nichols' own adolescence in wartime Bristol with a good deal of vaudevillian vivacity. But Nichols' next play, *Chez Nous* (1974), was a far more transgressive piece. Described as a 'domestic comedy', it hinged on the hypocrisy of our liberal values. It was set in a farmhouse in the Anglo-Dordogne occupied by a paediatrician, Dick, and his wife, Liz, and paid for by the success of the former's book on adolescent sexuality. But the credibility of Dick's argument that children should be entitled to experiment freely from puberty was undermined by the impregnation of his fourteen-year-old daughter. Worse still, his daughter's sexual partner turned out be his oldest friend, Phil. Clearly the play was an attack on the vanity of liberal intellectual theories which rebound on us disastrously when applied to our own lives. What was new was Nichols' ability to explore a tragic private hinterland; and there was a moment when Albert Finney's Phil, realising the implications of his actions, pressed his palms flat against the sides of his skull as if trying to beat down the awful truth that left one emotionally shattered. Because of our sensitivities concerning paedophilia and under-age sex, the play may languish in limbo. But it's a potent reminder of how in the Seventies even a sprightly anatomist of the national mood like Peter Nichols retreated into areas of private concern.

Disillusion and despair were the keynotes of the Seventies. Melancholia even invades a sex-filled farce like Alan Bennett's *Habeas Corpus* (1973). At first, the play looks like a cheerful romp: as English as a Donald Magill seaside postcard, celebrating the idea that 'King Sex is a wayward monarch' and filled with eccentrically hilarious situations. In one particular instance, an over-zealous falsie-fitter from Leatherhead mistakenly applies his prehensile fingers to the well-upholstered bosom of a Hove GP's wife. But Bennett is a far more complex writer than he is given credit for: one fascinated by formal experiment and emotional contradictions. And what he does in *Habeas Corpus* is to offer all the stock ingredients of a traditional farce – lust, panic, mistaken identity – while stripping away the familiar impedimenta of doors, beds, furniture and exploding props: another sign of the movement away from keyhole naturalism already seen in Pinter and Nichols. Bennett also links the Freudian imperatives of sex and death, introducing a choric char in the shape of Mrs Swabb who is never slow to point a moral and adorn a tale:

> The body's an empty vessel,
> The flesh an awful cheat,
> The world is just an abbatoir,
> For our rotting lumps of meat.
> So if you get your heart's desire,
> Your longings come to pass,
> Remember in each other's beds,
> It isn't going to last.
> The smoothest cheek will wrinkle
> The proudest breast will fall.
> Some sooner go, some later
> But death will claim us all.

This is not the doom-laden note you normally expect to hear in a trouser-dropping farce; nor do you habitually find one of the characters, at the end, confirmed in his terminal illness. Ronald Eyre's original production was also rounded off, at the suggestion of the lead actor, Alec Guinness, with an Astaire-like routine that, as the spotlight slowly dwindled, turned into a dance of death. I'm not suggesting that this new emphasis on mortality was directly attributable to Mr Heath or the three-day week. All the same, it is significant that a Seventies farce like *Habeas Corpus* contains dark shadows not found even in Joe Orton's wilfully offensive Sixties examples of the genre.

As all this work shows, there was a distinct change of tone in the drama of the Seventies: there was a sense of hopes dashed, of things winding down, of individual lives confronting intractable problems. It was as if the ebullient optimism of the Sixties had given way to an age of uncertainty in which, in the words of historian Norman Stone, 'all kinds of things just fell apart.' But, alongside the disillusion and melancholia, there was also a prophetic understanding of society's shift towards a self-seeking individualism that eventually came to be identified with Thatcherism. Before the 1970 election the Conservatives held a conference at Selsdon Park which abandoned the concept of One Nation Toryism in favour of free-market economics; and, even though some of the ideals were scuppered by subsequent events, big fiscal changes happened under Heath. Income tax was drastically reduced. Credit started to run wild. And 1971 saw an explosion in house prices which left them, within a couple of years, at double their former levels. Poets may or may not be the unacknowledged legislators of the world, but dramatists are certainly its prognosticators; and, although poles apart in many respects, Caryl Churchill and Alan Ayckbourn shrewdly foresaw the social consequences of the new Toryism.

Churchill was eventually to become something of a feminist figurehead and role model for women writers everywhere. But it's a sign of the male dominance of British theatre – and of the fact that she gave birth to three children in the Sixties – that Churchill took time to make her mark. Born in 1938, Churchill had begun writing plays at Oxford around the same time as her contemporaries, John McGrath and David Rudkin, and enjoyed similar student success. Where they quickly graduated into theatre, film and television, however, Churchill devoted herself to family and writing for radio: neither an activity, I hasten to add, to be taken lightly or downgraded. Indeed some of

Churchill's early radio plays stand up well to revival. *Not Not Not Not Not Enough Oxygen*, broadcast in 1971 and given a rehearsed reading at the Royal Court in 2002, is an eerily prophetic piece about a traffic-ridden, polluted world starved of air, food and freedom. But it was not until 1972 that Churchill produced her first professional stage play, *Owners*, and it confirmed the arrival of a genuinely original voice. As Churchill herself said, the play sprang from a collision of two ideas: one about landlords and tenants, the other about western aggressiveness and eastern passivity. What was extraordinary was the sharpness of Churchill's social antennae. She grasped the fact that the flood of money into the market was creating a wholly different scale of property values. She also saw that the new feminism could become a cloak for rampant acquisitiveness. Accordingly, Churchill presented us with a brutally exploitative landlord, Marion, who bought up houses, victimised tenants and even sought to appropriate a child belonging to a previous lover. At one point, Churchill's zealously individualist heroine expresses her philosophy of life: 'Be clean, be quick, be top, be best, you may not succeed, Marion, but what matters is you try your hardest' – a clear anticipation of the values of the Thatcherite Marlene in Churchill's *Top Girls*, written eleven years later. At the time I accused Churchill of bunging into *Owners* everything she could think of, including the kitchen sink; but what she cannily saw was that in the Seventies property was the path to economic progress.

Ayckbourn made exactly the same point in the remarkable *Absurd Person Singular* (1972). For Ayckbourn, comedy is always a technical challenge; and, as he has admitted, one of his prime motivations here was to give offstage characters and actions a life of their own. But Ayckbourn, partly by virtue of living in Scarborough, understands better than many metropolitan dramatists the daily realities of civic life. And what he captures here is the rise of the petty-bourgeois businessman at the expense of the middle-class architect and rogue and the lazy upper-class banker used to exercising social control. Set in three different kitchens over three successive Christmases, the play is still chiefly remembered for its incomparable central act: one in which Eve, the distressed wife of the philandering architect, makes a series of desperate suicide bids mistakenly interpreted by her guests as an attempt to clean her kitchen. But it is the final act, set in the freezing Victorian house of the upper-class Brewster-Wrights, that reveals Ayckbourn's darker purpose. The hostess lives in a state of alcoholic hibernation.

The middle-class architect faces professional ruin. It is the once patronised small-businessman, Sidney Hopcroft, who has risen to the top of
the heap by advantageously buying up many of the town's key properties. And Ayckbourn brilliantly embodies his point by showing
everyone, quite literally, dancing to Sidney's tune in a game of humiliating musical forfeits. What Ayckbourn also pins down, to his great
credit, is the cost-cutting tackiness that accompanied the capitalist
vigour of the Seventies enterprise culture. As a property developer, Sidney creates jobs and is a vital figure in the local economy; but, as the
architect waspishly observes, 'half his tenants are asking to be re-
housed and they haven't even moved in yet.' Behind Ayckbourn the
Contemporary Classicist, once dubbed by a German critic 'the
Molière of the middle-classes', lay an increasingly alert anatomist of
social change.

Ayckbourn and Churchill showed that good new plays were still being
written. A whole generation of great actors gave fine performances in
what was the inevitable twilight of their careers: Olivier in *Long Day's
Journey Into Night* and *The Party*, Richardson in *West of Suez*,
Ashcroft in Albee's *All Over*. Alternative theatre continued to expand.
Yet, underneath all the energy, there was a creeping uncertainty: a constant questioning both of the elaborate machinery of theatrical production and of the medium's hierarchies. And nowhere was this more
evident than in fluctuating attitudes to the two big national institutions. At a time of national economic crisis, the RSC under Trevor
Nunn became defiantly expansive while the National Theatre had to
cope with both a bungled transfer of artistic power and an impending
move to the South Bank. Championed by theatrical idealists in the Sixties, both companies became the object of sniping envy in the Seventies. Compared to their Continental counterparts, they were
subsidised only modestly. Yet in local terms, the sizeable sums needed
to keep them afloat opened up what John Elsom called 'a gap of privilege' between themselves and the burgeoning fringe.

In fact the RSC began the decade in fine shape. Three years into
Trevor Nunn's leadership they enjoyed a 1971 London season at the
Aldwych that represented an artistic perihelion. First came Peter Hall's
production of Pinter's *Old Times* with Colin Blakely, Dorothy Tutin
and Vivien Merchant. Pinter's themes were time, memory and our
ability to recreate the past according to the psychological needs of the

present and, in so doing, give that past a tangible reality. Pinter, in his flight from naturalism, also seemed to be creating a new kind of drama: one that forsook exposition and development and replaced it with a highly compressed image that gave the spectator maximum interpretative freedom. After *Old Times* came the London transfer of Peter Brook's magical, Meyerholdian *A Midsummer Night's Dream* and David Jones's no less remarkable production of Gorki's *Enemies*. This was a recreation of a 1905 play about a savage industrial dispute that combined an ensemble cohesion worthy of the Moscow Art Theatre with a set of richly individualised performances from John Wood as a flailing, vodka-soaked weakling, Patrick Stewart as a ruthless factory owner and Ben Kingsley as a professional revolutionary. And the season rolled on with Terry Hands' excellent revivals of Etherege's *The Man of Mode* and Genet's *The Balcony* and the transfer from the Mermaid of Harold Pinter's production of James Joyce's *Exiles*: a revival that proved that the century's most radical novelist was also one of its most pioneering dramatists.

Had Trevor Nunn been able to keep that group of actors from the 1971 season together, it is fair to say that they would have been a match for any company in the world. As it was, a handful of actors – including Wood, Stewart and Philip Locke – went into Nunn's ambitious 1972 Stratford season of 'The Romans' but the majority dispersed in the usual wasteful British way. But Nunn, to his credit, did something very significant in the early Seventies. Faced with the challenge of an expanding fringe and a perception of the big companies as money-devouring monoliths, Nunn decided to beat the alternative theatre at its own game: this meant showing that the RSC could also offer low-cost, affordable productions in small venues. In London this involved three seasons from 1971 onwards at The Place – headquarters of the Contemporary Dance Theatre – off the Euston Road. By normal fringe standards, even this 330-seat theatre was relatively upmarket; but it yielded Trevor Griffiths' *Occupations*, a sensational *Miss Julie* with Helen Mirren and a stage version of a David Rudkin radio play, *Cries From Casement*. However, the real breakthrough came in Stratford-upon-Avon with the transformation of a derisory tin hut in Southern Lane, originally built to house Michel St Denis's studio-work, into a performance space known as The Other Place. It was put into the hands of a radical feminist, Buzz Goodbody, who had worked her way through the male-dominated ranks of the RSC and who had a vision of an informal space that, through cheap tickets, would attract a new audience. After a trial run in 1973, TOP formally opened the following year with a season that included *King Lear*, Mike Leigh's *Babies Grow Old*, David Rudkin's *Afore Night Come* and Chekhov's *Uncle Vanya*. The magic of The Other Place was not just that it seated only 180 people: it was that it seemed to exist in a different world from the main theatre, in that performances were punctuated by the sound of church bells, hooting owls and the genial cacophony of nature. What the RSC couldn't have predicted was that The Other Place, through its rough-hewn intimacy, would call into question the scenic excesses of institutional theatre.

This was to become a constant theme of the Seventies: the war between small spaces and big stages. And one particularly vehement debate was prompted by something I wrote in the *Guardian* in the autumn of 1974. Returning from Paris where I had seen Peter Brook's inaugural production of *Timon of Athens* at the Bouffes du Nord, I opened the Sunday papers to read long, in-depth articles about the financial plight facing both the RSC and the National. When I sat down to write about the Paris trip I suggested that, in contrast to our own factory-like national companies, Brook had realised that the act of theatre had nothing to do with expensive hardware, hydraulic stages and drum-revolves and 'everything to do with narrative, language, ideas and physical skill'. This prompted Helen Mirren, then a member of the Stratford company, to write a letter to the editor in which she claimed that 'to myself and many colleagues of my generation who have been involved in work with the National and the RSC the expenditure on costumes, sets and staging in general has been excessive, unnecessary and destructive to the art of theatre'. Helen Mirren's brave letter opened the floodgates. Numerous theatre people – including Thelma Holt, Ralph Koltai, Michael Croft and James Roose-Evans – joined the debate. Some endorsed Mirren's plea for greater simplicity. Others argued that theatre was suffering from an insufficiency of funds rather than an excess of decoration. But the RSC's official reply – that production costs represented only a small proportion of its total outlay and that sixty-five per cent of its budget went on staff costs and maintenance of its buildings – served only to highlight the real problem: that theatre was in danger of becoming as much a vast administrative and architectural machine as a vehicle for producing plays. In one sense, my original article was unfair to our national companies. They were obliged to produce a large repertory of work on generally inadequate subsidy: in contrast, Peter Brook in Paris could devote all his resources to one-off, handmade productions. Trevor Nunn also had a point when he argued 'that the RSC was better when it was doing ten things and getting eight right than doing two or three things perfectly'. But the debate that was started in 1974 opened up issues that were to resound through succeeding decades. The need for our national companies to strike a delicate balance between expressive ferment and industrial treadmill. The difficulty of allocating resources fairly between 'official' and fringe theatres. The fear that buildings would come to dictate policy.

Criticism of the national companies was also related to their artistic standards. When things were going well, as with the RSC in 1971, one applauded how much they achieved on relatively modest grants: when things were going badly, as with the National in the same year, people started talking about waste and profligacy. It seemed an iron rule that, when one company was up, the other was down. While the RSC was enjoying its best-ever season at the Aldwych, the National was wrestling with an unpopular Arrabal, a minor Heywood revival and a *Coriolanus* that uneasily straddled the British and Berliner Ensemble traditions. The National also came under heavy fire for a 1971 West End season that included a frivolous Giraudoux, a mediocre revival of Buchner's *Danton's Death* and a populist musical about William Blake, *Tyger*, which alienated most critics (though not this one) and the middle-class, mailing-list audience. It was only Michael Blakemore's triumphant revival of *Long Day's Journey Into Night*, with Olivier at his finest as O'Neill's hollow Irish-American patriarch, that saved the day in 1971. The National recovered its nerve in the next two seasons with Stoppard's *Jumpers*, Michael Blakemore's ebullient revival of *The Front Page*, John Dexter's productions of *The Misanthrope* and *Equus*, and Franco Zeffirelli's *Saturday, Sunday, Monday*. But alongside these were a number of dull, middle-of-the road productions that stemmed, in part, from the lack of any sustaining vision. With Olivier's health failing and Tynan increasingly marginalised, the National seemed to lack either the moral fervour or radical faith of the RSC. It didn't help matters that, after the partial failure of the 1971 West End season, the question of seeking a successor to Olivier inevitably arose. Max Rayne, the incoming Chairman of the Board, bluntly told Olivier that he had his own reputation to consider; which led Olivier to remark privately that he thought his reputation might conceivably outlast that of Max Rayne. But, although it was necessary to find a successor to the battle-weary Olivier, the whole matter was handled with a brutal clumsiness and lack of finesse that recalled the removal of the post-war Old Vic triumvirate in 1947. Soundings were taken and secret approaches made to Peter Hall, who was formally appointed as Olivier's designated successor in April 1973. While Olivier was justifiably infuriated by the lack of consultation, the guerrilla campaign conducted against Hall by Jonathan Miller, Michael Blakemore and Kenneth Tynan was savage, unrelenting and counterproductive. And it has to be said that Hall, confronted by delays to the new South Bank building, a divided directorate and the angry shadow of Olivier, made an inauspicious start. His opening season at the Old Vic in 1974 included such spectacular duds as Peter Nichols' *The Freeway* and A. E. Ellis's *Grand Manoeuvres*. Even Hall's own production of *The Tempest* swamped John Gielgud under production values seemingly drawn from Baroque opera. Questions were raised about Hall's capacity to fill the giant maw of the new three-auditorium South Bank theatre. Maw, as I said at the time, often means worse; and, just as theatre was becoming more flexible and impermanent, the creation of a massive edifice on the South Bank seemed like an act of giant folly. Such was the uncertainty of the time that Hall, who had strenuously resisted earlier attempts to incorporate Stratford into the National Theatre scheme, even entered into secret talks about a possible merger of the National and the RSC.

The cultural climate in the early Seventies had decisively changed. Small was beautiful and big was now bad. Just as there was a growing cynicism about the efficacy of the two main political parties, so there was an accelerating scepticism about large-scale theatrical institutions: something fed by the proliferation of studio spaces and independent companies. But one of the most significant developments was the creation in 1973 of a company called Joint Stock. It was the brainchild of Max Stafford-Clark, David Aukin and David Hare. Its aim, according to its historian Rob Ritchie, was to form a company that could 'retain the flexible methods of the fringe yet have access to better facilities, reach a broader audience and achieve higher standards'. It also wanted to involve everyone in collective decision-making; and, with the inclusion of William Gaskill amongst its founders, it acquired the country's best Brechtian director. Working with an initial grant of

£12,000, Joint Stock made an instant mark with its adaptation of Heathcote Williams' documentary novel, *The Speakers*. Based on the public and private lives of Hyde Park soapbox orators, the production demanded new ways of working. In rehearsal the actors were asked to speak on set subjects for specific lengths of time to heckling colleagues. They were also sent out of the rehearsal room to go begging on the streets. And in performance, they had to compete for the attention of a promenade audience who could also use a tea-stall placed in the centre of the arena. In Birmingham Roger Lloyd Pack, after delivering the line 'Nothing you can say or do can startle me in any shape or form', found an elderly lady challenging this by throwing the contents of a tea-cup into his face. Quizzed as to her motives, she said, 'I've always wanted to do it, that's why.' But the real significance of *The Speakers* lay in its collaborative approach. The directors, Gaskill and Stafford-Clark, had literally done a scissors-and-paste job on Williams' book, laying the pages out on the floor and cutting them up into performable slivers. The basic text was then complemented by contributions from the actors. Other companies, such as 7:84, were working on similar lines at the same time, in defiance of the British theatre's traditional hegemonic individualism. In the past, either the producer, the actor or the director had been the one calling the shots. In a post-1968 climate, where authority figures were suspect, the theatre began to hunger for a semblance of working democracy.

By a neat piece of symbolism 1973 not only saw the birth of Joint Stock: it also witnessed the death of two glittering tsars of commercial theatre, Noël Coward and Binkie Beaumont. And it is not difficult to imagine what either of them would have thought of the new collectivist approach to theatre. Coward, who insisted on formal rehearsal attire and a working knowledge of the text from day one, would have been appalled by Max Stafford-Clark's approving note in his rehearsal diary about 'thirteen people wearing jeans, one not', and bemused by the idea of a text that emerged organically; for Coward the word 'workshop' doubtless meant a place to which the orphaned and indigent were consigned by a grateful society. And Beaumont, an autocrat to his elegantly manicured fingertips, would have been astonished by Joint Stock's idea of free-speaking, post-performance discussions in which everyone participated; just as he would have sacked an RSC star like Helen Mirren on the spot for writing to a national newspaper criticising the working practices of the company that employed her.

But, although Coward and Beaumont had contributed much to twentieth-century British theatre, by the time of their death their influence had palpably waned. Coward lived long enough to be knighted and to see *Hay Fever* enter the National Theatre repertory; but, although aged sycophants grovellingly dubbed him 'The Master', he was no longer a role-model for the new theatrical generation. And, long before his death, Beaumont's once-mighty Tennent empire had crumbled and with it the idea of a ruling impresario gazing out over Shaftesbury Avenue as if it were his personal fiefdom.

The new British theatre was pluralistic, questioning, fragmented and diverse. Figureheads like Peter Hall and Trevor Nunn exercised enormous power; but the soul of the British theatre was not confined to any one company or space. It hovered restlessly between the Old Vic, the Aldwych, the ICA, the shining new rep theatres in Birmingham and Sheffield, the Glasgow Citizens', Chichester, Exeter, the Almost Free, fringe groups like Freehold and the commando-like 'Theatre in Education' groups springing up all over the country. In the early Seventies theatre was geographically widespread and took a multitude of competing forms. If there was any unifying factor, it was a pervasive mixture of disillusion and fear. A disillusion with the political process and with the return of the Heath government to a form of bullying authoritarianism that had produced industrial anarchy. A fear that the workable theatrical structure that had emerged in the Sixties would be irretrievably damaged by rampant inflation and rocketing oil prices. People still went on making theatre out of ambition, conviction, idealism and ungovernable necessity. But, if the Sixties had been an era of high hopes and fervent optimism, the early Seventies produced only a resilient pessimism. For the first time in my experience, people even seriously began to wonder whether theatre could survive in its present form. What, after all, was the role of theatre in a nation suffering a collective nervous breakdown?

VII

1975–79
Winters of Discontent

The stock view of the late Seventies is that nothing really got better: that Britain continued on its relentless downward spiral in spite of changes at the top. In 1975 the Conservatives, after two election defeats, replaced Edward Heath with Margaret Thatcher: a famously abrasive figure as Heath's Minister of Education (I can still hear the cries of 'Thatcher, Thatcher, milk-snatcher' as she curtailed free supplies of playground milk), and regarded with a certain wary unease even in her own party. Meanwhile, to the surprise of almost everyone, Harold Wilson resigned as Prime Minister in March 1976. At the time, his resignation prompted all kinds of dark speculation: in particular, that it was the result of some impending sexual or espionage scandal. But the simple truth was that Wilson, after thirteeen years of leading a rancorous, constantly divided Labour Party, was mentally and physically tired. Of all the cautious tributes paid to his stewardship, perhaps the most apt was Anthony Howard's 'He kept the show on the road'. In other words, Wilson was an arch-pragmatist who held together the fractious coalition that constitutes the Labour Party both in government and opposition. But his successor, James Callaghan, inherited any number of problems. Wilson had put the European issue to rest in that, in a national referendum in June 1975, sixty-seven per cent of the country voted to stay in the Common Market; in stark contrast to the galloping Europhobia of a later generation, no national newspaper campaigned against staying in, the Conservative Party was broadly supportive and ninety-eight per cent of the CBI's membership was in favour. But Callaghan was still confronted by a wafer-thin parliamentary majority, high unemployment, rising inflation and recurrent financial crises. A low point came in the autumn of 1976 when the government had to go to the International Monetary Fund to borrow £2.3 billion to support the pound. Inevitably the IMF loan came with strings attached: public-sector cuts which provoked union strikes which led in turn to industrial chaos. And the Callaghan years are for-ever haunted by the so-called 'winter of discontent' in 1978–79, when public-sector workers refused an imposed pay ceiling of five per cent and dustmen went on strike and gravediggers refused to bury the dead. When one also recalls that, after seven IRA bombs exploded in London in January 1977, violence on the mainland became a regular feature of British life, it is fair to say that the late Seventies was an exceptionally turbulent and volatile period.

Yet, if you take the years from Labour's election victory in October 1974 to its eventual defeat in May 1979, the theatre miraculously weathered the storm. Moreover, it didn't merely survive. It even, in some areas, became measurably better. The RSC enjoyed what its offi-cial historian, Sally Beauman, called two 'anni mirabili' from 1977 to 1979, was endlessly productive and managed to wipe out its financial deficit. After more than a century of prevarication, delay and bureau-cratic pussy-footing, the National Theatre finally became a concrete reality with the phased opening of its new home on the South Bank in 1976. In the same year regional theatre got a symbolic boost with the opening of the Royal Exchange in Manchester. Fringe theatre was abundantly lively with a number of itinerant groups – Monstrous Reg-iment, Foco Novo, Hull Truck and Black Theatre Co-Operative – springing up to complement metropolitan buildings such as the Bush, the Soho Poly, the Orange Tree and the Almost Free. Not least, many of our playwrights were in prime form. This was the period of Harold Pinter's *No Man's Land* and *Betrayal*, David Hare's *Fanshen* and *Plen-ty*, Caryl Churchill's *Light Shining in Buckinghamshire* and *Cloud Nine*, Pam Gems's *Dusa, Fish, Stash and Vi*, Michael Frayn's *Alpha-betical Order* and *Donkeys' Years*, Edward Bond's *The Fool*, David Edgar's *Destiny*, Trevor Griffiths' *Comedians*, Peter Nichols' *Privates on Parade*, Alan Bennett's *The Old Country*, Alan Ayckbourn's *Bed-room Farce*, Simon Gray's *Otherwise Engaged*. Our theatre may have faced recurrent problems; but it obstinately refused, even in a time of crisis, to lie down and die.

How does one begin to explain this paradox: the fact that the thea-tre thrived while the country suffered? One has to begin by measuring the extent of the national crisis and by questioning the verdict of revi-sionist historians. Christopher Booker in *The Seventies: The Decade That Shaped The Future* describes the decade as the 'death throes' of English optimism: the time in which the belief in progress that had informed British life in the years since the Second World War seemed no longer tenable. But one has to make a distinction between the Heathite and the Wilson–Callaghan Seventies. In the former, there was a genuine sense of imminent collapse with the country reduced to a three-day week, petrol periodically rationed and a rise in oil prices sending the economy haywire. Whatever the vicissitudes of the late Seventies, and they were many, there was at least a sense of a government seeking to control events. In looking back at any decade, it is tempting to seize on the headline disasters. But Nick Tiratsoo, in the *Folio History* survey of the Seventies already quoted, rightly balances the bad news and the good. In particular, he says of the two Labour governments of the late Seventies that 'their achievements were at least as great as their lapses'. Inflation, as he points out, was running at twenty-four per cent in 1975 and just eight per cent three years later. The unemployment rate averaged four and a half per cent: high by comparison with the Sixties but low next to that of many other countries. The subject of women's rights was also addressed. The Sex Discrimination Act of 1975 saw women's earnings increase in relation to men's while the 1976 Domestic Violence and Matrimonial Proceedings Act made it easier for women to get legal protection against violent husbands. When we write off the Seventies as a dismal decade, we forget there was measurable progress. It is also received wisdom that, if Callaghan had called an election in October 1978 when Labour was three points ahead in the opinion polls, his government might well have continued in power.

Labour's gradual restoration of economic stability inevitably had its effect on the theatre: most obviously in the fact that Arts Council grants improved towards the end of the Callaghan years. It is also tempting to say that the theatre is always better off under Labour than the Conservatives. With the Conservatives, there are usually cutbacks. With Labour, as the subsidy rises, so does the opportunity for attacks on the party's ideological shortcomings. But there were many other reasons why theatre was so lively in the late Seventies. The Second Wave of new dramatists, directors and actors who had emerged around 1968, and who had been politicised by student unrest, were now reaching maturity. At the risk of endorsing the 'great men and women' theory of history, there were also a number of tenacious individuals who were determined to make the big institutions work even in difficult times: Peter Hall at the National, Trevor Nunn, Terry

Hands and David Brierley at the RSC, Michael Elliott and his colleagues in Manchester. One can also resort for an explanation to our old friend, the 'zeitgeist'. With devolution very much on the agenda, thanks to Labour's dependence for its survival on the votes of Scottish and Welsh nationalists, Britain was going through one of its recurrent bouts of self-examination. Did the United Kingdom have any meaningful identity or was it simply a convenient alliance of separate nations and tribes? And, if new powers were given to Scottish and Welsh assemblies, where did that leave England? Such were the fears about the potential break-up of the UK that the government issued a white paper, *The English Dimension*, intended to reassure English voters. I'm not saying that such issues were on everyone's lips or that saloon bars nightly rang with cries of 'Who are we as a people?' But the debate about national identity was very much in the air and was part of the intellectual context in which dramatists wrote. In short, the late Seventies wasn't quite the period of apocalyptic decay that many people have depicted. It was, however, a period of turbulence, contradiction and productive uncertainty; which may not be such a bad climate in which to create theatre.

The RSC is a prime example of an institution that both reflected the problems of the times and showed how, through initiative and enterprise, they could be transcended. At the start of 1975, the company seemed to be going through its own identity crisis. Funding could not match aspirations. Helen Mirren had gone public with her criticisms of the focus on costume and design. Severe cutbacks were announced. The 1975 season in the Royal Shakespeare Theatre was to contain only three new productions and one revival while at the Aldwych the repertory principle was to be abandoned in favour of one-off productions of plays by Charles Wood, Graham Greene, Granville-Barker and Shaw. These were clearly difficult times. And, when audiences assembled in Stratford in April for Terry Hands' opening production of *Henry V*, the signs of austerity were plainly visible. Where Peter Hall had used a cast of fifty for his *Henry V* in 1964, Hands had to make do with twenty-five. Farrah's raked stage looked like the bare deck of an aircraft carrier. And when Emrys James came on as Chorus he was wearing a leather jacket and corduroys. Then something miraculous happened. As the play opened out to admit us to the 'vasty fields of France', the drab floor-cloth ascended to the flies and swung round to achieve a billowing, glittering whiteness. What followed was a brilliant production that reflected the ethos of the times. The French, trapped in golden armour, seemed imprisoned in dated ideas of '*la gloire*' and a nostalgic militarism. The English, in contrast, were a tiny, ragged force filled with internal dissension, led by a man wracked by self-doubt and yet capable of emerging triumphant from national crisis. And the idea was followed through with great consistency. If Olivier in 1944 had given us Henry as glamorous heroic warrior, Alan Howard in 1975 suggested an introspective private man forced to subordinate his inner fears to the demands of public life. But Hands' production also implied that there was no excuse now, any more than there was in the early fifteenth century, for chauvinist triumphalism. There was a priceless moment, after Agincourt, when Howard's Henry and Oliver Ford Davies's French Herald movingly quit the field together surveying the human waste with shared regret. Once again *Henry V*, so often dismissed as a national anthem in five acts, proved the perfect mirror to our own world.

By showing how a dogged, ill-equipped group, combining English, Welsh, Scots and Irish, could overcome potential disaster this *Henry V* achieved the status of national metaphor. It also marked a turning point for the RSC itself. The only cloud over a vibrant Stratford season came with the suicide of Buzz Goodbody four days after the opening of her outstanding Other Place production of *Hamlet*: a radical, modern-dress version, starring a sober-suited Ben Kingsley, that showed how much the play gained from the microscopic intensity of a studio space. But, although Buzz's death was a tragedy for her family, friends and the company as a whole, she left behind a tangible legacy. As Colin Chambers says in his history of the RSC: 'Far from jeopardising the future of The Other Place, her death seemed to have the opposite effect and result in renewed commitment to the RSC's small-scale work.' And in 1976 the modest tin hut that Buzz had created housed not only a great classical production but the year's best new play.

The classical production was Trevor Nunn's *Macbeth*, starring Ian McKellen and Judi Dench. Olivier in 1955 had given a towering individual performance without altogether banishing the aura of ill omen that surrounded the play. But the persistent failure of *Macbeth* down the centuries had more to do with performance conditions than 'bad luck'. The real problem was that it always seemed to start on a note of nightmarish brilliance and dwindle into broken-backed spectacle. Also no one appeared capable of finding a visual image to match the play's fuliginous poetry. Nunn solved both problems instantly. By playing it without an interval, he gave the play a headlong momentum in which crime seemed to be followed immediately by punishment, guilt and remorse. By placing the actors on upturned beer crates inside a black circle, Nunn also lent the play a conspiratorial intimacy and allowed the audience to become imaginative participants in an occult ritual. It helped, of course, that he had two great actors and a stunning supporting cast. McKellen's warrior king was a man whose heroic mask seemed to disintegrate under pressure: confronted by Banquo's Ghost, his strong jaw slackened and juddered and his mouth foamed as if a once-whole man had been reduced to near-epileptic frenzy. And when Judi Dench's Lady Macbeth invoked the earth's dark spirits to unsex her and fill her full of direst cruelty, she suddenly leapt back with a stab of fear as if she had made direct contact with Satanic forces. In a big theatre this would have been a striking bit of business: in The Other Place it made us feel as if we were in the genuine presence of evil. Years later Dench recalled telling Trevor Nunn: 'We've got to remember that a lot of schoolchildren will come to the play and not know the Macbeths are going to kill Duncan.' Nunn's production not only restored the play's narrative excitement. It also gave it extraordinary emotional intensity – not least in the scene where Bob Peck's Macduff learned of his children's death with a slow-burning horror – and showed that great classics often yield up their secrets in scaled-down studio spaces where they become a shared experience.

If Nunn's *Macbeth* reclaimed a past landmark, David Edgar's *Destiny*, which appeared in the same Other Place season, showed that the RSC was fully alert to the present. In 1976 the extreme right-wing National Front had gained a sizeable share of the vote in a West Bromwich by-election; and here was a play that dealt, unexpectedly and intelligently, with the origins and nature of British fascism. But this was infinitely more than the kind of topical, headline-driven drama that Edgar had been turning out, and sometimess churning out, over the previous years. Born in 1948 into a Midlands media-based family – his father was a BBC producer, his mother an actress and radio announcer – Edgar had been active in student politics in Manchester before working as a journalist in Bradford. And it was there that he started pouring out plays for a company called General Will that embraced agitprop, documentary and environmental spectacle. Edgar certainly revealed a gung-ho aggression in his early writing: *Rent* (1972) was an assault on the Conservative government's Housing Finance Act and *A Fart For Europe* (1973) was an exuberant anti-EEC explosion. But, although Edgar described his political position at the time as 'soft Trotskyite', he also had a journalistic detachment and an ability to comment on the passing scene. Like many others, he soon recognised that the world was not going to be turned upside down by the act of writing socialist plays for select audiences who shared the dramatist's own assumptions. As Edgar later wrote:

> By the end of 1975, the '68 generation had lost its innocence and the section of that generation that had gone into theatre began to appreciate that anybody seriously attempting to represent the times that followed was inevitably going to be dealing with complexity, contradiction and just plain doubt.

Those elements of complexity are present in *Destiny*, which combines first-hand reporting with imaginative exploration of the seeds of fascism. 'If *Destiny* has a virtue,' Edgar once claimed, 'it is that it is true'; and it bears all the hallmarks of a well-researched play. It also places post-war fascism in its historical context by suggesting that the process of withdrawal from east of Suez instilled a nagging, unassuageable sense of loss. Starting in India in 1947, the play follows the contrasting but intertwined fortunes of three key representative figures in post-war Britain. Sergeant Turner becomes an antiques dealer who turns to the ultra-right Nation Forward party when his business is devoured by a property conglomerate. Khera is a Sikh servant who becomes a militant Midlands trade unionist. And Major Rolfe is a displaced army man who plots against the government, bankrolls Nation Forward and, in a neat plot twist, turns out to be the boss of the company that has swallowed Turner's thriving small business. But Edgar's achievement is to dispel the image of British fascists as jackbooted stormtroopers and show how the movement unites various strands of discontent. One particularly good scene shows a public meeting of the Taddley Patriotic League filled with wobbly banners and malfunctioning microphones. It is the kind of amateurish assembly you find in all strands of public life: what Edgar captures perfectly, however, is the way fascism becomes a magnet for anyone with a social grievance and sense of loss. At the meeting a Tory lady is appalled by the way Young

Conservatives 'look embarrassed when you talk about Empire or self-help or discipline'. The wife of a teacher from the local polytechnic echoes her husband's resentment at the influx of foreign students and far-left lecturers. A shop-steward from the local motor-foundry fears either foreign buy-out or the loss of his job to immigrant workers, since at dinnertime 'there's that many turbans in the canteen, it looks like a field of bloody lilies'. Edgar's play is a potent reminder that extreme right-wing parties provide an umbrella for all kinds of weirdly overlapping social and political resentments.

But *Destiny* is also an attack on both mainstream political parties for their failure to combat resurgent xenophobia. The Conservatives may have repudiated Enoch Powell for his 1968 'River Tiber' speech, but they did disproportionately well in the West Midlands in the 1970 election; Labour, in the late Sixties, had also used an earlier Conservative Immigration Act to deny passport privileges to Kenyan Asians and had subjected Ugandans fleeing the tyranny of Idi Amin to a discriminatory quota system. No one's hands were clean. Unusually for a radical dramatist, Edgar went even further in discerning unnerving parallels between extremists of right and left. 'It was like looking in a mirror, looking at him, me old mate Tony,' says the militantly left-wing Paul of an old friend who has turned fascist. It was a sign of Edgar's maturity and the tenor of the times that he could suggest there was a direct parallel between Paul's obsession with class and Tony's with race. And Edgar's mixture of accurate reportage and shrewd insight were seized on by most commentators. As Bernard Crick wrote in the *Times Higher Education Supplement*:

> Here was a project I have often imagined but never hoped to see: a strong and committed left-winger able to understand and to dramatise empathetically the psychology and doctrine of fascism; and, indeed, its working-class as well as its elitist appeal. Borkenau, Koestler, Orwell and Silone argued the need to know the other side's feelings and case as well as one's own; advice all too seldom taken today.

Even though it gained a place in the Stratford rep only thanks to the passionate advocacy of its director, Ron Daniels, *Destiny* benefited enormously from the imprimatur of the RSC. For a start it had a fantastic cast: Ian McDiarmid as the gnawingly discontented Turner, Michael Pennington as Major Rolfe, Bob Peck and John Nettles as warring fascists, Cherie Lunghi, Alfred Molina and Michael Cashman (subsequently a member of Labour's National Executive and an MEP) in key supporting roles. Because of its success in Stratford, *Destiny* also transferred to the Aldwych in 1977, where it played in rep with *King Lear* and caused a good deal of stir. On the last night of the play's run at the Aldwych – ironically, with the theatre decked with patriotic bunting for the Queen's Silver Jubilee – neo-fascists demonstrated outside the building and the police were eventually called: if they'd bothered to attend the play, the demonstrators might have realised that Edgar's dramatic achievement lay in refusing to demonise fascists or portray them as cloven-footed members of another species. What Edgar had done was seriously to examine the several strands which make up the extreme right in British politics. In writing a play for his times, he had also anticipated a world thirty years hence, in which the BNP would thrive in local council elections and find many of its anti-immigration policies endorsed by Britain's tabloid press and sections of the Conservative Party.

The manifest success of *Destiny* seems to have encouraged the RSC rapidly to expand its new-play policy. In 1977 it took over the former Donmar rehearsal rooms in Covent Garden and reopened them as a 180-seat theatre called The Warehouse – according to one spectator, it resembled a vandalised school gym. Under Howard Davies's direction, the venue became a home for transfers from The Other Place. More significantly, it also housed, over the next five years, a barrage of new plays by a wide variety of writers: Howard Barker's *That Good Between Us* and *The Hang of The Gaol*, C. P. Taylor's *Bandits*, James Robson's *Factory Birds*, Barrie Keeffe's *Frozen Assets*, Edward Bond's *The Bundle*, Peter Flannery's *Savage Amusement*. Taken together, the plays had a good deal in common. A belief that there was something rotten in the state of England. An extraordinary geographical freedom. A conviction that survival depended less on collective action than gestures of individual protest. The plays were all basically written from the standpoint of the left but pinned little hope on existing structures as a means of changing society. Even at the time one was aware of certain shared assumptions and stylistic features that led me to outline a scenario for an archetypal Warehouse play to be called *Scavengers*:

> It would feature a gang of articulate hobos on a savage journey through England in search of the killer of one of their clan. Their quest

would involve them in a brief encounter with a black-suspendered Cabinet minister's wife (the minister would be the one in suspenders) outside a motorway café; a scene where they shared out their rations in a ruined Presbyterian chapel; the gatecrashing of a bourgeois charity ball in Market Harborough; and a grim final confrontation in the forecourt of New Scotland Yard at midnight with a homosexual policeman who would turn out to be the killer.

I exaggerated; but only just. There was a sexual and political orthodoxy behind the plays that assumed, as in Barrie Keeffe's *Frozen Assets*, that if a man was Labour, a life peer and gay, he must automatically be a dangerous clown. And while it was good to see the RSC, at a time of national difficulty, expanding its output, too many of the Warehouse plays came and ephemerally went. The only two that could be said to have entered the national repertory both appeared, interestingly enough, after Callaghan had been replaced by Thatcher: C. P. Taylor's *Good* and Willy Russell's *Educating Rita*.

But there is little doubt that the RSC in the late Seventies was on a roll. Its Shakespeare work was outstanding; and, if I could bid time recall and pluck any one production from the period, it would be John Barton's *Love's Labour's Lost*. In Barton's exquisite production, we saw intellectual arrogance and posturing romanticism being punctured as the leaves began to fall from the trees and the evening shadows lengthened on the grass; and one can only marvel nostalgically at a cast that included Michael Pennington as Berowne, Jane Lapotaire as Rosaline, Richard Griffiths as the King of Navarre, Michael Hordern as Don Armado and David Suchet as a myopic curate. But while Barton – the supreme interpreter of Shakespeare's comedies – seemed haunted by the idea of transience, time and late-summer melancholy, Trevor Nunn was increasingly attracted by the idea of lyric Shakespeare. Immediately after his rigorous *Macbeth*, he turned *The Comedy of Errors*, with the aid of composer Guy Woolfenden, into a gag-filled, dance-bedecked Aegean musical. I was initially sceptical; but when the production moved to the Aldwych, its mock-Theodorakis tunes and Zorba-like dances induced the ecstasy that is the special province of the musical. The final moment, when the twin Dromios departed 'hand in hand, not one before another', was as communally celebratory as the climax to Brook's *Dream*. The show was also to prove historically significant. Amongst its London spectators was a young producer, Cameron Mackintosh, who spied in its director a man who could both animate a stage and fluently inter-weave Shakespeare's language with song and dance. Nunn seemed to combine the textual attentiveness of Cambridge's F. R. Leavis with the showbiz instinct of Hollywood's Busby Berkeley; and when the time came to find a director for a projected musical called *Cats* Mackintosh knew precisely where to look.

The RSC's adventures in musical theatre continued in 1977 with Peter Nichols' *Privates on Parade*, which managed to hit several targets at once. Like much of Nichols' previous work, it was an autobiographical memoir based on his own experiences with Combined Services Enter-tainments in Malaya in 1948. In the play this was transformed into an outfit called SADUSEA offering tat variety to listless troops or uncom-prehending Gurkhas. But the show was chiefly memorable for the figure of Terri Dennis: an acting (and frequently over-acting) Captain who embodied, in Denis Quilley's performance, a particular kind of showbiz queeniness that one could best describe as camp on the verge of being struck. I remember one militantly gay critic protesting about the perpet-uation of a sexual stereotype. But that overlooked both the social authenticity of a figure like Terri Dennis and his subversive humour. When the naive young hero invoked *Mrs Warren's Profession*, Terri unforgettably replied, 'That Bernadette Shaw? What a chatterbox! Nags away from arsehole to breakfast-time but never sees what's staring her in the face.' It was an observation from which Shaw's reputation never fully recovered. Aside from personal memoir, Nichols' play was also a political enquiry asking what the hell British forces were doing in Malaya in 1948. Were they saving a fragment of empire from the Chi-nese Communists or, as seems more probable, ensuring the commerical continuity of the highly profitable rubber industry? With the help of Denis King's excellent parodic score, Nichols also satirised various atti-tudes to Forties England ranging from Cowardesque anti-Attleeism to wartime nostalgia lewdly represented by a sub-Vera Lynn number:

Remember September
The country weekend
The yearning we felt inside?
And autumn recalls
Such wonderful balls
The organ at eventide.

Privates on Parade, which transferred to the West End and has been much revived since, was proof of both the eclecticism and expansiveness of the RSC in the late Seventies. Not only was the company operating concurrently in two Stratford and two London theatres. In 1977 it also inaugurated an annual tour of the complete Stratford repertory to Newcastle-upon-Tyne. And a year later it made good its commitment to reaching new audiences by launching a small-scale tour, led by Ian McKellen, to regional venues with a programme of *Twelfth Night*, *Three Sisters* and an anthlogy devised by Roger Rees. All this was happening at a time when the country was weathering a whole series of economic crises and the nation as a whole was supposedly going down the pan. So how does one explain this dichotomy between theatrical hyperactivity and national calamity? It was in part due to the unpredictability of talent. Trevor Nunn and Terry Hands, who became joint artistic directors in 1978, were both still relatively young men in their late thirties who seemed liberated by the challenges of both studio spaces and large stages. Just as Nunn gained a new lease of life from his Other Place *Macbeth*, so Hands' more visually exploratory style (many lights, as I once observed, make Hands' work) was ideally suited to the Shakespeare history cycle he explored on the main stage with Alan Howard as a sequence of kings. The labour-intensive nature of theatre also explains the company's expansiveness. 'Up to a certain point,' says Colin Chambers, 'the RSC became more efficient the more it did; broadly speaking, the same number of people worked harder for little or no extra cost.' But there was a crucial sense in which the RSC, while reflecting the national mood in much of its work, was consciously defying the zeitgeist. At a time of business contraction, it doubled its output. As Britain shed the last remnants of empire, the RSC expanded its artistic reach. It was almost as if the company, from the 1975 *Henry V* onwards, was seeking to become a role model and inspiration for the nation by proving that energy and productivity increased quality. There was no evidence that politicans were looking or listening; but, if they had taken note, they might have found in a Stratford-based theatre company both an example to business and industry and a symbol of national regeneration in difficult times.

As if by malign providence, the glorious renaissance of the RSC coincided with the long-awaited opening of the National Theatre on the South Bank in 1976. But, while the RSC basked in golden opinions, the National Theatre from the outset had to cope with guerrilla attacks from remnants of the Olivier regime, embedded hostility from the media and a rash of internal, wildcat strikes. An idea that had first been articulated in 1848 finally became in 1976 a concrete reality. But the fulfilment of a long-term dream was greeted not with an outburst of rejoicing but with sniping cynicism. We had campaigned for a National Theatre. Now that we had it, we didn't, if you believed the papers, seem to want it. There was even talk of a large-scale demo, which turned out to be a damp squib, by members of the fringe community on the day of the Lyttelton's official opening in March 1976 with Beckett's *Happy Days* and Ben Travers's *Plunder*. But there was one piece of good news. The paying public, after years of cramped conditions, high prices and churlish service in the West End, flocked to the building from its first day. And what they relished, apart from the productions, were the civilised amenities: the wide open foyers, the bars and bookshops, the riverfront outlook. Peter Hall in his *Diaries* records all the Dostoyevskyan angst that went into the opening of the National but he has a significant entry for 15 July 1976:

> Crowds of people milling around the theatre this lunchtime: a kite-flying festival by the river, a Dixieland band playing on the terraces, hordes of children watching a puppet show near the main entrance, a full house for the *Hamlet* matinee. Wine is flowing freely in the bars. It's the way this building has to be – a place for a party.

Denys Lasdun's grand architectural scheme was not the predicted white elephant to which no one would go, but an instant success; yet, far from silencing the attacks on the National, the opening of the Lyttelton served only to intensify them.

Why did the National Theatre, now accepted as part of the theatrical landscape, have such an anguished opening? The reasons were partly personal, partly political. There is little doubt that there was an entrenched opposition to Peter Hall that spread outwards from disgruntled Olivier loyalists to sections of the media led by the *Evening Standard*: then a paper of some influence. Admittedly the handover from Olivier to Hall had been handled with the usual Establishment clumsiness; and Hall didn't help his cause by combining his new role as the National's director with outside work such as hosting LWT's weekly arts programme, *Aquarius*. But the dislike of Hall was out of all proportion to his faults. He also became a convenient scapegoat for all those scraping a less privileged living up and down the country. As I wrote shortly after *Tamburlaine The Great* opened the Olivier Theatre in October 1976, the venom directed by members of the profession towards Hall had reached such an insane pitch that 'if an actor in Wrexham rep cannot afford a new pair of tights, it is all the fault of Hall and his sybaritic cronies who spend their days lolling on beds of down puffing on opium pipes and making bonfires of public money'.

But the opposition to the National was also deeply political. A building conceived and designed in the optimistic, expansionist Sixties had the misfortune to open in the miserabilist, nerve-wracked Seventies: even the very concept of a theatre expressing the spirit of the nation seemed anachronistic at a time when the United Kingdom was fragmenting into its constituent parts. Hall's stage-by-stage colonisation of the building was also in danger of being overshadowed by national events: March 1976 saw Wilson's resignation, the pound falling below two dollars for the first time, the collapse of constitutional talks with Ian Smith's Rhodesia. And, at a time of standstill or reduced grants, there seemed to many something offensively disproportionate about the National's financial needs: particularly the fact that, of the £2.9 million required in annual revenue grant to keep the National open, roughly half was swallowed up by maintenance before a play had been staged. The National was even prey to the industrial unrest that dogged British life in the Seventies: the dismissal of an inefficient plumber in 1977 led to a backstage strike by members of NATTKE (National Association of Theatrical, Television and Kine Employees) which dragged on through the summer, led to ugly picketing outside the building and disrupted several productions. Like the country itself, the National was plagued by industrial disputes and suffered periodic crises; yet Hall and his team, led by Peter Stevens as General Manager, got the building up and running.

In fairness, they did much more than that. Hall showed great tactical shrewdness in opening the building before it was fully complete and importing to the Lyttelton a proven bank of Old Vic productions: *Happy Days*, *Plunder*, *Hamlet*, John Osborne's latest national diatribe *Watch It Come Down* and a magnificent production of Ibsen's *John Gabriel Borkman*. This last, by Hall himself, effortlessly combined realism and symbolism: Ralph Richardson's Borkman, greeting visitors with one hand symbolically thrust inside his greatcoat, was a man living out an insane dream of himself as a Napoleon of commerce.

With the Lyttelton in business, the Olivier finally opened in October 1976. Even though it had been subject to appalling delays and the elaborate stage machinery was still not working ('It's like directing in the village hall,' Hall told me), there was something immediately inviting about the Olivier's large saucer-shaped stage and fan-like auditorium. Over the years it was to acquire a reputation as a 'difficult' space for anything but epic work; yet watching Albert Finney's smoke-wreathed Tamburlaine riding his huge chariot through the double doors of John Bury's set one was aware of its vast potential. And when the Cottesloe finally opened in March 1977 with Ken Campbell's sprawling, inordinate *Illuminatus*, one had a sense of completion. It had taken Hall a year to get all three auditoria fully operative and the cost, in nervous wear and tear, is amply recorded in his *Diaries*. The day after *Tamburlaine* opened to excellent notices, the *Evening Standard* ran yet another hysterical double-page spread demanding a public enquiry into alleged extravagances at the National. 'Home tonight feeling awful,' wrote Hall, 'and not wanting to continue with this life or this job.' But, of course, he did. And it is hard to think of any other figure in British theatre who would have had the tenacity, stamina, and sheer bloody-mindedness to have overcome the obstacles in his path: not least the insidious campaign of vilification conducted by personal enemies and philistine newspapers.

Apart from getting the building open, Hall's achievement in those early years at the National was to enlist the support of living writers: in particular, the younger generation of Howard Brenton, David Hare and Stephen Poliakoff as well as more established figures such as Pinter, Bond, Ayckbourn and Bolt. The National could easily have become a safe house or cosy museum. But, just as he had sought to bring Shakespearean disciplines to new work at the RSC, so at the National Hall created an internal dialogue between the classic tradition and contemporary drama. He also encouraged dramatists to write on a big scale and to address, if they so chose, the state of the nation; and, having been initiated by Hall, this idea became a central plank of the policy of two of his successors, Richard Eyre and Nicholas Hytner. It was, in fact, Eyre who, even before the new National building had opened, provided Hall with a vibrant new play: Trevor Griffiths' *Comedians*, which opened at Nottingham Playhouse on 20 February 1975, nine days after Margaret Thatcher's election as Conservative leader, and came down to the Old Vic in September. It was Eyre who discovered the play, Hall who gave it maximum exposure; and what was fascinating was how Griffiths, at a time when politics had lost some of its ideological passion and disillusion with the failures of 1968 was starting to recede, produced his most popular, durable and accessible work. As Griffiths himself wrote:

> *Comedians* eschews political theory, professional ideologues and historically sourced discourse on political revolution – all the perceived hallmarks of those earlier pieces (*Occupations* and *The Party*) in favour of a more or less unmediated address on a range of particular contemporary issues including class, gender, race and society in modern Britain.

Peter Hall put it more directly in his diary entry for 27 March 1975: 'Train to Nottingham to see Trevor Griffiths' *Comedians:* magnificent. I have liked Trevor's previous plays but they were cerebral, political, challenging the audience intellectually. This play fucks them: it achieves a full human congress with them. It is terrific.' As a result, he had no hesitation in presenting Eyre's production, starring Jonathan Pryce and Jimmy Jewel, under the National's banner.

One can see why Hall responded so enthusiastically to Griffiths' play: it applies the dramatist's dialectical method to the art of comedy. The play stemmed from a conversation Griffiths had in a Manchester bar with a couple of stand-up comics who had been taping sessions for Granada TV's popular show, *The Comedians*, which ran from 1971 to 1985. From these guys Griffiths learned of a class run by a veteran comic in the upstairs room of a local pub. That sparked the idea for Griffiths' play: of a night school for budding stand-ups which could be used to explore opposing views of the function of laughter. Eddie Waters, the old pro who runs the class, takes an idealistic view: 'A true joke, a comedian's joke, has to do more than release tension, it has to liberate the will and desire, it has to change the situation.' Bert Challenor, the line-toeing agent's man who has come to judge the apprentice comics in performance, is a pure pragmatist: 'I'm not looking for philosophers. I'm looking for comics. I'm looking for someone who sees what the people want and knows how to give it to them . . . A text for tonight. We can't all be Max Bygraves. But we can try.' Griffiths then throws a wild card into the debate in the shape of Gethin Price: a wilful individualist whose act is a mix of traditional Grock-inspired business and aggressive, working-class hatred. The play starts out as a battle between Waters and Challenor. It ends up as a duel between Waters and Price. And this is where it gets more contentious. Echoing Theodor Adorno's point that there could be no poetry after the gas-chambers, Waters implies that after Buchenwald and Auschwitz comedy has became an impossibility: Price, however, sticks rigidly to his belief that it can be an agent of revolution. Hall, in his *Diaries*, accuses Griffiths of 'bumming a free ride on the gas-chambers': I don't think that's quite fair, but the invocation of the death-camps introduces a whole new philosophical debate at a late point in a play that is otherwise remarkable for its tight-knit coherence.

The virtue of Griffiths' play is that it puts so much of contemporary Britain on stage. It begins and ends in a dilapidated Manchester schoolroom built in 1947 just after the passing of the Education Act: the same Act that helped transform many working-class lives, including that of Griffiths himself. The chipped and fraying desks, the torn and curling wall posters offer a potent reminder of the way the aspirational hopes and dreams of the post-war period have been insufficiently realised. Like Richard Hoggart's *The Uses of Literacy*, the play also shows a fascination with English popular culture and extra-mural education. Above all, it constantly reminds us that these amateur comedians exist in a world of real, day-to-day work: Gethin Price drives a van for British Rail and his fellow aspirants include a docker, a milkman, an insurance salesman, a builder and a smalltime club-owner. Comedy, for these men, is a mixture of career path, escape route, personal therapy: even, in the case of Gethin Price, an extension of some deep-rooted class antagonism.

But the play's real brilliance lies in the way Griffiths uses the aspiring comics' acts to articulate the racial, sexual and social prejudices of Seventies Britain. What is more, he exposes the basic contradiction of comedy: that it can appeal to dated stereotypes and at the same time be very funny. This is the risk the play takes. In the theatre we become the comics' audience. We thus find ourselves recognising the truth of Griffiths' point that 'some of the things you find funniest you also find most reactionary, most supportive of prejudice'. Sammy Samuels, the Jewish club owner who is one of the two apprentices to gain Challenor's professional approval, launches into a string of misogynist jokes: 'This Women's Lib woman collared me in a bar. She says: "You're a brutal, loudmouthed, irrational, sadistic, sexist, male chauvinist pig, you're nothing else." I said: "There's no chance of a quick shag is there?"' Offensive? Definitely. Outdated? Certainly. But because, in my experience, it makes a lot of the audience laugh, it confirms Griffiths' point that comedy often leaves us trapped inside our own prejudices. This is the eternal paradox that Griffiths explores in *Comedians*, reminding us that one of the most popular performers in the weekly Granada TV show was the late Charlie Williams: a performer who, precisely because he was black, felt licensed to tell jokes that reinforced racial stereotypes. But the prime vision that emerges from *Comedians* is of a Britain that has lost any sense of a cohesive working-class culture: what we are left with is a world that is deeply insecure about gender and race, that uses night-school as a source of self-advancement rather than self-improvement and that feels that, in the process of airing its prejudices, it has somehow decontaminated them. Intriguingly, however, Griffiths ends with a gesture of hope. By showing a new Asian applicant to the class telling a rather good joke about Hindu hypocrisy, Griffiths implies not only that Waters will overcome his disillusion but that multi-culturalism may reinvigorate our comic tradition. It would be nice to think this were true; but for every Meera Syal and Shazia Mirza there is still a Jim Davidson or Bernard Manning playing expertly on our existing prejudices.

Whatever one's qualifications, *Comedians* was a first-rate play that confirmed Griffiths was a major talent: a disillusioned Mancunian Marxist who, having provided Olivier with his farewell role at the National, also gave Hall one of his earliest hits. But Griffiths' belief in strategic penetration of the major citadels was a policy avidly pursued by the next generation of political writers, led by Howard Brenton and David Hare. Their determination to conquer the big stages, and appetite for maximum exposure, coincided with Hall's belief that the National should identify itself with the rising generation: something that never quite happened, for all Tynan's furtive insistence, during the Olivier years. But, although this alliance between the radical young and the National was to have a huge impact on the future, it still takes one by surprise. As early as June 1974, just after the opening of *The Churchill Play* at Nottingham Playhouse, Hall records in his *Diaries*:

> My first meeting with Howard Brenton. A huge man, shy, a little fat, delivering occasional knockout remarks like a gentle pugilist suddenly lashing out. He is very like his plays, a sure sign of a fine artist. He is the first of the new, young ones to be utterly enthusiastic about

the new building and the possibilities of reaching a big new audience at the new National. He will write a play for us and he wants David Hare to direct it.

And so it turned out, with *Weapons of Happiness* becoming, in July 1976, the first commissioned play to be staged in the brand-new Lyttelton Theatre. A somewhat disconcerting play it was too, in which Brenton contrasted the battered experience of an exiled Czech Communist, very well played by Frank Finlay, with the naive innocence of a group of anarchists who occupy a family-owned south London crisp-making factory. The right were alienated by the play's scatological language; the left by Brenton's attack on the false Utopianism of a group of disorganised rabble-rousers. Kenneth Tynan, admittedly no friend of the new National regime, with which he had parted company, was so insulted that he booed the performance he attended, claiming: 'The whole history of the Left – the great movement which has made life tolerable and tenable for working people over the last two centuries – is reduced to a choice between despotic Stalinists and idiot children whose idea of revolution is to shit on the factory floor.' Actually that was a wildly simplistic reading of Brenton's play, which argued that social change cannot be achieved without discipline, work and organisation. Possibly more significant than the content, however, was Brenton's voluptuous delight in the Lyttelton's enormous potential. As Brenton told Sheridan Morley in an interview: 'David Hare and I regard ourselves and our cast and production team as an armoured charabanc full of people parked within the National walls – we've brought our own concept in with us because we want consciously to use the National facilities to show our work off to its best advantage.' Which indeed they did. Long after one has forgotten the play's arguments, what one remembers is the way Hayden Griffin's design and Hare's production transformed the space, in a matter of seconds, from a London riverside wharf to a wintry Russian landscape or the London Planetarium. The National, one realised, offered a natural home for epic drama: plays that linked private and public worlds and that offered a panoramic, rather than a microscopic, vision of society.

The point was not lost on David Hare who, like Brenton, was quickly enlisted by Peter Hall in the National's new programme and who was, over the next three decades, to become an integral part of its repertory. Having directed *Weapons of Happiness* with such assurance, Hare deployed the spatial freedom of the Lyttelton in his own new play, *Plenty*, which opened there in April 1978. This was a play that transported its heroine, Susan Traherne, from wartime France in 1943 to a seedy Blackpool hotel in 1962. It also offered a wide-angled vision of post-war England, using Susan as a symbol of the disenchantment and disillusion that accompanied the peace. This was not, of course, a new theme. Several plays in the Forties and Fifties had dealt with the difficulty of adjusting to peacetime reality. But even the finest of them, Rattigan's *The Deep Blue Sea*, was confined by the demands of keyhole naturalism. Hare, writing a generation later, was able both to take a longer historical perspective and to deploy the epic possibilities of the Lyttelton stage. It doesn't mean Hare's play is better than Rattigan's; but its temporal and spatial freedom, heavily influenced by both Brecht and cinema, shows just how much playwriting had changed in a quarter of a century.

Hare's play is dazzling but problematic. It clearly suggests that there are two possibilities facing sentient beings in an imperfect world. You can accept the accommodations and compromises of a dishonest society, like the Foreign Office attaché whom Susan Traherne eventually marries. On the other hand, you can cling to your idealism, as Susan does, and thus destroy yourself and others. I have no problem with the starkness of the alternatives with which Hare presents us; but he himself was shrewd enough to see that the focus is almost entirely on Susan and that her husband, Brock, is a much less dramatically compelling figure. 'I was trying to say', Hare later admitted, 'that his fate is just as bad as the woman's but I didn't give it as much dramatic weight as I should have.' Particularly in his own first production at the National, you felt Hare was in thrall both to the character of Susan and its magnetic interpreter, Kate Nelligan.

For all that, *Plenty* remains a crucial play in post-war British drama. For a start, in spite of a set of largely chilly, uncomprehending notices, it was carefully nursed by the National: resisting strong pressures to yank it out of the repertory, Peter Hall kept faith in the play and was rewarded with an attentive young audience that turned up on the night rather than booking ahead. Extending Angus Calder's thesis in *The People's War*, Hare also showed how the upsurge of radical optimism that followed the cessation of hostilities in 1945 ran into the sand. To put it more simply, the promise of peacetime turned into the complacency, lies and hypocrisy that characterised the Churchill, Eden and Macmillan years of the Fifties and early Sixties. And, even though I believe Hare seriously underestimates both the difficulties faced by the Attlee government and its remarkable achievements, his play pins down very acutely his own generation's sense of betrayal. In fact, the play's pivotal scene is one set in a Knightsbridge drawing room in October 1956 when Susan confronts her husband's old Foreign Office boss, Sir Leonard Darwin, over the Suez debacle. Susan's own persistent tone is one of withering irony: 'Nobody', she cries, 'will say blunder or folly or fiasco. Nobody will say "international laughing stock". You are among friends, Leonard.' But Susan's insolent mockery pales beside Darwin's own anger at Britain's collusion with France and Israel in urging the latter to attack Egypt as a pretext for seizing the Canal. Hare, as he showed in *Knuckle*, had long been fascinated by tortured Establishment figures. And here there is real emotional weight behind Darwin's confession that he would have defended a stupid policy but not a dishonest one. At one point Brock accuses Darwin of hypocritically subscribing to anything, however murderous, as long as it is done in good faith. In response, Darwin says of the Suez adventure: 'I would have defended it had it been honestly done. But this time we are cowboys and when the English are the cowboys, then in truth I fear for the future of the globe.' It's a great scene; and, watching it in that first production where Basil Henson's poker-backed disillusion was confronted by Kate Nelligan's vituperative scorn, the penny suddenly dropped. *Plenty* was the *Look Back In Anger* of the Seventies. Colonel Redfern was the real hero of Osborne's play: similiarly I felt that the one figure whom Hare unequivocally admired was Darwin, the decent Foreign Office official who has been isolated and betrayed by his peers. Susan Traherne also became a modern Jimmy Porter: a fierce protagonist driven to madness by her alienation from post-war England. Even Brock's argument to Susan that 'you claim to be protecting some personal ideal, almost always at the cost of infinite pain to everyone around you', could be applied equally well to Jimmy. And, like Jimmy Porter, Susan was shadowed throughout the play by a devoted, Horatio-like friend, Alice, who provided a counterpoise to her own eloquent destructiveness. One critic at the time made the connection: the dramatist Ted Whitehead, writing in the *Spectator*, saw the play as a cry of disgust with Britain and wrote, 'I think we can say that David Hare, like

Osborne, has had a bellyful and again like him he compares the desolate present with a nobler and more heroic past.' More generally, however, the play was greeted with a quizzical puzzlement. Bernard Levin professed not to know what it was about. B. A. Young in the *Financial Times* claimed that 'Mr Hare has chosen for his subject the eternal favourite of the British theatre, the marital affairs of the middle classes'. Even the wise Irving Wardle felt: 'The details Mr Hare supplies do not accumulate into a portrait of post-war Britain, even with the help of Victor Sylvester and snide digs at the Third Programme.' This was one of those moments, quite frequent in post-war British theatre, when the critics both failed to recognise a significant play and proved to be out of touch with audience tastes. *Plenty* found an audience, lifted Hare to a new level as a playwright and reinforced his claim to be a spokesman for his generation. It also showed that the National Theatre was hospitable to epic drama and the ideal venue in which to debate the state of the nation.

But the late Seventies was a time when nearly everyone seemed preoccupied by the tensions and stresses of the country as a whole. And yet another of the National's elite cadre of young hopefuls, Stephen Poliakoff, took this subject on board in *Strawberry Fields*, which became the first brand-new commission in the Cottesloe Theatre. Poliakoff, through family background and personal temperament, was, however, a slightly different proposition to his radical contemporaries. As the precocious product of a Russian-Jewish family that had fled the Soviet Union in the Twenties, Poliakoff was less drawn to revolutionary romanticism or armchair Marxism. Instead he became the W. P. Frith of grotty urban culture, faithfully recording the drabness and desolation of inner-city life. He also started incredibly young. He wrote his first play while still at Westminster School, thereby attracting a favourable notice in *The Times*. And, although he had contributed in 1971 to the group-authored *Lay-By* dealing with a motorway rape case, he confessed himself bemused by some of the story's more arcane sexual terms. What really put Poliakoff on the map, however, were two plays produced by the Bush Theatre in 1975. The first, *Hitting Town*, was a study of incestuous siblings set in an echoing, graffiti-scarred, inner-city precinct. Suddenly, one realised this was a world that no one had pinned down on stage before: when the anarchic brother made a repulsively inedible mound out of the brown sauce, flavourless mustard and plastic tomato one finds in a

Muzak-filled Wimpy Bar, one got a sharp reminder of the tat and grime of the new materialism. Even better was *City Sugar* which showed a self-hating, manipulative local-radio DJ, played brilliantly at the Bush by John Shrapnel and less effectively in the West End transfer by Adam Faith, using his power to feed the undernourished dreams of lonely teenagers. 'You could drop anything over the air into that pool,' said the cynical DJ, 'and they'd gobble it up.' With commercial radio booming throughout Britain and the BBC extending its local radio outlets, Poliakoff seized unerringly on the media's capacity to bend minds and exploit loneliness. The principle of nation speaking unto nation, which underpinned the Reithian concept of broadcasting, had been replaced by the commercial reality of one solitary addressing another. Poliakoff was acutely sensitive to the mood of the times. And, looking back over his work from 1973 to 1979, he now sees his plays as a product of

> those grey years when the last residue of Sixties optimism was quickly fading and before the harsh, divisive upheavals of the Conservative Eighties. A period which already seems strangely distant: the years of Heath, Wilson and Callaghan, of Wimpy Bars, the Bay City Rollers, punk and the National Front. The plays, to some extent, lassoo the atmosphere of that time but they also look forward to many of the anxieties and desires of the late Eighties.

Atmosphere rather than analysis was certainly Poliakoff's forte. That much was clear from *Strawberry Fields*. It showed two young people – an upper-class county girl in a print frock and a nervy guy with a diseased retina, played by Jane Asher and Stephen Rea – meeting in a motorway café. As they journeyed northwards, and were joined by an unwanted hitch-hiker, it became clear that they were members of the quasi-fascist English People's Party and were opposed to rural pollution, urban wastelands, the tyranny of the car and black immigration. But Poliakoff's play, which appeared in April 1977, had none of the vivid, researched particularity of Edgar's *Destiny*. It never explained the young couple's precise relationship to the National Front nor the real purpose of their journey; and, when they killed a policeman in a Darlington café, the play lurched into melodrama. But what it confirmed was Poliakoff's gift for creating scenes that lodge unbudgeably in the memory. I think of one particularly, set in the sunlounge of a motorway café somewhere on the M1. The two young travellers make a pre-arranged rendezvous with a middle-aged woman surrounded by shopping bags and worried about collecting the kids from school. A scene of surpassing ordinariness, you might say. Except that the woman has raised funds for the new extreme right-wing party, has a scrapbook itemising examples of crime by black teenagers and articulates all the paranoia of middle England. Meanwhile, as the characters talk in the sun-lounge, anonymous voices come over the tannoy insistently announcing, 'The coach to Crewe will depart in one minute.' It's the kind of scene, much replicated in Poliakoff's later film work, where he pins down the oblique weirdness of English life: the idea that an airport-like motorway café might be a meeting ground for fascist malcontents. And, even if Poliakoff's play lacked the political weight of *Plenty* or *Weapons of Happiness*, it confirmed that Hall's National was in the business of dissecting Britain and was fast becoming a second home for young writers.

I make no apology for dwelling so far on the RSC and the National in the late Seventies. The former showed it was possible to thrive even in a time of crisis. The latter historically established itself on the South Bank, survived the snipers and the strikers and attracted young writers. But was there a real danger that these two monoliths might eventually swallow up too much of the available talent and resources? Between them, they took roughly half of the Arts Council's available drama budget. With seven auditoria to run, and no sign of the RSC's expansionist urges slowing down, might they achieve an unhealthy dominance and kill off other companies?

There were certainly times in the Seventies when other institutions began to look shaky. The Royal Court, for instance, had long been a pace-setter. But under the stewardship of Oscar Lewenstein from 1972 to 1975 it often seemed to be marking time and out of touch with the post-1968 generation. And when Robert Kidd and Nicholas Wright took over in the autumn of 1975 they soon ran into trouble. They were both intelligent men: the one a Scottish director, the other a South African writer-director with a wide knowledge of world drama. And they could hardly be blamed for the current grant squeeze that forced them to close the Theatre Upstairs for six months from October 1975 to May 1976. But some of their choices were expensive: Edward Bond's *The Fool*, a fine play about John Clare, required a cast of twenty-two wearing seventy costumes, and came in way over budget. Others were just plain flops: a Nigerian play called *Parcel Post*, a Richard O'Brien piece called *T-Zee*, even a David Storey play called *Mother's Day* which I, perhaps extravagantly, dubbed 'a stinker', resulting in a public cuff over the ears from the author and a good deal of media excitement (even though Storey and I quickly forgot about the incident and resumed cordially distant relations). The deficit at the Court mounted up. The Arts Council told the theatre it had to operate within existing cash resources. And, within eighteen months, Kidd and Wright had departed, to be replaced by the wily, pragmatic Stuart Burge, who at fifty-nine was four years older than George Devine at the time of his death. It wasn't a particularly glorious period in the Court's history but its problems had little to do with omnivorous national companies. They stemmed from a mix of directorial inexperience and a shortage of cash which applied across the board. In 1975 the Bush, a leading new writing venue situated over a raucous West London pub, was facing a deficit of seven thousand pounds and imminent closure. Over the next four years it steadily recovered by unearthing box-office hits like *The Fosdyke Saga* by Alan Plater and Bill Tidy, by showcasing satirical new writing talent like John Byrne and Tina Brown and by discovering new performers such as Victoria Wood and Robbie Coltrane. Today the Bush still bouncily survives.

It was true there was a good deal of belt-tightening around 1975: the first year in a decade in which the Arts Council grant had not gone up. But there was also a lot of activity in and around the fringe, much of it targeting highly specific audiences. The Women's Theatre Group, founded in 1974, was an agitprop company doing shows on subjects like sex education, work opportunities and equal pay strikes. Gay Sweatshop was founded in 1975 following a series of plays presented at the Almost Free. Its aim was to challenge pejorative gay stereotypes and it had some success with shows like *As Time Goes By*, co-written by Drew Griffiths and Noel Greig, dealing with different forms of homosexual repression over three different decades. Of even more significance was the foundation of the Asian company, Tara Arts, in 1977. Its initial impulse was again agitprop and its early shows concerned such subjects as racism in schools and the domestic difficulties caused by living in an uneasily multiracial society. But, under the guidance of Jatinder Verma, it eventually grew into a company capable of taking standard Western classics – such as *Tartuffe* or *The Government Inspector* – and revitalising them by putting them into an Asian context.

Far from being killed off by the big institutions or scrape-and-save funding, alternative theatre actually seemed to expand in the late Seventies: a glance at Cathy Itzin's *Stages In The Revolution* shows over four hundred productions listed in the period from 1975 to 1979 under the heading of political theatre. But far and away the most interesting development was the move towards some kind of documentary drama incorporating the actors' research. And the company that specialised in this was Joint Stock, which enjoyed a hugely productive period in the late Seventies. Its work included *Fanshen*, *Yesterday's News*, *Light Shining In Buckinghamshire*, *Epsom Downs*, *The Ragged Trousered Philanthropists* and *Cloud Nine*. All but one of these were sole-authored texts. Yet, in each case, the writer was able to benefit from workshops, in which the cast and the director pooled their experiences. It was the antithesis of the romantic view of theatre in which the author, after agonising for weeks or months in private, emerges with an impeccably unalterable text. It would also have been anathema to writers like John Osborne or Harold Pinter who possess an untrammelled personal vision. But, for some subjects, it was invaluable. A group of people could assimilate information about the Chinese revolution or the English Civil War far more quickly than an individual. The Joint Stock method also gave the actor a greater stake in the material and called into question the power structure that had developed in subsidised theatre: one in which the director was top dog and called all the shots.

Or so the theory ran. Simon Callow, who appeared in four Joint Stock productions in the late Seventies, later wrote a book called *Being An Actor* in which he questioned whether the company ever achieved a genuinely collective approach. In company meetings, the inquisitive Callow would constantly ask awkward questions: What is Joint Stock? What does it stand for? Callow concluded:

> The answer was simple: Joint Stock stood for the taste of its directors. The Joint Stock style was the Bill Gaskill style, the Max Stafford-Clark style. This style didn't stem from a political position or even an aesthetic theory: it was just their taste, what they liked to see . . . So once again, just as in any other non-collective, unfanshened company, those who stood on the stage were fulfilling the will of someone else, for reasons of which they were never altogether sure.

Callow had a point; and there probably was a certain amount of pious cant emerging from the Joint Stock rehearsal rooms as actors found themselves drawn into exploratory workshops. Yet Joint Stock did have an impact not just on political theatre but on working structures. Directorial taste remained a dominant factor. But it was also realised that, in addressing big public themes, historical movements or vast literary projects, some kind of collaborative approach was beneficial. Mike Leigh, though obviously a man of singular vision, put greater responsibility on the actor to explore and research invented characters. Shared Experience, in keeping with its name, sought to democratise the theatrical process. Even the big companies cottoned on to the changes. In the Eighties the RSC used the Joint Stock method as a means of harnessing a great baggy monster of a book when it launched into *Nicholas Nickleby*. Joint Stock didn't revolutionise British theatre. But it did open up a different way of working that enriched political theatre and helped the shift away from the easy simplifications of the Sixties.

You could see the results in *Fanshen* (1975), its distillation of William Hinton's massive six-hundred-page book charting the process of change in the Chinese village of Long Bow during the revolution from 1945 to 1949. The whole project began with an actress, Pauline Melville, recommending Hinton's book to Gaskill. Five weeks of intensive workshops followed. David Hare then went off for four months and mined a text out of the book. He later recalled:

> In shaping the play, I was very little influenced by any particular discovery in the workshop but I was crucially affected by its spirit. Although Bill had thrashed about seeking to find a suitable style for the work, often lapsing into long and sullen silences, he never relaxed his basic intention: that we should do justice to the sufferings of the Chinese peasants. His criterion for examining any given scene was to ask whether it was adequate to the experience the peasant had undergone.

The finished work was a soberly impressive, meticulously performed study of the process of revolution: one comparable in its effect to Alexander Dovzhenko's 1930 film, *Earth*, dealing with the collectivisation of the Ukrainian farmland. But this was Dovzhenko without his dubious propagandist heroics. The emphasis here was on continuing persuasion, self-criticism and reappraisal. The final image, after an ironically triumphalist unfurling of red banners, was of a solitary peasant interrupted in his hoeing by the demand to attend yet another village discussion. 'Under the Nationalists too many taxes, under the Communists too many meetings,' as one villager cynically observed.

Even if it didn't romanticise the Chinese revolution, *Fanshen* couldn't do full justice to its attendant horrors: no mention of the violence that accompanied the overthrow of the landlords, of the mass rallies in the major towns at which social enemies were denounced and sentenced, of the untold millions killed under the Maoist policy of purging the country of counter-revolutionaries. But, for all its omissions, *Fanshen* faithfully charted the long, laborious process of remaking society. It also left us in little doubt that the peasants were still manipulated by external forces and that the drive for productivity, under Mao, retarded the move towards equality. 'By sheer understatement,' wrote Kenneth Tynan, 'the play achieves by the end enormous power and moral authority. This is the first native offshoot of the Brechtian tradition that seems to me to stand comparison with the native tree.' And that Brechtianism had its effect on the actors. Pauline Melville, while recognising the absurdity of spending a morning pretending to be a Chinese peasant and then rushing off to the local café to stock up on grub, explained in *The Joint Stock Book* the positive side of rehearsals:

> It was the example of a beginning of a way of working that I had never come across in English theatre before where, instead of concentrating solely on character, individual motivation and so forth, we would undertake some sort of class analysis and look at the work from a political perspective . . . One crucial development that came about during rehearsals was the decision to look at each scene to discover what the political point of that scene was and how best to make it clear. This, in fact, was an extremely unusual if not revolutionary step for an English theatre company to take.

John McGrath might have pointed out that it wasn't that unusual north of the border. But Melville's point is valid. Joint Stock encouraged actors to think politically. It also – and this has been less noted – stimulated companies to seek their source material in fact: something that was to have enormously beneficial results for British theatre over the next quarter of a century.

The seductiveness of fact was seen in many of Joint Stock's shows after *Fanshen*. The riveting *Yesterday's News* (1976) was initiated when one of the company, David Rintoul, became fascinated by a newspaper story about the massacre of British mercenaries in Angola. Who were these men? How were they recruited? Did they subscribe to the regular military ethos? Rintoul and the actors set about finding out and even managed to scoop the whole of Fleet Street by getting an interview with a mercenary recruiting agent. The resulting show, scripted by the cast and Jeremy Seabrook, opened our eyes to a neglected facet of British life. And there was a similar investigative urge behind Caryl Churchill's *Light Shining in Buckinghamshire* (1976) which takes its place alongside *Destiny*, *Comedians* and *Plenty* as one of the best political plays of the decade. The subject here was the English Civil War of the seventeenth century and the millennial movements that it bred. As Churchill explained in her introduction to the published edition:

> The simple 'Cavaliers and Roundheads' history taught at school hides the complexity of the aims and conflicts of those to the left of Parliament. We are told of a step forward to today's democracy but not of a revolution that didn't happen; we are told of Charles and Cromwell but not of the thousands of men and women who tried to change their lives. Though nobody now expects Christ to make heaven on earth, their voices are surprisingly close to us.

The brilliance of Churchill's text lay in the fact that it was both historically informative and suffused with contemporary relevance. It caught the millennial optimism that followed the Civil War and the belief that anything was possible: a belief exemplified by the Levellers and Diggers who were crushed by Cromwell's army and the Ranters whose devotion to economic and sexual freedom was eventually destroyed by the Restoration. At the same time, the play carried its own oblique comment on the way the revolutionary hopes of the late Sixties and early Seventies had been followed by despair and disillusion. Like all good history plays, it found in the past a metaphor for the present. It also used fact to crystallise its argument. The pivotal scene became an edited version of the Army debates which took place in 1647 in the church of St Mary the Virgin in Putney. In her biography of Oliver Cromwell, Antonia Fraser notes: 'These debates must rank as one of the most extraordinary moots in British history . . . In their course the participants ranged over ideas which varied from the wild to the prophetic, many of them so far in advance of their times that they were not fulfilled until three hundred years later, if then.' On one side you had Colonel Rainborough, a Leveller from Cromwell's army who argued for liberty, male suffrage and equality under the law. On the other side General Ireton who claimed that it was impossible to achieve equality without the abolition of private property which he deemed undesirable. It was a crucial moment in English history and one faithfully recorded in Churchill's play:

RAINBOROUGH: Sir, I see it is impossible to have liberty without all property being taken away. If you will say it, it must be so. But I would fain know what the soldier hath fought for all this while.

IRETON: I will tell you –

RAINBOROUGH: He hath fought to enslave himself, to give power to men of riches, men of estates, to make himself a perpetual slave. We find none must be pressed for the army that have property. When these gentlemen fall out among themselves, they shall press the poor scrubs to come and kill one another for them.

IRETON: I will tell you what the soldier of this kingdom hath fought for. The danger that we stood in was that one man's will must be law. The people have this right, that they should not be governed but by the representative of those that have the interest of the kingdom. In this way liberty may be had and property not destroyed.

It was a fascinating piece of dialectic: a classic English contest between equality and property. But, even though the Levellers and Diggers were ultimately defeated, Churchill reminds us that the Ranters retained their Utopian vision: one in which God resided in each individual, there was to be no property in the flesh and the distribution of wealth would lead to spiritual liberation. Their inspiration was biblical and at one point they all sang from Ecclesiastes: 'Moreover the profit of the earth is for all: the king himself is served by the field.' Against that Churchill sets the pragmatism of a former military agitator, Briggs, who argues that Christ will not come and that life will continue much as it had before. 'England', he says, 'will still be here in hundreds of years. And people working so hard they can't grasp how it happens and can't take hold of their own lives, like us till we had this chance, and we're losing it now as we sit here every minute. Jesus Christ isn't going to change it.' With austere eloquence, Churchill's play pins down a crucial moment in history. Instead of heaven on earth, the Civil War led to an authoritarian parliament, massacres in Ireland, the development of capitalism. And, even as Max Stafford-Clark's production was being premiered at the Edinburgh Traverse in September 1976, Ireland was accusing British interrogators of torturing prisoners in Ulster and the Chancellor was going cap in hand to the IMF to prop up the pound. But what staggers me is that Churchill's play is not better known. It is never revived, never discussed and not, as far as I am aware, studied in schools. Yet it is one of the key texts of the Seventies in its portrayal of the failure of the revolutionary dream.

The Churchill play from this period that has survived is *Cloud Nine* (1979): a vibrant, playful, highly theatrical piece that forges a link between sexual and political imperialism. The original Joint Stock production was also famous for its cross-gender and cross-race casting and produced some fine performances from Antony Sher, Tony Rohr, Julie Covington and Miriam Margolyes. But although the play's first half, set in a colonial outpost of Victorian Africa, is very funny, the second half, which pursues many of the same characters through to a liberated Seventies London, strikes me as less successful. In apparently endorsing a late-hippy metropolitan bohemianism, Churchill ducks many of the hard questions. Does the erosion of the nuclear family automatically lead to happiness? What effect does gay parenting have on the children? And when an oppressed colonial wife leaves her husband to celebrate the joys of mature masturbation, isn't she sacrificing with one hand what she gains with the other? Michael Patterson in *Strategies of Political Theatre* takes a different line, arguing that Churchill shows that 'contemporary freedoms may prove as confining as imperial morality'. Maybe so, maybe not. But, although *Cloud Nine* has become a campus bible in American drama departments and is often revived in Britain, it is the historical *Light Shining in Buckinghamshire* that for me expresses more eloquently the confusions of the late Seventies.

Political theatre. Factual theatre. State-of-the-nation theatre. All expressing the fever-chart mood of a country racked with economic uncertainty. You could make that the key story of the late Seventies. But it would be slightly misleading since what is most striking is the perverse variety and vigour of a theatre that seemed capable not only of riding the economic and political storms but even of overcoming them. And, at the risk of lapsing into Panglossian optimism, I could point to any number of encouraging signs in the late Seventies.

One was the resilience of regional theatre, which got a big boost in 1976 with the opening of the Royal Exchange in Manchester. Architecturally, it was an astonishing feat: an uncompromisingly modern module set down inside the old Victorian Cotton Exchange. Michael Elliott, the theatre's pioneering director, aptly called it 'a glass lantern of a theatre that is lit from within and seen everywhere from without'. At the time the Royal Exchange was constantly compared, to its advantage, to the National Theatre. The National was massive, institutional, expensive to run and cost £14 million: the Royal Exchange was manageable, community-based, sensibly budgeted and cost a modest £1.2 million. The National's three auditoria were the compromised product of committee thinking: the Royal Exchange's theatre-in-the-round grew out of the shared obsessions of working colleagues. Even the openings of the two buildings, both graced by Laurence Olivier, were pointedly contrasted. The Royal Exchange kicked off on 15 September with a lively revival of *The Rivals*, prefaced by a speech from Olivier who described the occasion as 'one of the greatest joys I have known'. The official launch of the National took place a month later and was a bit of a disaster: the National Anthem was badly played, the Queen glowered and a stuffy audience stared at Bill Bryden's production of Goldoni's *Il Campiello* as if personally affronted. It was game, set and match to Manchester. But one has to say that, thirty years on, the picture looks a little different. The Royal Exchange happily survives: even the IRA bomb-blast that partially destroyed Manchester's city centre in 1996 was used to structurally improve, as well as rebuild, the theatre. But, while I admire the Royal Exchange's tenacity, I also find that its galleried space is not suited to all plays: to me the theatres-in-the-round that work best are those, like the Stephen Joseph in Scarborough and the Orange Tree in Richmond, that depend on a closeted intimacy. Meanwhile the National, perhaps because I spend more time in it, has acquired a comfortable durability. But the opening of the Royal Exchange was certainly an event and one that showed that regional theatre was in no mood to be swallowed up by the mighty National. Those opening seasons yielded some particularly unforgettable performances: Tom Courtenay in *The Prince of Homburg*, Albert Finney and Leo McKern in *Uncle Vanya*, Michael Hordern in *The Ordeal of Gilbert Pinfold*, Vanessa Redgrave in *The Lady From The Sea*.

Those last two shows transferred to London's Roundhouse. And, looking beyond the national institutions, it was possible to detect a good deal of metropolitan life in the late Seventies. That perennial invalid, the West End, certainly showed flickers of vitality, not least in the area of the musical. It absorbed, from the Mermaid, one of the best-ever musical revues in the shape of *Side by Side by Sondheim* which crisply established its subject as the wiliest, wittiest composer-lyricist of his generation: it also showed that Sondheim could be profitably liberated from the Broadway razzmatazz of his regular director, Hal Prince. Meanwhile Prince himself was imported to bring just that quality to Andrew Lloyd Webber and Tim Rice's *Evita*: a songspiel whose dramatic thinness was artfully disguised by Prince's production, with its rotating balconies and robotic soldiers, and by Elaine Paige's belting bravura in the title role of the opportunist adventuress with the fascist husband. As well as importing Broadway talent like Prince, the West End also acquired Broadway shows like *A Chorus Line* which again, thanks to Michael Bennett's choreography, was a triumph of style over substance. New plays even appeared in the West End, admittedly many of them transfers from the subsidised sector. Agatha Christie's long-time supremacy as the West End's only woman dramatist was thankfully challenged by two invigorating plays. One was Pam Gems's *Dusa, Fish, Stas and Vi* which provided an honest, accurate and moving account of the problems faced by liberated modern women. The other was Mary O'Malley's *Once A Catholic* which explored both the repressiveness and the rebelliousness of a Fifties girls' convent: it managed to be warm-hearted and gently subversive at the same time, with the final scene showing a girl affixing a plasticine penis to a statue of Christ in the school chapel. Ten years earlier, before the abolition of censorship, such an episode would have been unthinkable. Now no one, not even devout Catholics, turned a hair.

But, while women dramatists made serious advances in the Seventies, men were still setting the agenda. And it's striking how many of the best West End plays of the period revolved around one particular quality: *the emotional detachment of the English male*. If I emphasise this, it was because it was so pervasive; and, in the case of Simon Gray, you could argue that it was not just an occasional theme but a governing, lifelong obsession. Gray started writing plays while still a lecturer in English literature at Queen Mary's College in London's East End. And, not surprisingly, his chosen milieu was that of metropolitan academia and publishing. His heroes were invariably products of public school and Oxbridge, living in a state of arrested adolescence. For Gray it was as if a life of hermetic privilege drained one of emotional development. In his 1971 success, *Butley* – which, like much of his subsequent work, starred Alan Bates and was directed by Harold Pinter – the hero was a self-destructive academic whose whole life was based on a notion of male friendship derived from schooldays and consisting largely of 'abuse, jokes, games'. With *Otherwise Engaged*, which had a long run at the Queen's Theatre in 1975, that same theme acquired a darker tinge.

The hero is now a successful publisher, Simon Hench, who protects himself from reality through a calculated detachment, stony irony and verbal pedantry. As he sits down to listen to a recording of *Parsifal* during his wife's temporary absence, he finds his privacy invaded by a succession of visitors: his scrounging lodger, his resentful schoolteacher brother, a literary journalist called Jeff and a vengeful acquaintance from his schooldays whose fiancée he has seduced on the office floor. But, although he is casually promiscuous, Hench is also emotionally impervious. He rejects the breast-baring advances of Jeff's latest girlfriend as sternly as Wagner's Parsifal does those of Kundry. And when Hench's wife returns from a tryst with her lover, she quotes the latter's perceptive observation: 'You're one of those men who only give permission to little bits of life to get through to you.' Gray's point is that Hench's homo-social world is an extension of public school and university; and when he and Jeff, who initiated him into Wagner at Oxford, finally sit down to listen to *Parsifal* they are clearly retreating nostalgically into an undergraduate state of ecstasy.

In form, the play owes something to Osborne's *Inadmissible Evidence*. But, even if Gray doesn't possess Osborne's self-flagellating rawness, he is very astute on the flaws in the English male psyche. Hench represents a semi-detached attitude to life. His friend Jeff, meanwhile, is his crude alter ego, embodying both sexual chauvinism and curmudgeonly despair. At one point Jeff defiantly announces, 'I'm English, yes, English to my marrow's marrow.' And how does he define that Englishness? First by a hatred of the foreigners he has spent years encountering in his role as a cosmopolitan *littérateur*. Then by declaring, 'I detest women, love men, loathe queers.' Finally Jeff reveals he is most at peace in a solitary no man's land on his way to and from sexual encounters with his ex-wife:

When I'm caught in a traffic jam on an English road, under an English heaven – somewhere between London and Cambridge, on my way to Gwen, on my way back from her, rain sliding down the window, engine humming, dreaming – dreaming of what's past or is to come. Wrapped in the anticipation or the memory, no, the anticipation *of* the memory.

Taken together Jeff's remarks amount to a brilliant definition of a certain kind of male Englishness: one that depends on xenophobia, a repressed or latent homosexuality, an elevation of memory over lived experience and an almost obsessive self-awareness. Gray doesn't just probe the male ego. He implies that a concomitant of educated Englishness is a capacity to disengage from life itself and to retreat, at the first opportunity, into literature, music or a world of remembered privilege. And it seems wholly appropriate that Hench and Jeff should find communal solace in Wagner: a composer who notoriously appeals to those who lack their own internal emotional dynamic.

Harold Pinter, as director of both *Butley* and *Otherwise Engaged*, quickly became one of Gray's best interpreters and a loyal friend. And, although their careers in the Seventies had an entirely different trajectory – with Pinter working chiefly at the National and Gray in the West End – and although their perceived status was very different, the two men had a lot in common. Both, for instance, were deeply attached to poetry, cricket and drink. Pinter's preoccupations in the Seventies were also strangely similar to Gray's: male self-sufficiency, emotional isolation, the nature of memory. I wouldn't push the point too far but it's interesting that Pinter went straight from overseeing the opening of *No Man's Land* at the Old Vic in April 1975 to directing *Otherwise Engaged* in the West End in late July. Pinter's play is far bleaker and more poetically resonant than Gray's: it is, in fact, one of his most tantalising masterworks. But both deal with detached literary figures coping with the threat of external invasion. Both plays also invoke an Eliotesque world that hovers between dream and reality. And if Jeff is the other half of Gray's Hench, so Pinter's dual heroes, Hirst and Spooner, are umbilically linked. I've always seen them, in fact, as Pinter's fears made flesh. Hirst, the wealthy man of letters isolated from the reality that was his creative source, was the writer Pinter was frightened of becoming; Spooner, the minor poet inhabiting a world of small magazines, was the writer he might once have been.

But the kinship between Pinter and Gray is even more evident in *Betrayal*: a play whose reverberations I singularly failed to grasp on its first appearance in 1978. Behind Pinter's study of the insidious nature of sexual deceit lies the suggestion that Jerry (the lover) and Robert (the husband) are bound to each other by ties just as strong as their individual passions for Emma. As agent and publisher, respectively, both have also betrayed their undergraduate passion for literature. Over lunch Robert startles Jerry by announcing that he hates books and specifically modern prose. It's a scene that echoes a moment in *Otherwise Engaged* when Jeff, a literary critic, declares literature 'a bloody boring racket' and Hench, a publisher, reveals that he has written the blurb for one of his firm's best-sellers without actually reading the book. Neither Pinter nor Gray are denying the need for publishers and agents. What exercises them both, as lovers of literature, is the professional detachment of a publishing industry that sees authors as mere commodities and books as mere products in a market-driven world.

Detachment, whether emotional or professional, is a quality that haunts the Seventies work of both Pinter and Gray. It was also investigated, in relation to a lower social stratum, by Alan Ayckbourn, towards the end of the decade. Ayckbourn could be said, on the whole, to have had a very good Seventies in which he firmly established himself as both a popular commercial dramatist and an acute social commentator. *Absurd Person Singular* (1972) pinned down crucial shifts in the class system and the rise of the bustling, pre-Thatcherite entrepreneur. *Absent Friends* (1974) portrayed our social embarrassment in the face of death. *Bedroom Farce* (1975), proving that three beds are better than one, was a peerlessly funny study of what Schopenhauer called 'the tyranny of the weak' and the capacity of the neurotic to impose their condition on those with whom they come into contact. But Ayckbourn's work, by his own admission, acquired a perceptibly darker tinge in the second half of the decade. He attributed this to the altered rhythm of the Scarborough season and the fact that he was now composing plays in January while North Sea storms howled around his house and slates cascaded from the roof. Possibly so. But one can't help wondering if the peculiar astringency of *Just Between Ourselves*, written in the gloomy winter of 1975–76, may have been subconsciously influenced by the darkening national mood.

Whatever the motivation, *Just Between Ourselves* picks up on a theme explored by Simon Gray in *Otherwise Engaged*: the English vice of emotional detachment. There is, however, one key difference. The chief victim of the distancing irony dispensed by Gray's Simon Hench is the man himself. In contrast Ayckbourn's hero, a bullish suburban hearty called Dennis, uncomprehendingly destroys those around him: in particular his lonely, mentally disintegrating wife, Vera. And it is this that lifts Ayckbourn's play into the realms of tragicomedy. In the past Ayckbourn had shown the dark side of human nature but, as if keeping a shrewd weather-eye on audience expectations, had always managed to retrieve the situation. Here he resisted the temptation; and by doing so, as he himself said, 'I felt I took a large stride towards maturity as a playwright.' One particular scene, in which Vera (always addressed by her husband with the patronising diminutive of 'Vee') confronts Dennis in his garage and begs for help, is as good as anything in the Ayckbourn canon. It is not that Dennis is a monster. It is simply that, partly because of his upbringing by an omnicompetent father and a ferociously possessive mother, he is emotionally deaf to Vera's desperation. Dennis is also an obsessive handyman who spends all his spare time in his garage disastrously tinkering with do-it-yourself projects: an astute piece of observation by Ayckbourn that suggests a causal link between home improvement and domestic disintegration. This reaches its apotheosis when Vera accosts Dennis in his cluttered garage and pathetically begs him for help:

DENNIS: Yes, but don't you see, you're not being clear, Vee. You say help but what sort of help do you mean?

VERA: Just help. From you.

DENNIS: Yes. Well, look, tell you what. When you've got a moment, why don't you sit down, get a bit of paper and just make a little list of all the things you'd like me to help you with. Things you'd like me to do, things that need mending or fixing and then we can talk about them and see what I can do to help. All right?

(VERA *does not reply*)

How about that, Vee? All right? Does that suit you?

(VERA *moves to the door*)

Vee?

(VERA goes slowly out into the house).

Vee .Vee.

By the end of the play Vera has been reduced to a catatonic wreck while Dennis, his ogre-like mother and the neighbourly Neil and Pam, as if oblivious to her downfall, wanly sing 'Happy Birthday'. It is as sombre an ending as you'll find in Ayckbourn and indeed in most modern drama. It is also a reminder that in the late Seventies the master technician edged closer to Chekhov and showed that he was capable of building laughter out of suffering.

Where Ayckbourn and Gray explored the domestic consequences of emotional detachment, Alan Bennett in *The Old Country* (1977) examined its wider implications. This was a play about the very nature of 'Englishness'. And what Bennett suggested was that it was not dependent upon place. It was more a state of mind, implying a gift for ironic impenetrability. This was, of course, exactly the quality that had made the English past masters in the field of espionage. And, although Bennett claimed that *The Old Country* was as much about exile as about espionage and was inspired more by W. H. Auden than Kim Philby, it was nevertheless the first in a sequence of plays – including *An Englishman Abroad* and *A Question of Attribution* – in which Bennett explored the politics of deception.

Even the play itself practices a form of benign deceit. At first, what with books scattered around a country veranda and the sound of Elgar drifting through from an adjacent room, we assume we are in deepest Berkshire. Only gradually do we realise that we are in the Russian dacha of an old public-school Marxist, Hilary, who has betrayed his native land. But Bennett uses this situation to offer multiple perspectives on the changing character of English life. Hilary combines affiliation to the Soviet Union with the romantic nostalgia of the exile: he wanly regrets that the old Eucharist has been banished, that Lyons Corner Houses, Gamages and Pontings have all gone. Meanwhile Duff, his Establishment brother-in-law and a married Harold Nicolson-like homosexual who has come to summon Hilary home, suffers the pangs of the internal exile: he regrets the architectural despoliation of England's provincial cities and says, 'one's whole nature yearns towards the new yet time and again one finds oneself averting one's eyes from evidences of modernity.' But Bennett implies that elegiac regret is the prerogative of the privileged. And he sharply contrasts the upper-class head-shakings of Hilary and Duff with the unsentimental realism of Eric, an exiled Gosport draughtsman, and his Mittel-European wife, Olga. Although Eric is homesick he finds that his recollection of being picked up by Duff one afternoon in the National Gallery cuts little ice socially and that the old class barriers are as stiffly erect as ever. And Olga is given a pained and perceptive speech on the English capacity for embarrassment from which only the Queen is exempt:

> With the rest it's 'I won't make you feel bad as long as you don't make me feel bad.' Then everyone is happy. That is the way it works. That is the social contract. Society is making each other feel better.

But what makes Bennett such a complex and interesting writer is that he examines the whole idea of Englishness, and the ironic detachment it implies, with his usual bifurcated sensibility. At one point he puts the boot into the mandarin snobberies of English life, mercilessly exposing the sexual sentimentality behind E. M. Forster's remark that he hoped he would have the guts, given the choice, to betray his country rather than his friend. Dismissing this as 'nancy rubbish', Hilary sees the Forsterian notion of 'friendship' as a form of nostalgia for lost youth embodied by 'some fourteen-year-old tart giving them the glad eye during the service of Nine Lessons and Carols'. In contrast to this woozy definition of 'friendship', Bennett suggests there is a very real notion of Englishness: one that transcends circumstance and geography and is defined by a pervasive irony and the use of language as a protective mask. 'In England we never mean entirely what we say, do we?' enquires Hilary. 'Do I mean that? Not entirely. And logically it follows that when we say we don't mean what we say, only then are we entirely serious.' For Simon Gray this kind of verbal camouflage is a character flaw that in the end leads to emotional sterility. But Bennett is more equivocal. You feel that for him it lies at the very heart of Englishness – far more than the weather, Gilbert and Sullivan or cricket – and that it is to be acknowledged, scrutinised and deployed as one of a dramatist's most valuable weapons.

But the whole question of Englishness – of who we were as a people and what kind of lives we led – preoccupied just every about every dramatist in the late Seventies; and none more so than the pioneering author-director, Mike Leigh, who produced one of the decade's defining works in *Abigail's Party*. First seen at Hampstead

Theatre in 1977, it went on to be filmed by the BBC and has since become one of television's enduring classics; and, when revived in 2002 as the final production in the old Portakabin Hampstead playhouse, it confirmed its power as both social document and Strindbergian marital drama. If one stresses the content of Leigh's play, it is because far too much attention has been paid to his singular, collaborative method. After studying acting at RADA, art at Camberwell and cinema at the London Film School, Leigh set out to create a new kind of drama by utilising the observational and imaginative power of his actors. Each would be given the germ of a character whom they would research over a period of several weeks. Once they reassembled, secure in the knowledge of who they were, the dramatic action would be developed under Leigh's firm direction. Improvisation was simply a tool: the aim was to produce a finished script that would be as tight and controlled as that of any playwright. Alan Ayckbourn, speaking of Leigh's working methods, once joked, 'Mike's simply too mean to buy a typewriter.' But Leigh takes himself seriously as a writer and once upbraided me for ignoring the influence of Harold Pinter on his work.

But it is Ayckbourn with whom Leigh most obviously invites comparison. They were the only two writers willing to explore a territory disdainfully ignored by most dramatists in the Seventies: that of the newly prosperous, status-conscious suburbia. And what Leigh discovered, in creating *Abigail's Party*, was that many people, in spite of their increasing affluence, were living lives of joyless desperation. The pivotal figure, whom everyone remembers from Alison Steadman's hip-swinging, gin-swilling performance, was Beverly, who has invited guests round to her suburban parlour but whose overriding aim is to humiliate her sexually inadequate estate-agent husband. But, if the hosts are bound together by mutual loathing, so too are their guests: Tony, a taciturn computer operator whom Beverly seeks to seduce, so detests his own wife, Angela, that he has threatened to seal her mouth up with Sellotape. And completing this unhappy group is a crushed divorcee, Susan, in flight from her fifteen-year-old daughter's rumbustious party.

Leigh has often been accused of condescension: of mocking the tastelessness of people who fetishistically worship their rotisserie, who delight in the music of Demis Roussos and Donna Summer and who exhibit their social aspirations through their immaculately bound,

unread volumes of Dickens and Shakespeare. But, far from patronising his characters' pretensions, Leigh truthfully observes a world in
which people define themselves by their possessions. He also reminds
us of something too easily forgotten in all the talk of social disintegration in the Seventies: that the majority of people were much better off
as shown by the statistics about durable goods. Between 1970 and
1979 the percentage of UK households with a telephone rose from
thirty-five to sixty-seven, with a refrigerator from sixty-six to ninety-
two, with central heating from thirty to fifty-five and with colour television from two to sixty-six. Even in a time that witnessed the decline
of manufacturing industry and a good deal of anarchy in the work-
place, most households enjoyed a higher standard of living.

Leigh and Ayckbourn are virtually the only dramatists to record this
rising affluence. But Leigh goes on to suggest that material comfort is
no salve for an atomised society in which there is little sense of community and in which marriage is simply an institutionalised habit. In
fact, Leigh anticipates something that was to be a symptom of the
Thatcherite Eighties: the awareness that conspicuous consumption is
no solution to life's problems. Leigh also points to a more permanent
sense of insufficiency that Bernard Levin was one of the few critics to
understand. He wrote in *The Times* of Leigh's characters:

> In organic terms, these people lack roots; in terms of energy, they
> are unearthed. The problem is our world's; they are torn loose from
> history, faith, spirit, even language, because they are torn loose from
> themselves. Only when they (and they are we) can identify with
> themselves – not with the chromium-plated egos on show but with
> the true inner and incorporeal reality that is part of a universal
> human self – will they be able to abandon these lives of noisy des-
> peration. *Abigail's Party* offers no cure for its characters' sickness or
> for the contagion the audience feels; but its diagnosis is faultless.

There may have been a touch of the apocalyptic about Levin's column, but he expressed a fundamental truth about Leigh's play and
about much of Seventies theatre. It was, in many ways, a time of
extraordinarily productive growth. The National Theatre had at last
opened. The RSC hit a rich vein of form. New theatres had blossomed.
Working practices had been democratised. And dramatists, far from
being deterred by a succession of financial crises and prevailing national uncertainty, had been spurred into activity. Even the traditional male

dominance of theatre had been marginally dented. Anyone who had been alive in 1945 would have recognised that, while commercial theatre was continuingly precarious, subsidised institutions had broadened the possibilities. Yet running through the drama of the decade was a nagging sense of uncertainty. Who were we? Where were we going? How were we to survive? What values were we to live by other than those of material acquisition? By the end of the Seventies there was a sense that dramatists had deployed every possible means to analyse the state of the nation: epic, satire, social commentary, historical metaphor. Yet, although dramatists thrived on dissent and were stimulated by the perception of national decline, they mostly felt that their work had done little to change the situation. What British theatre needed was a fresh impetus, a new direction; or possibly a larger target to attack than the policy failures of successive Labour governments or the erratic rightward lurches of Conservative ones. But, as Callaghan went to the country in May 1979 shadowed by 'the winter of discontent', the theatre was soon to find that it was to be jolted into a new and disquieting reality: one that was to change its very nature, provoke fierce opposition and cause it to look back fondly at the underrated achievements of the supposedly grey Seventies.

VIII

1979–90

Scenes from an Execution

We can't say we hadn't been warned. Dramatists had for a long time been writing prophetically about an acquisitive society lacking in spiritual values. But even they couldn't have foreseen the devastating changes that were to accompany a long period of Thatcherite government. On 4 May 1979 Margaret Thatcher went to Buckingham Palace as the first woman Prime Minister in British history. On 28 November 1990 she was unseated not by the electorate but by her own party in a coup that was far more dramatic than anything at the time happening on British stages. In the eleven intervening years British society experienced a none-too-peaceful revolution in which the theatre mirrored, all too accurately, the changes taking place in the wider world. The post-war structure of subsidies may have remained precariously intact. In the late Eighties the theatre also recovered its capacity for dissent. But Thatcherism had a profound effect on both the style and content of British theatre; and in many ways the medium is still permeated by the influence of the market forces that dominated what the political commentator Alan Watkins once called 'a uniquely detestable decade'.

One thing that changed was the language in which we talked about theatre. At the start of the Thatcherite era the then arts minister, the highly civilised Norman St John Stevas, promised there would be 'no candle-end economies in the arts'. By 1987, after Mrs Thatcher had been elected for a third term and a decisive shift from subsidy to commercial sponsorship had taken place, his successor Richard Luce said of the arts that 'the only test of our ability to succeed is whether we can attract enough customers'. Customers, you notice, not audiences. But the word 'only' is the real giveaway. No one advocates empty seats. But, by Luce's test, George Devine's Royal Court would have been closed down, Pinter and Arden would have been consigned to the rubbish heap after early failures and *The Mousetrap* was the greatest

theatrical triumph of the twentieth century. It was all part of a philosophy that allowed the phrase 'bums on seats' to become the decade's
favourite mantra. Government ministers and Arts Council chairmen,
who became highly political appointees, no longer justified theatre on
grounds of its spiritual nourishment, intellectual stimulus or communal pleasure. Instead they spoke of 'an important strand in our export
drive' and of the 'quick and sizeable returns' that would follow any
increase in funding: a rare enough event usually achieved only in election years.

What, though, did we mean by Thatcherism? Hugo Young in *One of
Us* calls it 'a ragbag of ideas' often lacking intellectual coherence. Peter
Clarke in *Hope and Glory*, however, helpfully quotes Nigel Lawson's
definition: 'a mixture of free markets, monetary control, privatisation
and cuts in both spending and taxes, combined with a populist revival
of the "Victorian values" of self-help and nationalism.' At the heart of
Thatcherism also lay a belief in the sacredness of the individual
entrepreneur. Hugo Young recalls how he was once lectured by Mrs
Thatcher on a foreign trip and told that he should abandon journalism
and do something useful 'like setting up a small business'. And I can
reinforce that with anecdotal evidence of my own. In the late Seventies
I was a Kensington neighbour of the late Alfred Sherman who, along
with Sir Keith Joseph, was one of Mrs Thatcher's key intellectual men-
tors. Indeed it was in his flat that many of the ideas that were to govern
the Eighties were hatched. Over lunchtime drinks one day, Sherman
kindly suggested I was wasting my time writing for the *Guardian* and
working for BBC arts programmes. What I should do was set up my
own business in which I recorded taped interviews with leading theatrical luminaries and market them to American and global radio stations. Capping all that was the experience of Peter Hall. Taken to task
by Mrs Thatcher for complaining in public about the state of British
theatre, she pointed out that our theatre was famous the world over.
'Look', she triumphantly said, 'at Andrew Lloyd Webber!'

Mrs Thatcher's nomination of Lloyd Webber as a symbol of theatrical success is highly revealing. He embodied everything she revered:
entrepreneurial skill, a world-famous brand name, the priceless ability to make money. And it was no accident that in the Eighties it was
the musical – the most potentially profitable of all theatrical forms and
the ultimate celebrant of individualism – that came to dominate theatre: the musical was Thatcherism in action. In previous decades British

theatre had been largely identified by its writers and actors: Eliot and Fry, Osborne and Pinter, Olivier and Ashcroft. We had also boasted freely of the achievements of the RSC, the National Theatre and the Royal Court. And directors such as Tyrone Guthrie, Joan Littlewood and Peter Brook had radically influenced the physical shape and spiritual purpose of theatre across several continents. In the Eighties, however, the British theatre was synonymous with the achievements of two particular men: Lloyd Webber and the producer, Cameron Mackintosh. Between them – and sometimes in tandem – they provided the shows that defined the decade and put a girdle around the earth: *Cats* (1981), *Starlight Express* (1984), *Les Miserables* (1985), *The Phantom of the Opera* (1986), *Miss Saigon* and *Aspects of Love* (1989). Collectively these shows wrested the initiative from Broadway and turned London into the western world's leading song-and-dance factory: it was these shows that greeted visitors, in poster form, as they arrived at Heathrow, that confronted them on their journeys in from the airport and that were assiduously recommended by ticket agencies and hotel desk-clerks. The shows made vast fortunes for their creators and produced mind-boggling statistics. They also had a profound effect on our theatrical culture. One can easily forget that *Les Miserables* was a co-production between Cameron Mackintosh and the Royal Shakespeare Company, which was partly sustained by its continuing profits. One disastrous side-effect of this was that beleaguered subsidised companies came to regard the musical as a permanent goldmine: a notion severely dented by the National Theatre's production of *Jean Seberg* and the RSC's of *Carrie*, both of which turned out to be mega-flops. But more significant was the assumption that it was a mark of populist chic for the big national companies to work their way through the Broadway back catalogue: an ultimately debilitating assumption at a time when there were never fewer than twenty musicals already occupying West End stages.

The musical was the dominant form of the Eighties. But the groundwork had been done well before. Lloyd Webber had been writing musicals in conjunction with lyricist Tim Rice since 1966, when they joined forces on an unproduced show about Dr Barnardo's before going on to collaborate on *Joseph and the Amazing Technicolour Dreamcoat*, *Jesus Christ Superstar* and *Evita*. Cameron Mackintosh, after early struggles as a stage manager and chorus boy, had also been an aspiring producer since 1969, finally hitting the jackpot in 1976 with *Side by Side by Sondheim*. By the Eighties both Lloyd Webber and Mackintosh were in their early thirties. After a somewhat testy initial encounter at a theatrical awards ceremony, they were ready to achieve fulfilment as a creative team. But the ascendancy of the musical in the Eighties and its capacity to marginalise other theatrical forms was a product of the Thatcherite times. Musicals had the potential, with the aid of intensive marketing, to make bucketloads of money. They offered audiences both escape from social reality and spiritual uplift. In the hands of skilful creators they also transcended national boundaries. *Salad Days* and *The Boy Friend*, Joan Littlewood's joyous Theatre Workshop shows and Lionel Bart's *Oliver!* had been definably British. The hit shows of the Eighties – two of which were written by the Frenchmen Alain Boublil and Claude-Michel Schonberg – had less visible cultural roots and ultimately turned into the theatrical equivalent of multinational companies. In their wealth-making capacity and corporatism, musicals were the perfect expression of Thatcherite values: plays, on the other hand, were less immediately popular and often expressed the obstinately dissenting vision of cranky individuals. Mrs Thatcher herself was also aware of musicals' myth-making quality. Entertaining Lloyd Webber, along with filmmaker David Puttnam, at Chequers over the Christmas of 1984, she took them on a tour of the property. At one point she paused to observe, 'This is the chair in which I sat when I decided to sink the *Belgrano*.' Since Lloyd Webber had already turned one charismatic populist, Eva Peron, into a musical heroine, Mrs Thatcher presumably thought he might do the same for her own resolute self.

If the Falklands War showed how a potential fiasco could be turned into a public success, much the same, to make a somewhat frivolous comparison, could be said of *Cats*. Originally conceived as a solo song cycle, based on ten of T. S. Eliot's poems from *Old Possum's Book of Practical Cats*, the show was first staged in a simplified form at Lloyd Webber's own private Sydmonton Festival in 1980. The composer himself and his new friend, Cameron Mackintosh, instantly saw the show's theatrical potential. In this they were enthusiastically supported by Eliot's widow, Valerie, who provided them with a set of unpublished poems. Gillian Lynne was enlisted as choreographer, Trevor Nunn, fresh from his success with *The Comedy of Errors*, as director and John Napier and David Hersey as designer and lighting man. But it was Nunn who helped provide the skeletal storyline about the selection, by the night's end, of a single pussy to go to cat heaven. It was also he and Napier who saw the possibility of creating a colossal garbage dump, seen from a cat's-eye perspective, in the confines of the New London Theatre. But the prospect of a cat musical staged in an unfashionable venue by a predominantly classical director was deeply unseductive to potential backers. The show was capitalised at £450,000 but the money came together only in the last week of previews. Lloyd Webber also had to provide a personal guarantee of £75,000 (for which he received an additional five per cent of the profits) to ensure the theatre would honour its commitment. Even in rehearsal, *Cats* was paradoxically dogged by ill luck. Judi Dench, who was playing Grizabella, was hospitalised with a torn Achilles tendon; and, although she briefly returned, she eventually had to be replaced by Elaine Paige who went on at the first preview with four hours' stage rehearsal. And when it was decided to capitalise on Paige's musical gifts by supplying an extra song, Nunn chose his own Eliotesque lyric, 'Memory', in preference to one supplied by Tim Rice: a choice that had a permanently damaging effect on Rice's relationship with Lloyd Webber. The first night itself was also accident-prone. An IRA bomb scare, then a regular feature of metropolitan life, led to an unexpected clearance of the New London with only Milton Shulman, theatre critic of the *Evening Standard*, stoically staying put. 'I'm not moving,' he cried. 'This theatre has never had a hit yet.'

Milton's implied prediction was, of course, wrong; and it would be foolish either to patronise or underestimate *Cats*. For a start there was an overarching musical structure. As Lloyd Webber later told me:

> Nobody, I hope, notices that the beginning of *Cats* is a fugue and that the middle of the Jellicle Ball is a fugue and that the resolution comes in a later theme. But for me it's the crucial thing on which the score depends, just as the whole of *Evita* is based on a tritone and goes round in a complete circle.

Gillian Lynne's choreography also had a demonstrable ecstasy, not least in the Jellicle Ball number with its somersaults, spins and whirling catapult motions. But, although I stand by my overnight enthusiasm for the show, what none of us realised in 1981 was that *Cats* would lead us down the dubious trail of the 'concept' musical in which story and character were subordinated to spectacle and visual effect. *Cats* gave you an adrenalin rush while you watched it. What it didn't do, in the manner of great musicals like *West Side Story* or *Company*, was engage you with a propulsive narrative or the emotional dilemmas of human character. You didn't even need to know the language to enjoy it. Twenty years into its London run I came across a newly arrived Italian football manager who hardly spoke a word of English. He had taken a large family party to see *Cats* and they'd all had a high old time. What they'd discovered was a simple truth: that this was a show that transcended generational differences and linguistic ignorance.

Undeniably *Cats* was a statistic-busting phenomenon. In 1989 it became the longest-running musical in West End history. In 1997 it knocked *A Chorus Line* off a similar Broadway pedestal. By that time, in fact, it had been seen worldwide by fifty million people in forty-two productions and had grossed nearly two billion pounds. But a musical is more than an entry in *The Guinness Book of Records* and *Cats*, for all the pleasure it has given, had less-than-happy consequences for the ecology of theatre. It led to the industrialisation of the musical by pioneering the use of individual mikes for each singer instead of group microphones on or above the stage: the result was the banishment of the unaided human voice from virtually all musical shows and even the acceptance of visible mikes which curl over the singers' heads like fungoid growths. Even the use of TV monitors broadcasting the image of the offstage conductor helped to destroy the traditional rapport between the pit band and onstage singers. By its very success, *Cats* also encouraged the idea that the musical was the apogee of theatrical experience and the form most likely to attract overseas visitors: by 1985 tourists accounted for a staggering forty-four per cent of all seats sold in West End theatres. And *Cats,* which signified the start of the 'event musical' where the total experience mattered more than the libretto or the language, had an equally big impact on New York's theatrical culture. 'The fall-out', as Frank Rich wrote in the *New York Times*, 'eventually affected the commercial fortunes of straight plays since they found it harder and harder to compete for Broadway's increasingly dominant tourist audience.' Rich went on to observe that *Cats* led directly to the Disney Corporation's arrival on Broadway with shows like *Beauty and the Beast* and *The Lion King*, both of which took the theatrical premise of *Cats* to even more extravagant levels. It may seem hard to pin so much on a seemingly harmless show. But *Cats* changed the rules of the game by turning the musical into a mixture of ersatz religion and secular bonanza. And the ultimate paradox is that a show that did so much to replace the traditional 'book musical' with a form of showbiz spectacle was directed by the text-trained Trevor Nunn. When he accepted a Broadway Tony award in 1983 for his direction of *Cats*, Nunn announced, 'all I can do is purr,' adding that 'in England we dream of New York'. It was a remark that led the acerbic critic Robert Brustein to suggest that it was not the British who had conquered New York but Broadway that had totally debauched the British.

And not only Broadway: the next Lloyd Webber project, *Starlight Express*, as realised by the Nunn–Napier–Hersey team at the Apollo Victoria in 1984, bore the Hollywood imprint of both *Star Wars* and the Steven Spielberg canon in its mixture of monster spectacle and fake religiosity. Where *Cats* had a feline charm, this was a ghastly, over-produced show that turned a simple children's fable into a piece of showbiz kitsch. Loosely based on the railway stories of the Rev W. Awdry – creator of the Really Useful Engine which gave its name to Lloyd Webber's own Really Useful Theatre Company – it didn't make any narrative sense. It revolved, literally, around a race between Rusty (a steam train), Electra (an electric train) and Greaseball (a diesel). What was never clear was how Rusty managed to win a competition from which he had been eliminated in the heats. But the medium was the message. The actors were put on roller-skates and whizzed round a triple-tiered track that encircled the auditorium. Computerised gantries rose, descended and swivelled to create bridges and embankments. Michael Ratcliffe hit the nail on the head when he described the show in the *Observer* as 'the apotheosis of the High Tech masque'. It was an Inigo Jones spectacle for a modern audience. Deploying two million pounds and banks of machinery to celebrate the virtues of steam, the show seemed obtusely unaware of its own internal paradox. But the key moment came at the end when the back wall dissolved to introduce the mystical force expressed by the title. As Rusty discovered that the magical Starlight Express lay within himself, the show combined the now obligatory numinous climax with a hymn to Thatcherite individualism.

There was a certain grisly historical irony to all this. The show not only opened while London was in the grip of a transport strike, in late March 1984. It also coincided with a period when coal, the fuel that drove Rusty's train, was cruelly revealed no longer to be a crucial factor in the national economy. A few days after the premiere of *Starlight Express*, the National Union of Mineworkers called a national strike against pit closures, including that of the lately closed pit at Cortonwood in South Yorkshire, and in favour of a vastly increased basic wage. This led to a major trial of industrial strength. On one side you had Arthur Scargill, the militant miners' leader. On the other, the National Coal Board led by Ian McGregor, an elderly Scots-American metallurgist who had been offered the chairmanship after his success in downsizing British Steel. For all the government's pretence at non-intervention, McGregor had clearly been appointed to do a job: to enforce pit closures and see off Arthur Scargill, who had humiliated the Heath government in 1974 into fighting an election which it had lost. As one Thatcherite minister put it, 'Our leader will not be satisfied until Scargill is seen trotting round Finchley tethered to the back of the prime ministerial Jaguar.' The result was a bitter, bloody dispute that divided Britain and left permanent scars. But the ultimate victory, if such it was, went to the government, which saw a split in the NUM, the closure of ever more pits and the miners going back to work. The miners' strike lasted a year: *Starlight Express* ran for twenty. But the two events make a fascinating conjunction. While hymning the virtues of old-fashioned, coal-powered trains in a way Scargill might have approved, the musical clearly exemplified the Thatcherite belief that the road to salvation lay through self-fulfilment.

Like *Cats, Starlight Express* depended heavily on an alliance between talent drawn from subsidised theatre and commercial know-how. What had formerly been a promiscuous liaison, however, turned into a contractual marriage with *Les Misérables*, which opened at the Barbican in October 1985 as a joint venture between Cameron Mackintosh and the RSC. Mackintosh had fallen in love with the original concept album of *Les Mis*, created by Alain Boublil and Claude-Michel Schonberg, when he first heard it in 1980. He had hawked the idea of an Anglicised version around London and New York. Eventually he commissioned the poet and critic, James Fenton, to produce a revised scenario and new lyrics. He also talked to Trevor Nunn and John Caird who had shown that an epic novel could be regurgitated on stage with their walloping 1980 RSC success, *Nicholas Nickleby*. It was Nunn, however, who insisted that he would only come on board if *Les Mis* was presented under a joint RSC–Mackintosh banner and if a percentage of all profits went in perpetuity to the company: a shrewd move at a time when eyebrows were being raised at the freelance activities of both Nunn and Peter Hall at the National. For his part, Mackintosh insisted that *Les Mis* should enjoy a straight eight-week run at the Barbican, that it should be designed with an eventual transfer to the Palace Theatre in mind and that he himself, in consultation with the RSC, should be responsible for casting and musical decisions.

Looked at from one angle, this was a classic public-private partnership in which the brand name and technical expertise of the RSC were allied to the commercial flair of a West End showman. Seen from another perspective, however, it was rather as if the Old Vic of Lilian Baylis had gone into partnership with a flourishing entrepreneur like Charles Cochran. In the Thirties such an alliance would have been unthinkable: in the Thatcherite Eighties it was seen simply as a marriage of convenience. But, while the arrangement was of pragmatic benefit to the RSC, it set a dangerous precedent. It gave a commercial producer a large say in the artistic programming and policy of a subsidised national company; and, however well it accorded with the Thatcherite policy of stealthy privatisation of nationalised industries, it totally changed the rules of the theatrical game. Over the years Cameron Mackintosh was to develop a close working relationship with both of the country's big national companies. He co-produced a number of musicals with the NT and, as a theatre-owner as well as producer, now hosts the RSC's London seasons. But, while Mackintosh is a delightful man with an uninhibited schoolboyish passion for musical theatre, his power and influence tended to dilute the artistic independence of our national companies. In some ways, it was the result of a historical accident. It so happened that in the Eighties and late Nineties Trevor Nunn, Britain's best director of musicals, was running first the RSC and then the NT. This meant that if Mackintosh wanted Nunn's directorial services, he had to strike a deal with his respective companies. But Mackintosh's power was also a reflection of subsidised theatre's chronic shortage of funds and of our slavish obeisance to musicals. You can't altogether blame the cuddly Cameron. But one consequence of the RSC's partnership with Mackintosh over *Les Mis* was a shift of values. Increasingly our national companies were judged less by their obligations to the world repertoire than by the fundamental criterion of commercial theatre: is it a hit or a flop? Something in the culture radically changed in 1985; and changed for the worse.

Intriguingly, the blockbusting potential of *Les Mis* eluded most of us overnight critics back in 1985. Jack Tinker in the *Daily Mail* said that trying to condense Hugo's teeming novel into a three-hour musical was 'like attempting to pour the entire Channel through a China teapot'. John Barber in the *Daily Telegraph* spoke of a 'turgid panorama'. I myself wrote in the *Guardian* of 'cartoon characters' and 'vulgar melodrama'. Only Michael Coveney in the *Financial Times* hailed 'a piece that really does deserve the label "rock opera", occupying brand new ground between Verdi and Andrew Lloyd Webber'. Faced by a set of largely chilly overnight reviews, Mackintosh could easily have cut his losses and decided not to transfer the show to the Palace, thereby losing only his original £50,000 deposit. Wisely, however, he phoned the Barbican box office the morning after the first night to be told that there was a queue snaking all round the building that had been there since ten o'clock. It's hard to believe they were all dedicated readers of the *FT*. I suspect what attracted people was the mythical power of the title. Hardly anyone in England had read Victor Hugo's novel, including Cameron Mackintosh, but almost everyone had heard of it. It is, after all, the most filmed of all classic novels, dating back to a silent Pathé version made in 1907. And somewhere in the back of people's minds is a vague awareness that it has to do with obsessive pursuit and social injustice: as Trevor Nunn, who also hadn't read the book when he was first approached, pointed out to Cameron Mackintosh, 'it's a 19th century version of *The Fugitive*.'

But the global popularity of *Les Mis* doesn't mean the critics were automatically wrong: as Bernard Shaw said when accused of attacking a long-running piece of Gallic boulevard theatre, 'forty million Frenchmen can't be right.' What was so depressing about *Les Mis* was the way it reduced Hugo's epic structure and social detail to a few well-chosen banalities. Hugo, as V. S. Pritchett once pointed out, had a naturally dramatic eye that enabled him to 'bring things to life by implicating them with persons in the action in rapid takes'. Hugo also understood the drama of internal debate. When the pursued hero, who has swapped his old identity for a new one, is told by the obsessive Javert that a man answering to Valjean's description has been arrested, he undergoes a dark night of the soul. The real Valjean, we are told, 'strove in torment as another man had striven eighteen hundred years before him'. In the musical this potent image of Christ in the wilderness is lamely translated as 'Why should I right this wrong /

When I have come so far and struggled so long?' Even the musical's supposed identification with Paris's poor and oppressed amounted to little more than glamorised poverty: as Milton Shulman wittily observed, the death of the prostitute, Fantine, 'occurs on a bed as well made as anything supplied by BUPA'. As for the musical's evocation of the historic past, a survey of theatregoers conducted during the Broadway run revealed that the majority of them thought the action was set during the French Revolution. Somewhat defensively, Nunn and Caird wrote in the Barbican programme that the production took place against a background of traditional suspicions, 'for example that musical theatre cannot be serious and that classical companies cannot and ought not to attempt it'. But the notion that this kind of witless musical cartoon was inherently 'serious', as opposed presumably to the frivolity of *Anything Goes*, *Guys and Dolls* or *Girl Crazy*, showed just how much perfectly sane men had lost their critical judgement. *Les Mis* may have offered the RSC a vital financial lifeline: it also represented a degradation of standards and a vulgarisation of taste that seemed neatly to encapsulate the philistine spirit of the Eighties.

The next big musical of the decade, *The Phantom of the Opera*, presented no such problems. Composed by Andrew Lloyd Webber, jointly produced by Cameron Mackintosh and the Really Useful Company and opening at Her Majesty's in October 1986, this was a show that made no pretence at high seriousness. It delivered precisely what was promised on the packet: a piece of lavish romantic theatre in a style that might best be described as Metro-Goldwyn–Meyerbeer. But three things gave it distinction. It seemed to be driven by a strong personal imperative in that it was conceived as a vehicle for Lloyd Webber's beautiful young wife, Sarah Brightman, and dealt with the nature of amorous obsession; after cats and locomotives, we once more had a musical about the heart's affections. At the same time, Lloyd Webber's score was rich and closely textured. *Cats*, for all its unifying musical ideas, was essentially a 'numbers' show. 'Now,' as John Snelson wrote in his study of the composer, 'the emphasis was not on difference and structural separateness – with contrasting songs juxtaposed for deliberate contrast – but on dissolving such boundaries to create a more seamless whole.' But the real triumph lay with the late Maria Bjornson. Having worked frequently at the RSC and Covent Garden, she was recruited to design sets and costumes which gave *Phantom* its distinctive visual style. Inside the framework of Beerbohm Tree's handsome

Victorian theatre, she offered a stunning recreation of the Paris Opéra with its sweeping staircases, swagged curtains and gilt caryatids. As the hapless heroine descended into the underworld, Bjornson also led us via a tilting bridge towards a candle-filled lake reminiscent of those found in mad King Ludwig's Bavarian castles. Even if the ascent of the Opera House chandelier was more exciting than its ultimate descent, that was only because we all knew that what went up must come down. Bjornson's real achievement was to find a visual correlative to Lloyd Webber's ripe romanticism and to offer us an escape into a world of quilted horror. And escape was what audiences clearly craved in a year that saw the malfunctioning of a nuclear reactor at Chernobyl, the death of the crew of the US space-shuttle *Challenger*, the assassination of the Swedish prime minister Olof Palme and Cabinet ructions over the Westland helicopter affair. *The Phantom of the Opera* has continued to delight audiences over the decades. But it seemed especially comforting in a year of escalating catastrophe such as 1986 to sink into a world of artful hokum and romantic yearning where the only visible phantoms were those stalking the sewers of the Paris Opéra.

As *The Phantom* and its predecessors proved, musicals in the Eighties served a dual function: they distracted us from the daily realities of Thatcher's Britain while exemplifying the pursuit of profit that was its guiding principle. But the final big show of the decade was *Miss Saigon*, which opened at the Theatre Royal, Drury Lane in September 1989; and, although it came from the Boublil–Schonberg team that had given us *Les Misérables,* it was a decisive cut above its predecessor. For a start it had a mythic plot deriving from Puccini's *Madam Butterfly*. Not only that: it actually improved on the Puccini prototype. In the opera Lieutenant Pinkerton is a callous shit who marries the fifteen-year-old Cio-Cio-San in the knowledge that the contract will not be legally binding and that he will eventually sail for America. In the musical Chris, an American GI serving in Saigon in 1975, swears his love for the seventeen-year-old Kim in apparent good faith. What separates them is the enforced American evacuation of Saigon; and, when Chris returns to what is now Ho Chi Minh City three years later with his new Atlanta bride, it is less in a spirit of Pinkertonian imperialism than one of post-war guilt. In offering to support Kim and her child, Chris and his bride symbolise America's belief that financial aid will somehow compensate for a tragedy created by its own disastrous intervention.

This was popular theatre with a political edge. The point it made was that the Americans never remotely understood the people they were supposedly protecting in Vietnam. Meanwhile the inhabitants of Saigon had an image of America entirely based on celluloid fantasy. Through the Pandarus-like character of The Engineer, vividly played by Jonathan Pryce, the musical showed the capacity for survival of the pimps and middle-men who moved easily from the sleazy corruption of capitalism to the regimented inhumanity of Communism: as Mr Pryce cynically announced at one point, 'I speak Uncle Ho and I think Uncle Sam.' In once again raiding the subsidised sector to find a director, Cameron Mackintosh also made a shrewd choice in Nicholas Hytner. In Hytner's disciplined hands, the spectacle served a narrative purpose. The raising of a great golden statue to Ho Chi Minh exemplified the secular idolatry characteristic of Communism and reminded me of Hytner's use of totalitarian icons in his low-budget ENO staging of Wagner's *Rienzi*. And the famous moment when a helicopter descended onto the roof of the US Embassy was notable less for its theatrical engineering than for its image of Vietnamese women clawing at the wire compound begging to be evacuated. *Miss Saigon*'s critique of capitalism and its vision of the personal tragedies created by American foreign policy did not stop it making bundles of money or being a big success on Broadway; even though Mackintosh was forced into a disruptive row with American Equity which insanely decided that his decision to import Pryce to play the role of the Eurasian Engineer was somehow racist. What made *Miss Saigon* unique amongst Eighties musicals was that it had something interesting to say. Significantly, it came at the fag-end of the Thatcher era when the mystique of her 'special relationship' with Ronald Reagan was starting to wear thin – not surprisingly, in view of America's unilateral invasion of Grenada and a Reykjavik summit in which Reagan independently agreed to the abolition of nuclear warheads. Musicals distracted us from reality for much of the Eighties; but by the end of the decade there were reassuring signs that the public wanted something more than apolitical escapism and that the theatre was slowly recovering its traditional capacity for dissent.

Some would argue that the capacity for dissent had never gone away; but the stark fact is that it took a long time for the theatre to mount an intellectually coherent attack on Thatcherism. In the event two particular forms dominated the Eighties: the musical and the epic. The former, certainly until *Miss Saigon*, offered escape, spectacle and uplift: the latter yielded, more often than not, spiritual affirmation in a time of disillusion. But although the epic 'events' were seen as obliquely political in their emphasis on hope and redemption, they left the core of Thatcherism untouched. Even the prospect of a day spent inside the Aldwych or the National watching the work of Aeschylus, Euripides, medieval Mystery plays or a Dickens adaptation was ultimately a form of refuge. The epics yielded some great theatre and showed a refreshing ambition at a time of financial cutbacks. But we delude ourselves if we believe that they fundamentally altered the situation: what they did was provide a pleasurable, and sometimes inspiriting, alternative to the meanness of the times for middle-class audiences.

The most contentious, in terms of its impact, was David Edgar's eight-and-a-half-hour version of *The Life and Adventures of Nicholas Nickleby* for the RSC. I was amongst those who argued that, for all the abundant theatricality of the production by Trevor Nunn and John Caird, the whole venture was a substitute for the investigation of contemporary society or the world repertory that was part of the RSC's mission. It was undeniably well done; but should the RSC have been doing it? Counterclaims were made that the production demonstrated theatrical democracy at work and provided a subversive attack on the philosophical core of Thatcherism. Without doubting the sincerity of the company's aims, it is worth unpicking the legitimacy of both arguments. It is perfectly true that there was an unusual degree of company involvement. Each of the forty-five actors was invited to research some aspect of Victorian England. Rehearsal-room work even began with everyone sitting in a circle. Clearly Nunn and Caird were aware of the methods employed by Max Stafford-Clark and Bill Gaskill at Joint Stock. But Leon Rubin, who was part of the directorial team, later questioned the myth that *Nicholas Nickleby* was the product of creative equality:

> In cold reality, the contribution of the leading actors (and indeed their power) was vastly greater than that of those who played the small parts and the contribution (and power) of the directors was, in essence, as great as it ever was or is. So, superficially, the fact that we began the play sitting in a huge egalitarian circle, that everyone was encouraged to feel that they made an equal contribution, could be seen as a sentimental hypocrisy.

Rubin goes on to argue that the egalitarian myth was a necessary fiction if the play was ever to get on stage at all; but it was a fiction nonetheless and one that did little to alter the director-led structure of the RSC.

But did *Nicholas Nickleby* offer, as David Edgar has suggested, an oblique attack on Thatcherite values? In particular, on her notorious claim: 'There is no such thing as society. There are individual men and women and there are families.' I suspect there has been a good deal of retrospective rewriting of history. For a start, Thatcher's remark about society wasn't made until 1987 when she gave an interview to *Woman's Own*. Also at the time of *Nicholas Nickleby*'s debut, in June 1980, it would have been difficult to pin down the exact nature of Thatcherism. What is true is that Edgar and the directors changed the ending of Dickens's story in order to avoid the feelgood consolations of false optimism. In the novel the hero challenges the brutality of Wackford Squeers; befriends the victimised Smike; and outwits his rapacious uncle who plans to marry Nicholas's sister, Kate, to a revolting usurer. By the end of the story Nicholas has found happiness with the benevolent Cheeryble Brothers, married his sweetheart and seen his sister, Kate, hitched to the Cheerybles' nephew. Dickens's ending is a celebration of domesticity and philanthropic capitalism, and of what George Orwell described as his fundamental belief that 'if men would behave decently the world would be decent'. But Edgar sought to overturn Christmas-card cosiness by showing Roger Rees's Nicholas at the climax breaking up the symmetrical family composition. In the process the hero discovered a new Smike to replace the dead original and, holding the impoverished child out to the audience, brandished a militant and upraised fist. According to Edgar, the intention was to ask the audience the question 'whether the Cheerybles can exist, whether the solution is to be found in individual philanthropy and the message of the adaptation is, no, it probably isn't'. All well and good; except that Nicholas's solitary gesture of defiance seemed to underwrite, rather than question, isolated acts of liberalism. 'Is the newly affluent Nicholas', asked Robert Brustein, 'prepared for any personal sacrifices beyond taking one more social victim into his home?' Brustein, writing of the Broadway transfer, went on to point out that American audiences, having shelled out a hundred dollars for a ticket, probably did their best to circumvent the mass of suffering humanity just a few steps away on Eighth Avenue; and the same doubtless went for London audiences sidestepping the derelicts and beggars whose presence in the doorways of the Strand was to become a disfiguring symbol of the Eighties.

The virtues of *Nicholas Nickleby* were stylistic rather than socio-political. It had the wit to realise that Dickens's novel was itself essentially theatrical. As Peter Ackroyd has pointed out, 'The book was eventually dedicated to Macready and everything about it has the feel of the theatre; it is as if Dickens saw human life conducted among the bright lights of the stage, making it somehow larger and brighter than reality.' That is why one of the highlights of the production was the Crummles company's boisterous staging of *Romeo and Juliet* complete with rewritten happy ending: this was the RSC cocking an enjoyable snook at the populist techniques of nineteenth-century pomping folk. The self-referential approach even extended to Suzanne Bertish as Mrs Snevellicci deliberately parodying the vocal mannerisms of Dorothy Tutin: a legitimate device given that Dickens's own understanding of gesture, speech and character was influenced by contemporary acting. The production by Nunn and Caird also brought to a wider stage the techniques deployed by fringe companies since the late Sixties. If the rehearsal methodology came from Out of Joint, the use of collective narration was borrowed from Shared Experience's production of *Bleak House*. Ideas such as evoking London's fog-bound harshness through heavy-breathing actors were familiar from the physical-theatre techniques of Nancy Meckler and Pip Simmons. What we got from *Nicholas Nickleby* was a sustained piece of narrative theatre performed with gusto and attack and cleverly anthologising many of the theatrical styles of previous decades. But, far from providing a radical critique of the times, it offered a mild pinprick to the liberal conscience that left us more likely to offer a contribution to Oxfam than go out and change the world.

The real significance of Eighties epics was that they combined the pleasure of total immersion with proof that theatre had not lost its appetite for the inordinate: that, even in straitened times, it was possible to stage an event that challenged the reductive logic of financial cutbacks. But, although they defied the meanness of the times, the brute fact was that most of them had been conceived in the previous decade. As early as July 1973 Peter Hall recorded in his diaries that both he and John Barton were working independently on a project involving Greek drama. By 1978 Hall's concern about Barton's plan to do a cycle of plays about the Greeks for the RSC at the same time as he staged *The Oresteia* at the National had reached panic level. 'But surely,' Barton told Hall, 'it would be interesting for the two theatres to do the Greeks at the same time?' Hall's response was: 'This, though, is idiocy. I am absolutely shattered. The hopes of four years go down the drain. I can't do it now.' In the event, both projects went ahead. In February 1980 the RSC staged Barton's ten-play cycle, *The Greeks*, translated by Kenneth Cavander, as a day-long event at the Aldwych. And in November 1981 Peter Hall's production of *The Oresteia*, in Tony Harrison's translation, opened at the Olivier. Both turned out to be big successes: much to the astonishment of the RSC, in the case of *The Greeks*, who scheduled it for a pathetically limited run that occupied far fewer weeks than the rehearsal process itself. But, if both ventures touched a public nerve, it was clearly because they offered audiences something they craved: spiritual affirmation.

Affirmation may seem a strange quality to pick out of *The Greeks*: a story of war, bloodshed and revenge dealing with the fall of Troy, the murder of Agamemnon, the retribution exacted by and visited upon Orestes and Electra. Barton also deliberately highlighted its contemporary resonance. Sometimes legitimately, as when Agamemnon returned home from war in a juggernaut-like chariot propelled by bolted sten-guns; at other times rather heavy-handedly, as in the transformation of Orestes and Electra into gun-toting Baader–Meinhof terrorists. The latter device seemed limiting rather than illuminating. Sixties urban terrorists were driven by political rage and rejection of capitalist values: Orestes and Electra were motivated by filial revenge and hatred of Helen of Troy. Yet, in the end, there was something healing about Barton's audacious venture. It was partly to do with the structure of *The Greeks*. Instead of the random exposure to single plays that constituted our normal experience of Greek drama we were offered a consecutive narrative beginning with the sacrifice of Iphigenia and ending with her miraculous redemption. The music of Nick Bicat, scored for bouzouki, oud and Chinese membrane flute, also lent the plays an airy lightness. Above all, the Barton–Cavander text, drawn principally from Euripides, combined scepticism with hope. 'No man that is human ever lives his life through without pain and sorrow,' we were told in *Iphigenia at Aulis*. But the emphasis was on mankind's ability to survive both divine whim and individual cruelty. Advocating reason in the conduct of human affairs, Athena urged:

'You must find a balance between freedom and compulsion. You must accept that order, harmony and meaning only come to men in fragments.' The fact that these words were spoken by Billie Whitelaw, the epitome of Beckettian stoicism, only served to make them more moving. They also seemed highly applicable to the world outside the theatre: one of escalating tension in which, early in 1980, the Soviet Union invaded Afghanistan, Congress postponed ratification of the Strategic Arms Limitation Treaty and fifty-three American hostages were held by Iranian fundamentalists in Tehran. *The Greeks* was arguably the least celebrated of all the Eighties epics. It was also the most moving.

Peter Hall's NT *Oresteia* was a very different beast. For a start, it had a distinctive sound. Kenneth Cavander's text for *The Greeks* was plain, direct, even prosaic. In contrast, Tony Harrison's translation of Aeschylus's trilogy for Peter Hall was densely packed, full of Anglo-Saxon alliteration and vibrantly poetic. Even more crucially, Hall staged *The Oresteia* with an all-male cast wearing masks. Hall's justification for masks – which he has used in all his subsequent productions of Greek drama – is twofold: that they supply a strong external form comparable to Shakespeare's use of the iambic pentameter, and that they make aesthetically bearable the violence and suffering within the plays. I remain sceptical. The mask is a historical convention born out of the fact that in the vast Greek amphitheatres, seating up to fifteen thousand, the unadorned human face would have been scarcely visible to most spectators: today's theatres are built on a more practical scale. And the idea that we need to distance ourselves from the plays' suffering is highly dubious: an audience conditioned to watching the blinding of Gloucester in *King Lear* or the multiple mutilations in *Titus Andronicus*, let alone the medical materialism of *Pulp Fiction* or *Goodfellas*, can surely look without flinching at a blood-soaked Clytemnestra. My argument against masks is that they do precisely what Hall claims. They aestheticise Greek tragedy. In the process they also rob it of much of its raw power. Only in the third play in Aeschylus's cycle, *Eumenides*, did the masks justify themselves; and that is because the concluding work is highly ritualistic. Apollo and the Furies are locked in a debate over Orestes' matricide which is only resolved, after a juristic vote, by the divine intervention of Athena. It is an ending which Maurice Bowra once called 'not merely happy but radiantly positive and constructive'; and it is something that other directors of the trilogy, including Peter Stein and Katie Mitchell, have either fudged or invested with a layer of modern irony. Hall, however, played what Aeschylus wrote: a celebration of the birth of democracy, with the jurors dropping pebbles into one of two downstage urns, and the transformation of the Furies into benevolent beings. Democracy may have brought us Mrs Thatcher, for whom Hall himself had voted in the 1979 election. Without making invidious comparisons, it also allowed Germany to vote in Adolf Hitler in 1933. But, however much the democratic concept may have been misappropriated and misused, and for all the historical disasters it has produced, I applaud Hall for sticking to the original Aeschylean concept. It endorsed the democratic principle, admittedly aided by divine intervention, and ensured that *The Oresteia* ended on a note of hope.

Audiences in the Eighties looked to theatre to provide consolation in a time of increasing despair: in 1981, even as we celebrated a peaceful resolution to irrational bloodshed in *The Oresteia*, we were living with the consequences of civic riots in Brixton, Bristol, Toxteth, Birmingham, Hull and Wolverhampton. And the palpable need for some form of communal experience was further proved by the success of the National's three-part production of *The Mysteries*, directed by Bill Bryden with a text brilliantly hewn by Tony Harrison mainly from the York and Wakefield medieval cycles. It was a project that grew incrementally. First came *The Passion* in 1977. Then *The Nativity* in 1980. The third part, *Doomsday*, was added in 1985 to form a day-long trilogy in the Cottesloe Theatre. Such was the clamour to see the productions that they later transferred to the Lyceum Theatre, on the opposite side of Waterloo Bridge, which had been closed to drama since the Forties.

But why did these plays, dealing directly with the Christian story, achieve such popularity in a secular age? Obviously it had a lot to do with the aesthetic skill with which they were presented. Tony Harrison, laconically describing himself as 'a Yorkshire poet who came to read the metre', had fashioned a text that lovingly preserved the earthy regionalism of the medieval plays. Cain, marked for all eternity by his fratricide, bluntly announced: 'Farewell. When I am dead bury me in Wakefield by t'quarry head.' And Harrison's alliterative zest combined with the original's rooted realism in an indignant Judas's declaration: 'Bursar was I, balancing t' brethren's budgeting book.' The expressiveness of Harrison's language was matched by Bryden's production and William Dudley's design, which anchored these plays in a working-class culture. Banners of modern unions and guilds billowed down from the Cottesloe roof. The promenade action was performed under what Michael Ratcliffe vividly described as 'a smoky orange firmament flickering with lamps built from punctured utensils of everyday life – dustbins, braziers, colanders, graters, paraffin stoves, compost-burners and hurricane lamps'. The plays were also performed by a tight-knit company dominated by brawny, muscular actors with a strong Northern and Scottish bias and a reputation for heavy drinking; after the death of one of them, Brian Glover, in 1997, Richard Eyre wrote that 'anyone who'd seen him in The Mysteries would have been convinced that God was a big Yorkshireman'. No less vital was the music played by The Home Service under the direction of John Tams: when the town band, dominated by tuba, banjo and drum, turned a slow march into a jazzy stomp at the Virgin Mary's funeral Knaresborough suddenly seemed to unite with New Orleans.

None of that, however, fully explains the impact of The Mysteries. If you went to the all-day event you started in the morning with the Creation, went on to watch Christ's crucifixion after lunch and in the evening, having seen the souls of the damned writhing in torment, were offered the possibility of redemption through God the Son: 'But they that mended all their miss / Shall abide with me in endless bliss.' It is fair to assume that the bulk of the National Theatre audience were not practising Christians. By 1980 membership of the traditional British churches had shrunk to 7.33 million, the lowest figure in Western Europe. By 1990 only 11.7 per cent of the mainland population was attending church once a week or more. And yet, in the theatre, spectators responded to a Christian idea of punishment and redemption to which few formally subscribed. It may, if my own experience is anything to go by, have had much to do with religious nostalgia: ancestral memories of Sunday School, school chapel and family churchgoing bred into the bone. It may also have been a response to the aesthetic persuasiveness of theatre: because the writers of the original medieval plays were men of unquestioning faith, something of their belief transmitted itself directly to a modern audience. But I suspect there was a political element to our enjoyment in that The Mysteries offered an alternative creed to the culture of greed and the social Darwinism that dominated the Eighties. In 1985 – the year The Mysteries came together – the Church of England published a document called *Faith In The City*: it powerfully argued that inner-city problems were a direct result of a Conservative ethos which gave too much emphasis to individalism and not enough to the collective obligations of society. It was a document that deeply angered Mrs Thatcher but struck a chord with many people in Britain. By the same token, *The Mysteries* challenged our residual selfishness and invited us to celebrate a story based on sacrifice and redemption. It also operated on a deeper level than a secular myth like *Nicholas Nickleby* in that it went beyond endorsing individual charity to offer us a religious vision. 'My chosen childer, come to me,' cried God the Son, 'With me to dwell now shall you wend. / There joy and bliss shall ever be. / Your life in liking ye shall lend.' *The Mysteries* was not a missionary meeting or a Billy Graham-style conversion rally. But it operated at some supra-aesthetic level; and, even if it turned us only into day-return Christians, it left us emotionally moved and spiritually re-energised by the possibility of eternal 'joy and bliss'.

There was need for a bit of joy and bliss on earth as well in the early Eighties. 'Thatcherism', even if it was a less coherent philosophy than is sometimes claimed, fractured the post-war consensus and produced social division. The riots of 1981 led Lord Hailsham in Cabinet to evoke memories of Thirties Germany, in which unemployment had given birth to fascism: not so far-fetched a comparison when you recall that a record 2.7 million British citizens were out of work and that the government had presided over the biggest collapse in industrial production in a single year since 1921. Only two things saved Mrs Thatcher, whose personal popularity had plummeted in the polls, from political extinction. One was the fragmentation of the opposition. Following the election of Michael Foot as Labour leader in 1980 and the party's increasing move to the left, Shirley Williams, David Owen and William Rodgers abandoned Labour to form the Social Democratic Party. It was a clear attempt, in the words of their fourth partner, Roy Jenkins, to 'break the mould' of British politics; but, despite initial electoral successes, the only tangible achievement of the SDP was crucially to divide opposition to the Tory government. Even more vital to Thatcher's survival was the Falklands war, which lasted from 2 April to 14 June 1982, cost 255 British and over 650 Argentinian lives and released a spirit of gung-ho patriotism in Britain while giving Mrs Thatcher a reputation for brisk decisiveness. It also, in the words of a Cabinet colleague, 'fortified her conviction that she is right on every subject'. This view, however, conveniently overlooked several facts. One was that it was the government's withdrawal of the survey ship, HMS *Endurance*, from the South Atlantic in June 1981 that encouraged the Argentinian belief that the British government was not seriously committed to the defence of the Falklands. Another was that between January 1981 and April 1982 there was no meeting of the Cabinet Defence Committee to discuss the Falklands. As the *Economist* tartly remarked over twenty years later, 'The conclusion of the official Franks report in 1983 that Mrs Thatcher's government was in no way to blame for the invasion was nonsense.' Triggered by British negligence and Argentinian opportunism, the war was also shrouded in misinformation. The most notorious example was the sinking of the cruiser, *General Belgrano*, with the loss of 360 lives, when it was leaving the military-exclusion zone and heading back to Argentina. Only the radical Labour MP Tam Dalyell, Mrs Diana Gould in a famous televison phone-in, Clive Ponting who was a civil servant in the Ministry of Defence and Steven Berkoff in a vitriolic stage play seriously attempted to nail Mrs Thatcher for her personal responsibility over the ship's sinking. For the most part the Falklands war was seen as a national triumph and one that guaranteed Mrs Thatcher a second victory at the polls in 1983.

But what was disappointing, especially in Thatcher's first term, was the failure of the theatre to respond to new political circumstances. The threat of diminished grants made resident companies nervous. Mass unemployment and the assault on the trade unions robbed agitprop of its natural constituency. Even in June 1980 when Howard Brenton and Tony Howard came up with a satirical attack on Thatcher called *A Short Sharp Shock*, plans for simultaneous nationwide productions were quickly aborted. In the event, the play was staged only by the Theatre Royal, Stratford East, where it broke box-office records, and by a student group in Sheffield. It was also a sign of the times that one particular scene – an encounter between the mutilated ghosts of IRA victims Airey Neave and Lord Mountbatten – led to furious exchanges in the Commons, where Norman St John Stevas was forced to apologise for the play's presentation in a subsidised theatre. The Brenton–Howard play had its sparky moments: especially one surreal episode where Sir Keith Joseph gave birth to monetarism as Milton Friedman erupted from his stomach like a monster out of *Alien*. But the public and private scenes never fully meshed and the play faced one of the most familiar problems of satire: that the supposed target, through sheer demonic energy, became the most dynamic figure on stage.

Even if it wasn't a response to Thatcherism – indeed it had been written before the Prime Minister's accession – Brenton's next performed play, *The Romans in Britain,* revealed a good deal about the mood of the times: in particular the moral bullying and feverish sanctimony that were a by-product of a market-driven decade. The particular irony of Brenton's play, which opened at the Olivier in October 1980, was that people at the National were bracing themselves for a major political row. Here, after all, was a play that drew a direct parallel between the Roman invasion of Celtic Britain in 54 BC and the contemporary British presence in Northern Ireland. The defining moment of the play, in fact, comes at the close of the first half when the marauding Romans reappear in the uniform of the modern British army and proceed to shoot a female Irish terrorist. According to Richard Boon in his study of Brenton's plays, 'It is a breathtaking moment, a daring assertion that between Roman soldier and British there is no real difference bar technology and that the British are as much invaders in Ireland as the Romans were in Britain.' But while the sight of erstwhile Romans sweeping on in Centurion tanks may constitute a theatrical coup, it skews the argument. It ignores the basic fact that the British Army went into Northern Ireland, still a part of the United Kingdom, at the request of the Catholic community who feared Protestant persecution. Brenton also never explains how you banish the British presence and achieve a united Ireland without the full consent of people on both sides of the border. One of the twentieth century's most intractable political problems is reduced to a simple colonial issue.

But the politics of Brenton's play were hardly discussed. Instead it became the occasion for a display of moral outrage over a brief scene in the first act in which a Druidic priest is raped by a Roman soldier. However preposterous the row seems today, at the time it led to financial sanctions against the National Theatre, had a draining effect on both Brenton and the play's director, Michael Bogdanov, and signalled that we were in for a new wave of vindictive puritanism. Sir Horace Cutler, leader of the Greater London Council and a member of the National Theatre board, which had incidentally endorsed the play, walked out of a preview before the interval claiming that the work 'went beyond the bounds of decency'. This was the 'Dirty Plays' drama of the Sixties all over again; except that here Cutler was in a position to impose financial punishment and duly ensured that the GLC froze its grant to the National. Cutler's well-publicised walk-out provoked an inevitable media frenzy about anal rape on the Olivier stage. Some of the reaction was, in all honesty, quite funny: a cartoon in the *Evening Standard* showed a tremulous actor waiting in the Olivier wings (not that it actually has any) claiming, 'I'm buggered if I'm going on there.'

For those involved, however, the protests were anything but a joke. Having twice failed to initiate a public prosecution, Mary Whitehouse of the National Viewers' and Listeners' Association launched a private prosecution in 1982, invoking the 1956 Sexual Offences Act. Michael Bogdanov, the play's director, was charged with having procured an act of gross indecency by the actors involved, Peter Sproule and Greg Hicks, in a public place: a manifest nonsense since the act itself was simulated and belonged in the realms of art rather than life. The ensuing trial at the Old Bailey had a Beachcomber-like absurdity. Three days into it the prosecution announced that it did not wish to proceed and the case was withdrawn. But, although Bogdanov was acquitted and his £40,000 costs met from public funds, he remained angry that he had been denied the opportunity to put his case. Mrs Whitehouse, the bulk of whose £20,000 costs were met by an anonymous private donor, claimed that she had made her point. And, in a way, she had. The judge, Mr Justice Staughton, ruled that the 1956 Act could apply to events on stage, that even a simulated sexual act could still be grossly indecent and that sexual gratification need not be part of the offence. The aborted case left open a legal loophole. It also led to the withdrawal of projected productions of *The Romans in Britain* at Swansea and Warwick Universities and ensured that it had to wait twenty-five years until it received a major revival at the Crucible Theatre, Sheffield. And, even though Bogdanov and Brenton survived professionally, it meant, as Brenton said, that 'we all spent a lot of energy on an agenda we didn't set: the defence of my play'. But what it proved, above all, was that in Britain we much prefer a major moral kerfuffle to a debate about politics. As with Bond's *Saved*, and later with Kane's *Blasted*, all the hoo-ha about how far you can go on stage in terms of explicit sex and violence obscured any genuine discussion about what the author was actually trying to say.

That lack of debate was also a sign of the times. Through its mixture of moral bullying and punitive cutbacks, Thatcherism stifled intellectual discussion. And it's an appalling fact that only one play in Thatcher's first term seriously addressed the radically changed political landscape: Caryl Churchill's *Top Girls*, which became an instant success at the Royal Court in August 1982 and which, after being seen in New York, returned to Sloane Square in early 1983. It was no surprise that Churchill was one of the first dramatists to understand the reality of Thatcherism. As far back as 1972, in *Owners*, she had explored the impact of a powerful woman on a group of supine men and the danger of the unquestioned worship of money. But the achievement of *Top Girls* was that it went beyond local concerns. As Churchill told two American authors in 1987, the play was triggered by the question of whether it was an advance to have a woman prime minister with such aggressive social and fiscal policies. 'She may be a woman but she isn't a sister, she may be a sister but she isn't a comrade,' said Churchill. 'And in fact things have got much worse for women under Thatcher.' In another interview, Churchill said the play had also been stimulated by a visit to America in 1980, 'where I met several women who were talking about how great it was that women were getting on so well now in American corporations, that there were equal opportunities. And although that's certainly part of feminism, it's not what I think is enough. I'm saying there's no such thing as right-wing feminism.'

That was what made *Top Girls* such a resonant play: it went beyond the immediate present to argue that the replication by women of the ruthless male success ethic is counterproductive and that feminism has to be seen from a socialist perspective. It also revealed Churchill's familiar playfulness by placing Thatcherism in a broad historical context. Famously the first scene showed Marlene, the newly promoted managing director of a London employment agency, hosting a dinner party for five iconic females. Only gradually did it dawn on us that these women, ranging from the pregnant Pope Joan to Chaucer's Patient Griselda, were all social victims as well as pioneers. In a series of vinegary vignettes Churchill went on to explore the contradictions faced by the modern working woman. One high-flier was told by the go-getting Marlene to conceal her intention to get married if she wanted to get an upgraded secretarial post. Another woman, a forty-six-year-old middle-manager, had tragically suppressed her emotional and sexual life. And with what result? She had simply achieved modest promotion. Women, implied Churchill, are caught either way. They are seen as a long-term risk if they want to become wives and mothers. On the other hand, they are blocked by the glass ceiling if they sacrifice themselves to the firm.

But *Top Girls* was a work of art rather than a social tract; and it acquired real emotional momentum in the final act, where Churchill explored the dilemmas faced by so many women through a confrontation between Marlene and her working-class sister, Joyce. Marlene has escaped to pursue her career but has consigned her disadvantaged daughter, Angie, to the care of her sister. Joyce, meanwhile, has stayed loyal to her class but is filled with rancorous bitterness: she is even reduced to impotent gestures such as spitting at Rolls Royces and scratching a Mercedes with her ring. Although tied by blood, the two women clearly inhabit different worlds:

MARLENE: I don't believe in class. Anyone can do anything if they've got what it takes.
JOYCE: And if they haven't?
MARLENE: If they're stupid or lazy or frightened, I'm not going to help them get a job, why should I?
JOYCE: What about Angie?
MARLENE: What about Angie?
JOYCE: She's stupid, lazy and frightened, so what about her?
MARLENE: You run her down too much. She'll be all right.

What gives the scene its pathos is that Marlene is dimly aware of the dubious bargain she has made in sacrificing her child to her career. In the final moments the distraught Angie comes in and twice tells the brooding Marlene of a dream she has had that was 'frightening'; and that climactic word lingers in the air, suggesting that in the 'stupendous' Thatcherite Eighties, to use Marlene's own epithet, the Angies of this world face a dismal future. Admittedly there was something a touch schematic about Churchill's view of the polarised choices facing women: as Frank Rich noted, 'Even in England, one assumes, not every woman must be either an iron maiden or a downtrodden serf.' But what Churchill pinned down accurately was the emotional price women are still expected to pay for career advancement. She also understood that there was no necessary equation between individual success and female progress. Mrs Thatcher may have become Prime

Minister and a handful of women chief executives or boardroom boss-es. But, after two decades of feminism, women were still taking a sub-ordinate role in British life. The Department of Employment was charged with taking a symbolic lead in increasing opportunities for women; yet by 1994 only two of its top thirty civil servants were women and only three of its 719 typists were men. Churchill's play, however, was not about statistics or about the need for more neo-Thatcherite top girls. What Churchill was saying, with her usual for-mal audacity, was that feminism will never seriously advance until we restructure society.

Churchill's, however, was one of the few dissenting voices during Thatcher's first term: generally the theatre retreated into spectacular escapism or shocked subservience. It was only after Thatcher's re-election in June 1983 that writers began to raise their heads above the parapet. It seems that it took the miners' strike, mass unemployment and civil disruption for dramatists to become aware of the ghastly consequences of Thatcherism; and of the bland acceptance of the new ideology by the bulk of the British media. One of the most pugnacious plays of the period – *Pravda* by David Hare and Howard Brenton, staged at the National in May 1985 – addressed a key question: how a supposedly independent press had failed to offer any serious chal-lenge either to Mrs Thatcher or to an invasive tycoon in the shape of Rupert Murdoch. The influence of the Murdoch-owned *Sun,* which by 1979 had a circulation of four million, in promoting the Thatcher pro-ject as it unfolded can hardly be exaggerated. As Peter Clarke notes in *Hope and Glory,* 'through carefully cultivated links with the popular press, Thatcherite propaganda reached a down-market consistituency, traditionally Labour.' The success of the *Sun,* in particular, in acting as a Thatcherite hymn-sheet can be gauged from examining the famous front page for 4 May 1982. It announced the sinking of the *Belgrano* and the damaging of an Argentinian patrol-boat under the screaming headline 'GOTCHA'. But at the bottom of the page was a story head-ed 'Union Boycotts War'. What this amounted to, on closer inspec-tion, was a warning from an official of the National Union of Seamen that it would be dangerous for workers on the roll-on, roll-off ferries, requisitioned by the government and carrying troops and equipment to the South Atlantic, to join the task force. Perfectly proper union advice to civilian workers was presented as an act of wartime treachery.

Having turned the *Sun* into a vulgar and hysterical propaganda sheet, Murdoch's News International went on to acquire *The Times*: a crucial takeover that led to ugly confrontations at the newspaper's vast new fortified plant at Wapping and saw the print and editorial unions brutally stripped of their power. Whatever the failures of the print unions, which had become a byword for restrictive practices, Murdoch's takeover of *The Times* transformed it, in the words of John Campbell, 'from a proudly elitist paper of record into just another middlebrow broadsheet, taking readers from both its old rival the *Daily Telegraph* and from the middle-market *Daily Mail*, though its circulation trailed well behind both'. But what was depressing about the British press throughout the Eighties was its creeping uniformity of tone. At the 1983 and 1987 General Elections, the only papers to question the government line were the Maxwell-owned *Daily Mirror*, the *Guardian*, which leaned to the Liberal–SDP Alliance, and the *Observer*.

Such was the climate of conformity in which *Pravda* was written. As David Hare said to me at the time, 'if you were a visitor from Mars and read the bulk of the British press you would conclude that the relation of government to newspapers was much as it was in the Soviet Union.' It wasn't true but it was the impression given. It was a state of affairs that also cast doubt on the validity of the argument advanced by Tom Stoppard in his 1978 play about the press, *Night and Day*: namely that 'the whole country is littered with papers pushing every political line from Mao to Mosley ... and it is the very free-for-all which guarantees the freedom of each'. To suggest that the existence of the *Morning Star* somehow balanced the views promulgated in the *Sun* was, however, *faux-naïf* on Stoppard's part. In showing the power of a fictional tycoon, Lambert Le Roux, to ride roughshod over liberal opposition, Hare and Brenton's *Pravda* seemed far closer to reality than *Night and Day*. It also pinned down the pressure on editors from both interventionist owners and the state. Le Roux owns an upmarket paper, *The Victory*. At one point, a rival paper runs a story claiming the Minister of Defence has lied about the risks involved in transporting plutonium. When the paper's editor is paid a visit by Special Branch and threatened with prison unless he reveals his source, he duly succumbs: an incident that had direct parallels to one that occurred at the *Guardian*. Even the play's suggestion that Le Roux would trade his South African birthright for commercial advantage proved prophetically true. Shortly after *Pravda* appeared, Rupert Murdoch swapped Australian for American citizenship in order to buy into the lucrative TV and press industry of the United States.

Unsurprisingly, *Pravda* was panned by most of the press's big panjandrums. They claimed it was professionally inaccurate and impugned their legendary integrity. But *Pravda* aired a vital topic: who really runs Britain in an age of monopolistic media ownership? It also followed a classic model. As in *Richard III*, we saw an outsized hero methodically removing all obstacles between himself and his chosen goal, going mad in the process and ultimately confronting the isolated vanity of power: what Le Roux calls 'the great melancholy of business'. Admittedly there were times when one felt that Hare and Brenton, having let this particular spider out of the bottle, were unable to control him. But the play drew from Anthony Hopkins one of his last great stage performances before his inevitable defection to Hollywood. The precise Afrikaans over-articulation of each sentence, the bull-like thrust of the massive head, the smiling satisfaction at the conquest of spineless editors and journalists: all these were exactly caught, making one wish that Hopkins had dared to challenge Olivier's famed supremacy as Richard, Duke of Gloucester. Hopkins was, of course, playing Le Roux, not Murdoch. But the uncanny accuracy of Hopkins' portrait of a tycoon only became apparent when one read Harold Evans' account of Murdoch in *Good Times, Bad Times*: 'The flip side of the charm is a bleak hostility expressed through highly charged language or brutal curtness. He is well aware of his ability to win or to frighten and exploits this by switching personae unpredictably to create insecurity.' Murdoch, in short, was something of an actor himself; and it was precisely that ability to keep his victims guessing as to whether they would receive flattering balm or foul disfavour that lay at the heart of Hopkins' monumental Lambert Le Roux.

Hare and Brenton looked at the big picture in *Pravda*: what they wrote was an epic. In contrast, the following year a brand-new playwright, Jim Cartwright, born at Farnworth just outside Manchester, offerered a minutely detailed picture of a desolate pocket of north-west England in *Road* at the Royal Court. Opening at the Theatre Upstairs in March 1986, the play made such an impact that it transferred to the main house a few months later. Cartwright's setting was a road in a bleak industrial town that had never known boom times. But the significance of his play, which showed how unemployment had drained people of hope, was that it highlighted the deep divide in Thatcher's Britain between north and south and between those in and out of work. As Hugo Young pointed out in *One Of Us*, in the period from 1983 to 1987 inflation never rose above five per cent and average weekly earnings rose, in real terms, by fourteen per cent. At the same time unemployment never fell below 3.1 million. Although unemployment topped people's list of publicly expressed concerns, Young astonishingly described this as a meaningless piece of evidence. 'One of the successes of the Thatcherite enterprise', he wrote, 'consisted in re-educating the public not to care seriously about unemployment. The longer it lasted the more it was accepted as a seemingly unalterable fact of life.' But, with all respect to Young, that was the view of a salaried metropolitan commentator. And the triumph of Cartwright's play was that it showed how, in large sectors of the once-industrial north, the prevailing mood was one of disillusionment and despair.

Road was like a de-sentimentalised *Under Milk Wood*. With Ian Dury's hobbling Scullery acting as our guide (though the role was initially created by Edward Tudor-Pole), the play exposed the thwarted lives and cultural tackiness of a declining northern blackspot. 'All of life is chucked here,' said Scullery. But two particular episodes brilliantly highlighted the mood of hopelessness. At the end of *Road*'s first Act a young boy called Joey took to his bed, in company with his girlfriend Clare, to starve himself to death in protest against a world that had denied him work. Clare's plight was especially moving as she dwelt on the consolations of the office routine of which she had been deprived:

> Making order out of things. Being skilful. Tackling an awkward situation here and there. To have a destination. The bus stop, then the office, then the work on the desk. Exercise to my body, my imagination, my general knowledge. Learning life's little steps. Now I'm saggy from tip to toe. Every day's like swimming in ache.

Unregarded and unemployed, Joey and Clare slip into oblivion, making an unromantic suicide pact born of the Thatcherite era. Cartwright also shows that the jobless are not the only victims: the relatives of the unemployed suffer too. Without a hint of condescension, he gives a powerful second-act speech to Valerie, who blends exasperation towards a husband who spends much of his Giro on booze with anger at a system that deprives him of work:

When he's in all day, he fills up the room. Like a big wounded animal, moving about, trying to find his slippers, clumsy with the small things of the house, bewildered. I see this. I see the poor beast in the wrong world. I see his eyes sad and low. I see him as the days go on, old damp sacks on top of another.

Amidst all the praise that greeted Cartwright's poetic evocation of human waste, there were some dissenting voices. Francis Wheen in the *New Statesman*, while invoking *Look Back In Anger*, commented on the absence of black people and added, 'Cartwright's Britain is not the land of crumbling tower-blocks and inner-city riots, Samantha Fox and George Michael, skag kids and video nasties.' But Cartwright was not writing a panoramic survey of modern Britain: he was focusing on a typical street in a run-down Lancashire city and getting behind the soap-opera clichés to show the bleakness of unemployed lives. He also caught the blighted hopes of a young generation. In an elegiac final scene two binge-drinking boys pick up two girls and the sozzled four-some, after listening to Otis Redding's version of 'Try A Little Tender-ness', allow their feelings to emerge. For one of the despairing boys 'England's in pieces. England's an old twat in the sea,' while one of the girls vainly cries for 'a Jesus to come and change things and show the invisible'. Unemployment may have been accepted in parts of the cos-seted south as a seemingly unalterable fact of life. For Cartwright's characters it was a grim reality. The result, according to the *Independent*, was 'perhaps the most inspiring and exciting state-of-the nation piece that the eighties have seen'.

Given the paucity of public plays at the time, that wasn't a very big claim. But during the final months of the second Thatcherite term two works emerged that challenged the prevailing values. One was an ebullient satire that was instantly absorbed and neutralised by the very system it was attacking; the other was a traditional comedy, by a sup-posed boulevard writer, that turned out to be a surprisingly durable critique of the Eighties and all it stood for.

The first play was Caryl Churchill's *Serious Money*, which began when Max Stafford-Clark, the author's best and most faithful inter-preter, suggested a play about the City of London and the mysteries of finance. It was certainly a timely topic. The privatisation of British Tele-com in 1984 and British Gas in 1986 ushered in a period in which pub-lic utilities were placed on the market; the main beneficiaries, however, often appeared to be the directors of the businesses concerned, who granted themselves inflated pay rises, rolling payments and share options that offered total insurance against being dismissed. The stock market was also fundamentally reformed by the 'big bang' of October 1986, which ended restrictive practices. 'Henceforth,' wrote Kenneth O. Morgan, 'the old spectacle of brokers milling around on the Stock Exchange floor was replaced by silent, almost invisible, computerized networks for dealers, reflecting the new internationalism of the stock market.' It also put a premium on youth, with its instant grasp of technology and readiness to suffer physical burn-out for the sake of bumper profits. Stafford-Clark saw the theatrical potential in all of this. In classic Joint Stock fashion, he took Churchill, a group of actors and the Royal Court's literary manager down to the City for a two-week workshop. Out of this came a play, written with dash and verve, that had two interlocking strands. One, with echoes of Hare's *Knuckle*, involved the investigation of a Sloaney futures dealer into the mysterious death of her brother. The other dealt with the takeover by a sharp East End corporate raider of a plodding company symbolically named Albion.

Churchill's play, which opened at the Royal Court two months before the May 1987 election and transferred to Wyndham's two months after it, certainly caught the spirit of the money-making times. It produced a memorable catchphrase that epitomised the zeitgeist: 'Sexy greedy *is* the late eighties.' It also caught the laddish coarseness of the City, where one of the male rituals was to despatch innocent female newcomers with the message 'I'm looking for Mike Hunt' before they realised its implications. But what was unnerving was the rapturous way in which this socialist play about capitalist pleasure was received by its targets. During the run at the Royal Court, the minimal parking space around the theatre was thronged by City traders' Porsches and BMWs. And at Wyndham's, after Thatcher's third successive election victory, Ian Dury's climactic, tongue-in-cheek anthem took on new resonance:

> Five more glorious years, five more glorious years
> We're saved from the valley of tears for five more glorious years
> Pissed and promiscuous the money's ridiculous
> Send her victorious for five fucking morious
> Five more glorious years.

What to some sections of the Royal Court audience had a vestigial irony became in the West End a triumphalist hymn. As Thomas Sut-cliffe wrote in the *Independent*, 'It is now a bit like going to see *The Resistible Rise of Arturo Ui* with a coach party of SS men.' Max Stafford-Clark gamely challenged that view by linking *Serious Money* to Restoration comedy, in which audiences relished seeing their vices and follies ridiculed. But Churchill's play wasn't about sexual rapaci-ty: it was about a world in which greed was sanctified and virtually any amoral action was vindicated by profit. The fact that London – and later New York – audiences responded so enthusiastically testified to a shift in sensibilities: in a world where public image was crucial to a sense of personal identity, any recognition was better than none. When the play moved to New York in December 1987 Michael M. Thomas wrote in *Vanity Fair*: 'What once no normally brought-up person would have liked to see in his psychological mirror is now – in the City and on Wall Street – cause for admiration.' If that were true – and it largely was – then Thatcherism and Reagonomics had not only rendered satire superfluous. They had changed the moral climate by abolishing guilt and shame.

That idea lay at the heart of Alan Ayckbourn's *A Small Family Busi-ness*, which has not only outlasted *Serious Money*. It now seems, in the words of Ayckbourn's biographer, Paul Allen, 'the central political play of the decade'. Some still find it hard to believe that a comic dramatist should have written such an astute analysis of Thatcherism. But one shouldn't be surprised. For a start Ayckbourn has an un-rivalled capacity for turning technical challenges into creative opportu-nities. In 1986 he was invited by Peter Hall to create his own company under the umbrella of the National Theatre. And, after a near-definitive production of *A View From The Bridge* in the Cottesloe, Ayckbourn was confronted with the daunting task of writing a new play for the vast Olivier Theatre. His response was to create a 'family' play that put a complete cross-section of a house on stage. He was thus able to exploit the possibilities of simultaneous action, show how events in one room had consequences in another and deploy a cast of thirteen in a way that would have been unimaginable in Scarborough. The National commission not only enabled Ayckbourn to work on a big-ger canvas. It also allowed him to explore the moral concerns that had long nagged at his conscience. As far back as 1973 in *Absurd Person Singular*, Ayckbourn had analysed the rise of a new entrepreneurial class driven by the dictatorship of the free market. And in *Way*

Upstream in 1981 he explored the Manichean conflict between good and evil in a world existing off residual memories of faith.

All these concerns – moral, political and practical – came together in *A Small Family Business*, which opened at the Olivier in May 1987 in the last weeks of the election campaign. The timing was neat since the play offered a scathing portrait of a society where the profit motive was primary, where lifestyles had replaced real human contact and where the 'family' was a cover for chicanery, fraud and murder. I was reminded of Dürrenmatt's savage Fifties morality, *The Visit*: a play that showed the respected burghers of a Mittel-European town first rejecting and then slowly succumbing to a rich woman's suggestion that they kill the man who wronged her as a youth. We see a similar progressive moral collapse in *A Small Family Business* in that Ayckbourn's hero, Jack McCracken, makes impressive speeches about the need for moral probity when inheriting the family furniture business. But, having banished the culture of petty theft, 'whether it's raw materials from the shop floor, an extra fifty quid on our car allowance or paper clips from the office', Jack gradually caves in to the communal amorality. It starts with Jack bribing a slimy private dick, Benedict Hough, who has evidence of his daughter's shoplifting. When it transpires that Hough has also uncovered the family's illegal furniture-flogging racket, Jack is forced to act as bagman, offering Hough ever larger sums of dosh. And, although Jack draws the line at murdering Hough, his sister-in-law shrewdly remarks, 'Oh, he'll come round to it. You know Jack . . .' Ayckbourn's point is clear: that even a good man like Jack will shed his principles, like so many articles of clothing, in order to protect his family's interests.

Ayckbourn was the first dramatist to pin down an essential contradiction of Thatcherism: its worship of traditional family values and its sanctification of individual greed. You can't, Ayckbourn implies, have it both ways. Or, if you do, you will end up with one of two things: a corrosion of human relationships or a notion of 'family' that owes more to the Mafia than to morality. Ayckbourn's McCracken family is, in every way, dysfunctional. Jack can barely communicate with his doped-up daughter. Jack's brother, Cliff, not only lives off his prostituted wife's earnings: he openly announces that his Porsche, his boat, his digital wrist computer mean more to him than she does. And Jack's brother-in-law combines an Epicurean love of food with a deep detestation of his dog-infatuated wife. Through their devotion to dishonest profit, the family enjoys all the comforts that money can buy; at the same time they will stop at nothing, even murder, to protect themselves. Obviously Ayckbourn is not suggesting that, in deepest Surrey or Yorkshire, we are all conniving at killing. What he does do is explore the contradictions inherent in the Thatcherite ideal of the 'small family business' and show how 'corruption, mining all within, infects unseen', in a way that harks back not just to Dürrenmatt but to an explicitly socialist post-war play like *An Inspector Calls*. Hardly anyone understood this in 1987 when the play was treated as one more product off the Ayckbourn assembly-line, even though created in a different and larger factory. It was only with later revivals that people woke up to a basic truth: that Ayckbourn had nailed the essential contradictions of Thatcherism.

But what about the contradictions within Mrs Thatcher herself? In so far as she was represented on stage in the Eighties – which was surprisingly rarely – it was simply as a demonised hate figure. It wasn't until David Hare's *The Secret Rapture*, which opened at the Lyttelton in October 1988, that any attempt was made to explore the psychological foundations of Thatcherism; and even then it was done not through a direct portrait of the woman herself but through the fictional character of a rising right-wing politician, Marion. And what Hare suggests, with considerable subtlety, is that the tragedy of Marion, and all those like her, lies in her lack of imaginative empathy: as she herself says, 'I can't interpret what people feel.' In terms of the dramatic action, this has disastrous consequences. First Marion foists onto her humane sister, Isobel, their boozy, feckless stepmother. Then Marion and her husband encourage Isobel to expand and modernise her small, successful design firm, with ruinous results. But Hare's play is much more than a simple confrontation of good and evil. It suggests that the modern Marions are fuelled by an anger not just at the vacillating uncertainty of other people and their refusal to accept the ethos of competitive individualism. They are also frustrated by some perceived deficiency within themselves. That was certainly the quality that came across in Penelope Wilton's superb display of charcoal-suited fury. And Hare's point about the emotional and imaginative limitations of the Thatcherites is confirmed by Hugo Young's vivid portrait in *One Of Us* of the Grantham childhood of the young Margaret Roberts. 'The Roberts children', wrote Young, 'had few possessions and were indulged in fewer fripperies. They had no bicycles and visits to the cinema were a rarity. But this was the result not of poverty so much as thrift carried to the point of parsimony.' The impression you get of the Roberts household, with its double doses of chapel, banning of Sunday newspapers and ignorance of art, is of a world where civic duty and utilitarian values took precedence over feeling and fancy. It is precisely the world described by Dickens in the opening chapters of *Hard Times* where Tom and Louisa Gradgrind are reared on facts and statistics. And it is that sense of exclusion from the world of passion and imagination that nourishes the anger of Hare's Marion and, by implication, of Mrs Thatcher herself.

For all that, the striking feature of *The Secret Rapture* was its faith in the tenacity of virtue: its belief that the Marions of this world would not ultimately conquer and that the Eighties would come to be seen as an historical aberration and a deviation from the path of tolerance and compassion. It was an idea that Hare went on to explore in *Racing Demon*, which appeared during the last months of the Thatcher era and which I'll explore later in the context of what came to be known as the 'Hare Trilogy'. And, if one looks for shreds of hope in a dismal decade, it lay in the emergence of three adventurous companies which defied the economic logic of the times. It wasn't a good decade for new dramatists and one can point to only a handful who made any significant mark. One was Timberlake Wertenbaker, an unusually cosmopolitan figure of mixed British and American parentage educated in France and the Basque region, who scored a big hit with *Our Country's Good*. Another was Charlotte Keatley whose *My Mother Said I Never Should* was a technically adventurous piece about four generations of mothers and daughters. And a third was a young Irish actor-writer, Billy Roche, whose *Wexford Trilogy* at the Bush explored the cramping effects of small-town culture in minute, Chekhovian detail. But, of the three writers, only Wertenbaker went on to enjoy a long, productive career. Steady, organic growth was difficult for dramatists in a decade when subsidy was short and instant acclaim was prized above continuous development.

Companies that sought to offer some alternative to the style and ethos of mainstream theatre did, however, prosper in the Eighties: you could at least say that Thatcherism, by undermining institutions, opened the way for maverick groups and individuals to pursue their own singular vision. 1981, for instance, saw the emergence of Cheek by Jowl. Founded by Declan Donnellan and Nick Ormerod, partners in life as well as art who first met when studying law at Cambridge, it quickly established itself through its rigorous visual simplicity and eclectic Europeanism: its repertoire embraced Racine, Corneille, Ostrovsky, Sophocles and Calderón. A similar Europeanism informed the work of Théâtre de Complicité which moved in the Eighties from cult company to international success. It was created in 1984 by a group of performers – Simon McBurney, Annabel Arden, Marcello Magni and Fiona Gordon – who were all graduates of Jacques Lecoq's Parisian mime school. But what was heartening was watching a comic mime troupe develop to the point where it could apply its physically expressive skills to a modern European classic such as Dürrenmatt's *The Visit*. It was almost as if the Little Englandism that characterised the Thatcher years bred its own defiant antibody. But if Cheek by Jowl and Complicité – as it eventually became known – enjoyed an international outlook, the Renaissance Theatre Company worked along more traditional British lines. It was set up in 1987 by Kenneth Branagh and David Parfitt with the aim of making Shakespeare available to a broad popular audience and giving actors a greater say in the staging process. It owed much of its success to the charisma of Branagh himself who, having been catapulted to fame as an RSC Henry V in 1984, essentially belonged to the actor-manager tradition of a previous generation. There was no doubting Branagh's charm, energy or talent; and he went on to make a startling debut as a film director in 1989 with his own version of *Henry V*. But far from being a repudiation of Thatcherism, Branagh with his entrepreneurial flair and go-getting spirit could be classified as one of its happier embodiments.

It would, in fact, be myopic to write off the Eighties as a theatrical wasteland. New companies appeared. Epic shows were mounted. Musicals addressed a popular audience. The theatre is a resilient institution which never gives in. What changed in the Eighties was the context in which it operated and the criteria by which it was evaluated. The subsidy principle, which had been accepted by every post-war government since 1945, was radically questioned. And the notion that work should be judged by its inherent worth, rather than by its commercial potential, was seriously undermined. But the full extent of the theatre's difficulties only came home to me in 1986 when I was recruited as part of an Enquiry into Professional Theatre in England: a process

319

that resulted in the publication of the Cork Report, named after our volatile chairman, Sir Kenneth Cork. Compiling the Report produced a spirit of camaraderie amongst the enquirers themselves. One of its many pleasures was being sent to Coventry with Diana Rigg to look at youth theatre or despatched to Bolton on a Saturday night to see *No Orchids For Miss Blandish*. But, as we stumped the country assembling oral and written evidence, I was struck by the fact that much of English theatre – outside a handful of privileged companies – was run like a glorified sweatshop. People often worked in dingy, overcrowded offices. The pay structure was appalling, with most actors on the Equity minimum of £120 to £140 a week. Even multitasking directors of big regional companies earned little more than £18,000 a year. Designers were often forced to take on five or more commissions at once in order to scrape a living. Statistics assembled for the Enquiry by its Secretary, Ian Brown, and his assistant, Rob Brannen, also revealed disquieting trends. In Arts Council-funded theatres, the proportion of new work staged went down from fifteen per cent in 1971 to eleven per cent in 1985. Classics (i.e. any play written before 1945) went down from eighteen to eight per cent over the same period. Musicals, meanwhile, had doubled in number. But the prevailing emphasis on one-set, small-cast plays meant that the whole classic tradition, outside Shakespeare, was in danger of being wiped out at regional level. It also transpired that the English theatre was not only subsidised by its low-paid workers. It was increasingly turning into a cheap recruiting ground for television: actors, writers, directors, designers and technicians, having learned their craft in theatre, were sucked into the remunerative small-screen factory. In our Report we proposed that a levy of one per cent on the BBC licence fee and the profits of ITV companies be ploughed back into the theatre. Perhaps we were hopelessly naive. But I remember, even now, the patronising contempt with which Sir William Rees-Mogg, then Chairman of the Arts Council, kicked our idea into touch.

Our Report concluded that the English theatre was cripplingly under-financed, that workers were badly paid and that new money was urgently needed both to sustain the existing structure and to increase touring, youth, education and ethnic-minority work. We costed our modest proposals at £13.4 million. To restore subsidy to the levels it had achieved by 1970 would, in fact, have required a total of £23.2 million. But our case that many people struggled to earn a living was not helped by the impression given in the media that a few people were making a killing. While we were assembling our evidence, in the summer of 1986, the *Sunday Times* came up with a devastating assault on Peter Hall and Trevor Nunn headed 'Laughing All The Way To The Bank'. The allegations, broadly, were that they had profited improperly from commercial exploitation of their work for the NT and RSC; that they had used prolonged leaves of absence to increase their personal fortunes; and that they had abused the baronial power they exercised over British theatre. Hall answered all the allegations publicly and showed that they sprang from baseless gossip. Nunn kept his counsel and used due legal process to sue the *Sunday Times*. Undeniably there was a serious issue to be debated about what happened when subsidised work enjoyed a commercial life; and the Cork Report recommended that half the earnings from any transfer should go to the originating theatre. But the charges made against Hall and Nunn were vitiated by their inaccuracy. Hall had not made two million pounds from Peter Shaffer's *Amadeus*, as the paper alleged, but £720,000: half the amount earned by the National Theatre itself. And Nunn, far from illicitly moonlighting from the RSC in order to make money, had been given sabbatical leave after sixteen years' continuous service. But the mud stuck. Right-wing papers like the *Daily Telegraph* and *Daily Mail* joined the witch-hunt calling for Hall and Nunn to resign. And the impression lingered that people in the subsidised sector were living off the fat of the land. Conspicuously neither Richard Luce, the Arts Minister, nor Sir William Rees-Mogg came to the defence of two of the key shapers of post-war theatre; and the whole grisly charade turned into a victory for the philistines and a defeat for the subsidised sector. At worst, Hall and Nunn were naive in not foreseeing the problems involved in engaging with the commercial world while enjoying the privilege of running national companies; and, although there were legitimate questions to be asked about the cosy relationship between private entrepreneurs and big institutions, nothing that Hall and Nunn did was either improper or extortionate.

Significantly, Trevor Nunn resigned from the RSC in 1987, leaving Terry Hands as sole artistic director. Peter Hall quit the National Theatre a year later, handing over the reins to his anointed successor, Richard Eyre. And, although both Nunn and Hall departed voluntarily, their joint exit was a sign of the increasing pressures of running a big national company. Nunn in his eighteen years at the RSC had built progressively on the foundations created by Peter Hall, steered the company into its new London home at the Barbican and overseen a massive expansion of output. Hall, in his fifteen turbulent years at the National, had successfully colonised its new home on the South Bank, turned a Utopian dream into a living reality and vigorously championed a new generation of writers. Yet two organisations that in the Sixties represented the hopes and dreams of idealists were perceived very differently in the late Eighties. By 1985–86 they were consuming forty-seven per cent of the Arts Council of England's total drama budget: an unhealthy imbalance that reflected not their greed but the puny nature of government allocations. For Thatcher and her loyal mouthpieces in the right-wing press, the two companies also embodied, like the BBC, subsidised permanence in a free-market culture. The steady erosion of state funding raised a familiar question: could we actually afford to sustain two national companies? I remember a draft paper that was submitted for discussion to the Cork Enquiry recommending the abolition of the RSC in order to release new money to the regions. At the time I offered to resign if we incorporated the idea into our final report. But it's a sign of the gravity of the situation, as well as of the anti-institutional bias of the Eighties, that such an idea could even be countenanced.

This, then, was the Eighties. A decade that saw a modest proposal that one of our two big national companies be sacrificed. A decade that, despite the denial of 'candle-end economies', began with a 4.8 per cent cut to the Arts Council grant and ended with another one of 2.9 per cent. A decade that witnessed the Arts Council itself transformed from an independent funding body into a pliable instrument of government. A decade that saw 'bums on seats' changed from a vulgar Barnumesque mantra into a form of ministerial holy writ. A decade that sanctified the musical for its ability to make high, astounding profits. I could continue with the melancholy litany. But if one thing especially characterised the Eighties it was the gradual shift from a creative to an interpretative culture. Obviously the classics were a vital part of the British theatrical tradition, and one deplored their gradual disappearance from regional theatres. But the single most important factor that had made British theatre the envy of the post-war world was its continuing ability to produce new writers. In the Eighties, although the stubborn and tenacious older writers nagged, criticised and questioned, the well looked in danger of drying up. What we witnessed was the gradual displacement of new writing from the centre of theatrical activity; and if the decade is remembered it is more for a procession of hit musicals and for productions like *Nicholas Nickleby*, *The Mysteries* and *The Greeks* than for the commanding vision of individual dramatists. This was the measure of the times and reflects the success of the Thatcherite enterprise in pervading and shaping the whole culture. And, as her reign came to its abrupt and dramatic end, one wondered whether the theatre could recapture its old radical ebullience or whether there were still worse times around the corner.

IX

1990–97
Picking Up the Pieces

The year of Thatcher's downfall certainly began ominously. In January the British Isles suffered hurricane-force winds, tumultuous coastal waves and severe flooding with rivers reaching their highest levels in two decades. And that was simply the meteorological prelude to a momentous year. In March 1990 the imposition of the 'poll tax' or community charge, which replaced the old-fashioned rates, prompted massive public disorder in central London. Police charged demonstrators with riot shields and truncheons. Cars, buildings and workplaces were set on fire. In May the crisis over BSE – popularly known as 'mad cow disease' – led to the banning of exports of live cattle from Britain to the European Community. In August Saddam Hussein's forces enterered Kuwait: an event that initiated the first Gulf War in 1991 and that prompted an obsession with the Iraqi dictator that was to have lasting repercussions for both American and British politics. In October Britain formally applied to join the European Exchange Rate Mechanism (ERM). But, after attending a meeting of heads of government in Rome, Mrs Thatcher gave a rattily unstable performance in the Commons in which she seemed to renege on the idea of the 'European Monetary Fund and a Common Community Currency' to which she had just signed up. She attacked the hard ecu as unworkable, implied it would lead to loss of sovereignty and suggested that the European Commission was trying to 'extinguish democracy'. It was a febrile performance that exposed the Conservative Party's deep divisions over Europe; and it was that unbridgeable Tory rift, along with the massively unpopular poll tax, that led to Mrs Thatcher's enforced departure from office on 22 November.

It was one of those moments in post-war British life that opens up a host of memories. I first became aware of the threat to Thatcher, prompted by Geoffrey Howe's House of Commons resignation speech as Chancellor on 13 November, while sitting in a comfortable Giza hotel close to the Pyramids. Christopher Hampton, who had belatedly arrived from London to join a party of British Council guests at a Cairo conference, arrived like a rather more elated version of the messenger in a Greek tragedy bearing momentous news. Back in London I found myself, like everyone else, glued to the television watching the unfolding drama of the Tory leadership crisis. On 20 November I was due at a revival of Pinter's *The Birthday Party*; but even that seemed momentarily less exciting than the spectacle of Mrs Thatcher rounding on the BBC's John Sergeant, outside the British Embassy in Paris, to announce that she intended to fight on despite a poor showing in the first leadership ballot. And, on the morning of her resignation, I happened to be lunching at the Ivy where even the celebrity diners, who might be thought to be beneficiaries rather than victims of Thatcherism, seemed visibly euphoric.

Thatcher's fall, for which commentators sought parallels in everything from *Julius Caesar* to *Macbeth*, was followed by the rise of John Major. But the immediate sense of relief that followed Thatcher's departure was short-lived. On the international front there was a period of continuing turbulence: the Gulf War, the Maastricht Treaty, the ousting of President Gorbachev by the unstable, drunken, pseudo-democratic Boris Yeltsin. And on the home front, there was little sense of quietude. By the spring of 1992 Britain found itself in its longest-running recession since the Second World War. Manufacturing was down, inflation was up and unemployment stood at 2.6 million. It was hardly the ideal context, from a Conservative viewpoint, for an April election campaign in which there were palpable signs of a Labour resurgence. But there was a key moment when John Smith, Neil Kinnock's shadow Chancellor, rashly published the outline of a budget that he would introduce in the event of a Labour victory. This was meat and drink to the Tory press which perpetuated the image of Labour as a tax-and-spend party. And when the results came in – with the Conservatives on 336 seats compared to Labour's 271 and the Liberal Democrats' twenty – Rupert Murdoch's noisiest organ proudly, if somewhat illiterately, claimed 'It Was The *Sun* Wot Won It'.

Looking back over the Major years, from late 1990 to 1997, it is possible to see them in one of two ways. Major was undoubtedly a more emollient figure than Mrs Thatcher, even if he was viewed with a snobbish condescension that led one commentator to describe him as 'the kind of man one would meet in the car park of any DIY store loading veneered clipboard shelves into his hatchback'. But Major's stated aim was to reintroduce collegiate government and to produce a nation 'at ease with itself'. He even, in one speech, evoked a Baldwinesque vision of deep England: a place with 'the long shadows falling across the grass, the county ground, the warm beer, the invincible green suburbs, dog lovers and pools fillers and, as George Orwell said, old maids bicycling to Holy Communion through the morning mist'. This was Major as the promoter of peace and stability. Admittedly this image was shattered by the events of 16 September 1992: the so-called 'Black Wednesday' when Britain pulled out of the ERM, allowing world markets to decide sterling's value rather than pegging it to the Deutschmark. The impression was of panicky indecision, in the face of sterling's catastrophic fall, and of economic incompetence: something that was to haunt the Conservatives for well over a decade. What many people forgot was that it was the Thatcher government that had taken us into the ERM in the first place. Nevertheless Major's period in office was seen by hard-line Thatcherites as a retreat from everything her administration had stood for: endemic opposition to Europe, a condition of 'permanent revolution', the dismantling of existing institutions.

Yet, although Major was viscerally loathed by right-wingers for his supposed moderation, there is another way of looking at his years in office. Major may have been elected as a one-nation, middle-of-the-road Tory. But, according to *The Major Premiership*, edited by Peter Dorey, it didn't turn out like that. 'Far from betraying Thatcherism,' Dorey argues, 'Major's premiership constituted a consolidation of it.' Majorism was simply Thatcherism without the handbag and 'the abrasive and strident rhetoric'. And the evidence for that argument is impressive. The Major government privatised the coal industry in 1994 and the railway system, with frenzied speed and disastrous long-term consequences, in 1996–97. The Civil Service, hoping for a period of tranquillity and ease, found it was subject to the same old mantras of 'market testing' and 'contracting out'. The gulf between rich and poor continued to widen. And, while Major was open to constitutional advance in Northern Ireland, he remained rigidly opposed to devolution in Scotland and Wales. In short, Major was just as much an ideologue as Mrs Thatcher. He simply adopted a more accommodating manner.

Even if Major was in office, Thatcherism cast a long shadow over

British life – and by extension over British theatre. Despite a welcome pre-election increase in Arts Council funding in 1992, the theatre was faced with four more years of standstill grants or sharp cuts. The establishment of the National Lottery in 1994 meant that it was easier to gain money for capital projects than for day-to-day operations. The tension between high and low art, ever present in British life and in some ways vitally necessary, escalated to the point where the latter's commercial power gave it a startling ascendancy. And the prevailing freelance culture, with its bias towards competitive individualism, meant that the idea of loyalty to an institution began to look distinctly old-fashioned. All this was reflected in British theatre, which was torn between its role as an oppositional force and its need to survive in a post-Thatcherite world. It was, in short, an uncertain period. But significantly, even theatre's major achievements in the field of new writing were largely dictated by events of the previous decade. The 'Hare Trilogy', produced at the National Theatre in 1993, was a direct response to the ideological assault on institutions witnessed during the Eighties. And the explosion of new writing that occurred at the Royal Court in the mid-Nineties was entirely the work of a generation that had grown up in the Thatcher years and was appalled by its unchecked materialism. Discarding direct-action politics and apparently oblivious to religion, it was a generation that seemed to be flailing around in search of something in which to believe. And if one had to characterise the Nineties it would be as an era marked, unless you were a Conservative ideologue, by an absence of faith.

One faith that disappeared in the Nineties was a belief in state socialism. The progressive disintegration of the USSR from 1989 to 1991 and the collapse of communism throughout Eastern Europe was obviously an historical watershed; and one that had a huge impact on left-wing intellectuals throughout the world. The Marxist historian, Eric Hobsbawm, addresses the issue honestly and directly in *Age of Extremes*. Analysing the reasons for the system's collapse, he comes up with several explanations. One is that 'Communism was not based on mass conversion but was a faith of cadres or (in Lenin's term) vanguards'. Another is that, exactly as Marx predicted, a crisis occurs when the forces of production come into conflict with the ideological superstructure of the state. But Hobsbawm goes on to reject the nineteenth-century optimism of Marx who believed that the overthrow of the old system must lead to a better one, because 'mankind always sets itself only such problems as it can. solve'. Writing in 1994, Hobsbawm was as unsure as anyone as to what the future would hold.

In Britain very few dramatists were outright Marxists but most were left-wing by inclination and had to confront a new situation; and, to their great credit, many of them did so successfully. The first response to the collapse of European communism came with *Moscow Gold*, written by Tariq Ali and Howard Brenton and staged by the RSC in 1990. In part, the play was retrospective. It treated East European politics of the past decade as a vast Meyerholdian pageant: a meeting of the Soviet Politburo was represented by half-masked old men in black Homburgs, the fall of the Berlin Wall was symbolised by GDR citizens clawing their way through a paper screen. All that was lively enough. But, writing as events were unfolding, Ali and Brenton pinned their faith in Gorbachev as a man who had emerged from a mummified party hierarchy and who was trying 'to devise a socialism that nature can handle'. In the end, the authors were simply overtaken by reality. They were not to know that by Christmas 1991 Gorbachev's attempts at glasnost and perestroika would have failed because gradualist reform could not take place in a society that was dismembering itself. Caryl Churchill's *Mad Forest* (1990) was more substantial in that it was based on first-hand research. It evolved, in fact, from a trip to Romania by Churchill and eleven students from the Central School of Speech and Drama. And what they discovered was that the so-called Romanian revolution was something of a shadow affair, in that the Ceauşescus had been overthrown only to be replaced by remnants of the previous regime. It was not the fault of Churchill or the group that any keen reader of newspapers or watcher of television might have come to the same conclusion.

The problem theatre faced was not just that of matching reality. It was how to explain and interpret events and relate them to our own experience. The dramatist who succeeded best in this was David Edgar, whose play, *The Shape of the Table*, opened at the Cottesloe in November 1990 even as Britain was experiencing its own domestic political coup. Edgar had always been fascinated by the language and process of politics: he had something of Schiller's preoccupation with shifting patterns of power even if he lacked the German master's understanding of the human heart. As someone steeped in socialism, Edgar was also forced to confront the failure of his own political dream. Setting his play in a fictional country, with strong echoes of Czechoslovakia, he showed a communist puppet regime collapsing through a mixture of Muscovite string-pulling, its own internal power struggles and the influence of satellite TV beaming pictures of street demonstrations around the world. Edgar was accused by some of writing an elegy for communism; and it was true that Stratford Johns as the Party's First Secretary elicited a measure of sympathy in his transition from Stalinist ogre to powerless martyr. But Edgar's point was that all politics is a matter of compromise and that the new velvet revolutionaries would eventually be subject to the same pressures as the old communists. In a sense, Edgar was asking the same question as Hobsbawm: what comes next? And the play's most powerful speech came from a sceptical politician who remarked:

> You see I wonder if 'out there' they've really grasped what's going on. If they realise that they're exchanging the Red Flag for the pop-song. *Pravda* for *Playboy*. The hammer and sickle for the strip-joint, cola-tin and burger-bar. To have expelled the Germans and the Russians to hand the whole thing over to America.

Aside from the specifics of Eastern Europe, Edgar was also raising the issue of how the world would cope without explanatory narratives. As he told his biographer, Susan Painter: 'There are many ways in which the Marxist story and the fairy story are equivalent. But now that the grand story is off the agenda – a story that we have all ingested even without realising it – it will be interesting to see how we live.'

That absence of grand narratives was a theme that was to recur throughout Nineties drama. Religion had supplied the nineteenth century with its own encompassing narrative. Freud and Marx fulfilled the same function for much of the twentieth century. Even Thatcherism and the Milton Friedman gospel of the free market had, in a crude, simplistic way, provided a story for the Eighties. But, although that was still the official government credo, there was a strange lack of any coherent value system or guiding philosophy in the Nineties. There was, as Beckett had once written, 'no lack of void'. One answer to that vacuum, of course, was to look back and see just where Britain as a society had gone wrong. And that was the response of David Hare, who provided the National Theatre with a remarkable trilogy incrementally assembled over a three-year period. First came *Racing Demon* (1990). Then *Murmuring Judges* (1991). The set was completed, as a day-long event, with *The Absence of War* in 1993. It was astonishing to see the British theatre offering a living writer the same kind of platform that had been granted to Aeschylus, Shakespeare and Dickens in the Eighties; and in a sense, Hare was constructing his own contemporary epic narrative to explain the Thatcherite transformation. He told Hersh Zeifman:

> The basic idea that it came out of was of realising that we have had, for the last ten years, ideological prima donnas who are dancing on the top of the society, producing an ideology which they say the society is meant to believe in – as it happens an entrepreneurial ideology. And at the bottom or middle of society, we have all the people who are actually dealing with the tensions that are created by that ideology.

That was very much Hare's starting point: to look at the clergymen and policemen who had had to do the dirty work to keep the system running. Unusually, Hare also turned the research that fuelled the trilogy into a separate book, *Asking Around*, published in 1993. It's an excellent book: a first-hand piece of reporting on the church, the law and the state that echoes Anthony Sampson's various anatomies of Britain and the unvarnished truth-telling of George Orwell. But, although Hare claims that the plays that resulted from his research are pure fiction, it is fascinating to see how close the parallels sometimes were between life and art. *Asking Around* not only illuminates the trilogy. It even mirrors its strengths and weaknesses. The sections of the book on the Church Synod of 1987 and the 1992 General Election make gripping reading. Only the middle chapters on the law seem weighed down by too many statistics and pluralistic viewpoints. In the same way, *Racing Demon* and *The Absence of War* are the outstanding plays of the trilogy. By comparison, *Murmuring Judges*, with its survey of the separate worlds of the police, the judiciary and the prisons, seems information-heavy.

What Hare learned about the Church of England from his research was that it was an institution in crisis: riven with divisions between pragmatists and evangelicals, filled with arguments about the ordination of women and gay priests, unsure of its role in a militantly secular society. Not all those divisions, of course, were new. Samuel Butler in *The Way of All Flesh*, written at the end of the nineteenth century, had satirised the evangelicals in the person of the fiery Rev. Gideon

Hawke. 'We should,' concluded Butler, 'be churchmen but somewhat lukewarm churchmen, inasmuch as those who care very much about either religion or irreligion are seldom observed to be very well bred or agreeable people.' In the course of asking around, Hare had met Hawke's modern equivalents. He had also come across a priest called Walter who had been leader of a south London team ministry where he had crossed swords with his bishop, who had dismissed such ministries as 'a refuge for the inadequate'. Wanting to appoint one of his more zealous protégés to the team, the bishop had consigned Walter to a job in Thamesmead. And when Walter asked a junior bishop what would happen if he took legal advice, he was roundly informed: 'I can tell you what will happen. You will never get a job in the Church of England again.'

All this is closely echoed in *Racing Demon*. Like Walter, the Rev. Lionel Espy is a good man doing valuable work in a south London parish. But his substitution of social amelioration for proselytising vigour is attacked by Tony, a firebrand evangelist. As a result, Lionel is despatched by the Bishop of Southwark to outer darkness – or at least to a school chaplaincy. But, even if Lionel suffers, Hare pursues his fascination with the tenacity of virtue in dark times through the character of the Rev 'Streaky' Bacon: a man who finds God in people's happiness, the taste of a drink and the love of friends. Hare also shows a mature, broad-based sympathy that allows him to explore contradictions of character. Lionel, endowed by Oliver Ford-Davies at the Olivier with just the right crumbling charm, is a decent man but one so wrapped up in his community work that he neglects his wife and alcoholic daughter: another variation on a theme of Samuel Butler, who pointed out that 'it is a matter of common observation that the sons of clergymen are frequently unsatisfactory'. Even the evangelical Tony is both a mischief-making nuisance, who disastrously intervenes in the case of a battered Jamaican woman, and a man driven by a crusading ideal. And the Bishop of Southwark, 'whose brass balls clang as he walks', emerges as a political ecclesiast whose humane instincts are vitiated by the demands of office. In a powerful scene directly modelled on Brecht's *Galileo*, his attitude towards Lionel perceptibly hardens as he is robed to conduct a cathedral service.

Like all good plays, *Racing Demon* works as metaphor as well as on a literal plane. Quite obviously, it is about religion: a rare enough event in a theatre that, from *See How They Run* to *Beyond The Fringe*, had always tended to see Church of England vicars as comic buffoons. But Hare is also writing about the nature of power. The Bishop of Southwark, attacking Anglican reformers, says that 'the church has been turned into a ghastly parody of government'. And I recall Hare himself saying to me in 1990 that 'anyone of any intelligence can see that the play is really about the current state of the Labour Party'. I hadn't quite spotted that myself but, in retrospect, I can see that the Church of England, with its internal factions, battles between moderates and militants and paralysing sense of impotence, had many parallels with Her Majesty's ineffectual opposition. Hare's play, however, takes on even wider resonances than that. It is about all the shabbily pressurised institutions of British life, from the BBC to the National Health Service, which were sustained in the Eighties by the hardworking and largely underpaid regular staff. Although he was rewarded rather better, there is even a prophetic hint of the future BBC Director-General, John Birt, in the evangelically reformist Rev. Tony Ferris: both red-eyed zealots ready to trample over a surrounding group of dismayed moderates.

Racing Demon was one of those plays that expanded its possibilities with every viewing. *Murmuring Judges*, the second play in the trilogy, was, in contrast, about precisely what it was about: the rigid compartmentalisation of the various male clubs that make up the English legal system. Hare had done his homework and banged across various points: that in Germany and Sweden prison sentences had been reduced without any visible increase in crime, and that our penal system avoids total breakdown only because a mere three per cent of all crimes reach the courts. Richard Eyre's Olivier production was suave and pleasing to look at: not least in the first-act climax where the masonic closeness of a pair of corrupt cops was counterpointed by the exultant opening bars of Mozart's *Magic Flute*. But Hare's play was up against several problems. One was that its plot hinged on a miscarriage of justice in which a bent cop planted semtex on a gang of Irish petty crooks: exactly the kind of thing that was a staple of TV drama, not least an excellent Peter Flannery series, *Blind Justice*. Reality, especially the imprisonment of the so-called Birmingham Six for a pub bombing in which they had no hand, also far outstripped anything in Hare's play. For all its implicit attack on Thatcherism and defence of the ordinary desk sergeant, Hare's play also failed to make a basic political point: that if the crime rate rose by forty per cent in the Eighties, it was 'largely owing to a deep and lasting recession'. That observation came not from a left-wing commentator but from the late Sir Stephen Tumim, a senior judge and HM Chief Inspector of Prisons.

Of the three Hare state-of-the-nation plays, it is *The Absence of War* that now looks the most accurate and perceptive: one of those works that genuinely perceives a shift in the political culture. At the time, however, no one got the point. Coming as it did, only eighteen months after Labour's fourth successive election defeat, it was widely seen as a semi-documentary analysis of Labour's flawed strategy and a dissection of Neil Kinnock's personal failings: almost an intrusion into private grief. I recall Hare, on a singularly skewed and unpleasant discussion of the trilogy on BBC2's *The Late Show*, claiming that he had written a classically structured tragedy about the political downfall of a decent man. His claims were pooh-poohed by the show's arrogant chairman and largely ignored by a panel of pundits of whom I was regrettably one. What we missed at the time was that Hare had written a shrewd study of the faults endemic in the British electoral system: that, in a media-driven age, party leaders are programmed to stick unwaveringly to the prescribed hymn-sheet and are never permitted to show their feelings. In particular, Hare pinned down the fear that governs any Labour electoral campaign: the paralysing dread of being exposed as unsound on the economy. Neil Kinnock defined that fear for himself in *Asking Around*, when he observed that 'the labour movement has one basic fault. It denounces the capitalist press on the one hand yet on the other accepts what it reads in it. This is a terrible self-inflicted weakness among us.'

But *The Absence of War* is much more than a catalogue of Labour failings. It is based on a simple proposition, hardly noticed at the time but a clue to everything that has happened in politics since: that Thatcher changed the rules of the game and that, in her wake, Labour was forced to fight elections on Tory terms. And there is an ironic coda to that idea: that the very reasons Hare adduces for Labour's shattering defeat in 1992 – its conformism and anxiety not to offend middle England – were the keys to its eventual success in 1997. It's all there in Hare's play. He shows Labour's increasing reliance on advertising agencies, focus groups and spin doctors who issue grim dictats such as 'Never use the word equality. The preferred term is fairness.' Attempting to rebut the media myth that Labour is shaky on the economy, the shadow Chancellor is programmed to make constant use of the word 'fiscal' to denote gravitas. Hare also perceives how Labour leaders, sensitive to charges that they are soft on defence, become aggressively militaristic: when George Jones, the fictional leader, jokingly says, 'I'm afraid there's a sense in which I even quite like a war,' one gets eerie intimations of Tony Blair. But Hare plays his trump card at the end. A defeated George Jones looks ahead and sees a life of perennial opposition. Then he has a bright idea: 'You know what I think? I think, let's all just be Tories. After all, they always win. So what's the point of having other parties? Given that they never get in?' Obviously, there is self-mockery behind those lines. To argue that Labour and Conservatives would eventually become indistinguishable is also too easy. There were many areas – from massively increased public spending to the minimum wage – on which the two parties differed. But Hare hit on a fundamental truth: that, after four successive defeats, Labour could only win elections by occupying the centre ground. What Hare saw as a misfortune, Blair was to seize on as an opportunity. And it is this that makes *The Absence of War* one of the few political plays that, far from dating, gains more resonance with time. Long before the rest of us, Hare saw the extent to which Thatcherism had permanently changed British politics.

Starting as a grand retrospective narrative, the 'Hare Trilogy' ended up looking uncannily prophetic. But, of all British dramatists, Hare is the one who has always seemed to have the sharpest awareness of what is going on around him, which is what makes him such an eagerly sought-after journalist. In an earlier, and happier appearance on BBC2's *The Late Show*, which in the Eighties became the epitome of hip trendiness, Hare had remarked that, in an age of cultural relativism, it had now become heretical to suggest that Keats was actually a better poet than Bob Dylan. Coming from a young or old fogey, such a comment might have passed unnoticed. Coming from a progressive dramatist like Hare, it reverberated through public life. What Hare had put his finger on was not just a contemporary nervousness about value judgements. He opened up a whole debate about the opposition of 'high' and 'low' art that had sharpened in the Eighties. And that opposition was not just the product of academic relativism. If commercial success was regarded as the ultimate criterion of value, then it logically followed that a Hollywood product was of more interest than European art movies, TV soaps had more validity than single plays, the Sex Pistols were more significant than Schoenberg or Stockhausen, blockbuster fiction more important than the latest William Trevor or Anne Tyler. You could argue that such cultural stratification had been a constant factor in post-war life. But something changed in the Eighties and Nineties for a variety of reasons: sanctification of profit, the expansion of the media, the decline of the middlebrow market, the supineness of the intellectual classes. 'High' and 'low' art became rigidly defined terms. The former supposedly occupied a privileged ghetto; the latter spoke for the people. The idea that there might be any easy crossover between the two – such as T. S. Eliot showed in his enjoyment of the music hall and Groucho Marx – suddenly became anathema.

The one dramatist to address this subject head-on was Tony Harrison in a play seen at the Olivier in 1990: the richly stimulating *The Trackers of Oxyrhynchus*. At the time, the play achieved a certain notoriety for the magnificent spectacle of a group of clog-dancing satyrs endowed with proudly erect prosthetic phalluses: something that I know caused certain *Guardian* readers to gulp over their breakfast tables. But Harrison's play was really an attack on the division between 'high' and 'low' cultures in Britain and the association of artistic appreciation with a self-perpetuating minority. And it made its point by showing two classical scholars, Bernard Pyne Grenfell and Arthur Surridge Hunt, turning into leading characters in a lost Sophoclean satyr play, *The Ichneutae*. Grenfell became Apollo, who loses a crucial contest. Hunt was turned into Silenus whose brother, Marsyas, is flayed alive for daring to defeat Apollo. As Silenus says, 'It confounded the categories of high and low when Caliban could outplay Prospero.' But Harrison's point was that those who are excluded from the delights of high culture will in the end get their revenge through a destructive triumphalism. After Marsyas has been punished for his presumption, we see a contemporary generation of satyrs emerging in the guise of soccer hooligans, kicking ghetto-blasters into angry life and using a rolled-up bundle of papyrus as a football. I was reminded of the observation of Alan Bennett – like Harrison a working-class scholarship boy from Leeds – at the end of *Forty Years On*, that 'the crowd has found its way into the secret garden'. For Bennett that was a source of wan regret. For Harrison it was a matter of historical inevitability. Deny people high culture because of their class and background, says Harrison, and they will not only find their way into the secret garden. They will ultimately desecrate and vandalise it.

You could quarrel with aspects of Harrison's analysis. He assumes that culture in Britain is inexorably tied up with class: that an educated minority keep the best to themselves while the masses are left to feed off pap. But, while there might be a grain of truth in that, Harrison leaves several things out of the equation, especially the economic factor. Enjoyment of high culture in Britain is determined as much by money as by class or education. Where art is made freely available, as in our national or civic galleries, there is ample evidence that it is enjoyed by a cross-section of the public. It is only when a high price-tag is put on it, as in most of our major opera houses, that it becomes uncomfortably elitist. Harrison's play also posits a world where 'culture' is still handed down from on high. In the Eighties and Nineties, however, it was, as Auden said of another age, more likely to spread from the bottom up. But the virtue of Harrison's play is that it seeks to demolish the artificial boundaries between 'high' and 'low' and craves the wholeness of vision that was part of the Greek experience, in which a tragic trilogy was always followed by a satyr-play. To understand Harrison's point fully, one needs to read his introduction to the published version of *The Trackers*: a crucial text that deserved much wider discussion than it got. I question Harrison's plea for a return to daylight open-air theatre: something far more practical in Greece than in drizzle-soaked Britain. But Harrison dreams of a unified culture and undivided sensibility that can embrace high and low, tragic and comic, the mystic and the mundane. And he rightly extends his argument from fifth-century Athens to the Elizabethans. Harrison pertinently cites Dr Johnson who said that Shakespeare depicted neither 'tragedy' nor 'comedy' but the real state of 'sublunary nature', in which 'at the same time the reveller is hastening to his wine and the mourner is burying his friend'. The conclusion is that we have lost the social and aesthetic unity that nourished both Greek and Elizabethan theatre: partly through our acceptance of neo-classic forms but also through our division of dramatic texts into high and low art. Harrison's *Trackers*, however, united panto and politics, scatology and social comment. In so doing, it not only created an exhilarating piece of contemporary theatre but added to the cultural debate that Hare had ignited.

It is no accident that the bulk of the plays so far mentioned – *The Shape Of The Table*, the 'Hare Trilogy', *The Trackers of Oxyrhynchus*

– were all products of the National Theatre under Richard Eyre. After an uncertain start when he took over in 1988, Eyre ran the National until 1997 with both artistic integrity and moral vigour. As it happens, Eyre was never a great classicist: only with his intimate Cottesloe production of *King Lear,* starring Ian Holm, did he reveal any deep psychological or textual insight into Shakespeare. Eyre's great achievement was to follow Peter Hall's example in making the National Theatre a natural venue for new drama. Not only Hare, Harrison and Edgar but Stoppard, Bennett, Hampton, Churchill, Storey, Griffiths, Gill, Patrick Marber, Martin McDonagh and Robert Holman all had their work done at the National. The door was also opened to Jatinder Verma's Tara Arts and to black writers such as Mustapha Matura and Winsome Pinnock. Eyre premiered new American work of the calibre of Tony Kushner's panoramic *Angels in America* and Arthur Miller's *Broken Glass.* And, without abandoning his personal commitment to text, Eyre encouraged the visual experimentation of directors like Robert Lepage, Simon McBurney and Martha Clarke. As Simon Callow noted in his potted history of the National:

> Paradoxically Eyre, the champion of lucidity, was the driving force behind this stress on the non-verbal. Admitting that he had once been less visually aware than he might have been, he had since undergone a Pauline conversion; now he went on record as saying that he would rather a play were over- than under-designed.

It all made for a rich and stimulating mix in which the National, to its credit, maintained its critical, sceptical role. Indeed I remember an official lunch at which Eyre used the precise word 'oppositional' to describe the theatre's role in society, only to be greeted with an archly raised eyebrow from the Chair of his Board, Mary Soames. Yet, without questioning Eyre's passion or commitment, there was still a sense in which he was inevitably working to an agenda set during the Eighties and fighting battles with Thatcherite values. Reading Eyre's stress-filled diaries, *National Service,* you certainly get an impression of a man wrestling with budgetary restraints and his own uneasy role as someone who is part of the Establishment but also constitutionally at war with it. The diaries are also permeated by a sense of frustration at the survival of the Eighties ethos into a new decade. At one point, in 1993, Eyre approvingly quotes a postcard he has received from Max Stafford-Clark:

The Eighties have been like trench warfare fighting endlessly on the same miserable yards of territory and, of course, being pushed slowly backwards. It's the English inclination to celebrate defeats: Corunna, Dunkirk but, in truth, 'marketing' and 'security' have been the only growth areas.

In the same year, Eyre also quotes a significant conversation with Peter Brook in Paris:

We spoke of the change of climate in Britain: it's very competitive now in all the arts, as if there's a small patch of territory that we're all fighting over and we're all afraid of being pushed off it. Like Borges's view of the Falklands War: two bald men fighting over a comb.

This may simply reflect the doomy nature of directors when they get together. But there was a basic truth in the observations of both Stafford-Clark and Brook. There was an attritional spirit about theatre in the Eighties which carried through into the Nineties. And any sense of a theatre community engaged in one mighty enterprise had been replaced by an anxious competitiveness in which each organisation was concerned primarily with its own survival. Even the structure of the National itself in the Nineties tended to confirm this. Although it played host to groups like Complicité and Tara Arts, it was less hospitable than in the past to visiting companies from the regions. There was no semblance of a real acting company: each production was simply cast from the available pool of talent. And, although Eyre had a loose-knit team of associates and relied heavily on the expertise of David Hare and Nicholas Wright, there was little sense of a permanent directorate. Indeed one of the saddest features of Eyre's tenure was his sacking of Peter Gill as head of the Studio: a man brought up in the ethos of the Devine–Gaskill Royal Court simply didn't seem to fit in at the new National.

Within these parameters, Eyre produced and promoted an abundance of good work; and much of it inevitably revolved around the question of England's identity past and present. Alan Bennett's *The Madness of George III* (1991), although lacking metaphorical resonance, was a witty historical drama offering an unfashionable vindication of monarchy: like virtually all works on the subject, from Shakespeare's *Richard II* to Peter Morgan's *The Queen*, it exposed the essential solitude of sovereignty. Christopher Hampton's *White Chameleon* (1991) was a deeply moving memory-play about the author's experience of growing up in Alexandria and England between 1952 and 1956. One particular moment, in which the hero's English prep-school headmaster burned the tarboosh that was a gift from the family's loyal Egyptian servant, brilliantly encapsulated the chauvinist hysteria provoked by the Suez crisis. Stephen Daldry's famous 1992 Expressionist revival of *An Inspector Calls* both released Priestley's play from its schematic naturalism and struck a public chord. The passionate nightly response to the Inspector's declaration that society is larger than the individual and that we are members one of another suggested that, on the part of theatre audiences at least, if not the mass of voters, there was a hunger for a new beginning. And Tom Stoppard's ingenious *Arcadia* (1993), owing a good deal to both Thomas Love Peacock and A.S. Byatt's *Possession,* was not just about chaos theory, biographical fallibility and the tension between the unpredictable and the determined. It was also a love letter to the continuing beauty of the English landscape. All these works explored, in different ways, the nature of national identity. Except for one half of *Arcadia*, however, they were not set in contemporary England. It was as if theatre, still living off the Thatcherite inheritance, was reluctant to address the realities of Major's world.

Even David Hare's *Skylight* (1995), although set in the present, was very much an attack on the guiding philosophy of the Eighties: one in which the public-sector workers who keep society functioning are constantly insulted and downgraded. You could say that Hare was fighting old battles. Equally you could argue that his need to make the point yet again was proof of the insidious persistence of the Thatcherite legacy. In the end it didn't matter which argument was right because the play was written and performed with such verve. Essentially it was about the relationship between a thriving restaurateur and a penurious East End teacher. Michael Gambon, for a man of such bulk, played the former with extraordinary lightness and grace: I shall never forget him tripping about the teacher's bedroom, the morning after the night before, with a dainty post-coital glee. And Lia Williams – in what Paul Taylor dubbed the dramatist's 'Hare-shirt' role – endowed the teacher with just the right touch of faintly puritanical idealism. It was a sign of Hare's maturity that he was scrupulously alert to the strengths and weaknesses of both characters; yet he

339

also expressed people's growing anger at the journalists and politicians who condemn those who do society's dirty work. The teacher had one particular speech on the subject that was greeted with volleys of applause both times I saw the play:

> I'm tired of these sophistries. I'm tired of these right-wing fuckers. They wouldn't lift a finger themselves. They work contentedly in offices and banks. Yet now they sit pontificating in parliament, in papers, impugning our motives, questioning our judgements. And why? Because they themselves need to feel better by putting down everyone whose work is so much harder than theirs. You only have to say the words 'social worker' . . . 'probation officer' . . . 'counsellor' . . . for everyone in the country to sneer.

The speech was magnificently delivered by Lia Williams. But the sheer intensity of the reaction to it is what was intriguing. It suggested that, even if we were living in an age of uncertainty without any positive political faith, people were sick and tired of the hangover from a bankrupt Conservative ideology. It was one of those moments when theatre offered a surprisingly accurate barometer of the public mood. And I met yet another when, in the winter of 1996–97, I heard an audience in suburban Bromley wildly applauding an attack by John Bird and John Fortune on Tory plans to use private finance for the building of public hospitals. Little did they know that this was a policy Labour would actively prosecute. But, if *Telegraph*-reading middle England was openly contemptuous of Tory health proposals, it was clear the Conservatives' number was up.

That delicious prospect, however, was still to come. For much of the Nineties the theatre battled on, struggling to do good work in the face of dwindling grants and the spiritual ennui of the time. But, while one could commend the National for its oppositional stance and commitment to new work, the RSC retreated into a reactionary mode totally alien to the spirit of its founding fathers. Taking over from Terry Hands as artistic director in 1991, Adrian Noble inherited considerable financial and artistic problems. But his solutions were based on the shakiest of premises. Central to Peter Hall's conception of the company in the Sixties had been the vital cross-fertilisation of classical and contemporary work. Noble's aim, in contrast, was simply to make the RSC 'the best classical theatre company in the English speaking world'. That, however, was to ignore the historical evidence that the

RSC was at its best, as in the golden late Seventies, when it was actively engaging with modern society. Noble also disbanded the team of associate directors, which again denied the fact that the company had always thrived through continuity, artistic consistency and internal criticism. Instead Noble embraced the prevailing freelance culture in a manner that reached its nadir with the engagement of Griff Rhys Jones, a funny man but a Shakespearean tyro, to direct *Twelfth Night*, which he turned into a Gilbert and Sullivan-style operetta. On top of this, Noble expanded middle and senior management to the point where the planning committee became so large it was forced to hold meetings in Stratford Town Hall. The old RSC may have been guilty of paternalism and empire-building. But, as Sally Beauman points out, at its creative peak in the Seventies it was run by a small 'family' unit including general manager David Brierley, head of finance Bill Wilkinson and planning controller Genista McIntosh. Under Noble, it become less a centralised family business than a sprawling managerial enterprise designed to put on plays.

Artistically, Noble's choices were not all bad. He kicked off his regime with his own productions of *Henry IV Parts I and II* in which Robert Stephens brought out, for the first time in my experience, both the predatory cruelty of Falstaff and the pathos of his childlessness. Sam Mendes was also revealed to be a major classical director who built on a fruitful working relationship with Simon Russell Beale in *Troilus and Cressida*, *The Tempest*, *The Alchemist* and *Richard III*: in the last of these Russell Beale resembled some swollen, demonic version of Mr Punch. New approaches to Ibsen were also discovered through Katie Mitchell's *Ghosts*, in which the inspissated gloom seemed to have a determining effect on character, and through John Barton's *Peer Gynt*, in which the entire action was a remembered dream occurring inside the head of Alex Jennings' beguiling hero. But, although there were fitful splendours, one looked in vain for either the turbulent energy of the Nunn–Hands era or any hint of the radicalism that had informed the company's work in the past. This was a troupe that in the Sixties had staged *The Marat/Sade*, *The Homecoming* and *Afore Night Come* and had been embroiled in the 'Dirty Plays' controversy. In the Seventies it had staged *Destiny*, pioneered studio Shakespeare and turned the Warehouse into an anti-capitalist cell. Even as late as 1990, under Terry Hands, it had risked a play like Peter Flannery's *Singer*, which showed a Holocaust survivor turning into a

Rachmanesque slum-landlord. And although Noble sanctioned some perfectly decent new plays – Shaffer's *The Gift of the Gorgon*, Ayckbourn's *Wildest Dreams*, Peter Whelan's *The School of Night* and *The Herbal Bed* – they were not conspicuous for their political edge. Even in the classics there was a marked failure to mine the works for their political relevance. Peter Holland, in his book *English Shakespeares*, seizes on the specific example of David Thacker's promenade *Julius Caesar* at The Other Place in 1993. Thacker himself was an instinctively left-wing figure and his production relied on loose associations with the civil war in Bosnia. But the analogies were inexact and hazily pursued. As Holland argued:

> Like the RSC's ambivalent (effectively reactionary) attitude, under Noble's guardianship, towards making visible its cultural or political readings of Shakespeare, Thacker offered generalised connections whose implications the production consistently evaded. This is of a piece with a post-Thatcherite position which renders oppositional theatre almost impossible within the massive institutions of centrally-funded and business-sponsored theatre.

That last was a big claim belied by the work of Richard Eyre at the National Theatre. But it was certainly true of Noble's Stratford stewardship, during which the RSC became a safe classical company. And, while it may have reflected the contemporary world in its management practices, it signally failed to engage with it in its artistic policies.

It is always difficult to determine how much changes of policy are due to individual temperaments and how much to shifts in the political climate. But theatre in the Nineties undeniably reflected the culture at large in that it saw the dissolution of the collective ethos and the growth of a peripatetic individualism. It also witnessed the rise of small-scale theatres that had no defined public role. Their job was simply to pursue an individual artistic vision through a mixture of modest subsidy and generous private sponsorship. These theatres were light, flexible, quick on their feet and, because of their short-run policy, capable of attracting the kind of star names who might be reluctant to commit themselves to National or RSC contracts. In London the two outstanding examples were the Almeida and the Donmar Warehouse. They were the big theatrical success stories of the decade. And what they had in common was a small seating capacity, an enterprising directorate and an indefinable air of glamour. Depending heavily on private finance, they were perfect products of the post-Thatcherite era; and it was not their fault if they made one sigh occasionally for the days when flair and imagination were accompanied by the delights of a permanent company.

Of the two key Nineties venues, the Almeida had the racier history. Built in 1837, it had at various times been Victorian musical hall, Salvation Army Citadel and factory for carnival novelties. Then in 1972, shortly after Peter Brook had reclaimed a similarly neglected building in Paris's Bouffes du Nord, it was rediscovered by an independently wealthy, artistically imaginative producer: the Lebanese-born Pierre Audi. It is Audi who deserves the credit for spotting the Almeida's potential and for turning it into a progressive venue for international imports, avant-garde music and off-the-wall plays. Capitalising on Audi's success, Jonathan Kent and Ian McDiarmid took over the building in 1990 with the intention of making it a centre of theatrical excellence. Significantly, Kent and McDiarmid were both actors who had emerged from the company system of the Seventies and Eighties. They had worked for the expressionist Glasgow Citz and the more institutional RSC. And what they clearly wanted was to recreate the former's artistic panache without the latter's bureaucratic machinery. They also understood the vital importance, given the Almeida's Equity minimum wage and primitive backstage conditions, of making actors feel welcome. And it helped that their talents neatly complemented each other. McDiarmid was a shrewd Scot with an Edinburgh degree and a sinister, vulpine stage presence. Kent, who had forsaken acting for direction, was part of the South African diaspora (including Janet Suzman, Antony Sher, Nicholas Wright and David Lan) that has had a huge impact on British theatre. He also possessed an easy-going charm that was vital in wooing commercial sponsors.

What Kent and McDiarmid shared was impeccable taste, an international outlook and a large book of contacts. That much was clear from a brilliant opening season that kicked off with Glenda Jackson in Howard Barker's *Scenes From An Execution*, written for radio and easily Barker's best play. It was followed by Claire Bloom in Ibsen's rarely seen *When We Dead Awaken*; Jonson's *Volpone* directed by Nicholas Hytner and starring McDiarmid; and a classy revival of Anouilh's *The Rehearsal* that transferred silkily into the West End. An Almeida first night quickly became a different kind of event to one at the National or the RSC: you could smell the money and almost feel the taffeta sheen of the sponsors' wives, who seemed the embodiment of metropolitan chic. One night in St Petersburg, where they were touring a typically lustrous production of Chekhov's *Ivanov* starring Ralph Fiennes and Harriet Walter, I asked McDiarmid what was the secret of the Almeida's success. He attributed it to the fact that it was more 'fleet of foot' than the national companies. On one occasion, for example, Harold Pinter's agent, Judy Daish, offered the directors his latest play on a Monday night. By the following lunchtime, it had been read, accepted and given a provisional production slot – something unthinkable at the big houses.

Pinter was, in fact, pivotal to the Almeida's success in the Nineties. Equally the theatre gave him the kind of semi-permanent home that every dramatist craves. The Almeida staged excellent revivals of *Betrayal* and *No Man's Land*: in the latter Pinter himself appeared as a burly Hirst to Paul Eddington's moulting eagle of a Spooner, thus proving that the play didn't depend on the luminous presences of Richardson and Gielgud. But the Almeida also gave the premieres of *Party Time* in 1991, *Moonlight* in 1993 and *Celebration* in 2000. And what the association with Pinter confirmed was not merely the Almeida's hospitality to a great writer but its willingness, for all its reliance on commercial sponsorship, to toss in the odd hand-grenade.

Party Time is one of Pinter's most fascinating late 'political' plays and, oddly, one rarely seen since its premiere. It also confronted its first-night audience with a group of people not unlike themselves. Pinter's characters are the fashionable, smart upper-bourgeoisie. They rejoice in their membership of an exclusive new health club. They boast freely of their sexual affairs. They brag of their island retreats and the pleasures of fucking on boats. Yet beneath the banter lies a constant thread of unease. A helicopter is heard whirring overhead. Fleeting references are made by the host, Gavin, to a 'round-up' of social and political nuisances. A row suddenly erupts between Terry, an Essex bruiser, and his wife, Dusty, who naggingly enquires after the fate of her missing brother. Only at the end, as a fierce white light burns into the room from an upstage door, do we realise that the brother is a victim of the oppression to which the partygoers have turned the blindest of eyes. As Irving Wardle wrote at the time, 'the play reflects the reported iniquities of Africa and Latin America in the perspective of a London that Pinter knows inside out.' For some, this

344

importation of state violence into the capital was proof of Pinter's paranoia. But Pinter wasn't literally suggesting that the tanks were about to roll through Holland Park. He was creating a potent poetic metaphor: one that suggested that a society that sanctifies personal fulfilment while ignoring the encroachment of the state is likely to discover one day that its freedoms have disappeared. Paranoia? Hardly. Not after a decade that had seen the banning of trade unions at GCHQ in Cheltenham, internment without trial in Northern Ireland, a police raid on BBC studios in Glasgow, the hidden vetting of BBC employees by MI5. If you want security, governments constantly argued, you have to sacrifice certain liberties; and Pinter's play, witty, concise and prophetic, was a warning about the dangers of allowing our basic freedoms to slip away unnoticed. Taken to its logical conclusion, its argument was that health fascism can be a step on the road to state fascism.

Pinter's association with the Almeida continued in 1993 with *Moonlight*: an exquisite tone-poem about dying, separation, loss and the yearning for contact between the living and the dead. For Pinter the play was inspired by a number of external factors: suspended grief over the loss of his mother (which occurred while he was rehearsing *No Man's Land*), awareness of his own mortality, sadness at his estrangement from his son. But a play is more than a collection of sources and what made *Moonlight* so moving was both its emotional candour and aura of mystery. Towards the end there was a scene where Anna Massey, as the wife of Ian Holm's dying civil servant, telephoned their two estranged sons who resolutely pretended to be a Chinese laundry. It was a scene that, unusually for Pinter, tore at the heart, because you felt not only the grief of the parents but the spiritual cost to the sons of cancelling one of nature's deepest bonds. What added an extra dimension to the play was the visible presence of Bridget, the parents' dead daughter, who was fitfully seen in a gauze-covered chamber. You felt that Bridget, through her ghostly solicitude, represented the tender concerns the dead have for the living. This, again, was something new in Pinter; and it was an idea that was brought out even more forcefully in Peter Zadek's later production at the Berliner Ensemble where Angela Winkler as the mother seemed to possess an extra-sensory awareness of her daughter's ethereal presence. *Moonlight*, which Pinter started working on when acting every night in *No Man's Land*, was a direct product of his association with the Almeida.

It was also proof of that theatre's rapport with the best of living dramatists. But the Almeida, in its first few years, rarely put a foot wrong. At a time when the RSC was ossifying and even the National seemed more at home with contemporary than classical work, the Almeida stepped into the breach. With a programme that included Euripides, Molière, Racine, Dryden, Jonson, Chekhov, Ibsen, Shaw, Pirandello, Brecht and Lorca, it explored the canon of world drama. And that it did so with star actors – with Diana Rigg virtually becoming a house fixture – only added to its lustre.

Parallel to the success of the Almeida in the Nineties was that of the Donmar Warehouse in Covent Garden. Like the Almeida, it was a building with a chequered past. Over the years it had been, variously, a hops-brewery, banana-ripening warehouse and rehearsal room. Like the Almeida, it was pleasingly intimate: it seated 250 at most and confronted its audiences with a bare brick wall. But, unlike the Almeida, the Donmar had strong associations with particular companies. From 1977 to 1981 it had been the RSC's London studio base and offered a host of angry analyses of English decadence. Then from 1984 to 1989 it provided a London home for cutting-edge classical companies like Cheek by Jowl and Deborah Warner's Kick Theatre. By the Nineties it lost some of its circumambient scruffiness, finding itself in the midst of an expensive shopping complex. I recall taking part in a debate there with John McGrath, who was dismayed to find that the old RSC home had lost its quondam roughness and was now part of London's equivalent of Los Angeles's Rodeo Drive.

The real sign of changing times, however, is that when Sam Mendes and Caro Newling took over as artistic director and executive producer of the Donmar in 1992, they had no stated policy nor public subsidy. They simply had a guarantee from Roger Wingate and George Biggs, whose Maybox Theatres owned the site, that they would underwrite the project for three years. After that it would have to become self-financing or externally subsidised. There was a half-expressed hope that Donmar shows would move into the West End; but, although some of them did, they rarely earned enough to sustain the parent theatre. From the start Mendes and Newling were working within tight commercial parameters and, in the circumstances, they mounted some impressively stylish productions. They kicked off with the British premiere of Sondheim's astringent *Assassins*: it was a show that seemed perfectly suited to the Donmar's focused intimacy, analysing the American urge to achieve self-definition and celebrity through presidential murder. The success of the Sondheim opened up a highly fruitful exploration of American musical theatre. Mendes himself gave us a brilliantly de-glamorised *Cabaret*: the first I'd seen that highlighted the tawdriness of Thirties Berlin rather than its kitsch glamour and also the first to suggest that Sally Bowles was not some glittering sexpot but a culpable airhead in her apolitical indifference to the surrounding fascism. Later Mendes gave us an equally revisionist version of Sondheim's *Company*, which emphasised the bachelor hero's existential doubt and nagging rootlessness: something with which Mendes, himself a hetero singleton at the time, seemed to empathise. Classic American plays like *The Glass Menagerie*, *Glengarry Glen Ross*, *True West* and *The Front Page* were also revived alongside neglected works from the modern repertory such as Brian Friel's *Translations* and Alan Bennett's *Habeas Corpus*. You went to the Donmar in the Nineties in the expectation of a class act, which you almost invariably got. But, even if the productions were exemplary in their ability to make us see familiar work in a new light, Mendes's repertory was essentially conservative. This was a quintessentially post-Thatcherite theatre, heavily beholden to its sponsors and rarely concerned either with the shock of the new or the European tradition.

Things eased up a little after 1996, largely thanks to an emergency Arts Council grant of £150,000 engineered by the Drama Panel's ubiquitous chairperson, Thelma Holt. But, although the Donmar was a Nineties success story and mirrored the Almeida in its ability to attract top actors, it also embodied the paradox of the time. Mendes himself, in a startlingly candid introduction to Matt Wolf's history of the theatre, *Stepping Into Freedom*, says that in an ideal world theatres like the Donmar shouldn't have to exist. Mendes contrasts the Sixties and Seventies, where theatres had definable aesthetics, policies and methodologies, with the harum-scarum, free-for-all present (he was writing in 2002):

> It's a world now of freelance directors, all working in the same few theatres, all discussing the same few plays. A world where the desired theatre contract for a young actor or actress is a short one that can be fitted in between television and film commitments so, at the very least, he or she can pay the mortgage. It is a world buckling under the weight of a new disease: celebrity obsession.

Mendes goes on to ask whether the Donmar is a product of this new obsession or, in some small part, a cause of it; and the honest answer is a bit of both. But Mendes also puts his finger unerringly on one of the key issues of the Nineties: the impact of freelance culture on the theatrical ecology. Since the mid-Fifties, with the visit of the Berliner Ensemble and the creation of the English Stage Company, an essential part of the visionary dream, for every director, had been a team of like-minded associates and a more or less permanent company working in harmony. That was the classic European model and that was how great theatre was created: through stability, subsidy and constancy. Now, by the Nineties, that dream had dissolved, to be replaced by the success of the individual project. This is not to deny that both the Donmar and the Almeida had their own distinctive repertoires. They also expressed the taste of the individuals who ran them. But they were the outward symbols of a new cultural world in which a growing army of freelance directors transported their own particular aesthetic, and often their own favourite designers, lighting experts and even actors, from one venue to another. You might, like Deborah Warner, Katie Mitchell or Phyllida Lloyd, turn up variously at the National, the RSC, the Royal Court, Welsh National Opera or Opera North. You might, like the late Steven Pimlott, enjoy a fruitful association with the RSC while still staging opera and musicals at home and abroad. You might, like Stephen Daldry, move rapidly from the tiny Gate Theatre to the National and thence to the Royal Court. But running a regional theatre was no longer an intelligent career move. Far better, in the peripatetic Nineties, to keep your options open and commute between the elite subsidised theatres and the major opera houses. None of this was morally reprehensible. Directors have to live and, unless they have a percentage of a hit musical, are often surprisingly poorly paid: I remember Jonathan Miller telling me, after he had left the National, that he might have to remortgage his house in order to carry on working. But the growth of the freelance culture had one simple consequence. Where in the past it had been companies and buildings that possessed a defining aesthetic, now that was something imported by individual directors who came bearing their own particular brand and style.

I've dwelt a good deal so far on the negative aspects of the Nineties. The loss of belief. The spiritual ennui. The search for identity. The prevalence of the freelance ethos. But it's worth stressing that, aside from the internationalism of the Almeida and the oppositional tone of Eyre's National, there were also positive aspects to the Major years. And one, at a time when the whole notion of Englishness was under scrutiny, was the emergence of a brace of plays that hymned the moral virtues of English landscape and literature. It is almost superfluous to point out that both plays came from writers who, for different geographical reasons, regarded themselves as outsiders: Timblerlake Wertenbaker and Frank McGuinness. Few native dramatists in the Nineties would have had the temerity to stand up for cherished aspects of our national life, for fear of appearing to endorse Major's own sentimental view of deep England.

Wertenbaker's *Three Birds Alighting On A Field*, which appeared at the Royal Court in September 1991, was one of Max Stafford-Clark's final productions as artistic director. His tenure, which began in 1979, had coincided almost exactly with that of Mrs Thatcher in government; and it says much for Max's obduracy and vision that his commitment to new writing remained untarnished during those fretful years. And, even if he couldn't conjure into existence epic anti-Thatcherite plays that didn't exist, he deserves the highest praise: in particular for his championship of women writers and his assiduous loyalty to a great Irish dramatist in Brian Friel. One of Max's greatest bonds was with Caryl Churchill; and at first it seemed as if Wertenbaker's *Three Birds* might be a social satire on the lines of Churchill's *Serious Money*. Its theme was the self-education of an upper-class girl: the Benenden-reared Biddy, who starts out as the trophy wife of a Greek millionaire. Looking for a purpose in life, Biddy takes an interest in contemporary art, which gives Wertenbaker licence to attack its association with status and power. The play actually begins with a London art-auction at which the final lot is an illuminated billboard proclaiming 'ART IS SEXY, ART IS MONEY, ART IS MONEY-SEXY, ART IS MONEY-SEXY SOCIAL CLIMBING FANTASTIC', which is purportedly a quote from 'the director of a great national museum across the water'. But, having spelt out her theme in capital letters and explored the insecurity of the art world, where everyone is trying to second-guess the next international trend, Wertenbaker shifts her ground. In *Our Country's Good*, she had demonstrated the redemptive power of drama. Here she shows how Biddy's growing love of art gives definition to her life. Admittedly Biddy's ability to see art as something more

349

than a monetary symbol is the product of her private passion for a North Country landscape artist, Stephen Ryle – but there is nothing wrong with that. And it was Stephen who, in trying to capture the changing English landscape on canvas, expressed the play's positive values:

> I paint what is vanishing. As it vanishes. Sometimes I only paint the memory of something that was there long ago. A shape. We drool over the Aborigines because they hold their land sacred. But we must all have done that once. Even the English. Particularly the English. Islands are mysterious, our land is so watery, that is its beauty.

What made the play moving was Wertenbaker's suggestion that we needed to reject the money-mad Eighties and rediscover enduring qualities such as the romance of English landscape. Having started out as Churchillian satire, Wertenbaker's play echoed Priestley's *Summer Day's Dream* in its reverence for deep England and endorsed David Hare's argument that there was an indestructible virtue that would survive the Thatcherite assault. At the end, as Stephen integrated Harriet Walter's memorably bare-breasted Biddy into his impressionistic vision of nature, one of his questions lingered poignantly in the air: 'When England began doubting itself, why did it have to stop loving itself?'

Why indeed? Why could we not see beyond contemporary politics to appreciate the things that really mattered such as England's language, landscape and literature? One answer might be that our perception of their virtues had been inescapably altered by a market-driven culture: what chance was there for a younger generation to grow up to enjoy the delights of English poetry if it was progressively edged off the school syllabus, was alien to the world of television and regarded as a frivolous irrelevance in a utilitarian age? One person who took a more sanguine view was the Irish dramatist Frank McGuinness, who was born in County Donegal. You could say that as a lecturer in English, first in Maynooth and later at University College Dublin, McGuinness had a vested interest in the subject. But what is remarkable about *Someone Who'll Watch Over Me*, which first appeared at Hampstead Theatre in 1993 and has had a considerable after-life, is the sincerity of its testament to the moral character of the English and the enduring power of their literature. Inspired by the experience of Brian Keenan, who had been held hostage in the Lebanon, the play shows an American doctor, Irish journalist and English academic holed up together in a Middle Eastern cell. The American's ingrained self-belief and the Irishman's love of family, horses and drink both buckle under the strain. Unexpectedly, it is the prissily English Michael who posseses an irony and resilience that sees him through the ordeal. McGuinness is clearly making a sexual point about the inherent toughness of the apparently fey as against the falli-bility of the outwardly macho. But crucial to the play is Michael's equation of love of country with a passion for its literature. As an aca-demic, Michael has the capacity to recollect in detail the Anglo-Saxon poem *The Wanderer*, the medieval tale of Sir Orfeo and George Her-bert's beautiful 'Love bade me welcome; yet my soule drew back. Guiltie of dust and sinne'. McGuinness's point was that Michael's love of literature gave him an imaginative freedom that enabled him to tri-umph over immediate circumstance. But what was impressive, at a time of national self-doubt and entrenched philistinism, was seeing an Irish writer asserting the glories of the English literary inheritance.

One aspect of that inheritance is its ability to permeate the present. And Terry Johnson, who wrote two plays that adorned the Nineties in the shape of *Hysteria* and *Dead Funny*, elicited a rich tribute from his fellow writer, Nicholas Wright, in the introduction to the Methuen edition of his works. For Wright, Johnson belongs firmly in the pre-Civil War English Puritan tradition of Webster, Tourneur and Middle-ton. Like them, he is obsessed with sex. 'And what makes this obsession a fatal one in the Puritan cosmology,' argues Wright, 'is not guilt or the threat of damnation neither of which, after all, has any rational basis. It is the fact that, in flesh, sex shares a common denom-inator with death.' It is a highly perceptive argument reminding us that living dramatists are part of a tradition. But it is also possible to see Johnson, who came of age as a writer with *Insignificance* at the Royal Court in 1982, as part of another, more recent movement: that of intellectual farce. Using the familiar properties of panic, conceal-ment and disguise, a generation of British writers had shown that farce could become more than a piece of self-delighting theatrical engineer-ing. After Peter Shaffer's *Black Comedy* and Joe Orton's *What The Butler Saw* had come Michael Frayn's *Noises Off* which memorably demonstrated that even the rehearsal and performance of a stock rep farce could embody the thin dividing line between order and chaos.

Terry Johnson was squarely in that tradition in that he used farce both to explore ideas and analyse the English psyche. In *Hysteria*, superbly staged by Phyllida Lloyd at the Royal Court in 1993, he showed an ageing Hampstead-based Freud suffering a guilt-haunted dream in which he was accused of suppressing evidence of child abuse amongst the Viennese middle classes in order to save his career. What made the play so startling was the way Freud's fears were expressed in Daliesque terms as clocks melted, solid doors turned to rubber and a swan descended from the ceiling. And in *Dead Funny*, which appeared at Hampstead Theatre a year later, Johnson turned his clinical eye on the English character as expressed through its popular comic tradition. Prompted by the death of Benny Hill and Frankie Howerd within a few days of each other in the early Nineties, Johnson suggested that our well-established love of saucy innuendo and *double entendre* masks a deep-seated mixture of fear and sexual chauvinism. But Johnson's genius lay in his ability to, as it were, have it both ways. He pointed up the pathos and hypocrisy of a group of comedy-worshipping anoraks who formed their own Dead Funny Society. Yet his first-act climax showed Richard, one of its supposedly impotent members, rogering a friend's wife, Lisa, over the back of a sofa. At which moment a fellow member, the campy Brian, passed cheerily by while dressed as a Fred Scuttle lookalike in long mac, beret and pebble spectacles. This produced a superb pay-off in the next act when Lisa apologetically said 'Just now . . . I don't know what came over me.' To which Brian sardonically replied, 'Well, Richard presumably.' In his ability to get extravagant laughs, explore the supple filthiness of the English language and at the same time suggest that we use comedy as a camouflage for our deep-seated national deficiences, Johnson wrote a play that rivalled *Noises Off* in its hilarity and *Comedians* in its social resonance.

Dead Funny rightly won every award going and transferred to the West End. And Johnson, whose work had appeared since 1979 at the Bush, Hampstead, Stratford East and the Royal Court, was a prime example of a writer who used the new-writing circuit to hone his craft even in difficult times. All the theatres on that circuit had undergone financial crises, yet they survived, and in the mid-Nineties two of them even witnessed a highly dramatic flowering of talent. The Bush, under Dominic Dromgoole, enjoyed a golden period during 1995–96: a season called 'London Fragments' offered plays by David Eldridge, Samuel Adamson and Simon Bent flanked by imports from Scotland (David Harrower's *Knives and Hens*) and from Ireland (Conor McPherson's *This Lime Tree Bower* and *St Nicholas*). Meanwhile the Royal Court, where Stephen Daldry had succeeded Max Stafford-Clark, bombarded us in the mid-Nineties with new plays by then unknown writers: Sarah Kane, Mark Ravenhill, Joe Penhall, Martin McDonagh, Jez Butterworth, Nick Grosso, Judy Upton. These seasons were to give the British theatre a fresh impetus and would even yield a handful of plays that later achieved fame throughout Europe. And the inevitable question is why this happened at a time when British society, during the long, slow adagio of the Major government's expiry, seemed in such a pitiful state.

One can point to both external and internal reasons. In the case of the Royal Court, Stephen Daldry, on assuming control in 1992, took a radical look at both the building and its programme. He was told that the old wooden fly-tower grid was on the point of collapse and that the danger-fraught backstage area needed a complete overhaul. This prompted a decision to modernise the whole Royal Court, front and back, without destroying its essential character. A lottery grant of £18.8 million was received from the Arts Council. That left the Court itself to raise matching funding of £7 million. It also had to continue the production cycle uninterrupted while the theatre was closed from 1996 to 1998. But alongside renovating the building, Daldry also raked through the Court's history to determine the secret of its success. He realised that a key quality of the Devine era was the sense of creative tumult and of new plays following each other in quick, pell-mell succession. Accordingly he decided to programme as many as nineteen productions a year in the Court's two auditoria and, where possible, to showcase brand-new writers. To do this, he raised extra funding from the Jerwood Foundation and raided the bank of new plays commissioned by the National Theatre Studio. If the Royal Court suddenly became a creative powerhouse in the mid-Nineties, it was because of Daldry's mixture of vision and pragmatism (always the crucial qualities for any artistic director), the Jerwood's rock-solid support even when the new plays provoked a storm of bad publicity, and the generosity of the National Theatre in releasing a host of work it would never be able to schedule on its own stages.

But there were was another, less tangible reason for the avalanche of

353

new plays that appeared primarily at the Court but also at the Bush: the peculiar nature of the times. If the first New Wave of writers in the Fifties were reacting against the cramping frustrations of British life, the Second Wave was driven by a rejection of the materialism of the Eighties: the decade in which most of the new writers had moved from adolescence to maturity. Anyone born around 1970 was, by definition, either a victim or a beneficiary of Thatcherism: possibly both at once. As Ian Rickson, Daldry's successor at the Court, put it:

> The writers who grew up under Thatcher experienced two things: they were disempowered and simultaneously empowered. On the one hand, the state was strengthened at the expense of the individual: on the other hand, the only way of achieving anything was to do it yourself. Thatcherism provided both a climate of anger and the motivation to do something about it.

Along with Thatcherism, the Nineties writers also discarded the formal models of their predecessors. In a sense, they were reacting just as strongly against the public-issue plays of Hare, Brenton and Edgar as against their own poisoned social inheritance. And, while there may be a strong vein of oppositional anger running through their work, it is more often explored through damaged personal relationships than anti-government rhetoric.

You saw this at its best in Joe Penhall's *Some Voices*: the play that launched a landmark season at the Theatre Upstairs in September 1994 and was artistically superior to much of the work that followed it. Although born in Surrey, Penhall had spent much of his childhood in an Australian suburb, returning to London only in 1987, when he was twenty. Working as a reporter on local newspapers in south London and Hammersmith, Penhall saw at first hand the consequences of the Conservatives' 'Care in the Community' programme, under which the depressed, the mentally ill and the schizophrenic were often released back into society. Had he been born a generation earlier, Penhall might well have been tempted to write a big public play attacking Conservative social policies. But his models were less Hare, Brenton and Edgar than Buchner's *Woyzeck*, the short stories of Raymond Carver and Hanif Kureishi's *My Beautiful Laundrette*. And what impressed one about Penhall was his sympathy with a broad range of disenfranchised characters. His hero, Ray, is a certified schizophrenic glibly discharged into the Shepherd's Bush jungle. Once in the outside world, Ray finds himself surrounded by misfits and outsiders guaranteed to reinforce his shaky sense of stability. He befriends a fellow schizophrenic whom he first met in a mental hospital and who is full of unfocused rage. And, although Ray takes up with the pregnant Laura, he finds that she is being tormented by a psychotically jealous lover. Even Ray's brother, Pete, is too busy trying to turn his father's caff into a chic new eaterie to be a full-time carer. Not surprisingly, Ray goes to pieces. But, although he is re-institutionalised, the play ends with a measure of hope as he is taught by his brother how to cook an omelette on a specially imported hot plate. It's an image that has all sorts of echoes. It reminds one of the fraternal protectiveness at the end of *The Caretaker*: also of Arnold Wesker's perennial faith in cooking as a healing symbol. Penhall, however, was very much his own man in his compassionate quietude and his belief that we release people into a community that no longer meaningfully exists.

Penhall's impressive Theatre Upstairs debut was quickly followed by Nick Grosso's *Peaches*, dealing with laddish insecurity, and Judy Upton's *Ashes and Sand*, which was about seaside girl gangs. But it was Sarah Kane's *Blasted*, which opened at the same venue in January 1995, that promoted Daldry's new-play season onto the front pages and provoked a moral hullabaloo and media panic unmatched in British theatre since the premiere of Bond's *Saved*. Writing about it now, one has to disentangle personal guilt about one's initial incomprehension of the play from honest assessment of its virtues and faults. And the difficulty is compounded by the knowledge that Kane's tragic suicide was to occur only five years after her debut. But there is little doubt that, arriving unprepared for *Blasted* on a bleak January night, all the critics were caught on the hop. Writing about the play the morning after, I took refuge in a defensive irony of which I have long felt ashamed. Charles Spencer in the *Daily Telegraph* more directly called *Blasted* 'a lazy, tawdry piece of work without an idea in its head behind an adolescent desire to shock'. The late Jack Tinker in the *Daily Mail* said he was disgusted by a play 'which appears to know no bounds of decency yet has no message to convey by way of excuse'. We were all wrong. Sarah Kane, as became clear from her later work, was driven by a strong moral animus. Yet, although *Blasted* remains an important theatrical phenomenon, it is one with the defects of its qualities.

Its first half is acutely gripping. Ian, a middle-aged tabloid hack, is holed up in a Leeds hotel room with the naive, epileptic twenty-one-year-old Cate. Ian is both seriously ill and sexually exploitative. He constantly protests that he loves Cate yet forces her into a series of sexual acts and, during the night they spend together, rapes her. It is deeply disturbing, yet there is something strangely compelling about Ian's mixture of brutality and paranoia and about Cate's inbuilt resilience. The age gap between the two characters and the mixture of hostility and spasmodic tenderness also implies they are more than two lovers: we seem to be confronted by a metaphor for an abusive father-daughter relationship. But the real problems start in the second half when a rifle-wielding Soldier bursts into the hotel room. The Soldier, part of some unspecified civil war raging in the streets, proceeds to bugger Ian and suck his eyes out before killing himself. Cate, who has drifted into the battle zone, returns holding a baby which dies and is buried under the floorboards. After masturbating and defecating, the starving Ian cannibalises the dead baby. Buried up to his neck under the floorboards, Ian is reduced to a shrivelled wreck of a human being. But, as Cate feeds him sausage and pours gin into his mouth, he at last treats her as a human being and utters the final words of the play: 'Thank you.'

Kane told Aleks Sierz that she was writing a play about two people in a hotel room when she switched on the television in March 1993 and saw Srebenica under siege. She was moved by the powerlessness of an old woman looking into the camera and demanding a help that was not forthcoming. Kane felt compelled to incorporate this into her existing structure, at the same time acknowledging the difficulty:

> I asked myself 'What could possibly be the connection between a common rape in a Leeds hotel room and what's happening in Bosnia?' And then suddenly the penny dropped and I thought 'Of course, it's obvious. One is the seed and the other is the tree.' And I do think that the seeds of full-scale war can always be found in peacetime civilisation and I think the wall between so-called civilisation and what happened in central Europe is very, very thin and it can get torn down at any time.

The key question is whether Kane establishes an iron-clad connection between personal abuse and the larger image of civic chaos; and I am not persuaded she does. On the purely narrative level, she tries to justify the Soldier's suspicions of Ian by making the latter a gun-carrying government agent. But it's hard to believe that a homophobic, cancerous red-top hack like Ian would be in the paid employ of even our own notoriously unreliable Whitehall agencies. More seriously, Kane's argument that there is an umbilical connection between the pain individuals inflict on each other and civil war never goes beyond a convenient *donnée*. In the case of Bosnia, there were very specific reasons for the violence: not only the whole history of the former Yugoslavia, but the decision by the European Community in January 1992 that Croatia and Slovenia be recognised as independent states, thereby provoking Serbian retaliation. Kane's play obviously has a raw visceral power. It can also be adapted to fit different political circumstances, as Thomas Ostermeier proved in his sensational Berlin Schaubune production in 2005 when it became an oblique comment on Iraq. And, like Dennis Cannan in a famous speech in Peter Brook's *US*, Kane uses shock tactics to bring home to us the reality of global violence. But, while I can now see the virtues of *Blasted*, its assertion of the link between personal and public brutality seems imposed rather than inevitable.

For me that link was more persuasively suggested in Harold Pinter's *Ashes to Ashes* which the Royal Court presented in September 1996 in its temporary home at the Ambassadors. Pinter, like Edward Bond and Caryl Churchill, greatly admired Sarah Kane; and it is more than possible that his own play owed a surreptitious debt to *Blasted*. It was sparked initially by Pinter's reading of Gitta Sereny's biography of Hitler's armaments minister and favourite architect, Albert Speer. And the image that haunted Pinter was that of the duality of Speer's life: in particular the discovery that the man responsible for slave-labour factories later carried on a clandestine affair with a German married woman who was half his age. How is it, Pinter seems to ask, that the agents of fascist cruelty can function simultaneously as adoring lovers? But, like Kane in *Blasted*, Pinter introduces a world of calamitous European suffering into an English setting. In her case, it was a Leeds hotel room. In his, it is a country-house drawing room with a garden beyond. However, where Kane's shock tactics are largely physical, Pinter's are almost entirely verbal. As we watch a man, Devlin, obsessively interrogating his partner, Rebecca, about her relationship with a former lover, both the eroticism of power and the corrosiveness of evil are conveyed through language. At one point Rebecca refers to a condition known as mental elephantiasis, which 'means that when you spill an ounce of gravy, for example, it immediately expands and becomes a vast sea of gravy'. Eventually you suffocate in a voluminous gravy. 'But', she continues, 'it's all your own fault. You brought it upon yourself. You are not the *victim* of it, you are the *cause* of it. Because it was you who spilt the gravy in the first place.' As an expression of the way intimate violence expands into public barbarism, that seems to me more dramatically effective than Kane's image of hotel walls collapsing to admit civil war.

Understatement, indirectness, poetic suggestiveness of the kind practised by Pinter were not, however, the prevailing modes of the Nineties. This was the decade of In-Yer-Face Theatre, described by Aleks Sierz as 'a theatre of sensation: it jolts both actors and spectators out of conventional responses, touching nerves and provoking alarm'. In some ways, it was reminiscent of the High Sixties when Artaud was the ruling deity and assaulting the senses was considered a legitimate way of rousing audiences from their bourgeois complacency. But, for various reasons, the ante had been decisively upped since the Sixties. Young dramatists no longer found a censorious Lord Chamberlain breathing down their necks. Audiences had also become conditioned, especially in cinema, to the graphic representation of sex, drugs and violence. The days when we could be shocked by the spectacle of butter-aided anal penetration, as in *Last Tango In Paris*, were now quaintly a thing of the past. Fellatio, cunnilingus and self-mutilation were the stuff of weekly movie-going. Danny Boyle's version of Irvine Welsh's *Trainspotting*, with its working-class Edinburgh druggies and toilet-bowl vision of humanity, won awards everywhere and received the imprimatur of a Conservative Minister of Arts. Above all, Quentin Tarantino in *Pulp Fiction* had lent criminalised violence a glamorous sheen and tactile excitement. In such a climate it was hardly surprising that stage dramatists should exploit the new expressive freedoms. But what is interesting about the In-Yer-Face writers is that they appropriated, and even extended, the possibility to say and do virtually anything while endowing it with their own brand of moral disgust. There may have been a strong '*épater les bourgeois*' element in their work. At the same time they were driven by a contempt for the values they had inherited and a critical attitude to the surrounding culture.

This criticism took many forms. In some cases, it was demonstrably violent and shocking. Sarah Kane followed *Blasted* with *Phaedra's Love* (1996), which used Seneca's tragic story of misplaced passion to satirise Britain's own dysfunctional royal family and at one point had its high-born hero masturbating assiduously into a sock. Jez Butterworth's *Mojo* (1995), although set in the seedy Soho gangland of 1958, was a jazzily written, biliously funny attack on a violent, patriarchal culture, during which the hero suggested that 'there's nothing like someone cutting your dad in two for clearing your mind'. And Anthony Neilson broke one of the last taboos of all in his dark, disturbing play, *The Censor* (1997). In this a boundary-breaking female film-maker tried to cure the hang-ups of an anally fixated movie censor by enacting his secret fantasy, which was to watch women defecate. But if Neilson's play left its palpable mark on the British stage, it was not merely through the actions of its heroine but through her philosophy that 'anything can be shown anywhere'.

If any one play defined the theatre of the Nineties, however, it was Mark Ravenhill's *Shopping and Fucking*. Co-produced by Max Stafford-Clark's company, Out of Joint, and the Royal Court, it survived the bowdlerisation of its title, in accordance with London laws and local susceptibilities, to become one of the great success stories of the decade. It initially played at the Theatre Upstairs at the Ambassadors in the autumn of 1996. After a regional tour, it was revived in the larger Ambassadors space in January 1997. It moved into the Gielgud Theatre in the West End in June 1997 and then went on an arduous regional and international tour, taking in Sweden, Italy, Australia, New Zealand and Israel, before undertaking a second UK tour in 1998. At the same time, there were dozens of independent productions worldwide. Although objections were raised in the Antipodes to its explicit title and theme, it was loyally supported by the British Council and became an international advertisement for the inherent vitality of our culture.

But what is it about Ravenhill's play that so caught the popular imagination? Stephen Daldry argued on a public platform that audiences no longer wanted old-fashioned thesis plays but preferred 'a personalised internal search without necessarily a clear answer'. And there is much truth in that. Even if the plays of a previous generation hadn't supplied the answers, they assumed political solutions existed. Ravenhill's play, however, captured the mood and language of a dysfunctional, disillusioned post-Thatcher generation struggling to make sense of a world without religion or ideology. Above all, it was a world without any grand narrative to make sense of the randomness of experience. If you take away God, Marx and Freud, what have you left?

That point is explicitly made in Ravenhill's play in a keynote speech by Robbie. He is a hapless bisexual who shares a flat with two friends, Mark and Lulu. He fecklessly squanders three hundred Ecstasy tablets he has been hired to sell by a middle-aged entrepreneur. He is also party to the penetrative wounding of a masochistic rent boy, Gary. When Gary confesses that he is looking for a strong, hard man to punish him, Robbie speculates that this may just be a convenient fiction:

> I think . . . I think we all need stories, we make up stories so that we can get by. And I think a long time ago there were big stories. Stories so big you could live your whole life in them. The powerful hands of the Gods and Fate. The Journey to Enlightenment. The March of Socialism. But they all died or the world grew up or grew senile or forgot them. So now we're all making up our own stories. Little stories. But we've each got one.

Ravenhill is a learned, allusive writer and Robbie's lament for the death of grand narratives clearly echoes Jimmy Porter's famous despairing cry in *Look Back In Anger*:

> I suppose people of our generation aren't able to die for good causes any longer. We had all that done for us in the thirties and forties, when we were still kids. There aren't any good, brave causes left. If the big bang does come, and we all get killed off, it won't be in aid of the old-fashioned, grand design. It'll just be for the Brave New-nothing-very-much-thank-you.

Forty years separate Osborne's Jimmy and Ravenhill's Robbie. What links them is a hunger for the days of coherent beliefs that made sense of people's lives. Both also suggest that the only response to the mean time is to create a world of one's own: a Strindbergian sexual antagonism in the case of Jimmy, a recourse to small private fictions in the case of Ravenhill's Robbie. To my ear – and perhaps to someone of my generation – there is more tang and savour in Jimmy's *cri de coeur* than in Robbie's all too palpable authorial message. But, looking at the young audiences that attended *Shopping and Fucking*, I got a similar sense to that experienced in the Fifties: of people's delight at hearing their own concerns and preoccupations reflected on a public stage.

Where Ravenhill's play also scored was in its illustration of Robbie's point about our dependence on solipsistic private narratives. Brian, the junk-dealer who gives Robbie, Mark and Lulu three hundred

Ecstasy tablets to sell, has his own consoling stories: he takes refuge from reality in the Disneyfied myth of *The Lion King* and a dream of encouraging his son to become a cellist. Mark embroiders a scabrously hilarious fantasy of having sex in a public toilet with Princess Diana and 'Fergie', the Duchess of York. Lulu lives out her own personal fears by telling a story of how she saw a shop assistant attacked by a knife-wielding customer. The masochistic rent-boy, Gary, recalls how his stepfather perpetually raped him. Even the way Robbie and Lulu are forced to sell telephone sex in order to raise the money they owe Brian becomes part of the dominant motif of fragmented fiction. In an age without grand narratives we survive, Ravenhill implies, by creating our own private myths and by making necessary compromises with the materialism of the time.

Ravenhill, blessed with sharp antennae, clearly caught the public mood. His play reflected a world in which sex had become a negotiable transaction and shopping had acquired a tangible sexual excitement: what George Steiner once called 'the fascism of the supermarket'. Max Stafford-Clark's production, beginning with Mark spewing up the contents of a carton of takeaway food, was also pervaded by the pungent aroma of cheap, microwaved meals. And, not unlike Sarah Kane in *Blasted*, Ravenhill showed how conspicuous consumption could be transformed into a peace-offering and signal a kind of fragile redemption. At the end, as Robbie, Mark and Lulu took it in turns to feed each other with ready-made meals, one felt they were breaking out of their individual straitjackets. As a social document, Ravenhill's play was impeccable: it bottled the essence of its period in a way that will make it an invaluable source of study for future generations. But, although the play ended on a gesture of hope, I was left hungering for some concrete notion of a better society: some indication that there were large-scale remedies for the characters' urban angst. What *Shopping and Fucking* lacked, like so many plays of the Nineties, was any vision of Utopia. But maybe that was part of its point and why it was such a success wherever it played. In the drifting, desolate Nineties, argued Ravenhill, there were no ready-made Utopias and no grand narrative schemes. The best that we could hope to do was construct our own private dreams and tell each other stories.

X

1997–2006

New Labour, New Theatre?

We had stumbled through the Nineties under John Major: a decent enough man but, like the schoolmaster cast as Alexander in *Love's Labour's Lost*, 'a little o'er parted'. And, when an election was finally called for 1 May 1997, the country was clearly in a mood for change. But, although we all expected a Labour victory, the scale of the triumph, evoking memories of 1945, took most of us by surprise. I remember driving back on election night from Newcastle-under-Lyme, where I'd been to see a play by Peter Whelan, and letting out a yelp of delight as I switched on the ten o'clock news and heard the Tory Chancellor, Kenneth Clarke, conceding that a Labour landslide was in prospect. And, back in London, the night simply got better as it wore on. There was a wicked pleasure in seeing Tory totems such as David Mellor and Michael Portillo bite the dust in seemingly safe seats. Next day, as the scale of the victory became clear, one detected a palpable euphoria on the streets of London. Outside the gates of Downing Street, crowds sang and danced. Tony Blair and his family, posing on the steps of Number 10, seemed to embody a bright new future. Later that day, as I made my way to a first night at the Bush, faces were wreathed in smiles. Glancing up at the cloudless summer sky, the theatre's PR ironically remarked that 'even the weather seems better under Labour'.

After the euphoria came the reality; but it is a lazy untruth to say that nothing whatsoever changed after the victory of what Blair insisted on calling 'New Labour'. Almost immediately the Chancellor, Gordon Brown, announced that the Bank of England would take over responsibility for setting interest rates. And, within the first hundred days, Blair flew to Northern Ireland to set up a new peace initiative and to the Netherlands to advertise his commitment to Europe. White papers were published outlining details of a Scottish Parliament and a Welsh Assembly. Plans were also announced for a new Greater London Authority and a directly elected mayor. Less happily, Blair decided, in spite of heavy Cabinet opposition, to press ahead with the Millennium Dome. For all the flurry of activity, however, there was a certain caution about New Labour, symbolised by the famous five pledges printed on an election card. There were commitments to reduce NHS waiting lists, cut class sizes for five- to seven-year-olds, get a quarter of a million young people off benefit and into work. But there were no promises to build the new Jerusalem. In his July budget Gordon Brown announced an extra £1.3 billion for schools and £1.2 billion for the NHS. But, remembering how the City and international markets had panicked when Harold Wilson arrived in Downing Street in 1964, Labour in its first two years stuck, overall, to the spending limits prescribed by the Conservatives.

This inevitably had an impact on the arts; and, most acutely, on the theatre. In January 1997 – four months before the election – Tony Blair earned ringing applause when he told an audience at the *South Bank Show* awards that 'the arts should not be an add-on on page 24 of the manifesto but something that is central to a decent country'. A year later Sir Peter Hall got a standing ovation when he told precisely the same audience: 'I know both political parties are excellent supporters of the arts when they are in opposition. Come the dawn, what happens? A cut in the Arts Council grant. Why? It saves tuppence and it's going to ruin a number of small theatres and dance companies.' And Hall was right. In London, the fate of the Gate, the King's Head and Greenwich Theatre (existing within the shadow of the Millennium Dome) hung in the balance following cuts in funding. Outside London, the Liverpool Playhouse and the Chester Gateway were forced into temporary closure. A large number of other regional theatres faced bankruptcy. It seemed almost inconceivable that a newly elected Labour government could allow this to happen at a time when the Arts Council was spending a staggering £14.7 million on the administration of National Lottery capital grants.

Peter Hall had particular reason to be angry. In March 1997 he took over the Old Vic, owned by the Mirvish family of Toronto, to create a permanent company doing a seven-day-a-week season of classic and contemporary plays. By December, he was forced to vacate the building after the Mirvishes had put it up for sale. Appeals by Hall – to the new Arts Minister, Chris Smith, and to the Arts Council – to rescue the project fell on deaf ears. Their argument was that London had quite

enough theatres already and that the Peter Hall Company was superfluous to requirements. It was a big blow not just to Hall's pride but to
his conviction that he was offering London something different: a
rotating repertory in which standard classics like *King Lear*, *The Seagull*, *Waiting For Godot*, *Waste* and *The Provoked Wife* were mixed
with new plays by April de Angelis, Sebastian Barry and Samuel
Adamson. By cutting production costs and simplifying design, Hall
had fulfilled his mission 'to give the stage back to the actors'; and he
had assembled a formidable group including Ben Kingsley, Alan
Howard, Michael Pennington, Felicity Kendal and Victoria Hamilton.
He had also shown that there was a sizeable public for Sunday theatre: it had always seemed crazy that while cinemas, concert halls and
galleries were packed on Sundays, London's theatres stood stonily
silent as if still in thrall to the Lord's Day Observance Society. After the
collapse of the Old Vic dream Hall, as usual, moved on. At the time he
told me, with a degree of bitterness in hs voice, 'I feel I have done the
state some service'; but any hopes of a tangible reward, in terms of a
public rescue of the Old Vic, were brutally dashed. The result was that
Hall, the single most influential figure in post-war British theatre,
became an itinerant outsider and vocal opponent of the existing arts
bureaucracy, even threatening to create an Alternative Arts Council.
As he learned to his cost, Cool Britannia – as it was officially dubbed
– was no country for old men.

What is startling is how long it took New Labour to realise that, in
the arts, a relatively modest investment can yield massive rewards.
Chris Smith, a genuinely innovative Arts Minister, wanted to abolish
museum charges for all national collections. Instead he got a tranche
of new money, £100 million, to admit first children and then pension-
ers for free, which led to a rise in admissions. As Polly Toynbee and
David Walker say in *Did Things Get Better?*, 'that is New Labour for
you: they missed a grand gesture which would have won sackfuls of
brownie points but did some good with scant recognition.' In the theatre, however, there weren't even these small consolatory offerings. In
the summer of 1998, only fifteen months after the Labour landslide,
the National Campaign for the Arts put out a chilling document
detailing the consequences of declining funding. The value of annual
Arts Council grants to producing theatres had fallen by thirteen per
cent since 1992. There had been a cumulative loss of £12 million in
core funding over a decade. Thirty-three English regional reps had

deficits totalling over £10.3 million. Theatres were also driven to increasingly desperate straits to survive. In 1998 Nottingham Playhouse put out a booklet called *Theatre in Industry* in which it offered tailor-made shows for local firms that could be used for training staff and managers and which offered – the big draw – 'a chance to increase your profits'. Under Richard Eyre, Nottingham Playhouse had put on shows like *Brassneck*, *Comedians* and the multi-authored *Deeds*, offering a critique of contemporary capitalism. Now Nottingham had become capitalism's unwilling accomplice.

This could be taken as symbolic of a Blair administration that believed in a Third Way that would navigate a path between market capitalism and old-style socialism. In reality, it was a sign of a general crisis. And it seemed strange that it was happening under Blair, who was far more theatrically inclined than previous Labour leaders such as Clement Attlee and Harold Wilson. As a schoolboy at Fettes, Blair had shone as Mark Antony and as Stanhope in *Journey's End*. At Oxford, he had acted in student revues and, as the whole world knows, was part of a rock band called Ugly Rumours. He was even one of those rare politicans who went to the theatre. Yet, under his watch, the medium seemed to be suffering. But it is my contention that the theatre, in the most astonishing way, reflects the different phases of the Blair premiership. From 1997 to 1999 the theatre was inevitably stifled and checked by the government's tight hold on public spending. In the next four years, as public spending dramatically rose, it enjoyed a period of expansive growth. And, during the long period of Blair's decline dating from the Iraq war of 2003, the theatre became once more a strenuously oppositional voice. Blair was well known for his admiration of Mrs Thatcher. And, just as her ideology decisively shaped the theatre of the Eighties, the same was true of Blair in his period of office. It was Blair's, and Gordon Brown's, eventual commitment to increased spending that rescued the theatre from the doldrums. Ironically, it was also that new-found stability that enabled the theatre to recover its political voice as trust in Blair's foreign policy disappeared to vanishing point. From 1997 on theatreland was, for good or ill, a reflection of Blairite beliefs and deeds.

For an example of Blairism in action one need look no further than the National Theatre. During the tenure of Trevor Nunn, from September 1997 to March 2003, the National provided an uncannily accurate mirror of Blairite philosophy and practice. For a start, there was an obsession with fiscal prudence that, in the early stages of the Nunn regime, put a severe brake on reforming possibilities. Just as Labour in its first two years was so concerned with balancing the books that it seemed to lose sight of its *raison d'être,* much the same could be said of the National. For me a low point was reached when, in the summer of 1998, one was offered a choice between straight runs of *Oklahoma!* in the Olivier and *The Prime of Miss Jean Brodie* in the Lyttelton. An institution for which idealists had campaigned for over a century was presenting nothing more imaginative than a well-known American musical and a middlebrow adaptation of a Muriel Spark novel.

Throughout his tenure, Nunn's attempt to reconcile the public-service ethos of the National with commercial popularity resembled a direct replica of Blair's Third Way approach. Classics and new plays were combined with a steady stream of musicals: seven in all during Nunn's five and a half years, with *Oklahoma!* quickly followed by *Candide, The Villains' Opera, Honk – The Musical, My Fair Lady, South Pacific* and *Anything Goes.* Only a puritan killjoy would argue that the musical has no place in the National's repertory; and I would put Nunn's production of Cole Porter's *Anything Goes* high on the list of the most pleasurable experiences I've had in post-war theatre. But Nunn's personal attachment to the musical unbalanced the National repertory. And the marriage of public subsidy with private finance – so dear to the heart of New Labour – reached its apogee, or possibly its nadir, with *My Fair Lady.* This was a musical Cameron Mackintosh had long wanted to revive under Trevor Nunn's direction. As a result, it got a three-month straight run at the National – in effect a pre-West End 'try-out' – before moving on to its predestined home at the Theatre Royal, Drury Lane. But, even if the National made a healthy profit from the transfer, I doubt that Granville-Barker and William Archer had ever envisaged that one day the home of the nation's theatre would operate as a safety net for commercial producers. The frequent absences during the National run of the Eliza, the soap star Martine McCutcheon, also made the production a standing joke. It was alleged that Jonathan Pryce, exasperated one day by the unavailability of both Ms McCutcheon and her understudy, came before the Lyttelton front curtain and asked in Higgins-like tones if there was anyone in the house who had sung Eliza Doolittle. But throughout, the parallels between Nunn and Blair were extraordinary. The same initial determination to stick to prescribed spending limits. The same inclusive 'Big Tent' approach stripped of anything resembling an ideology. Even the same paranoia about the press, and the same concentration of power in a few hands at the expense of collegiate decision-making. As political commentator Peter Riddell said of Blair, he 'adopted a deliberately presidential style, trying to stay above the fray: no longer first among equals but rather first above equals'. And if Blair was presidential in his approach to politics, Nunn seemed, to all outward appearances, to treat the National as his personal fiefdom, in which he was free to direct the classics, musicals and new plays of his choice.

Yet, as with Tony Blair, there were positive as well as negative aspects to the Nunn years. There was a definite sense of expansion as the purse-strings were loosened. Nunn's own productions of *The Merchant of Venice*, *Summerfolk*, *The Cherry Orchard* and *A Streetcar Named Desire* were of the highest class. And, although new writing was never Nunn's strongest suit, one contemporary classic and several estimable works emerged. There was some territorial argument about whether Michael Frayn's *Copenhagen* was a legacy from the Eyre regime or a discovery of the Nunn era. Either way, this was a major work about the meeting in wartime Denmark between Niels Bohr, Europe's leading quantum theorist, and Werner Heisenberg, his ex-colleague working on the German atomic-bomb project. What actually happened in 1941? Why was the meeting so brusquely aborted by Bohr? Was Heisenberg seeking information, absolution or endorsement? And why did Heisenberg fail to make the final calculation that would have enabled Nazi Germany to develop its own atomic bomb? Frayn's play not only posed a number of riveting questions. It also became a profound exploration of a theme that runs through modern drama and that had excited many of Frayn's contemporaries, such as Pinter, Stoppard and Bennett: the subjectivity and fallibility of memory. But Frayn's play offered something even more remarkable than that. Unlike earlier plays by Shaw, Brecht and Dürrenmatt, it didn't simply talk about science. It applied it through the act of performance. Kirsten Shepherd-Barr in her invaluable book, *Science on Stage*, traces the history of scientific theatre from Marlowe's *Doctor Faustus* to Complicité's *Mnemonic*. But she is particularly astute on Frayn's merging of theme and form in *Copenhagen*: 'The dialogue', she notes, 'brims with vivid demonstrations of the applicability of the uncertainty principle to the workings of memory and as they talk, the actors orbit the stage like the electrons, neutrons and protons they signify.' All this was made brilliantly clear in Michael Blakemore's Cottesloe production; and he himself later wrote of *Copenhagen*, after it had moved from the National and the West End to New York, that 'it was extraordinary the way the act of theatregoing supports the various concepts in the play'.

Frayn's masterpiece stood head and shoulders above the new writing that emerged in Nunn's first two years at the National: a period in which even good dramatists produced work that ranged from the mildly indifferent to the downright awful. Frank McGuinness's *Mutabilitie*, Stephen Poliakoff's *Remember This*, Nick Stafford's *Battle Royal*, Hanif Kureishi's *Sleep With Me* were among the plays that sank without trace. But honour was restored in April 2000 with Joe Penhall's *Blue/Orange* which richly confirmed the promise shown in his earlier *Some Voices*. Once again, Penhall was concerned with society's treatment of the marginalised and mentally disturbed. This time, however, his setting was a psychiatric hospital where two doctors treated a black patient, who believed that oranges were blue and that Idi Amin was his father, as a ping-pong ball in a private battle of egos. One doctor wanted the patient thrust back into the community. The other, believing that he was on the border between psychotic and neurotic, wanted to keep him in for further treatment. One's heart bled for Chiwetel Ejiofor as the victim of their professional arrogance and personal competitiveness. But what cheered one was the sight of a young dramatist making the Shavian point that, even in our brave new millennium, the professions were 'a conspiracy against the laity'. And, even if it was deeply flawed, there was a creditable ambition behind Tom Stoppard's massive trilogy, *The Coast of Utopia*, which Nunn impressively staged in the Olivier in the summer of 2002. The work itself sprawled and didn't always seem to have fully digested the stories of Russia's romantic exiles that it borrowed from works by E. H. Carr and Isaiah Berlin. But it touchingly revealed Stoppard's awareness of mortality and faith in children as a moral litmus test. In its distrust of dogma, the trilogy also suggested a convergence between Stoppard's own temperamental bias and the spirit of the age.

By this time the Blair government had been re-elected with another massive majority. And the public-sector expansiveness and belief in accessibility that characterised Blair's second term was duly reflected in the National's own Transformation Project. Conceived by Nunn and produced by Mick Gordon, this involved carving up the Lyttelton into two spaces. The main theatre itself was changed so that stalls and circle were connected in a single sweep. Above it, a new hundred-seat space called the Loft was created out of the circle foyer. And between May and September 2002 some thirteen new works were premiered in the two auditoria at much-reduced ticket prices. Some, such as a version of Jeanette Winterson's *The Power Book* and Kathryn Hunter's physical-theatre staging of Aristophanes' *The Birds*, were extravagant flops. Others, such as Richard Bean's *The Mentalists* and Tanika Gupta's *Sanctuary*, were highly skilful although not substantially different from the kind of work you might have seen at Hampstead or the Bush. But at least the National was trying to connect with a new audience and counter its own greying constituency. And one highly durable play emerged from the season: Roy Williams' *Sing Yer Heart Out For The Lads*. Set in a London pub on the October afternoon in 2000 when England played Germany in a crucial World Cup qualifier, this was a vigorous, combative piece about the limitless nature of English racism. Everyone, as they watched England's defeat, fell instinctively into a tribal, anti-German chauvinism. But, since the pub's soccer team depended on a black striker and the son of the pub landlady had been duffed up by a black gang, Williams was able to explore white Anglo-Saxon attitudes ranging from crude xenophobia to the articulate bigotry of a senior BNP member. The play presented the rough and smooth faces of English fascism while being equally unforgiving to young black men who tried to show their cultural assimilation through violence. After an unusual national tour, sponsored by the Football Association, Williams' play was brought back for an extended run in the Cottesloe. Its presence also said a lot about the transformation that had overtaken the Nunn regime. It had begun by reflecting, all too closely, Blair's cautious pragmatism. Towards the end of its time it echoed, more happily, New Labour's commitment to social inclusion.

Blairism, in its less happy aspects, also pervaded the RSC during the second half of Adrian Noble's tenure from 1997 to 2002. There was much talk of 'modernisation' and 'reform', of restructuring the company, of redefining the working model. There was even a New Labour emphasis on presentation with the creation of Project Fleet, which would have included the demolition of the original Royal Shakespeare Theatre and its replacement by some Disneyfied monstrosity called a

'Shakespeare Village': had it happened, it might well have turned out to be Stratford's equivalent of the Millennium Dome. To be fair to Noble, a decent man wrestling with difficult circumstances, there were genuine problems the RSC had to address. Star actors were increasingly reluctant to commit to a renewable sixty-week contract. In servicing three Stratford and two London theatres, the company sometimes seemed to be on a relentless treadmill. There was a rumbling dissatisfaction with the company's two main stages at Stratford and the Barbican. But Noble's solutions to the RSC's malaise seemed to be worse than the disease. His answer was to create shorter contracts, alter the rhythm of the Stratford season so that it ran from November to August, operate a phased withdrawal from the Barbican and talk of demolishing Elizabeth Scott's art deco Royal Shakespeare Theatre. His biggest mistake, however, was to negate the company ethos by creating what were often called 'stand-alone' productions. A particularly grisly example was a production of *Richard III* in the autumn of 1998 that took us back to an age of star-led, pictorial Shakespeare. The production was built around Robert Lindsay, who turned Shakespeare's savage ironist into a sly, ingratiating charmer. It was also directed by Elijah Moshinsky, best known for his apolitical readings of Verdi operas and a total stranger to the RSC, who ignored Peter Hall's crucial discovery in *The Wars of the Roses* that Richard and Buckingham stage a carefully planned, legally sound coup d'état. And an ad hoc supporting cast could not disguise the intellectual vacuity of a production that tore up everything the RSC had learned over the course of four decades. The fact that it was co-produced by Duncan Weldon and transferred straight from Stratford to the Savoy suggested that the RSC was going further down the road of public–private partnerships in a manner that both Thatcher and Blair would have approved.

Clearly something was going wrong. But the extent of the impending crisis only became clear to me when the late Lord Alexander of Weedon, who was to replace Sir Geoffrey Cass as chair of the RSC, invited me to his box at Lord's during a Test Match. In that nod-and-wink manner so typical of British life, the amiable Bob Alexander told me that the RSC was going to concentrate in future on 'solus' productions. It hardly seemed the time or place to protest that the whole spirit of the RSC depended on creating work that was unified by the presence of a permanent team of actors and directors. And what one witnessed, as we entered a new century, was the slow unravelling of the company. Noble's idea of replacing the Barbican with short-term seasons in diverse spaces proved costly and ill-fated. Stratford's main house became full of discrete, isolated productions devoid of any governing aesthetic. And for no obvious reason The Other Place, which had long been a forging-house of thought, was arbitrarily closed in 2001.

Even when the RSC had a bold, imaginative idea, it wasn't particularly well handled. In 2000 Noble and his associates decided to celebrate the millennium by staging a complete cycle of Shakespeare's histories from *Richard II* to *Richard III*. In 1964, when the cycle had last been attempted, it was the product of a unified historical and directorial vision. Now, as if in recognition of our fractured sense of national identity, the productions were assigned to individual directors and spread across three performance spaces. Some of the productions were outstanding. Steven Pimlott's *Richard II* brilliantly deployed the intimacy of The Other Place to eschew pageantry and relate the play to contemporary European power struggles. But it was a sign of the growing gulf between artists and administrators that Chris Foy, the RSC's new general manager, told Samuel West, who played Richard, that he just wished such a popular production could have played in a bigger venue. An exasperated West replied, 'But then it wouldn't have been the same fucking production!'

The other dominating event was Michael Boyd's staging of the complete *Henry VI* trilogy and *Richard III* in a radically reconfigured Swan Theatre. Much was made of the fact that David Oyelowo, as Henry VI, became the first black actor to play a king in a Stratford production: far from being a pious liberal gesture, however, it seemed a proper recognition of the actor's natural grace and authority. Even more striking was Boyd's ability to direct vertically and think laterally. In the old days actors used to enter from left and right: in Boyd's production they were frequently required to descend from the heavens like SAS men (and women) on a combat mission. Death, in Boyd's vision, also became an entrance as well as an exit with characters constantly returning from the grave to watch and oversee the embattled living: an idea with strange echoes of Pinter's *Moonlight*. For all the impressive quality of its constituent parts, however, the full eight-play cycle never achieved the public resonance of previous stagings of Shakespeare's histories. You could see that as a reflection of England's own sense of uncertainty in 2000. In reality, it had more to do with the fact that, when the productions transferred to London, there were only two occasions on which it was possible to see the cycle in its entirety; and even that required a good deal of frantic commuting from one theatre to another. The failure of the cycle to make a big impression told us more about the RSC's muddled thinking than about the state of the nation's morale. And there was a general sense of relief when the beleaguered Noble resigned in 2002, leading to the abandonment of Project Fleet and Shakespeare Villages and the appointment of Michael Boyd as artistic director, with a mission to take the company back to first principles: something he achieved with startling success in the first four years of his tenure.

If Noble's Dome-like dreams and Nunn's National pragmatism both seemed to reflect different aspects of Tony Blair, the Royal Court had a more complex attitude to New Labour. I recall asking Ian Rickson and Stephen Daldry at a conference in Taormina in 1998 – the year in which the former succeeded the latter as the Court's director – whether the election of a new government posed a problem. Routine Thatcher-bashing was now becoming obsolete. Was it more difficult for writers to sustain an oppositional stance with a government in power on whom many pinned a good deal of faith? They saw the point but suggested writers still had to analyse society and ask awkward questions. And Max Stafford-Clark argued that the cuts to single-parent benefits – one of the fiascos of Labour's early years in office – proved there was a need for constant vigilance. But there was a detectable shift in emphasis at the Royal Court during the early Blair years. It was partly because, with the company still performing at the Duke of York's and the Ambassadors, the chief preoccupation was the successful refurbishment of the home base. Ian Rickson was also a patient, skilled consolidator where Daldry was a more flamboyant innovator. During the transition period one detected no great urge to dissect the Blair Project. Instead the focus was more on Ireland or the new mood of apocalyptic, millennial gloom.

If there was a particular attention to Ireland in the Daldry–Rickson period, it had much to do with the coincidental emergence of two exceptionally gifted young writers: Conor McPherson and Martin McDonagh. McPherson, a quiet-spoken graduate of University College, Dublin, had shown himself a skilled monologuist in *This Lime Tree Bower* and *St Nicholas*; but he raised his game substantially in

The Weir, which opened under the Court's aegis at the Ambassadors in 1997 and went on to have a long international life. This was one of the outstanding plays of the decade: one that, while capturing the pathos of a group of yarn-spinners in a Sligo bar, also told us a good deal about contemporary Ireland. In particular, it exposed the gulf between sleepy rural backwaters and rackety modern Dublin, and the Irish male's reverence for, and nervous apprehension of, women: the residue of a Marian religious faith. In *The Weir* it was the eruption of a newcomer from Dublin, Valerie, that prompted McPherson's habitual boozers to launch into a series of vauntingly self-advertising ghost stories: bombastic fictions which Valerie herself easily trumped with hair-raising fact. But McPherson wasn't just a natural storyteller. He also had a gift, reminiscent of both Chekhov and William Trevor, for detailing the long littleness of life. There was a heartbreaking moment when Jack, a cantankerous old garage-owner, explained to Valerie why he had never married. As he described the mortification of attending his ex-lover's Dublin wedding and the consolation he found in a small act of kindness from a city barman, you felt the holiness of the minute particular. McPherson was clearly a real writer in the great tradition; and no praise was too high for Jim Norton's Jack in his stoic acceptance of a wasted life ('Down in the garage. Spinning small jobs out all day. Taking hours to fix a puncture') or for Rickson's flawless direction, which proved he was Daldry's ideal successor.

No one disputed McPherson's gift for observant realism. But British critics have a tendency to use McPherson as a stick with which to beat his showier contemporary, Martin McDonagh: a pity, since McDonagh is a highly talented writer who views contemporary Ireland with the sardonic eye of a metropolitan outsider. Shortly after the Royal Court had premiered *The Weir*, it played host to Garry Hynes's Druid Theatre company productions of a remarkable McDonagh trilogy: *The Beauty Queen of Leenane* (already seen at the Theatre Upstairs), *The Skull in Connemara* and *The Lonesome West*. Part of the pleasure of the trilogy lay in a postmodernist recognition of McDonagh's sources: most especially Beckett, Synge and Sam Shepard. While plundering other writers, McDonagh also offered his own individual vision. His aim was to explode the myth of rural Ireland, perpetuated in movies like John Ford's *The Quiet Man*, as a place of whimsical gaiety and folksy charm: the reality he suggested was a compound of spite, ignorance, solitude and rain where festering hatreds were acted out against the background of the banalities of the global village. McDonagh may lack McPherson's quiet compassion and fastidious detail. But he has an extraordinary sense of theatre: something manifested in *The Beauty Queen of Leenane* where a vengeful old harridan destroys her daughter's one chance of happiness by burning a crucial love letter. Writing from the vantage point of south London, McDonagh sees Ireland today as a place where lip service is still paid to the old religion but where Christian values are constantly denied and cruelty prevails.

From Restoration drama onwards, English theatre has been dependent on Ireland for injections of verbal energy and coruscating wit. But McPherson and McDonagh reminded us, in their different ways, of the lost pleasures of linear narrative, something that most of their English contemporaries actively disdained. To its credit, the Court also gave us a glimpse of life in Northern Ireland today through its championship of Gary Mitchell: a writer who lived on a working-class estate in North Belfast's Rathcoole and was later to suffer grievously for his attempts to tell the truth about Protestant loyalists' ferocious resistance to change. Mitchell's power lay in his ability to report from the front line and, like his southern peers, to offer gripping stories. This gift was seen at its best in *The Force of Change* (2000). Set in the interview rooms of a Belfast police station, it showed the collusion between diehard members of the Royal Ulster Constabulary and UDA terrorists, and also the male clannishness of a culture that left a dirt-digging female detective out on a limb. Some claimed the play was simply good television; but it's hard to imagine British television, in its current state of wet-nelly nervousness, having the courage to show such an acute dissection of the RUC.

Even if Mitchell's work had obvious political implications, the late Nineties was a time when dramatists seemed primarily concerned to explore localised pockets of experience or write apocalyptic mood-pieces. Sarah Kane's *Cleansed*, seen at the Duke of York's in 1998, was emphatically one of the latter. It was a dark, disturbing, extremely violent play about the precarious survival of love in a state institution designed to enforce social conformity. Once again, this was territory Pinter had explored much earlier in *The Hothouse*. And, while acknowledging the sombre power of Kane's theatrical imagination, it was difficult to relate her play to the mildly reformist, social democratic Blairite Britain of the late Nineties. Only later, with the imprisonment of suspected terrorists without trial, did it gain unexpected political resonance. Caryl Churchill's brief, cryptic *Far Away* (2000) was even more alarmist. It started, brilliantly and unnervingly, with a night-time encounter between an aunt and a young niece who had seen her uncle hitting people with an iron bar and bundling them into the back of a lorry: an image as arresting as that in Pinter's *Ashes to Ashes* of babies on station platforms being torn from the arms of their screaming mothers. But Churchill's opening impression of a localised fascism broadened out into a vision of a whole world at war and of nature itself absorbed into a cycle of unending destruction. If Kane had been influenced by her forebears, you felt they in turn had appropriated something of her despairing vision. Without in any way denying the authenticity of Churchill's pessimistic world-view, I still felt in the case of *Far Away* that it was a theatrical given rather than something to be persuasively argued or rationally justified. As we entered a new millennium, what struck me was the new note of determinist gloom. Where theatre had once admitted the possibility of social progress and political change, there seemed a growing assumption that civilisation itself was on the point of meltdown.

One excellent thing, however, happened to English theatre during Blair's first term: a radical overhaul of funding that was to be liberating for individual companies, good for the theatre community at large and, in the fullness of time, an enabling factor in the criticism of government. After the imposition of a destructive two-year straitjacket on arts funding, there was a dramatic turnaround in 1999 in line with the government's increase in public spending. In September the Arts Council of England announced a review of regional theatre to be conducted by Peter Boyden Associates, an arts management consultancy. Those of us intimately associated with the Cork Report of 1986 felt this might be just another cosmetic exercise. There would be much hand-wringing and an array of statistical evidence about the state of regional theatre followed by token dribs and drabs of money. But Boyden meant business. His report was published in May 2000. Two months later the Arts Council published a National Policy for Theatre in England, based on £25 million of new money that it had extracted from government and that was specifically earmarked for theatre. And in March 2001, just in time for another general election, details of how the extra £25 million would be allocated were released.

The Boyden Report was a landmark in post-war theatre. It was both practical and idealistic. You could tell it was no dry-as-dust blue book from the fact it was prefaced by the words of Federico Garcia Lorca:

> The theatre is one of the most expressive and useful instruments for building up a country, it is a barometer of its greatness or decline. An intelligent theatre, well orientated in all its branches, can change the sensibility of a people within a few years; a disintegrated theatre, with clumsy hooves instead of wings, can cheapen and lull into sleep an entire nation.

Poetic metaphors in an official report? We weren't used to this. Boyden was also unashamedly political in his judgements. What did he have to say, for instance, about the Thatcher years, with their mission to commercialise?

> Like the rest of the arts, the theatres received about as much sympathy from central government as did local authorities, the nationalised industries and the steel, coal and rail unions. The long term impact of a series of 'behind inflation' funding agreements over this period cannot be overestimated.

Having itemised the resulting problems – frozen grants, higher ticket prices, smaller audiences – Boyden then gave Blair's New Labour a good kick up the bum: 'Over the recent period a "sticking plaster" response has reacted erratically, unevenly and without strategic context to some of these concerns.' Once he had analysed past problems Boyden made an iron-clad case for future investment. Standstill funding, he pointed out, would lead to a four per cent decline in artistic activity. In contrast, a ten per cent funding increase could lead to a twenty-six per cent increase in levels of activity and attendance. But a twenty per cent increase in public investment could produce a massive fifty-seven per cent addition to artistic output. This was music to the theatre community's ears. At last, someone had got the point. Attritional funding was ultimately counterproductive. An increase in subsidy would produce better value for money and release artistic energy. Bully for Boyden!

The results of Boyden were instantly visible both in the hard-pressed regions and in London. In the 2001 spending round there were exponential funding increases across the board. Manchester's Royal Exchange got a rise of thirty-six per cent, Derby Playhouse eighty-two per cent, London's Almeida ninety-six per cent , Salisbury Playhouse a hundred per cent, the Palace Theatre, Watford 147 per cent, London's Gate Theatre (admittedly starting from a tiny base) a staggering 381 per cent. Even if these increases inevitably bottomed out over the three-year cycle from 2003 to 2006, there was a sense that theatre was in business again. After decades of backs-to-the-wall funding and crisis management, theatres could now start to plan a rational, realistic, long-term programme. I recall Nicolas Kent, who as artistic director of London's Tricycle Theatre saw a subsidy of £291,576 in 2000 increase to one of £633,149 by 2003, spell out the difference the new money made: he could now create at least half a dozen in-house productions a year rather than the usual two supplemented by touring shows. It wasn't Utopia and salaries for actors and staff still remained at uncompetitive levels. But at least, thanks to Blair, Brown and the determined advocacy of both Boyden and Chris Smith, subsidised theatre recovered its ability to function. In the process it also proved, *pace* Mrs Thatcher, that there were a good many problems you could solve by throwing money at them.

Under New Labour, regional theatre was released from years of captivity. New money by itself, however, wasn't enough. There needed to be someone imaginative at the helm. And Sheffield Theatres – a troika combining the Crucible, its Studio and the Lyceum – showed just what could be done. In the past, Sheffield had been a problem area. Richard Eyre's diary entry recording a visit made in 1988 for an Arts Council assessment strikes a suitably gloomy note:

> To keep the work consistently good seems more difficult than ever. Resources to the regions have diminished and a whole generation of directors has stuck at the RSC and the NT without ever running regional theatres. And we've lost that haphazard apprenticeship for actors: those that might have done a year or two in a regional theatre now look for parts on TV, in films or the national companies while they're still at drama school.

Ten years on everything changed. Sheffield Theatres got a ninety-one per cent funding increase as part of the new financial deal. The appointment of Michael Grandage as Associate Director in December 1999 also led to a dramatic upsurge in fortune. Grandage was a good middle-range actor who had suddenly swapped careers to become a director. More importantly, he had a producer's instinct for what

worked and a total faith in Sheffield audiences to respond to excitingly cast classical theatre. He attracted Joseph Fiennes – fresh from the
movie, *Shakespeare in Love* – to the Crucible to play Marlowe's
poker-backed Edward II. He persuaded golden boy Kenneth Branagh,
who had scarcely been seen on the British stage since the disbandment
of Renaissance, to don the caliper as Shakespeare's Richard III. And he
enticed Derek Jacobi to Sheffield to play Prospero in *The Tempest* and
Philip II of Spain in Schiller's *Don Carlos*. This last was an extraordinary venture: a rare revival of a German classic staged by Grandage
with minimal furniture and designed by Christopher Oram with a
dark, claustrophobic power that evoked the idea of imperial Spain as
a religious prison. Following rave notices, it packed out the Crucible
in 2004 and transferred to the Gielgud in London for a sold-out
twelve-week run that could easily have been extended but for the
actors' other commitments. The real point, though, was that an austere masterpiece like *Don Carlos*, demanding a cast of fourteen actors,
would have been unthinkable in a regional theatre during the previous
ten years when retrenchment became a way of life – or even a form of
slow death.

It was a mark of Grandage's confidence, however, that he didn't
simply schedule star-led classics. One of his achievements was to
devote a four-week season in the summer of 2002 to Peter Gill, primarily as playwright but also as director: four old Gill plays in the Studio, a brand new one, *Original Sin*, in the Crucible. For a long time,
Gill had been one of the unsung heroes of British theatre. At the Royal
Court in the Seventies he'd rediscovered the plays of D. H. Lawrence.
He'd set up the Riverside Studios as a performance space and later
kickstarted the National Theatre Studio. His plays, largely dealing
with Welsh working-class life, had also achieved a cult following without ever gaining massive circulation. But 2002 proved to be a vintage
year for Gill. In January his English Touring Theatre production of his
own play, *The York Realist*, had swept triumphantly into the Royal
Court. It was a beautifully tender, honest account of a hesitantly loving relationship between a Yorkshire farm labourer and a London-
based theatre director. It was also a meditation on Englishness and the
relation between culture and class. After a visit to the York Mystery
Plays, the labourer's family were almost embarrassed to display their
enthusiasm for a project that grew out of their own community. 'It
was very Yorkshire, wasn't it,' cried Anne Reid as the labourer's moth-

er before carefully adding: 'Not that I mind.' Gill's understanding of Welsh working-class life emerged with equal clarity in the course of the Sheffield season. *Small Change* was a beautiful study of frustration and disappointment built around the drama of two boyhood friends and their mothers. *Kick For Touch* showed a mesmerising Ruth Gemmell as a Welsh woman torn between two men: the one to whom she was married, and his brother with whom she was in love. Only *Original Sin*, which translated Wedekind's Lulu into an eighteen-year-old boy on the prowl in eighteen-nineties London, disappointed. But Sheffield's Gill Festival showed just what could be achieved by giving extended exposure to a living writer. In Gill's case, you were able to trace the arc of his career, admire his ability to manipulate time and see how his belief in the inescapable influence of the past was a reflection of his own surprisingly puritanical Cardiff Catholic working-class origins. One only wished more writers could get the seasonal treatment: an honour we reserve exclusively for Shakespeare.

Admittedly not all theatres survived the regional shake-up that followed the advent of new money. The Swan in Worcester, which had served its community decently, was excluded from the hand-out and sadly closed. The Chester Gateway also turned from a producing theatre into a multipurpose receiving house. But most theatres profited from Boyden's benison. Birmingham Rep, built in 1971 as a nine-hundred-seat single-arc auditorium, had struggled under a succession of artistic directors. Yet the combination of a grant increase of fifty-six per cent and a new director in Jonathan Church, who succeeded Bill Alexander in 2000, gave the Rep fresh impetus. Not the least of Church's gifts was to prove that there was an audience in Birmingham for political theatre. He revived the 'Hare Trilogy', discovering new resonance in *The Absence of War*. He imported from America's West Coast two plays by David Edgar, *Continental Divide*, about the current state of US politics. And he followed that with a satire by Alistair Beaton, *Follow My Leader*, about the Bush–Blair collusion over the Iraq War. Everywhere you looked there was new life. Derby Playhouse, long in the doldrums, not only did its first Shakespeare in years. It also offered an unusual version of *The Entertainer*, starring David Threlfall and spliced with black-and-white newsreel footage of the Suez debacle. Osborne's play cropped up again in Liverpool where Gemma Bodinetz and Deborah Aydon revived the flagging fortunes of the Playhouse and Everyman Theatres with an opening season that included

Calderón, Coward, Behan and new plays by local writers in the shape of Katie Douglas and Tony Green. And even before the influx of new money, Jude Kelly countered the pessimism of the Nineties by turning the West Yorkshire Playhouse into a venue that, while serving a local audience, acquired a national identity: its profile was raised even higher in 1998 when Ian McKellen headed a company offering a three-play repertory of *The Seagull, Present Laughter* and *The Tempest*. A post-Boyden grant increase of forty-seven per cent enabled Kelly to hand over to Ian Brown in 2002 a model regional theatre mixing new plays, classics, musicals and large-scale community projects.

But, if regional theatre was revivified under Blair, London's West End was faced with a series of running crises. The biggest problem concerned the decaying structure and rotting fabric of the playhouses themselves. In 2003 the Theatres Trust commissioned a report into the capital's commercial theatres which confirmed what habitual playgoers had long known from their own strained eyes, cramped limbs and frayed tempers. That sixty per cent of West End theatres had seats from which the stage was not fully visible. That forty-eight per cent had inadequate foyers and bars. That forty per cent needed major restoration work. That twenty-six per cent had inadequate legroom. The report went on to praise individuals such as Cameron Mackintosh who was spending thirty million pounds refurbishing the theatres under his control. Following his restoration of the Prince Edward, Mackintosh turned both the Prince of Wales and the Strand (rechristened the Novello at the end of 2005) into bright, fresh, spacious venues that it was a pleasure to enter. But the Theatres Trust estimated that it would cost at least £250 million over the next fifteen years to ensure that West End theatres were safe, usable and attractive. The question was who was to pay. Not all theatre owners had the deep pockets and altruistic instinct of Mackintosh. Accordingly, the Theatres Trust called on the government to intervene: a simple rewriting of the Lottery rules would enable public money to be spent on modernising London's theatres. And, while £250 million was undoubtedly a lot of bread, it didn't look so much when set in a wider economic context. The West End theatre generated over £200 million in tax each year. It also produced an estimated £400 million spending in the wider economy. Although in the past I would have been sceptical about public money being spent on privately owned theatres, it seemed the only solution; and, with London preparing for a massive facelift in time for the 2012 Olympics, work needed to start soon on refurbishing the capital's decaying playhouses.

That in itself raised a larger question. What exactly was the role of West End theatre in a changing world? Did we still need forty-two central London theatres, thirty-eight of them occupying an area around a third of a square mile? And, if we did, what should we put in them? Andre Ptasynski, Chief Executive of Really Useful Theatres, came refreshingly clean when he suggested that London probably had as many as six superfluous theatres. The problem was that some were listed buildings. Others, such as the Duchess, were of an ideal size for small-scale plays. And, although economic logic was on Ptasynski's side, everyone becomes a sentimental conservationist at the prospect of a disappearing theatre. Would we really want to see the Garrick, the Apollo or the Lyric transformed into a gaming house, lapdancing venue or Wetherspoon's bar? Even the temporary closure of the tiny Arts Theatre in Great Newport Street, with its long and honourable record stretching back to the Alec Clunes–Peter Hall Forties and Fifties, was a sad loss. The real problem with the West End – or so it struck me – was not the excess of venues. It was the dearth of enterprising and imaginative producers, following in the wake of the Mackintoshes and Lloyd Webbers, the Codrons and Kenwrights, capable of filling them. New young producers, such as Sonia Friedman and Matthew Byam Shaw, had emerged with the capacity either to devise or import attractive projects. But the real flair and imagination, in the modern world, seemed to have fled from the private to the public sector.

The best one could say about the West End in the Blair years was that it had periods of fitful vitality. In 1997 it was cheering to find *Shopping and Fucking*, *Popcorn* and *Skylight* all playing simultaneously to predominantly young audiences. A year later the Almeida expanded its empire into the West End to include a season at the Albery of Racine's *Phèdre* and *Britannicus*: an event about as likely, according to one critic, as a Ray Cooney retrospective at the Bouffes du Nord. But what made it possible was the drawing power of Diana Rigg, who did everything but chew the carpet in order to give the customers their money's worth. And, over the years, imports from America or from our own Donmar or Almeida gave the illusion that the West End was still a place of serious dramatic endeavour. In 2005, for instance, it was possible to see *Death of a Salesman*, *Don Carlos*, *Mary Stuart* and *Hedda Gabler* in the West End. 2006 was the year of the musical, as tune-and-toe extravaganzas poured out in ceaseless profusion: *Daddy Cool*, *Wicked*, *Spamalot*, *Cabaret*, *Dirty Dancing*, *Porgy and Bess*, *The Sound Of Music*. What could be wrong with a private sector that one year could offer a wide range of classics and the next a profusion of musical crowd-pleasers?

The short answer was 'Plenty'. The dramatists who had once been the backbone of Shaftesbury Avenue – Alan Bennett, Tom Stoppard, Michael Frayn, Simon Gray, Ronald Harwood and John Mortimer – now either owed their prime allegiance to the subsidised theatre or had sought other literary outlets. Even when one of them did write a potentially commercial play, it had little chance unless fronted by a Hollywood or TV star. A classic case was Simon Gray's *The Late Middle Classes* which, despite being directed by Harold Pinter and boasting a first-rate cast headed by Harriet Walter and Nicholas Woodeson, failed to get any nearer to central London than Watford and Richmond. It provided Gray with scope for one of his biliously entertaining autobiographical books, *Enter a Fox*, but was deemed less financially viable than *Boyband* which usurped its allotted slot at the Gielgud. Even Alan Ayckbourn, a mainstay of West End theatre since the late Sixties, ceased to be a safe bet and finally lost patience with the commercial ineptitude and bungling deviousness of the new generation of producers over a trilogy called *Damsels in Distress*. Originating in Scarborough, this was a highly enjoyable trio of plays all set in a chic Docklands apartment and deploying the skills of a versatile seven-strong cast. All the actors were good but Alison Pargeter was outstanding. First she was a gawky schoolgirl posing as a teenage tart. Then she was a sexually desperate actress caught up in some secret service malarkey. Finally she was a good-hearted gangster's moll. When the plays came to the Duchess Theatre in September 2002, many critics compared them favourably to the Tom Stoppard trilogy, *The Coast of Utopia*, which had opened a few weeks previously. Yet the delight in seeing the original Scarborough cast display its diversity was short-lived. When one of the three works, *RolePlay*, was singled out for special praise, the producers jettisoned the repertory principle without informing the author himself. Ayckbourn was left incandescent with fury and vowed never to work in the West End again. Instead he established new relationships with the Yvonne Arnaud, Guildford and the

Orange Tree, Richmond, which he regarded as ideal bases for his work. The truth is that the West End needed Ayckbourn more than Ayckbourn needed the West End; and the loss of his talent was a symbol of a commercial theatre that was becoming increasingly inhospitable to living writers.

Did it matter? As long as the box-office tills were ticking over merrily and people were packing into the West End, wasn't that enough? But a West End dominated, as it was in 2006, by no fewer than twenty-six musicals was one that was ceasing to offer the range and variety it once had. In essence, it was becoming more like Broadway where a basic diet of musicals was leavened by the occasional play imported from the non-profit sector. Even straight plays were also increasingly dependent on the presence of star names from film or TV. The intertwining of theatre and television became particularly conspicuous in 2006. The well-intentioned idea of discovering a new West End playwright through a Channel 4 series called *The Play's The Thing* backfired disastrously when the winning entry by fifty-one-year-old Kate Betts was exposed to critical gaze. The play itself, *On The Third Day*, might have been received quite calmly if it had been seen at the Bush or Hampstead. But, after all the ballyhoo surrounding the TV series, the play was savaged by the majority of critics and died a fairly speedy, unlamented death. Even more controversial was the use of the TV reality show *How Do You Solve A Problem Like Maria?* to discover an unknown name to play the lead in Andrew Lloyd Webber's production of *The Sound of Music*. Connie Fisher, who got the part, was the people's Maria in that a million and a half viewers voted for her. But casting by popular acclaim seemed a slap in the face for hardened professional performers everywhere and for the authority of the show's director, presented with a fait accompli. It also created a dangerous precedent. After *How Do You Solve A Problem Like Maria?* what next? *You Too Can Be A Lear* or possibly, in the quest for a unknown Ibsen star, *Taking a Hedda?* It would be palpably foolish for theatre to shun or ignore TV. Some of us felt there were equal dangers for theatre in clambering into bed with it.

One way and another the West End, whatever its changes, survived the Blair years. But the big story lay elsewhere. If the Blair decade was defined by anything, in theatrical terms, it was by the post-Boyden boost to the subsidised sector and the resurgence of political drama.

Obviously the two things were not unconnected. More money meant it was possible for the theatre to resume its oppositional role. But the main factors in the reinvention of political theatre were disillusion with New Labour spin and dismay at the consequences of the Bush–Blair foreign policy. At first the Blairite belief in 'humanitarian intervention' in the world's trouble spots was given a certain credence. It was even naively hoped that Blair's support for President Bush and the neocons surrounding him might lead to American prosecution of the road-map for peace in the Middle East. But, in the end, everything fell apart. Military intervention in Iraq and the toppling of Saddam Hussein produced only bloodshed and chaos. Under-resourced troops were left fighting a seemingly unwinnable war against the Taliban in Afghanistan. And the ill-conceived, Bush-led, post 9/11 'war on terror', enthusiastically endorsed by Tony Blair, predictably acted as a recruiting agent for al-Qaida. As Jonathan Freedland wrote in *The Guardian* in September 2006, 'The horrific truth is that the application of the Bush doctrine has helped vindicate Osama bin Laden and his ilk in the eyes of the Arab and Muslim world.' Harold Pinter, John Pilger and many others dubbed Tony Blair a 'war criminal' for the deaths his policies provoked. A perfectly tenable viewpoint. But to me Blair towards the end of his term seemed less a contemptible than a tragic figure: a political equivalent of Ibsen's Gregers Werle in *The Wild Duck*, whose idealistic interventions produced fatal consequences for everyone else. But, whatever history's judgement on the Blair decade, there is little doubt that it reactivated political theatre. In itself 'political theatre' is a vague term, implying something monolithic. But the striking fact about the Blair years, where political theatre became a vital necessity rather than an optional luxury, was the variety of forms it took: Factual, Satirical, Historical and Classical.

The fact vs. fiction debate had been going on since the Sixties; and no sensible person would deny there is room for both forms. If we watch documentaries as well as made-up stories on television, read non-fiction as well as fiction, why should theatre be immune to the enticements of fact? But the argument acquired new urgency in the Nineties, which witnessed an extraordinary resurgence of factual theatre. It was as if people felt a growing distrust with politicians, press, and the new rolling news outlets in which an endlessly repeated 'Newsak' replaced the aural wallpaper of Muzak. Feeling that once-reliable sources of information were either tainted or untrustworthy, audiences increasingly turned to theatre for raw information about public events. But no movement happens without some inspirational figure behind it. And, with what came to be known as 'verbatim theatre', it was Nicolas Kent at Kilburn's Tricycle Theatre who led the way with some assistance from Max Stafford-Clark at Out of Joint. Kent belonged to a familiar group in British theatre: white, middle-class, Cambridge-educated. But he was also a radical fired by a strong sense of social justice and a fascination with actuality. This first bore fruit in 1993 with *Half The Picture*: co-written by John McGrath and Richard Norton-Taylor, it reconstructed the Scott inquiry into the sale of arms to Iraq with dazzling precision. It was followed in 1998 by a production based on the Nuremberg Trials and by *Srebenica*, offering edited transcripts of the International Criminal Tribunal hearings into the Bosnian civil war.

It was, however, *The Colour of Justice* in 1999 that really showed the potential of verbatim theatre: that it could operate simultaneously as source of information, work of art and instrument of social change. The play was based on the Macpherson inquiry into the Metropolitan Police's handling of the killing of Stephen Lawrence, a black teenager stabbed to death in south London in 1993. Out of the eleven hundred pages of transcripts – reported on but never televised – Richard Norton-Taylor fashioned an enthralling, tight-knit play that posed endless questions. Why had the police failed to administer first aid to the dying Lawrence? Why were the murder suspects, named by a police informant, not put under surveillance until three days after the attack? Would the police have acted differently had it been a young white male found bleeding to death at an Eltham bus-stop? But the play was much more than an indictment of the Metropolitan Police. It also opened our eyes and ears to the racial hatred in our society. The most shocking moment came when one of the murder suspects was asked to give evidence. His stonewalling answers to questions from Macpherson and Michael Mansfield QC revealed little but smug contempt for an inquiry that had no judicial power. But we heard about the cache of arms found in the house where the suspect lived. We also heard taped extracts from conversations inside the house. 'Every nigger', said the suspect's brother, 'should have their arms and legs chopped up and left with fucking stumps.' It was one of the most shocking utterances ever heard on a British stage. And, as the witness left the stand, Michael Culver, who was representing Macpherson, shielded his eyes in an involuntary gesture of disgust.

Norton-Taylor had not invented anything. He had simply selected crucial incidents or testimonies. But David Hare, in a provocative essay entitled 'Why Fabulate?', got to the heart of the matter:

> In that act of editing, he [Norton-Taylor] laid before a live audience all the subtleties and intricacies of British racism, all its forms and gradations, with a clarity which I had never seen emulated by television, documentary or newspaper. The play seemed not just a rebuke to the British theatre for its drift towards less and less important subject matter: it also seemed to expose other forms by the sheer seriousness and intensity with which it was able to bring the theatre's special scrutiny to bear.

It did so precisely because fact was fashioned with great dramatic skill. By peeling off successive layers of official evasion, lies and incompetence, *The Colour of Justice* followed the classic rules of Ibsenite drama. Like Ibsen's social dramas, it also did its work in the world. It acquired a life beyond the Tricycle when it played in the West End and on tour. Eventually it was also shown on BBC2. That in itself was proof of theatre's political power. No cameras had been allowed into the Macpherson inquiry: only when it was recreated by a small north London theatre was it made available to the nation at large. As Kent, who co-directed *The Colour of Justice*, said:

> It really did change things. I don't just want to cause controversy. I want to highlight injustices and move towards a solution. The Stephen Lawrence play was part of the solution . . . it changed many people's views on the issue of racism. It's even used as teaching material by the Met.

Not all verbatim shows achieved quite that impact. *Justifying War*, which Norton-Taylor adapted in 2003 from the Hutton inquiry into the death of the government scientist, Dr David Kelly, took us behind closed doors. But, while undeniably interesting, it pre-empted the publication of Hutton's own surprisingly pro-government report. *Guantanamo*, compiled by Victoria Brittain and Gillian Slovo from interviews with detainees in the American prison camp for suspected terrorists, was far more shocking. Where previous Tricycle shows had revealed the intricate workings of the tribunal system, the power of *Guantanamo* lay in its exposure of what Lord Steyn called the 'utter lawlessness' of the discredited American prison camp. *Bloody Sunday*, which appeared in 2005, was also deeply disturbing. Drawn from the Saville inquiry into the deaths of thirteen civil-rights marchers in Derry in 1972, it revealed the enormity of what happened on that particular day and its dire political consequences. 'This is not the time for TV-style documentaries about politics,' said Deborah Warner, who happened to be directing *Julius Caesar* at the time. But Warner set up a false and needless distinction. No one denied the political relevance of classic drama or the right of living dramatists to create their own fictions. What the Tricycle tribunal plays showed was that political theatre could relay facts, break news, stir consciences. Sometimes the post-show discussion was just as important as the play. When, late in 2006, the Tricyle staged a series of short plays about Darfur, it was the debate afterwards that exposed a profound ideological divide about the best way of dealing with a humanitarian crisis.

Within the broad framework of factual theatre, there was also scope for different approaches. The Tricycle focused on verbatim accounts of tribunals. David Hare's *Via Dolorosa*, first presented by the exiled Royal Court in 1998, was a brilliant piece of subjective reportage performed by the author himself. And it was partly that which made it so moving: although Hare proved a perfectly competent actor, his lack of drama-school technique added to the sense of authenticity in the same way that a poet's rendition of his own work often surpasses that of a practised reader. The evening also took on the air of a personal pilgrimage. As a good reporter, Hare told us a lot about life in the Middle East. About the conflicts within, as well as between, the Israeli and Palestinian communities. About the gulf between secular, liberal Jews and those families living in the Occupied Territories who felt they had a biblical claim to the land. About the contrast between the endemic corruption of Yasser Arafat's PLO and the intellectual rigour of Arab intellectuals. In exploring the internal conflicts, Hare never let us forget a fundamental truth: 'that driving from Israel into the Gaza Strip is like moving from California into Bangladesh'. But, while the information was valuable, it was Hare's personal investment in the material that made this an exceptional piece of political theatre. You felt that Hare had faithfully reported what he had seen and heard. But you also sensed the palpable relief with which he returned to his Hampstead home after a series of scorching encounters with people living in a political crucible where conviction and certainty exact their own terrible price.

Via Dolorosa also raised a fascinating philosophical question. Does there come a point where the material being investigated is so monumental that art becomes an irrelevance? Visiting Yad Vashem, the museum of the Holocaust, Hare was struck by the idea that the sculptures and paintings on view seemed superfluous when one was confronted by the matchless horror of fact. It is a serious point of view. And we have all sat through enough bad Holocaust drama and cinema to know what Hare means. But when some years later I asked Harold Pinter, in a public interview, if there was any way in which art could encompass the Holocaust, he thought for a very long time and then cited the poetry of Paul Celan and Nelly Sachs. And the real answer to Hare's question is that, at a certain level of achievement, documentary itself acquires the lineaments of art. Primo Levi's *If This Is A Man*, Claud Lenzmann's *Shoah* and Marcel Ophuls' *The Sorrow and the Pity* are all, in the technical sense, non-fiction or documentary works. Yet, in the way they are shaped and presented, they also make a momentous aesthetic impact. I am not placing *Via Dolorosa* in that category nor, I guess, would Hare himself wish me to do so. But, if it worked as theatre, it was for the same reason they worked as literature and cinema. Although Hare may have had to will himself into being an actor, *Via Dolorosa* was constructed with all the dramatic technique at his command. In short, fact, no less than fiction, requires the harmony, balance and proportion of art.

Factual theatre – including such notable Out of Joint works as *The Permanent Way* and *Talking To Terrorists* and the Royal Court's *My Name Is Rachel Corrie* – was a key strand of the Blair years. It was as if theatre, in the constant need to justify itself, had to address big issues. Audiences also craved pure fact without the mediation of media egoists like Paxman and Humphrys. But, alongside the resurgence of fact, satire also made a comeback. For a long time, the genre was regarded as the natural province of television where it could be quick, sharp and topical: *Spitting Image*, in the Thatcher–Major years, showed the power of puppet caricatures and, under Blair, it was worth putting up with the feeble TV mimicry of Rory Bremner for the probing duologues of his accomplices, John Bird and John Fortune. But theatre also got in on the act by showing that it could explore the weaknesses of the Blair Project at greater length and in more depth. It all started with Alistair Beaton, himself a practised writer for TV satire shows as well as a serious Russian scholar. His play *Feelgood* opened at Hampstead Theatre in January 2001 five months before Labour's second election victory. It was a major event in that it became the first play to attack New Labour's obsessive news management and sacrifice of principle to the demands of power. Like all good satire, Beaton's play was based on a moral positive: a belief in the need to return to a long-term socialist strategy based on redistribution of wealth. It was also scathingly funny. The hero, a lightly disguised version of Alastair Campbell with a hint of Peter Mandelson, was a control-freak press secretary who would stop at nothing in his desire to manipulate the news agenda: at one point, you saw him happily shopping the Deputy Prime Minister in order to prevent Green activists hogging the six o'clock news bulletins. Obviously there was a malign pleasure in watching Henry Goodman's hip-swivelling performance as this back-stage Machiavel. But the play hit Labour where it hurt; and it ended with an imagined Tony Blair conference speech that was so deadly accurate – 'what we want is a job culture, not a yob culture' – that it sounded as much prophetic as parodic.

Beaton's later post-Iraq satire, *Follow My Leader*, failed to make the same impact: it lapsed into the smug certainty which it derided in Bush and Blair themselves. Beaton had, however, once more made theatrical satire a possibility; and where he led, others followed. The torch was taken up by a young Oxford-educated writer-director, Justin Butcher, who was driven by indignation about the Iraq war to stage a trio of satirical revues all based on existing works. The first of them, *The Madness of George Dubya*, was easily the most successful. It opened at a tiny north London venue, Theatro Technis, in January 2003, two months before the invasion of Iraq occurred. It didn't take a genius to work out that war was inevitable, but Butcher shrewdly tapped into Britain's oppositional mood and on the first night the audience cheered the play to the echo, as if relieved to hear someone say in public what they themselves believed in their hearts. It helped, of course, that Butcher deployed a first-rate prototype: Terry Southern's script for Stanley Kubrick's movie, *Dr Strangelove*. So we had the crazed head of a US British air base deriding UN weapons inspectors as 'pinko, degenerate subversives' and itching to launch a pre-emptive nuclear strike against Saddam Hussein. But Butcher went far beyond his cinematic model to explore the history of Britain's relationship with Iraq, from our installation of a puppet regime under King Faisal to our supply of weaponry during the war with Iran. Butcher's play was lively and funny but it pinned down the essential contradiction of the Bush–Blair invasion: that by making a military strike against terror, we actually increased its likelihood.

Factual and satirical theatre were both galvanised by public events. So too was the history play: a genre that brings a speculative imagination to recorded events. And, again, this was something that happened in both small and large venues. Descend into the converted crypt of a Wren church in the City of London in 2003 and you could see David Williams' *Warcrime*: a play that re-enacted the horrors of Slobodan Milosevic's policy of ethnic cleansing. At the other end of the spectrum, the National Theatre in 2004 staged David Hare's *Stuff Happens*, described as 'a history play which happens to centre on very recent history'. Hare's theme was Iraq; and what he showed was the Bush administration's preoccupation with regime change, its cynical use of the tragic events of 9/11 as a pretext for invasion and its crushing of internal opposition from Colin Powell who, as Secretary of State, was the one senior figure who saw the military folly of a pre-emptive war. Some columnists – notably Polly Toynbee, who thought the play should be called *Stuff Happened*, and Mary Riddell – argued that Hare's play had already been overtaken by events: the growing chaos on the ground in Iraq and terrorist outrages in other sectors such as the slaughter of three hundred children in a Russian school in Beslan. But it seemed somewhat perverse to argue that a history play dealt with the past. A more serious objection was to the mixture of verbatim dialogue with imaginative speculation. But historians since Thucydides, dramatists since Aeschylus and novelists since Sir Walter Scott had established the right to interweave the easily authenticated with the personally invented. In practical terms, it was also not difficult to work out when Hare was using recorded speech and when, as in a private conversation between George Bush and Colin Powell, he was relying on his dramatic imagination. What Hare did, successfully, was to examine the political processes that prompted the United States, with British support, to go to war. And what too few remarked upon was the extraordinary fact of the play itself. Here was a heavily subsidised National Theatre, under the direction of Nicholas Hytner, using its most prominent space to examine the causes of the most divisive war in British society since Suez. It would have been unimaginable in most countries, and was a measure of the British theatre's maturity and political alertness in its ability to react swiftly to public events.

Hytner, who himself directed *Stuff Happens*, was in fact a cultural hero of the later Blair years. Taking over a National Theatre that was fiscally prudent but only spasmodically adventurous, he rapidly turned it into a building that seemed to mirror the concerns of the nation itself. Suceeding Trevor Nunn in 2003, Hytner's first and boldest gesture, achieved with the help of sponsorship from Travelex, was to offer two thirds of the seats in the Olivier Theatre for £10: a radical move that enlarged the National's constituency and changed the ethos of theatregoing. Hytner gave flesh and meaning to the Blairite policy of social inclusion. At the same time, he showed how the classic repertory could be explored for its political resonances and even turned into a sustained critique of government. Hytner's opening production in the Olivier was of *Henry V*: staged only three months after the coalition forces' premature celebration of 'victory' in Iraq, his production brimmed with topical life. It not only addressed the meaning of nationhood. It also, through its use of modern dress, constantly reminded us that Shakespeare was portraying the multiple facets of a war of occupation based on legally dubious foundations. 'All the youth of England are on fire,' announced Penny Downie's cardiganed Chorus: a claim instantly undermined by the image of a pub-based Nym zapping TV channels and opting for the snooker rather than the bellicose rhetoric of Adrian Lester's king. In France itself Lester's morale-boosting cry of 'Once more unto the breach' was met with a universal groan from his battered troops. Embedded TV journalists conspicuously failed to report Henry's savage threats to the citizens of Harfleur: at the same time, the king's infamous order to kill the French prisoners was met with mutinous refusal by the soldiers until the Welsh toady, Fluellen, came along and did the job for them. Not for the first time, it struck me that you could learn a lot about the history of post-war Britain simply by studying productions of *Henry V*: the journey from Olivier's romantically heroic 1945 movie to Hytner's portrait of a nation divided by a messy, violent and ill-founded war reflected a startling shift in attitudes in under sixty years.

And if Shakespeare offered a direct reflection of a changing Britain, so too did the Greeks. In the immediate post-Second World War world Sophocles was the favoured figure, largely for his portraits of the suffering individual *in extremis* and the opportunities he afforded heroic actors. Then, as our own domestic troubles in Northern Ireland escalated and as the Israeli–Palestinian conflict worsened, we looked to Aeschylus for images of the cyclical nature of revenge. Latterly, however, it has been Euripides, with his pervasive scepticism about the gods and war, who has seemed to accord with the contemporary mood: hence the extraordinary rash of revivals in the wake of the Iraq war. Katie Mitchell directed a fine *Iphigenia at Aulis* at the National in 2004 which prompted Susannah Clapp to write in *The Observer*: 'A British audience looking for a reflection of itself will find it in the chorus who observe destruction and are helpless to prevent it; who warn and go unheeded.' The following months also brought us not one but two revivals of *Hecuba*: a classic study of the aftermath of war. The Donmar production, starring Clare Higgins, was the more successful. But Tony Harrison's translation, for an ill-fated RSC version, was the more immediate. Priam's son announced that his father feared that Troy would 'end up occupied by the Greek coalition', and the captive Trojan women recalled how the slaughter-gutted Greeks cried, 'let's finish it off and fuck off home.' The Iraq war made Greek tragedy, and Euripides especially, essential. Both the illegality of the war and its disastrous aftermath also turned political theatre, in all its manifold forms, into a necessity rather than an optional extra.

Iraq will always be part of Blair's legacy as Suez is of Anthony Eden's. Even more so, in fact. Blair's belief in 'humanitarian intervention' helped turn Iraq into a permanent disaster zone, cost countless lives and destabilised the Middle East while doing nothing to diminish international terrorism. But the unacknowledged, and slightly uncomfortable, paradox of the Blair decade is that it was very good for theatre after the wholesale depredations of the Thatcherite years. Blair's foreign-policy failures stirred the British theatre to creative protest. And, once Blair and Brown shed the cautious financial pragmatism of 1997–99, theatre, like the arts in general, experienced a sense of renewal. New money changed the cultural climate and had many positive effects: the regional revival, the expansion of the repertory, the quest for new audiences through cheap tickets. People often attacked New Labour for its focus on accessibility and social inclusion and accused the Arts Council of judging companies less by their artistic excellence than by their ability to tick politically correct boxes. But British theatre, if it was not to ossify, urgently needed to become more representative of the nation at large without compromising its capacity to deliver high-quality work. And, as Blairism reached its twilight period, it was possible to detect ways in which theatre had become both more socially inclusive and more artistically inquisitive.

When one talks of inclusion, one is really speaking euphemistically of race; and British theatre's record in this area had long been chequered. There had been spasmodic flurries of work, from the late Fifties onwards, from the first generation of Caribbean immigrants including Errol John, Barry Reckord, Mustapha Matura and Michael Abensetts. Later, British-born black and Asian playwrights such as Tunde Ikoli, Trevor Rhone, Edgar White, Hanif Kureishi, Winsome Pinnock and Ayub Khan-Din had addressed the tensions that existed amongst first- and second-generation immigrant communities. Companies devoted to culturally diverse work had also come and gone, with only Tara Arts, under Jatinder Verma, and Tamasha weathering the various funding crises. But, unless one followed such companies religiously or was a constant attender at the Royal Court, Stratford East, the Tricycle or the Young Vic, you could easily assume we were a racially monolithic society in which ethnic minorities lived largely invisible lives.

That situation was squarely addressed at a two-day conference that took place at Nottingham Playhouse in June 2001, set up by the theatre itself and the Arts Council. It produced the Eclipse Report and contained fierce condemnations of British theatre's alleged racism. A young director, Femi Elufowoju Jnr, said: 'It is an indictment of the profession that there is not one Black or Asian director of a repertory theatre or a producing house in the entire country.' Tyrone Huggins pointed out that no black actor could enjoy the same career trajectory as his white counterparts. David K. S. Tse, artistic director of the East Asian Yellow Earth Theatre, recalled his own experiences as an actor: 'More often than not,' he said, 'one is there to give a white-led project an international feel . . . One director at the BBC asked me to play a character in a "typically Oriental way, you know, inscrutable".' But perhaps the most poignant comment came from Rukhsana Ahmad who pointed to the problem of living and working in an artistic ghetto: 'Of being confined to a playpen where we play our own games of pretend art that no one can assess because they have only perceived us as "the other".' In short, the Nottingham Conference pointed to the sense that most black and Asian artists felt of exclusion from the mainstream, of existing on the margins.

No one could claim that there has been a total revolution since the Eclipse Conference. There still remains a shocking dearth of black and Asian artistic directors, chief executives and board members. But at

least modern Britain's multiculturalism is being more widely acknowledged and writers drawn from ethnic minorities are enjoying a higher
profile. There were two significant breakthroughs in 2005 when
Kwame Kwei-Armah's *Elmina's Kitchen*, which dealt with the realities
of life in Hackney's 'Murder Mile', and a musical about the Fifties
generation of Caribbean immigrants, *The Big Life*, both played in the
West End: shockingly, it was the first time any of us could remember
an indigenous black play or musical enjoying commercial exposure.
Kwei-Armah's fine play had originated at the National and *The Big
Life* at Stratford East, but their transfer was an occasion for genuine
celebration. Alongside these were a number of other encouraging por-
tents. Roy Williams has emerged over the last decade as a prolific
chronicler of black urban youth: what he pins down brilliantly are the
tensions within, as well as between, communities and the resentment
often felt by black underachievers for those who have got on and got
out. If Williams is a realist at heart, Debbie Tucker Green is a young
black writer with a poetic gift that reminds one of the African-American
Ntozake Shange. Tucker Green also has a Sarah Kane-like talent for
shock tactics, as she showed in *Stoning Mary*, which imagined what
might happen if the crises afflicting Africa today were transposed to
modern Britain. And the power of factual drama was grasped by Tanika Gupta in *Gladiator Games*, which was widely praised at both the
Sheffield Crucible and Stratford East in 2005. This was a play that
explored, with forensic precision, the death in custody of Zahid
Mubarek, an Asian teenager who had been sentenced to ninety days
for a minor offence and who was killed by his violently racist cellmate.
It was only persistent pressure from the Mubarek family that led to a
government inquiry; and, as with the Stephen Lawrence case, the theatre played a vital role in heightening public awareness of a racial scandal. None of this means that Paradise has been regained or that the
British theatre is anything like as racially inclusive as it might be. It is
also obvious that the so-called 'war on terror' has led to terrifying tensions within Britain between the mass of the population and militant
Islamic groups: tensions that produced the London bombings of July
2005 and an alleged plot to blow up a number of transatlantic airlin-
ers in the summer of 2006. A whole sequence of events, many of them
relating to Blair's own foreign policy, have made Britain a nervous,
edgy place in which Muslims are often viewed with suspicion as if
tainted by collective guilt. But, if theatre is to escape from its former

oppressive whiteness and explore what it means to live in a multicul-tural society, it will only be because writers of genuine talent emerge; and the signs are that there is a new generation of dedicated truth-tellers who have escaped from the ghetto so vividly defined by Rukhsana Ahmad at the Eclipse Conference.

I would go further and say that these young black and Asian writers are offering us vital social evidence every bit as important – probably more so – than that provided by their white counterparts. What is more, they rejoice in the power of language. And, if I stress this, it is because the authority of text-based work has been increasingly chal-lenged in recent years by the growth of what is variously described as 'physical' or 'visual' theatre. This is a movement that has undeniably widened the vocabulary of theatre, liberated generations of actors from traditional inhibitions and produced some good work. At its very best, it has led to a harmonious alliance of text and image and, from several examples in recent years, I would cite a memorable pair. The first was *Mnemonic*, a show conceived by Simon McBurney and produced by Complicité in 2000, which used the company's kaleido-scopic skills to explore the nature of memory and which skilfully inter-wove two stories: one involved a woman (played by the late Katrin Cartlidge) in a trans-European quest in search of her lost father, the other concerned the corpse of a Neolithic man discovered in 1991 in a glacier on the Austrian–Italian border. Eventually the two stories con-verged, as if to suggest that the history of Europe over the past five thousand years had been one of constant migration and upheaval. This was an unforgettable piece of theatre that showed how a troupe that had started out doing improvised physical comedy had matured to the point where it could explore complex ideas. And in the autumn of 2006 the Lyric Hammersmith staged an astonishing adaptation of Kafka's short story, *Metamorphosis*. This represented a fusion of the talents of Gisli Orn Gardasson, exuberant star of an Icelandic compa-ny called Vesturport who had visited Britain with productions of *Romeo and Juliet* and *Woyzeck*, and our own David Farr. The result was a radical reinvention of Kafka's famous fable about a man who wakes up to find himself transformed into a giant insect. Clever tricks were played with visual perspective. Gardasson's Gregor Samsa expressed his transformation by hanging from the ceiling and leaping from one precarious toehold to another. But the dazzling physical invention was at the service of an idea: that Kafka's story, written in

395

1912, offered a prophetic vision of the European nightmares to come and that Gregor Samsa, marginalised, isolated and finally destroyed by his family, provided a specific symbol of the persecuted Jewish race. This was visual theatre endowed with a clear political message.

If I am sceptical about much that is categorised as 'physical' or 'visual' theatre, it is for several reasons. The most basic is that all good theatre, from *The Oresteia* to *Noises Off*, depends on a fusion of text and image. We 'read' a play semiotically through its visual signifiers as well as through the language spoken. To create a separate area of theatre that is primarily 'visual', and to endow it with a sanctified purity as many of its apologists do, is simply to create a meaningless ghetto. What we loosely call 'physical' or 'visual' theatre also seems to me essentially conservative. It rarely does anything to change the situation, stir one's conscience or alert one to the injustices of the wider world. More often than not it offers a mildly titillatory sensory experience that leads to frequent use of that overworked critical word, 'scary'. A classic example, which symbolises many more, was a show called *Tropicana*, staged by the Shunt collective in the vaults under London Bridge station in the winter of 2004. I had heard Shunt spoken of with quasi-religious awe by its many admirers. It had also attracted the attention of Nicholas Hytner, who lent this particular production the imprimatur, and some of the resources, of the National Theatre. But what did one actually find? We, the audience, were taken on a mystery tour through the subterranean vaults beneath the Tube station. At first we seemed to descend in a lift to fathomless depths, although this turned out to be a mere illusion. Milling around in the underground darkness, we found ourselves gaping at surreal images. A horizontal elevator floated past. Feathered showgirls loomed out of the gloom. Disembodied feet passed by. Eventually we found ourselves in a cavern where chorines danced acrobatically around a hearse from which tepid beer was disbursed. After a suitable interval, we were invited to sit in a sepulchral operating theatre where a team of mock doctors jokily dissected a corpse, hacked their way through the bones and produced a number of bizarre objects from its innards. After half an hour or more of this lame student-revue stuff, we were then decanted into the Tropicana Bar for a drink and finally released into the reassuring bustle of the London night. But how had the show changed us? For some, assuming a *faux-naïf* wonderment, the show offered a magical sense of disorientation; but so does a fairground ride on a ghost train or a trip to the London Dungeon. For others, I assume the show was simply a prelude to a drink with fellow travellers in the bar afterwards; and, while there is nothing wrong with that, I feel that theatre should offer something more than the facilities of a dating agency. I seize on this one example because it is sadly typical. But, while I accept that theatre is a vast mansion with many different rooms, I find that this particular kind of let's-all-go-on-a-journey experience affords little illumination. Although supposedly appealing to our sense of adventure, what it really offers is infantile shock and sensation for jaded theatrical appetites.

Theatre is full of different possibilities; and I have no wish to deny people their pleasures. What concerns me is the growing assumption that the future of theatre lies in physical or visual work and that site-specific events create a frisson impossible to reproduce in conventional playhouses: that it is somehow more meaningful to take your audience on a journey round a disused railway station or to the top of a tower-block and give them glimpses of angels than it is to do a boring old play by Shakespeare, Chekhov or Beckett. For me the glory of theatre lies in the prospect of an encounter with a visionary intelligence or an inquiring mind. More specifically, the excitement of British theatre over the past sixty years has lain in its ability to investigate, explore and even to influence the society we actually inhabit. And it seems fitting to end this chapter with a celebration of plays that have recently accomplished this task. I have talked about the resurgence of political theatre in the Blair years. But that has been part of a wider renewal of faith in big ambitious plays that have examined not only the state of the nation but also the condition of the culture at large. Again, there are external reasons for this: the boost given by Boyden, Nicholas Hytner's consistent adventurousness at the National, even the creation by dramatists themselves of a group called the Monsterists, designed to escape from black-box plays dealing with tiny shards and fragments of experience. Above all, however, an assertive belief in the medium of theatre itself has been combined with a prevailing post-millennial disquiet about the rootless materialism of western society. Theatre, in the late Blair years, reminded us of its capacity not just to entertain but also to epitomise our own unsettling anxieties.

Of all the plays of the period, none was more popular than Alan Bennett's *The History Boys*. After opening at the National in 2004, it won cascades of awards and enjoyed wide circulation: it went on national tours, triumphed on Broadway, was turned into a film and finally came into the West End. At first, it seems strange that a play set in a northern grammar school in the Eighties and dealing with the relationship between a pederastic teacher, Hector, and his pupils should have enjoyed such vast popularity. Its success on Broadway also came as a shock to me. In London I encountered several Americans, young and old, who puritanically felt that Hector should have been severely punished for pursuing what they termed 'improper relationships'. So how does one account for the play's universal success? Obviously, it is laced with Bennett's characteristic humour. It also deals with the process of teaching, which is something we all know about, and addresses the larger purpose of education. But I am convinced that the real reason for the play's success is that Bennett deals with a decisive shift in cultural values. Calculatedly set in the Thatcherite Eighties, the play pins down a particular moment when virtually everything, not just education, was assessed for its material benefit rather than its inherent worth. And, suggests Bennett, the significance of that shift transcended both time and place. If Blair in the Nineties chanted the mantra 'education, education, education', it was, as Polly Toynbee and David Walker have argued, more for practical than idealistic reasons. Blair wanted education to sharpen up the labour force, offer universal access to the Internet and serve as an antidote to social exclusion. For all their nervousness about the play's sexual politics, the American Ivy League students I teach instantly understood the notion that everything is now subordinate to the demands of the market. But, in the end, Bennett's play offers a joyous and moving alternative to that reductive assumption. And it is perfectly expressed in a deeply emotional scene where Hector takes a shyly precocious pupil through Hardy's poem, 'Drummer Hodge'. Hector's transmission of his delight in the poem is totally superfluous to exam requirements. What it symbolises is an almost-vanished world in which enrichment of the heart and mind, and joy in precision of language, take precedence over league-table requirements and objective measuring-rods of success.

By being rigorously specific, and writing out of personal knowledge, Bennett was able to touch on universal themes; and much the same was true of Mike Leigh's *Two Thousand Years*, which emerged from the National Theatre a year later. A lot of slightly spurious excitement surrounded the play's creation. It was Leigh's first work for the theatre in over a decade and his closed-door rehearsal methods fuelled a good deal of press speculation about his intentions. Even the play's title was, somewhat coyly, not revealed until the last minute. But, once we saw the play, all became clear. Setting the action in a divided Jewish family home in Cricklewood, Leigh was dealing with the bitter consequences of living in a world without faith. How, he asked, do we survive without a sustaining belief in politics, religion and the very idea of social progress? Like Bennett, however, Leigh addressed a prevailing crisis through intimate specifics: in this case, the rumbling tensions in a north London Jewish family. A left-wing grandfather lamented the death of socialism and the convergence of Britain's main political parties. A middle-aged dentist and his wife, wistfully remembering their youthful ideals, viewed contemporary Israel as a lost cause dominated by the Zionist right; and this was before Israel's latest disastrous incursion into Lebanon in its war with Hezbollah militants. Even the son of the house, Josh, found that his unilateral attempt to discover religion led only to tension and exclusion: as his father sadly muttered, 'It's like having a Muslim in the house.' Leigh's play left you with the same sliver of hope discernible sixty years before in post-war Priestley: namely that if idealism survives, it will only be through the agency of the young. But the abiding impression, as in much of Leigh's remarkable corpus of stage and film work, was of the fission inside the nuclear family and of the difficulty of living in a world where material possessions constitute nine tenths of the cultural lore.

The Leigh and Bennett plays both came from the National; but it had no monopoly on ambitious new work. After a run of chic, short plays of urban angst adhering to a standard ninety-minute format, in 2005 the Royal Court staged Richard Bean's *Harvest*. As a prime mover behind the Monsterists, Bean duly lived up to the prospectus with a three-hour play covering four generations of a Yorkshire farming family over the past eighty years. This was not only a play on an epic scale. It was also a warm, humane tribute to the dogged resilience of Britain's small farmers and their ability to withstand dilettante landed gentry, wartime Whitehall edicts and present-day Brussels bureaucracy. Whether Britain's farmers have been quite so permanently persecuted is open to debate. The post-war Attlee government introduced extensive price support. And even the supposedly anti-rural Blair administration gave £500 million for improved 'stewardship' of the countryside. But Bean, who had already taken us inside a bread factory in *Toast* and detailed the lives of North Sea trawlermen in *Under The Whaleback*, once more expanded the territory of the 'work-play'. He also restored the expansive domestic saga; and what he proved was that, by pursuing the fluctuating fortunes of a single family over four generations, you cover a large slice of British social history.

It was, however, left to Tom Stoppard, making a somewhat belated debut as a Royal Court dramatist at the age of sixty-nine, to raise some of the largest questions of all about the state of our culture in *Rock 'n' Roll*. Admittedly the theatre's invitation to Stoppard to come up with a new play in celebration of its fiftieth anniversary provoked rumbles from some old Courtiers who resented the intrusion of a writer who was not part of the building's history. But Stoppard's play was strong enough to silence the internal critics. And, although its action oscillated between Prague and Cambridge in the period from 1968 to 1990, it was much more than an investigation of the chequered history of Stoppard's own native land. In part, Stoppard's play was about the capacity of a rock group, the Czech Plastic People of the Universe, to subvert a rigidly autocratic regime through its music rather than its dissidence. Bursting at the seams with ideas, Stoppard's play was also a meditation on freedom. And at the heart of it lay the idea that, while the Czechs and Slovaks had struggled painfully to achieve democracy, in England we had witnessed a gradual erosion of our own hard-won liberties. There is a crucial scene towards the end of the play set in an idyllic Cambridge garden; and it is there that Lenka, a Czech exile, warns her fellow-countryman Jan, who studied at Cambridge in the Sixties, not to return. It is clear that she is speaking not of the university but of England at large:

> Don't come back, Jan. This place has lost its nerve. They put something in the water since you were here. It's a democracy of obedience. They're frightened to use their minds in case their minds tell them heresy. They apologise for history. They apologise for good manners. They apologise for difference. It's a contest of apology. You've got your country back. Why would you change it for one that's fucked for fifty years at least.

Two things strike me about the speech. One is that it's spoken in 1990 at the climax of a Thatcherism which Stoppard tacitly endorsed. But the other point is that it is clearly meant to apply to the England of 2006, which Stoppard suggests has sacrificed its old inquisitive freedom in favour of intellectual conformity.

It is a thesis one could endlessly debate. It is perfectly true that draconian new laws, prompted by the terrorist threat, have curtailed individual liberties. It is also true that new technology is helping to create a surveillance state in which our every movement is supervised. It is true again that the police, in the supposed interests of social order, are forever seeking extensions of their powers. And yet England is still a country in which you can call the Prime Minister a war criminal without getting banged up, in which a million people are free to turn out in protest against an illegal war and in which the government subsidises a theatre instinctively opposed to its foreign policy. Stoppard has a case; and it is one that Harold Pinter would probably state with even more polemical vigour. Yet, without lapsing into naive optimism, it seems to me that critical dissent is still a possibility and one that is still exercised by journalism, art and literature. One of the multiple paradoxes of Blairism was that it enhanced the financial security of theatre, thereby enabling it to examine the failings of our society and the plight of western culture at large; which is precisely what writers like Bennett, Leigh, Bean and Stoppard did in a series of vauntingly ambitious plays in the early years of our century.

In 1945 there was a clear danger that theatre might lapse again into a pre-war mood of benign escapism and revert to ancient forms and class attitudes. Over the succeeding six decades it has proved that, more than any other medium, it is a vehicle of moral enquiry. It has questioned structures, scrutinised attitudes, satirised individuals. It has, on occasion, erected signposts to the future suggesting that it was capable of shaping society as well as reflecting it. It has energised and renewed theatrical language, affirming the vitality of prose and the possibility of poetry. Above all, it has shown that, for all the rapid advances in technology, the growth of physical theatre and the move towards more collaborative structures, it is the individual dramatist who is best equipped to record the anxieties of the time. British theatre since the war has acted as a uniquely informative mirror to the shifts and changes in our society. But, for all the achievements of the interpreters, it is to the writer, in his or her truculent solitude, that we have looked to gain a greater understanding both of ourselves and of the insanely perplexing world that we all inhabit. In the beginning was the Word.

Afterword

I finished the bulk of this book in the autumn of 2006; and, looking back, I hope what emerges is a picture of the resilience of British theatre over six decades. But now, in the spring of 2007 when daffodils are in early bloom, I feel it might be sensible to stand back and address certain basic questions. What is the future of British theatre? Are the jeremiads that frequently appear in the press justified? And is my championship of the supremacy of the individual dramatist over-optimistic in an increasingly pluralistic theatre?

Futurology is a mug's game. But it's safe to say that the healthy survival of the British theatre depends heavily on one basic factor: money. If we can learn anything from the last sixty years it is that, in the words of Nicholas Hytner in a preface to a National Theatre report, 'subsidy works.' In its reliance on a mixture of modest state patronage and popular appeal, the British theatre has avoided either the feather-bedded excesses of its European neighbours or the brash imperatives of the American box-office. Artists have constantly complained, rightly enough, about fluctuations in funding; but the reality is that the nation-wide theatrical network that emerged in the early 1960s has, with the exception of a few sad casualties, weathered the various storms. For that to continue we need a stable economy. Plus, of course, the political will-power to ensure that the arts come high on the agenda.

No-one can predict where the economy is heading, although the West's dependence on Middle East oil-supplies undoubtedly rattles the nerves. As for political will, everything hinges on who is in power. Something of rare significance, however, happened in early March 2007. Tony Blair, in a clear attempt to ensure that he is remembered for something more than the disastrous legacy of Iraq, made a speech at Tate Modern in which he actually boasted of Labour's beneficence to the arts. One wished he had done it sooner. Yet, to be fair, Blair did have a good case. Arts Council funding had risen from £183 million when Labour took office in 1997 to £412 million ten years later. Admission to national museums and art collections was free. Opera, ballet and orchestral music were all thriving. And theatre wasn't doing too badly either. Post-Boyden, regional theatre had been saved from virtual extinction and had reached the point where it could present Shakespeare, Schiller and even the occasional new play. Advocates of subsidised theatre also pointed out that its talents enjoyed a high international profile. Tom Stoppard's *The Coast of Utopia*, although coolly received at the National, had become a hot ticket at New York's Lincoln Center. Of the five nominees for Best Actress at the 2007 Oscars, Helen Mirren, Judi Dench and Kate Winslet were all products of the subsidised sector. And Dame Helen's regal triumph in *The Queen* owed a big debt not just to Elizabeth Windsor but also to a vibrant screenplay by Peter Morgan who had proved his theatrical mettle with *Frost/Nixon* which started life at the Donmar.

But where do we go from here? Because of his impending retirement, Blair could offer only vague assurances rather than iron commitments. And his salute to an allegedly golden decade came in a troubling context. The Arts Council was being asked to look at a doomsday scenario of a 5 per cent cut in funding for each of the three years from April 2008: presumably on the grounds that anything less draconian would be seen as a sign of unparalleled Medici-like munificence. Gordon Brown is also a prudent Scot not renowned for his passion for the arts; although I cherish the memory of seeing him heroically sit, at the Edinburgh Festival, through a nine-hour Russian *Oresteia* for which he evinced much the same enthusiasm as he might for a Blair Conference speech. But, since Brown has already indicated that public spending in the three-year cycle starting in 2008 will bottom out at 2 per cent, it is fair to assume that the arts are not exactly going to be showered with loot. Behind everything also lurks the shadow of the 2012 Olympics, already costed at £9 billion, and the fear that they may be used as an excuse to rob our artistic Peters to pay for our athletic Paulas. As so often in our post-war history, the arts are at a turning-point. We can either capitalise on Labour's enlightened decade and the fact that the arts now account for more than 7 per cent of the economy; or we can go back to the bad old days in which politicians embraced the idea of public subsidy with all the limp reluctance of a lukewarm lover.

If the political and economic future is unguessable, so too is the artistic one. But, at least with theatre, it is possible to present the choices available. My book is based on the belief that the health of British theatre over the past sixty years has depended heavily on its dramatists and their ability to reflect the state of the nation. Is there any guarantee, however, that it will continue? We live in a rapidly changing culture where 'plays' are often seen as slightly passé when set against an inclusive, all-embracing concept of 'theatre.' The lonely eminence of the writer is also increasingly challenged by a number of external factors: directorial power, the celebrity culture, the growth of group-devised and site-specific work and advances in new technology. With the exception of our insane deification of minor celebrities, none of these things is inherently bad. To date, dramatists have also survived rather well our continuing re-definition of theatre. The big question is whether they will continue to do so.

Dramatists, like actors, sometimes speak darkly of the 'directocracy': the supposed band of power-maniacs who virtually control the means of production in British theatre. But, looking back, I would say that living writers have gained more than they have lost from partnerships with particular directors. They may not have been made in heaven, but the creative marriages between, say, Pinter and Hall, Shaffer and Dexter, Storey and Anderson, Nichols and Blakemore, Hare and Eyre worked to the benefit of both parties. With the exception of Alan Bennett and Nicholas Hytner, Tom Stoppard and Trevor Nunn, there seem to be rather fewer such alliances in our promiscuous, contemporary culture. Not only that: there are hints of a return to the principles of Artaud who envisaged a future in which the typical language of theatre would be 'constituted around the *mise en scène*' and where the director would became an all-powerful auteur.

It is instructive, in fact, to contrast the careers of two highly talented directors: Ian Rickson and Katie Mitchell. Rickson, who ran the Royal Court for eight years, has devoted himelf primarily to the business of realising a living author's vision: Mitchell has worked predominantly with classic texts on which she sets her own increasingly personal stamp. But both Rickson and Mitchell have lately revived Chekhov's *The Seagull* and it's worth comparing their productions. Rickson's Royal Court *Seagull* was a model of intelligent re-appraisal in which even the famous first line – Medvedenko's enquiry to Masha of 'Why do you always wear black?' – was invested with new resonance. We had already seen a preoccupied Konstantin alone on stage feverishly scribbling notes and an enthralled Masha picking up his discarded jottings; so it seemed entirely logical that, because she was absorbed in their perusal, Masha would hilariously interrupt the schoolmaster's opening enquiry. The play had hardly begun but Rickson had already established Konstantin's essential solitude, Masha's hopeless devotion to him and Medvedenko's willing subordination to Masha. It is fascinating to set against that Mitchell's production of Martin Crimp's 'version' at the National. Mitchell prefaced the first line with well over a minute of stage business and idle chat involving workmen hauling on a grand piano for Konstantin's play. Finally, we heard Medvedenko indignantly saying off-stage 'And the way you dress' to which Masha replied 'What do you mean: the way I dress?' before they eventually appeared. But, although you could argue that Mitchell was being faithful to Crimp's text and was showing life-going-on-in-the-background, little crucial had been established; and the query about Masha's penchant for wearing black was rendered absurd when you discovered it was a trait shared by most of the other characters.

Opinions were sharply polarised about Mitchell's *Seagull*. Some saw it as a radical stripping away of Chekhovian clichés: others as a self-indulgent piece of director's theatre. And the same heated division continued over Mitchell's subsequent work at the National. First came *Waves*, 'devised by Katie Mitchell and the company from the text of *The Waves* by Virginia Woolf': then a new version of Martin Crimp's 1997 play, *Attempts On Her Life*, which the author himself described as 'seventeen scenarios for the theatre'. Both productions revealed a preoccupation with the technical resources of TV and video in which literary and verbal images were illustrated on screen in magnified close-up. For some, this was a way of extending the vocabulary of theatre and creating an exciting multi-media spectacle. For others, of whom I was one, it turned theatre into a form of stylistic exercise and transformed actors into a hybrid mix of on-camera performers and scuttling technicians. What was undeniable was that Mitchell was the controlling figure and ultimate auteur in a continental European tradition: spectators were being drawn into the National to see what Katie did next. In Germany, France and Italy the dearth of living writers has inexorably turned the director into a form of superstar: someone whose conceptual reading of a classic text has become a substitute for new drama. In Britain, with its abundance of living dramatists, there is less motive for such directorial adventurism. But increasingly one finds directors enticed by the challenge of transforming an epic narrative, a film script, a short story or a recalcritant novel into a piece of 'theatre'. It may be honestly motivated. It may also be a means of displaying their own dexterity. One of the most intriguing examples is David Farr who has combined the roles of dramatist, director and artistic impresario at London's Gate Theatre, then at the Bristol Old Vic (in tandem with Simon Reade) and latterly at the Lyric Hammersmith. As a writer himself, you might expect Farr to be hospitable to the work of fellow-dramatists. But increasingly he has turned his talents to staging the apparently unstageable. Epics such as the *Odyssey* and *Paradise Lost* have been followed, less successfully, by the Indian *Ramayana*. But, irrespective of the merits of individual works, what is revealing is Farr's evident belief that theatre is primarily a director's medium and that young audiences are pining less for plays on contemporary life than for flamboyantly sensory spectacles.

In the end, I would gamble on the dramatist outlasting the auteur-like director: simply on the grounds that plays have an emotional resonance you rarely find in engineered spectacles and that in Britain there are few directors equipped to assume the role of Artaud's 'unique Creator'. Far more insidious is the cult of celebrity which corrupts virtually every aspect of British life and which certainly affects the theatre. It has become increasingly difficult for a straight play to succeed in the West End without a big name attached; and, where once that would have meant a star of the calibre of Maggie Smith or Judi Dench, it now refers to someone known simply through film, television or the all-pervasive gossip columns. It could be argued that the dramatist benefits from celebrity-casting and that the results are not always harmful. When Daniel Radcliffe played the horse-blinding boy in Peter Shaffer's *Equus*, he showed a surly authority even though there was something creepy about the slavering press attention to his brief moment of on-stage nudity; the world seemed astonished that the cinema's Harry Potter actually had a penis. But when Billie Piper – best known for her two seasons in *Dr Who* and her marriage to Chris Evans – appeared as Ann in Christopher Hampton's *Treats*, the play was upstaged by the traumas surrounding the star's private life. Admittedly Piper's failure to appear at two preview performances fuelled various rumours. But it was distressing to see the *Observer*, instead of asking its drama critic to review the play, despatch a showbiz columnist to cover the event and chart, in breathless detail, all the stories about Piper's mystery illness, suspected pregnancy and offstage relationship with one of her co-stars. Tittle-tattle replaced analysis and Ms Piper, like Radcliffe making her stage debut, was given an attention that Sarah Bernhardt in her heyday might have envied. Ms Piper may well turn out to be a fine stage actress. What troubles me is the tenuous connection between fame and achievement; something that prompted Dame Edna Everage to remark, in her latest guest-crushing TV show, that 'celebrity is the new nonentity'.

If the role of the dramatist is being undermined by what Robert Hughes has called 'the psychotic cult of celebrity', it is also being challenged by the growth of group-devised and site-specific theatre; two terms that are sometimes, but not necessarily, synonymous. I have touched on these in my final chapter. I would simply add that devised theatre has a long and honourable history often associated with radical protest. New York's Living Theatre, California's El Teatro Campesino and the Brazilian Augusto Boal's Theatre of the Oppressed, which he once described as 'rehearsal for revolution', have all demonstrated the potential subversiveness of collaborative theatre. Nearer home a number of companies have also shown the benefits of drawing on the pooled resources of the ensemble. *Oh What A Lovely War!* derived much of its power from the responsibility of the actors for their material. Joint Stock, although it usually relied on solo authors for its finished script, tapped into collective research. And, even if Mike Leigh is emphatically the author of his plays, he'd be the first to admit their dependence on information collectively received. But today there are a growing number of groups – including Punchdrunk, Improbable Theatre, Shunt, Frantic Assembly, Forced Entertainment, Forkbeard Fantasy, Kaboodle, the People Show, Peeplelykus, Total Theatres, Trestle and Volcano to name just a few – that not only cross the boundaries between drama, dance and mime but that also tend to rely on a collective approach rather than the vision of a single author. The results can advance the frontiers of theatre; and when Improbable's Phelim McDermott and Julian Crouch applied their collaborative techniques to Philip Glass's Gandhi-based opera *Satyagraha* at the Coliseum in 2007, the effect was truly liberating. But there they were working within a strongly-defined musical structure. And that doesn't disprove my thesis that you rarely find in devised pieces the same kind of political intensity that you discover in the solo-authored work of a Hare or a Churchill. Where a foreign practitioner like Boal uses devised theatre as an instrument of protest, too many of our own companies seem involved in an act of navel-gazing introspection. You may emerge from a devised piece discussing the nature of theatre. You rarely come out wanting to change the world.

Of all the challenges to the living playwright, however, arguably the greatest comes from new technology: something that can be either master or servant but that undeniably affects every aspect of theatre from audience behaviour to scenic and aural design and the nature of dramaturgy itself. As audiences, we have all become accustomed to advance exhortations to switch off our mobile phones. Richard Griffiths became something of a folk-hero when, during the run of a play called *Heroes*, he publicly shamed a persistent offender to wild applause from the rest of the audience. You could argue that, historically, theatre has always been a contest in which the actor and the playwright have to battle to gain an audience's undivided attention; but, in addition to coughing, chatting and sweet-rustling, they now have to contend with our constant hunger for communication with the outside world. One solution, already applied in St Petersburg, is for theatres to instal jamming devices to render mobiles temporarily inoperable; though that, we are told in London, has the disadvantage of blocking frequencies needed for emergency services. Mobiles aside, my own feeling is that playwrights have to respond both to changing patterns of audience behaviour and the dramatic potential of new technology.

Audiences today are different. They inhabit an interactive culture. They are also less passively obedient than in the days of illusionist theatre. It, therefore, makes increasing sense for the playwright to acknowledge their existence. Admittedly the process of destroying the fourth wall has been going on for the last eighty years. It started with Brecht, continued with celebrated British plays such as *The Entertainer* and *A Day In The Death of Joe Egg* and is now universal. On successive evenings in 2007 I saw characters in Edward Albee's *The Lady From Dubuque* turning to the audience to comment on the developing action and I witnessed the South African, John Kani, in *Sizwe Bansi Is Dead* inviting front-row spectators on stage to examine a set of mounted photographs. I'm not suggesting for a moment that the process should be mandatory; but, as stages become more open, it seems logical for the actor and the dramatist to talk directly to us. The more they do so, the less likely we are to retreat into our own private world of phoning and texting. But new technology also opens up tremendous dramaturgical possibilities. So far the writer who has made wittiest use of them is Patrick Marber in *Closer* where a doctor engages in obscene internet chat with a woman called 'Anna' who is, in reality, a young male journalist: a vivid demonstration of the idea that a website can be a source of both sexual excitement and assumed identity. Enda Walsh's *Chatroom*, originally seen as part of the Shell Connections season at the National, took the process a stage further by showing how a group of manipulative teenagers could collectively use the computer to drive a depressive fifeeen-year-old to suicide: 'In these rooms,' as one of the wired-up teenagers remarked, 'words are power.' Even Harold Pinter, not renowned for his love of new technology, has written a cryptically powerful sketch, *Apart From That*, showing how a couple conversing on mobile phones become ever more silkily evasive about the phantoms that haunt their lives. When we talk of new technology in theatre, we all too often associate it with video projections as in Bill Dudley's panoramic design for *The Coast of Utopia* or batteries of on-stage cameras and sound equipment as in Katie Mitchell's *Waves*. But, just as dramatists in the past used the landline as a vital narrative device, so present and future playwrights are confronted by the limitless possibilities for deception in an e-mail culture and our inability to make real contact in an era of instant communication. Technology, in short, is the dramatist's friend rather than enemy.

Behind that lurks an even bigger question. Will theatre survive in a world that offers ever-expanding sources of entertainment? As a sports-nut, I still find it vaguely miraculous that I can sit at home, as on a Saturday night in 2007, and zap my satellite TV remote control to switch between two one-day cricket matches in the Caribbean and an England v Israel soccer game in Tel Aviv. Those who want music wherever they go can can now have it by downloading their personal choices and packing their iPod in their pocket. And virtually the whole cinematic culture of the past hundred years, as well as the best and worst of British television, is available to us via DVD. If we're really bored, we can even sit at home in the evening and surf the internet or engage in electronic conversations with total strangers. And, if we're of a more sociable disposition, we might go to the pub, drop into a restaurant, have dinner with friends. Given the plethora of choices available to us, who needs theatre? It is, after all, a demanding process that requires dressing up, going out, paying sometimes exorbitant sums to disobliging box-office staff, sitting in not always comfortable seats and fighting in the interval for the privilege of buying a barely visible tot of whisky or a lukewarm beer. And even then there is no guarantee of aesthetic satisfaction.

This admittedly is a caricature view of the hazards of playgoing peddled at regular intervals by the British press; sometimes even by theatre people themselves. 'Boring an audience is the one true sin in theatre,' wrote Anthony Neilson in the *Guardian* in the spring of 2007. 'We've been boring audiences for decades now and they've responded by slowly withdrawing their patronage.' It seemed an odd claim to make at a time when the West End reported record attendances of over twelve million in 2006, when the National Theatre claimed that its £10 ticket-scheme was wooing first-time visitors, when the RSC's London season had people queuing round the block and when a revivified regional theatre was reporting a sharp rise in audiences. And, even if there is no guaranteee the current boom will last, there still seem to me rational grounds for hope. In a world where advanced technology often heightens our sense of isolation, it is no accident that the theatre, which satisfies our need for social contact, is enjoying a surge in popularity. Confronted by the sophisticated, dehumanised wizardry of so much visual entertainment, we are also drawn to theatre by the sight of real people in three-dimensional, spatial relationships. And, far from replicating what is easily available to us on television, theatre appears to have learned the vital lesson of playing to its strengths: after a surfeit of medical soaps and routine *policiers* in which human nature is planed and shaped to accomodate existing formats, it is bracing to encounter the unresolved angularities of a straight play.

Theatre, as I've argued earlier, is a rambling mansion with multiple rooms. In theatre's diversity lies its glory; and it is large enough to embrace *Boeing Boeing* as well as *Britannicus, The Sound of Music* as well as Strindberg, Ken Dodd as well as Kafka, Pinero as well as Pinter, site-specific as well as stand-up and any other alliterative combination you care to name. If, in this book, I have stressed the contribution of the dramatist it is because I believe plays reflect not just individual temperaments but the form and pressure of the time. And, since I finished the main text, my instinct about the tenacity of the straight play has been underlined by events. Conor McPherson's

The Seafarer, explicitly invoking an eighth-century Anglo-Saxon poem about exile and solitude, transported us unforgettably to a booze-filled, all-male Dublin basement, untouched by the benefits of the Irish economic boom. Caryl Churchill's *Drunk Enough To Say I Love You?* was another of her radical formal experiments that conveyed the jagged history of the Anglo-American special relationship through a sado-masochistic, gay love affair. Roy Williams's *Days of Significance*, given a promenade production in Stratford-on-Avon's Swan, expanded his usual territory to offer a chilling portrait of the ignorance and prejudice of a younger generation exporting its Asbo values to the battlezones of Iraq. And, out of the blue, a 24-year-old Belfast writer, Lucy Caldwell, emerged at the Royal Court with a play called *Leaves* that touchingly explored the impact on her family of a female student's attempted suicide. Why, the play implicitly asked, at a time of such apparent plenty and opportunity, are so many people unhappy?

Other commentators would doubtless cite other plays. But what these four had in common was a sharply individual vision, an ability to connect personal dilemmas with the wider world and the capacity to haunt one long after one had left the theatre. All four were utterly different in form and style; yet they reminded one that a play, at best, is an event that happens in the present and resonates in the future. Spanning several generations, they also confirmed our theatre's ability to embrace the young without banishing the old. Of course, theatre will change in tune with the society around it, becoming, in future decades, both more physically interactive and dependent on technology. It will also, at another level, continue to offer fantasy, reassurance and escape. But, if theatre continues to matter, it will, I believe, be because of its linguistic richness, its thematic urgency and its ability to link our private hopes and fears to the state of the nation. In the end, the future of the theatre rests with its playwrights.

Bibliography

In the course of writing this book, I have read, dipped into and borrowed from a large number of historical works, theatrical studies, critical biographies and play-texts. I cannot list them all. But below I offer a selection of the history and theatre books on which I have most frequently relied.

History

Peter Clarke, *Hope and Glory: Britain 1900–90* (Penguin, 1996)

Felipe Fernandez-Armesto, *England: 1945–2000* (The Folio Society, 2001)

Antonia Fraser, *Cromwell* (Weidenfeld and Nicolson, 1973)

Philip French and Michael Sissons (eds.), *The Age of Austerity: 1945–51* (Hodder and Stoughton, 1963)

Kenneth Harris, *Attlee* (Weidenfeld and Nicolson, 1982)

Peter Hennessy, *Never Again* (Jonathan Cape, 1992)

Eric Hobsbawm, *Age of Extremes: 1914–91* (Michael Joseph, 1994)

Christopher Lee, *This Sceptred Isle: Twentieth Century* (Penguin, 2000)

Bernard Levin, *The Pendulum Years* (Jonathan Cape, 1970)

Peter Lewis, *The Fifties* (Book Club Associates, 1978)

Arthur Marwick, *British Society Since 1945* (Penguin, 1982)

Arthur Marwick, *The Sixties* (Oxford University Press, 1998)

Kenneth O. Morgan, *The People's Peace* (Oxford University Press, 1990)

John Pilger, *Hidden Agendas* (Vintage, 1998)

Anthony Sampson, *The New Anatomy of Britain* (Hodder and Stoughton, 1971)

Anthony Sheldon, *Blair* (The Free Press, 2005)

Polly Toynbee and David Walker, *Did Things Get Better?* (Penguin, 2001)

Hugo Young, *One Of Us: A Biography of Margaret Thatcher* (Macmillan, 1989)

Theatre Studies

Paul Allen, *A Pocket Guide to Alan Ayckbourn's Plays* (Faber and Faber, 2004)

Peter Ansorge, *Disrupting The Spectacle* (Pitman, 1975)

Peter Ansorge, *From Liverpool to Los Angeles* (Faber and Faber, 1997)

Eric Bentley, *What is Theatre?* (Methuen, 1969)

Kitty Black, *Upper Circle* (Methuen, 1984)

Richard Boon, *Brenton The Playwright* (Methuen, 1991)

Richard Boon (ed.), *About Hare* (Faber and Faber, 2003)

Howard Brenton, *Hot Irons* (Methuen, 1995)

Peter Brook, *The Empty Space* (Penguin, 1968)

Simon Callow, *Being An Actor* (Methuen, 1984)

Simon Callow, *The National* (Nick Hern Books, 1997)

Humphrey Carpenter, *That Was Satire That Was* (Victor Gollancz, 2000)

Humphrey Carpenter, *The Angry Young Men* (Allen Lane, 2002)

Colin Chambers, *Inside The Royal Shakespeare Company* (Routledge, 2004)

Sandy Craig (ed.), *Dreams and Deconstructions* (Amber Lane, 1980)

Dominic Dromgoole, *The Full Room* (Methuen, 2000)

Charles Duff, *The Lost Summer* (Nick Hern Books, 1995)

Richard Eyre, *National Service* (Bloomsbury, 2003)

Richard Eyre and Nicholas Wright, *Changing Stages* (Bloomsbury, 2000)

Richard Findlater, *The Unholy Trade* (Gollancz, 1952)

Richard Findlater (ed.), *At The Royal Court* (Amber Lane, 1981)

Ben Francis, *Christopher Hampton: Dramatic Ironist* (Amber Lane, 1996)

Stanton B. Garner Jr, *Trevor Griffiths* (University of Michigan, 1999)

William Gaskill, *A Sense of Direction* (Faber and Faber, 1988)

John Goodwin (ed.), *Peter Hall's Diaries* (Hamish Hamilton, 1983)

Howard Goorney, *The Theatre Workshop Story* (Eyre Methuen, 1981)

David Hare, *Asking Around* (Faber and Faber, 1993)

David Hare, *Obedience, Struggle and Revolt* (Faber and Faber, 2005)

John Heilpern, *John Osborne: A Patriot for Us* (Chatto and Windus, 2006)

Philip Hoare, *Noël Coward: A Biography* (Sinclair-Stevenson, 1995)

Harold Hobson, *Theatre* (Longman's Green, 1948)

Peter Holland, *English Shakespeares* (Cambridge University Press, 1997)

Richard Huggett, *Binkie Beaumont* (Hodder and Stoughton, 1989)

James Inverne, *The Impressarios* (Oberon, 2000)

Catherine Itzin, *Stages In The Revolution* (Eyre Methuen, 1980)

Nicholas de Jongh, *Politics, Prudery and Perversions* (Methuen, 2000)

Laurence Kitchin, *Drama In The Sixties* (Faber and Faber, 1966)

James Knowlson, *Damned To Fame* (Bloomsbury, 1996)

Michael Kustow, *Peter Brook* (Bloomsbury, 2005)

John Lahr (ed.), *The Diaries of Kenneth Tynan* (Bloomsbury, 2001)

John Lahr, *Coward The Playwright* (Methuen, 1982)

Charles Landstone, *Off-Stage* (Elek, 1953)

Joan Littlewood, *Joan's Book* (Methuen, 1964)

Gareth and Barbara Lloyd Evans (eds.), *Plays In Review: 1956–1980* (Batsford, 1985)

Charles Marowitz, Tom Milne and Owen Hale (eds.), *New Theatre Voices of the Fifties and Sixties* (Eyre Methuen, 1981)

John McGrath, *Naked Thoughts That Roam About* (Nick Hern Books, 2002)

Murray Melvin, *The Art of the Theatre Workshop* (Oberon, 2006)

Sheridan Morley and Ruth Leon, *Hey Mr Producer! The Musical World of Cameron Mackintosh* (Weidenfeld and Nicolson, 1968)

Sheridan Morley, *A Talent To Amuse* (Pavilion Books, 1985)

John Osborne, *Damn You, England* (Faber and Faber, 1994)

John Osborne, *Looking Back* (Faber and Faber, 1999)

Susan Painter, *Edgar: The Playwright* (Methuen, 1996)

Michael Patterson, *Strategies of Political Theatre* (Cambridge University Press, 2003)

J. B. Priestley, *Theatre Outlook* (Nicholson and Watson, 1947)

Dan Rebellato, *1956 and All That* (Routledge, 1999)

Frank Rich, *Hot Seat* (Random House, 1998)

Tony Richardson, *Long Distance Runner* (Faber and Faber, 1993)

Rob Ritchie (ed.), *The Joint Stock Book* (Methuen, 1987)

Peter Roberts (ed.), *The Best of Plays and Players: 1969–83* (Methuen, 1989)

Dominic Shellard, *British Theatre Since The War* (Methuen, 1999)

Dominic Shellard, *Kenneth Tynan: A Life* (Yale University Press, 2003)

Kirsten Shepherd-Barr, *Science On Stage* (Princeton University Press, 2006)

Aleks Sierz, *In-Yer-Face Theatre* (Faber and Faber, 2001)

John Snelson, *Andrew Lloyd Webber* (Yale University Press, 2004)

J. C. Trewin, *Dramatists of Today* (Staples Press, 1953)

Kenneth Tynan, *Tynan on Theatre* (Penguin, 1964)

Geoffrey Wansell, *Terence Rattigan* (Fourth Estate, 1995)

Irving Wardle, *The Theatres of George Devine* (Jonathan Cape, 1978)

Matt Wolf, *Stepping Into Freedom* (Nick Hern Books, 2002)

Brian Woolland, Dark Attractions: *The Theatre of Peter Barnes* (Methuen, 2004)

T. C. Worsley, *The Fugitive Art* (John Lehmann, 1952)

Index

Coward, Noël, 35–8, 58–60, 88–91;
Ayckbourn and, 201; *Cavalcade*,
159; death, 239–40; Eden and,
106; egocentricity, 70; Festival of
Britain, 48; 'talent to amuse', 130;
VE Day, 5, vulgarities, 64
Cox, Dr Alfred, 8
Cox, Brian, 195
Crazy People, 56
Cries From Casement (David Rudkin),
235
Crimp, Martin, 405
Cripps, Sir Stafford, 13, 22, 47
Criterion Theatre, 84
Crompton, Richmal, 72
Crouch, Julian, 407
Crucible, The (Arthur Miller), 97,
146, 150
Crucible Theatre, Sheffield, 306, 377,
378
Cuba, 144
Culver, Michael, 385
Cutler, Sir Horace, 305–6
Cyprus, 116

Daish, Judy, 344
Daldry, Stephen, 17, 339, 348, 353,
359, 372
Dale, Jim, 192
Damsels in Distress (Alan Ayck-
bourn), 382
Daniels, Ron, 248
Davidson, Bill, 25
Davies, Howard, 249
Dawson, Geoffrey, 193
Day By The Sea, A (N. C. Hunter), 70
Day In The Death Of Joe Egg, The
(Peter Nichols), 190–1, 408
Days of Significance (Roy Williams),
411
de Gaulle, Charles, 125

de Jongh, Nicholas, 163
Dead Funny (Terry Johnson), 351,
352
Declaration (ed, Tom Maschler), 120,
126
Deeds, 365
Deep Blue Sea, The (Terence Ratti-
gan), 60, 63, 65, 66, 260
Delaney, Shelagh, 111, 112
Delderfield, R.F., 44
Dench, Judi, 245, 246, 287
Denning Report, 126
Dennis, Nigel, 109
Derby Playhouse, 379
Destiny (David Edgar), 246–9, 263,
341
Devils, The (John Whiting), 136, 150
Devine, George, 75–7, 96–7; Arden
and, 114; Berliner Ensemble, 93–4;
Daldry influenced by, 353; death, 265;
influence of, 73; *Luther*, 149;
Osborne play turned down, 121;
Rattigan, 68; Thatcher and, 283;
Wesker and, 118, 156; Young Vic,
11, 35
Dexter, John, 95, 118, 119, 140–3,
157
Diaries (Peter Hall), 253, 255, 257,
258
Diaries (Harold Nicolson), 48
Diaries (Joe Orton), 176–7
Dickens, Charles, 210, 297–8, 318
Did Things Get Better? (Polly Toynbee
and David Walker), 364
Dingo (Charles Wood), 184–6, 222
Disney Corporation, 288
Disrupting The Spectacle (Peter
Ansorge), 221
Dissolution of Dominic Boot, The
(Tom Stoppard), 199
Divided Self, The (R. D. Laing), 178